Materialising the

Materialising the Roman Empire

Edited by Jeremy Tanner and Andrew Gardner

UCLPRESS

First published in 2024 by
UCL Press
University College London
Gower Street
London WC1E 6BT

Available to download free: www.uclpress.co.uk

A CIP catalogue record for this book is available from The British Library.

ISBN: 978-1-80008-400-1 (Hbk)
ISBN: 978-1-80008-399-8 (Pbk)
ISBN: 978-1-80008-398-1 (PDF)
ISBN: 978-1-80008-401-8 (epub)
DOI: https://doi.org/10.14324/111.9781800083981

Printed and bound by CPI Group (UK) Ltd, Croydon, CR0 4YY

Contents

List of figures

List of tables

Abbreviations

Unless otherwise specified, abbreviations of Classical texts and reference works follow the conventions of *The Oxford Classical Dictionary* (4th edition), edited by Simon Hornblower, Anthony Spawforth and Esther Eidinow (Oxford: Clarendon Press, 2012) and the *Année Philologique.*

List of contributors

Ton Derks is associate professor in Roman Archaeology at the Vrije Universiteit Amsterdam. He was trained in classics as well as archaeology, and developed a strong interest in Latin epigraphy. He earned a doctorate from the University of Amsterdam for his dissertation *Gods, Temples and Ritual Practices: The transformation of religious ideas and values in Roman Gaul*. He has published extensively on Roman religion in the provinces, including site reports on the sanctuaries of Empel, Elst and Born-Buchten, all in the Netherlands. His recent work has focused on the material dimensions of rituals of the human life course. He has also co-edited volumes on *Ethnic Constructs in Antiquity* (2009), *Roman Villa Landscapes in the North* (2011) and *The Roman Villa of Hoogeloon and the Archaeology of the Periphery* (2015).

Andrew Gardner is Professor of the Archaeology of the Roman Empire at the UCL Institute of Archaeology. He has research interests in the archaeology of Roman frontiers and of late antiquity, and in archaeological theory, particularly issues of power, identity and social change. In addition to publishing and teaching across these fields, Andrew is active in the wider discipline, and currently co-chairs University Archaeology UK, the subject body for archaeology in British universities. Andrew studied at the UCL Institute of Archaeology, then worked in Reading, Leicester and Cardiff, before returning to UCL as a lecturer from 2005.

Chris Howgego is Research Keeper in the Ashmolean Museum and Professor of Greek and Roman Numismatics in the University of Oxford. He was the founding Director of Roman Provincial Coinage Online and, with Professor Andrew Wilson, of Coin Hoards of the Roman Empire, and continues to co-direct both projects. He is also an editor of the series Roman Imperial Coinage and Roman Provincial Coinage. He is the author of *Greek Imperial Countermarks* (1985) and of *Ancient History from Coins* (1995), and edited *Coinage and Identity in the Roman Provinces* (2005) and *Coin Hoards and Hoarding in the Roman World* (2022). He has written widely on Roman coinage and history. He is currently working on *Roman Provincial Coinage vol. IV.4 (Egypt in the Antonine period)*.

Ray Laurence is Professor of Ancient History at Macquarie University (Sydney). His book *The Roads of Roman Italy: Mobility and cultural change* (1999) provided the disciplines of Ancient History and Archaeology with a fully developed analysis of Roman roads within the framework of the spatial turn. He has also published extensively on Roman urbanism: *Roman Pompeii: Space and society* (2007); *Rome, Ostia, Pompeii: Movement and space* (2011); *The City in the Roman West* (2011); and *Written Space in the Latin West* (2013). His most recent books have been *The Cultural History of Shopping in Antiquity* (2022) and *Mediterranean Timescapes: Chronological age and cultural practice in the Roman Empire* (2023). He edits the Routledge series *Studies in Roman Space and Urbanism.*

David J. Mattingly is Professor of Roman Archaeology at the University of Leicester, UK. He has written extensively on the history and archaeology of Britain and Africa in the Roman Empire and is well known for his work on identity, post-colonial approaches to empire and imperialism, the ancient economy, landscape archaeology and urbanisation. He has also researched the Saharan neighbours of the Roman Empire, notably the Garamantes in south-west Libya and the Gaetuli in southern Morocco.

John Pearce is Reader in Archaeology at King's College London. His research interests lie in Roman archaeology, especially for what it reveals of the societies of north-west Europe and their responses to becoming part of the Roman world. Having worked on the Vindolanda writing tablets as a post-doctoral researcher, he maintains an interest in writing as a Roman provincial phenomenon, in particular the insights which study of material attributes brings to the interpretation of inscriptions. He has published inscriptions reported to the Portable Antiquities Scheme and his current projects link epigraphic to visual and archaeological evidence to characterise Roman spectacle and hunting culture in northern Europe.

Rebecca Redfern is Senior Curator of Archaeology at the Museum of London, and is also a Fellow of the Society of Antiquaries and a Visiting Research Fellow at Newcastle University. She has published extensively on bioarchaeology and the Roman world for over 20 years, including

Injury and Trauma in Bioarchaeology: Interpreting violence in past lives (Cambridge University Press, 2016). Her current research examines inequalities in the Roman world, with a focus on enslavement.

Louise Revell is Associate Professor in Roman Studies at the University of Southampton. Her research focuses on Rome's western provinces, looking at questions of imperialism, identity and incorporation. She is the author of *Roman Imperialism and Local Identities* (2009) and *Ways of Being Roman: Discourses of identity in Rome's western provinces* (2015) and co-editor of *The Oxford Handbook of Roman Britain* (2016). She is currently working on urban citizenship as a mode of integration into the Roman Empire.

Peter Stewart is Professor of Ancient Art and Director of the Classical Art Research Centre at the University of Oxford. His research deals with many aspects of Greek, Roman and ancient Central Asian art, as well as the history of collecting. He has worked largely on ancient sculpture, particularly Roman provincial art. His past publications include *Statues in Roman Society: Representation and response* (Oxford University Press, 2003), *Roman Art* (Classical Association, 2004) and *The Social History of Roman Art* (Cambridge University Press, 2008).

Jeremy Tanner is Professor of Classical and Comparative Art at the UCL Institute of Archaeology. His research focuses on the history of Greek, Roman and early Chinese art, from a sociological and comparative perspective. Amongst his publications are *The Sociology of Art: A reader* (2003), *The Invention of Art History in Ancient Greece* (2006) and *Art's Agency and Art History* (2008, co-edited with Robin Osborne). His article 'Michael Baxandall and the sociological interpretation of art' won the Sage Cultural Sociology Prize in 2011. He is currently completing a project funded by the Leverhulme Foundation on 'The Axial Age and the Institutions of Art in Ancient Greece and Early Imperial China'.

Astrid Van Oyen is Professor of Roman Archaeology at Radboud University Nijmegen. Her research focuses on the archaeology of Roman Italy and the Western provinces, with a particular interest in the socio-economic history of non-elites, craft, rural economies and human–thing relations. She is author of *How Things Make History: The Roman Empire and its terra sigillata pottery* (Amsterdam University Press, 2016) and *The Socio-Economics of Roman Storage: Agriculture, trade, and family* (Cambridge University Press, 2020).

Andrew Wilson is Professor of the Archaeology of the Roman Empire at the University of Oxford, and Fellow of All Souls College. His research interests include the economy of the Roman Empire, ancient technology, ancient water supply and usage, Roman North Africa and archaeological field survey. Recent publications include *Trade, Commerce, and the State in the Roman World* (edited with Alan Bowman, Oxford, 2018), *Recycling and Reuse in the Roman Economy* (edited with Chloë Duckworth, Oxford, 2020), *Coin Hoards and Hoarding in the Roman World* (edited with Jerome Mairat and Chris Howgego, Oxford, 2022), *Simulating Roman Economies: Theories, methods, and computational models* (edited with Tom Brughmans, Oxford, 2022) and *The Economy of Roman Religion* (edited with Nicholas Ray and Angela Trentacoste, Oxford, 2023).

Preface

Jeremy Tanner

This volume represents the somewhat delayed fruits of a conference held in Beijing in April 2018, in collaboration with the School of Archaeology and Museology at Peking University, under the auspices of the joint ICCHA (International Centre for Chinese Heritage and Archaeology), the institutional vehicle for a collaboration between archaeologists at UCL and PKU for almost two decades. The title of the conference was 'Materialising Empire in Ancient Rome and Han Dynasty China'.

Although the archaeology of empires has been a notable focus of research in recent years, archaeologists have not made a significant contribution to contemporary developments in the comparative analysis of the ancient Roman and Han Dynasty empires, a project which has been dominated by historians, largely reliant on textual evidence (Dettenhofer 2006; 2009; Scheidel 2008; 2015). For archaeologists, in addition to the language barriers impeding communication, the rate of new discoveries, particularly in China, makes it extremely difficult for any individual scholar to gain sufficient mastery of the primary evidence to undertake comparative analysis. There have, of course, been several notable exhibitions with the ostensible theme of comparing the material culture of the Han and Roman Empires, but these have had a superficial, largely antiquarian character, simply juxtaposing comparable objects (coins, statues, examples of writing), without any sustained comparative analysis (Ru and Xun 2009; De Caro and Scarpari 2010). Apart from these, there are only a handful of scattered and isolated articles (Brennan and Hsing 2010; Razeto 2014; Norena 2015), which have not proven sufficient to stimulate the kind of sustained comparativism characteristic of the work of historians of the Chinese and Roman Empires, most notably the Stanford Ancient Chinese and Mediterranean Empires Comparative History Project, led by Walter Scheidel.

The conference was structured to facilitate, indeed require, comparison. Ten pairs of speakers addressed specific topics within five broad themes which the organisers considered central to understanding the way in which empires shaped material culture, and transformations in material culture conditioned the development of empire: Communication (transportation networks, archaeologies of writing); Money, Trade and Economies (archaeologies of coinage and of exchange); Urbanism and Transformations in Craft Production; Materialising Ideologies (art and empire, archaeologies of religion); and Center and Periphery (archaeologies of frontiers; imperial integration and resistance). Each contributor was asked to give a state-of-the-art account of the specific field their talk addressed, covering something of the history of the ways in which each particular field had been approached, as well as current questions, approaches and methods, including case studies from their own research to give some sense of how the field is situated today. In addition to delivering papers on their own area, each speaker was required to comment on the materials and arguments presented by their counterpart, highlighting what they saw as the most significant similarities and differences, and how we might begin to account for them. This was facilitated by precirculating PowerPoints (all made bilingual thanks to the exceptional efforts of the students at PKU), so each speaker on both sides had some basic knowledge of their counterpart's materials beforehand.

From the inception of the project, both sides had agreed to pursue a publication of the conference, in both Chinese and English versions, in order to provide some kind of baseline for future comparative archaeological studies of the two empires, and to reflect on the ways in which Chinese and Euro-American archaeologies of empire might learn from each other. The state-of-the-field articles from each side were to be 8000 words (or 6000 Chinese characters) each, with the comparative commentaries and reflections being 2000 words (1500 characters). The conference itself made use of simultaneous translation to facilitate discussion, and each side agreed, when we reached the publication stage, to translate the other's papers and circulate them to each author's thematic counterpart, in order to obviate any linguistic difficulties that might hinder the comparative reflections in the supplementary short essays. The final goal was two parallel publications, one in English, the other Chinese, in order to ensure the widest possible circulation of the discussions and thus provide impetus to further, hopefully collaborative, comparative archaeological projects on the two imperial traditions.

As it turned out, this plan proved over-ambitious. Although all the Roman 'state-of-the-art' papers were delivered by the agreed deadline (end of September 2018), or very shortly thereafter, only two Chinese papers arrived by that date, one with no references, another with no illustrations. Over the following two years, further papers arrived in a trickle, but often in unpublishable form: the Chinese contributor on roads and communication spent two-thirds of their allotted space discussing Roman roads, on the basis of recent Chinese translations of late nineteenth - and early twentieth-century publications by Theodor Mommsen and Tenney Frank, as if these were the latest word on Roman roads. In a way, this amply illustrated the obstacle to high-quality comparative study that the project was designed to overcome, and both sides agreed this essay had to be replaced, only to receive a new essay this time focusing on the Chinese material but at a length of almost 40,000 characters, more than six times the maximum permitted length. By the spring of 2021, three years after the conference, notwithstanding the valiant efforts of our PKU collaborators, we still had only a handful of the Chinese papers, not all of them yet in publishable form. At this stage, bearing in mind that each of these initial papers needed to be translated and then commented on by the Roman counterparts (and vice versa for the Chinese contributors), it became clear that there was no chance of completing our original plans before the papers would have become anything of more than historiographic interest.

We share this disappointing history partly in the hope that others may learn from what in some respects was clearly a failed experiment in collaboration, partly because we think that the model, for developing an informed and critical comparative archaeology of the Roman and Han Chinese empires, remains a good one. A number of colleagues have asked why we had not asked Euro-American specialists in the archaeology of Han China to participate in the project instead. By the time we had to abandon the original project, it was simply too late. Furthermore, in terms of the original collaboration, part of the initial attraction of the project from the UCL end, in line with current agendas for decolonising the curriculum, was to have the opportunity, through translation, to introduce more indigenous Chinese voices into the discussions both for our students in the UK and for non-Chinese-reading archaeologists with an interest in archaeologies of empire. There are of course significant numbers of archaeologists of Chinese origin working in universities in Europe and America, but by and large they have been heavily acculturated to Euro-American intellectual agendas and styles of research, and part of the interest in the project was a dialogue with long-standing and in many respects distinctive traditions of thought and practice in archaeology in mainland China.

Notwithstanding our disappointment (shared by our colleagues at PKU) that our initial ambitious plans had not been realised, both the editors of this volume and our contributors felt that a volume focused on the Roman Empire could still be something of value. While introductory texts on classical archaeology cover some of the same ground, their discussions of Roman archaeology do not have the same sharp focus on empire as the current volume, nor are they informed by the recent 'material turn' which gives the current set of studies added intellectual coherence. We particularly hope that it may, in due course, come into the hands of colleagues and students in China, and that they may find both the theoretical frameworks and the methodological approaches relevant to their explorations of the Han empire, and perhaps be inspired by the rich materials presented here to engage in the kinds of comparisons the conference was intended to stimulate.

Both editors would like to thank our hosts at PKU for their warm welcome and exceptional hospitality during the period of the conference, and in particular their wonderful students who did so much to make the event run smoothly, from their work on bilingual PowerPoints and handouts, to their organisation of the ample and delicious refreshments which punctuated the proceedings. We are also indebted to generous funding from UCL Institute of Archaeology Awards and from the UCL Peking University Strategic Partner Funds. We are grateful to UCL Press for agreeing to publish something very different from the initial prospectus which we offered them, and particularly to our commissioning editor, Pat Gordon-Smith, for her unfailing patience and enthusiasm, particularly in helping us through some of the complexities entailed by open-access publishing. Readers for the press have significantly improved the volume with their helpful suggestions. In light of these, we were delighted to broaden our range of coverage by adding Rebecca Redfern and Lisa Lodwick to our roster of contributors, though sadly Lisa's final illness and tragically premature death prevented her from being able to complete her chapter on botanical imperialism.

References

Brennan, T. Corey and Hsing I-tien. 2010. 'The Eternal City and the City of Eternal Peace'. In *China's Early Empires: A re-appraisal*, edited by Michael Nylan and Michael Loewe, 187–212. Cambridge: Cambridge University Press.

De Caro, Stefano and Scarpari, Maurizio. eds. 2010. *I Due Imperi: L'Aquila e il Dragone*. Exhibition at the Palazzo Reale, Milan, 15 April to 5 September 2010. Milan: Federico Motta Editore.

Dettenhofer, Maria H. 2006. 'Das Römische Imperium und das China der Han-Zeit: Ansätze zu einer historischen Komparatistik', *Latomus* 65(4): 879–97.

Dettenhofer, Maria H. 2009. 'Eunuchs, women, and imperial courts'. In *Rome and China: Comparative perspectives on ancient world empires*, edited by Walter Scheidel, 83–99. Oxford; New York: Oxford University Press.

Noreña, Carlos F. 2015. 'Chang'an and Rome: structural parallels and the logics of urban form'. In *Chang'an 26 BCE: An Augustan age in China*, edited by Michael Nylan and Griet Vankeerberghen, 75–97. Seattle, WA: University of Washington Press.

Razeto, Anna. 2014. 'Comparing East and West: aspects of urban manufacture and retail in the capitals of the Roman and Han Empires'. In *Making Ancient Cities: Space and place in early urban societies*, edited by Andrew T. Creekmore III and Kevin D. Fisher, 337–69. Cambridge; New York: Cambridge University Press.

Ru Xin 汝信 and Xun Ji 孙机. 2009. *Qin Han – Luo Ma: Wenming Fazhan*. 秦汉-罗马文明发展. *Qin-Han and Roman Civilization*. Beijing: Cultural Relics Press.

Scheidel, Walter (ed.). 2008. *Rome and China: Comparative perspectives on ancient world empires*. Oxford: Oxford University Press.

Scheidel, Walter (ed.). 2015. *State Power in Ancient China and Rome*. Oxford: Oxford University Press.

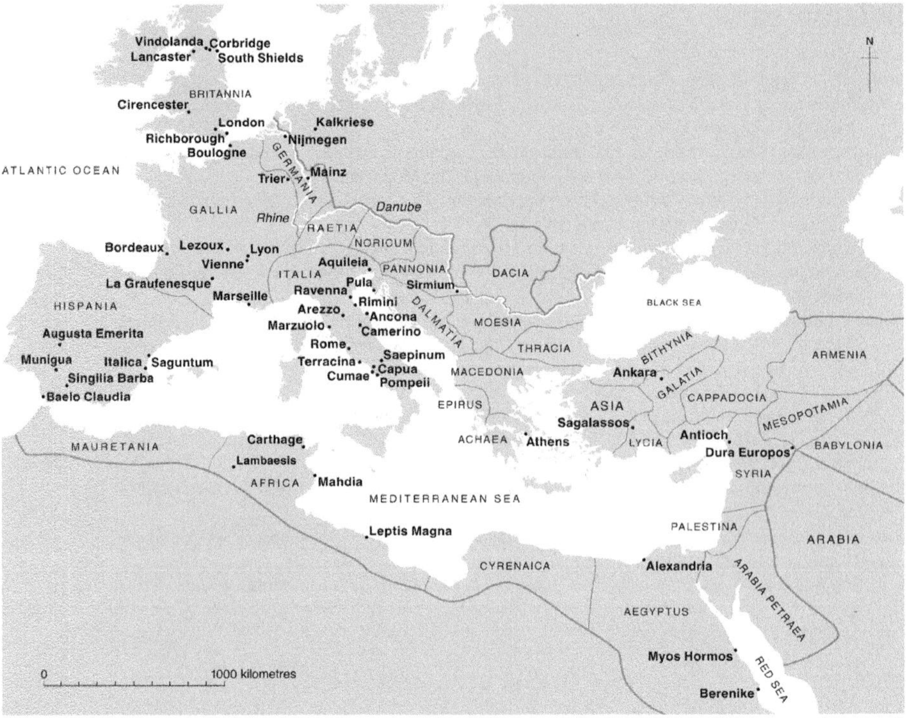

Figure 0.1 Map of the Roman Empire in the reign of Trajan. © Christina Unwin.

Introduction: Roman archaeology and the materiality of empire

Andrew Gardner

Materialising the Roman Empire defines an innovative research agenda for Roman archaeology, highlighting the diverse ways in which the Empire was made materially tangible in the lives of its inhabitants. Chapters in the volume explore how material culture was integral to the process of imperialism, both as the Empire grew, and as it fragmented, and in doing so provide up-to-date overviews of major topics in Roman archaeology. This introductory chapter will situate the volume within current, and recent, debates in Roman archaeology, and beyond. Beginning with a broad review of the state of the discipline – primarily in the Anglosphere – and highlighting research trends since the turn of the millennium, Roman studies will be positioned within an increasingly fragmented theoretical landscape across archaeology. The chapter will then consider the major themes which the volume directly addresses: the archaeology of empire, the role of materiality in social life and the comparison of different forms of evidence. Roman archaeology has engaged with a number of explicit approaches to empire in the last 30 years, from post-colonial theory in the 1990s to globalisation theory in the 2000s, reflecting different contemporary perspectives on imperialism that have flourished since the passing of modern European empires in the mid-twentieth century. The merits of, and interaction between, these approaches, as well as the insights that can be derived from comparative archaeologies of empire, will be explored. Materiality has also become a topic of interdisciplinary interest in recent years, and new approaches to the complex relationships between people and things are major subjects of debate across archaeology, as well as in anthropology, history of art, and sociology. The ways in which Roman archaeology has, or might, engage with these will be discussed, before concluding with an overview of the chapters in the volume, and their contributions to the understanding of the materiality of the Roman Empire.

Roman archaeology today

Roman archaeology is, depending on your perspective, in a period of comfortable continuity, or profound crisis. Like archaeology more generally, there is currently a lack of either a unifying paradigm or its obvious alternative, a deep ideological rift between competing schools of thought. Rather, there appears to be a state of benign fragmentation which allows multiple perspectives to prosper and seems able to smooth over the rhetorical – at least – differences between them to let archaeologists just get along, and get on with their work. This might be perfectly acceptable, but in the world in which archaeology is practised, there are real crises. For the discipline to remain vital, intellectually and pragmatically, and not simply resort to what it has been before – a nostalgic retreat from the present-day world – recognition that this comfort might conceal our own crisis is needed. For our discipline, whether at the level of archaeology itself, or the Roman sub-field, to attract new intakes of students, be enhanced with new jobs or take part in current debates, its critical relevance to the twenty-first century challenges of pandemic disease, imperialism, nationalism and climate change needs to be argued and articulated within and beyond the academy. Roman archaeology specifically has much to contribute to significant aspects of understanding these problems, but to do so will require unsettling some of the comfortable habits we have become used to in the last generation or so.

The time is ripe for this transformation because it is indeed about 30 years since a break with traditional Roman archaeology was forged in the era of the first Theoretical Roman Archaeology Conferences, at least in the Anglophone world. The fortunes of this specific gathering, and its uneven successes, are documented elsewhere (e.g. Laurence 1999; 2006; Gardner 2006; 2016), but it serves as a benchmark for the transition of Roman archaeology into a post-colonial era in the later 1980s and early 1990s, certainly in the sense of its practitioners no longer being familiar with life in a modern imperial power. More specifically, post-colonial theory in the vein of Said and Bhabha was actively deployed, at least in some quarters and for a little while, partly as critique and partly as a constructive approach providing an alternative to the stale, regressive and simplistic 'Romanisation' paradigm which had dominated much of the twentieth century. Even here, though, fragmentation crept in with the array of broadly post-colonial approaches deployed by key scholars in this wave of innovation, from creolisation (Webster 2001) to discrepant experience (Mattingly 2004). By the turn of the millennium, the kind of calendrical milestone which naturally prompted some reflections on the state of the field (James 2003; Woolf 2004), this revolution was seen as incomplete, alongside a considerable amount of continuity and indeed a degree of reaction, both of which have continued to the present, albeit the latter sometimes coming from a different angle now (e.g. Versluys 2014). In terms of more innovative approaches, post-colonialism began to be eclipsed by globalisation as the buzz-word at conferences (and not just at TRAC) from the mid-noughties, and it remains a significant presence (e.g. at the postponed RAC/TRAC 2020, in Split, Croatia, April 2022). What precisely these changing perspectives mean for our understanding of Roman imperialism will be explored further below.

The key point here is that neither of these over-arching theoretical positions has become a major locus for consensus, while at the same time critique of them has been insufficient to steer our field in a different direction; academic representation has rather emerged as the key theme of debate in recent years (Kamash 2021; cf. Gardner 2013; Versluys 2014). Thus we arrive at the fragmented condition already referred to, and reflecting a similar situation, albeit with different contours, in the wider discipline (cf. Johnson 2020: 265–83; Mizoguchi 2015). Some of those different contours are attributable to the particular character of Roman archaeology (post-colonialism, for example, has been explored more fully in our sub-field than many others, except for heritage studies). Fault-lines also persist between different regional traditions in Roman archaeology, along a 'classical–provincial' contiuum. Even in the more progressive sectors of the field, however, and as has frequently been the case in the past, debates within Roman archaeology lag behind those in mainstream archaeological theory, and so the most important trend of the last decade in that sphere, the cluster of approaches variously referred to as the new materialism, the ontological turn, or post-humanism, has yet to make a widespread impact (though cf. Gardner 2014; Versluys 2014; Van Oyen and Pitts 2017). Whether this trend is a productive one for Roman archaeology to follow is debatable – and this issue will be addressed later in this chapter – but at least that debate needs to be happening at conferences and in publications, where it is not very visible right now. Another major theme in the wider discipline which certainly demands attention in Roman archaeology is decolonisation, which is indeed an emerging agenda in the field (Kamash 2021). Engaging with these issues, and indeed entwining them as we tackle the material and human impact of imperialism in the past and in the present, might be just the kind of debate which re-energises Roman archaeology and galvanises it for the challenges of the century ahead. This volume seeks to launch a wider commitment to exactly this kind of project.

Empire in the twenty-first century

That there is still much work to do in understanding the nature of Roman imperialism might seem unlikely after well over a century of academic archaeological investigation, but the pervasive influence of modern imperial attitudes in scholarship for a large proportion of that time must be accounted for. There is no need here to rehearse all of the 'Romanisation' debates of the 1990s (see e.g. Hingley 2005: 14–48; Millett 2014; Versluys 2014; cf. Mattingly, Chapter 11 this volume). Suffice it to say that the predominant interest, across classical and provincial Roman archaeologies, in the apparently homogenising 'civilisation' of the Roman Empire, dominated by elite culture and influenced also by a handful of written sources, was clearly as much an echo of the self-justifying narratives of Western empires in the nineteenth and early twentieth centuries as any kind of account of Rome. In an international but generally conservative field, the long shadow of mid-twentieth-century syntheses well into the 1980s took considerable effort to escape and there remains uneven progress and a considerable risk of regression to simplistic descriptions, rather than critical analyses, of Roman imperialism – partly, as will be touched upon later, because of the demands of the materiality of the empire. In the rest of this section, I will review some of the perspectives deployed since that point, their strengths and weaknesses, and their connections and blind spots, some of which are particularly highlighted by recent political trends in the wider world.

The post-colonial turn in Roman archaeology, introduced already above, encompassed a number of characteristic approaches. Some of these were evident in the first TRAC proceedings in 1991 (Scott 1993), alongside an eclectic mixture of other strands of broadly post-processual theory (and notably this volume had a foreword by Ian Hodder). The clearest articulation of these approaches came, though, in a pair of mid-90s volumes, *Roman Imperialism: Post-colonial perspectives* (Webster and Cooper 1996) and *Dialogues in Roman Imperialism* (Mattingly 1997), followed of course by numerous other publications in subsequent years by

Richard Hingley, David J. Mattingly, Jane Webster and several other key figures, dealing particularly – but certainly not only – with Roman Britain. The post-colonial trend in Roman archaeology in this period developed along at least three major lines. The first – and indeed the earliest to be deployed – addressed the possibility for recovering the archaeology of resistance to Roman imperialism, not simply in overt rebellion but in more subtle forms, including disinterest or disengagement from cultural changes arising from Roman occupation. This kind of work developed particularly in a North African context (e.g. Bénabou 1976), and was picked up in the archaeology of Roman Britain in, for example, some of Hingley's early work on non-villa rural settlement (Hingley 1989). More recent research highlighting the long-lasting diversity of settlement forms in Roman Britain, for example (such as Smith et al. 2016), suggests that this is still a highly relevant theme.

However, other post-colonial developments sought to move more firmly away from the cultural dichotomies of the 'Romanisation' paradigm. One important strand here echoes much of the work in more contemporary post-colonial studies seeking to deconstruct the literature and other cultural media of the European imperial age (e.g. Said 1978). This has involved the engagement of Roman scholars in deeper critical analysis of the literary and other texts produced in the Roman Empire, so often used in the past as the main, and largely unquestioned, framework of understanding in Roman archaeology (e.g. Alston 1996; Forcey 1997). This vein of reappraisal aligns somewhat with other approaches in historical archaeologies to treat texts as material culture, situating them more firmly in their context of production and use (e.g. Moreland 2001). In a related development, the critical historiography of the field of Roman archaeology has been much expanded (e.g. Hingley 2000); both of these aspects of deconstructing ancient and modern texts find strong resonances in Classics (e.g. Goff 2005). The other, more conventionally archaeological, post-colonial strand encompasses a number of approaches to 'decentring' the Roman Empire, striving to complicate understandings of the nature of being 'Roman', across the diversity of times and places encompassed by the Empire, and embracing the even greater range of other dimensions and foci of identity that might have been significant in people's lived experience (cf. Dench 2005; Given 2004). Particular manifestations of this kind of perspective were articulated by Jane Webster, in her work on creolisation, deploying theories of cultural hybridity developed in American historical archaeology, and David J. Mattingly, whose adoption of Said's notion of 'discrepant experience' has been worked through in bottom-up studies of the multiplicity of identities at play in Roman Britain and North Africa (Webster 2001; Mattingly 2004; 2011; cf. Mattingly, Chapter 11 this volume). This kind of work aligned broadly with post-processual/interpretive interests in multi-vocality and agency, and with the political context of knowledge production, but stopped short of fully exploring decolonisation of the field, which has risen up the agenda much more recently. In the intervening period, a different set of approaches framed Roman archaeology in relation to another lens on the modern world: globalisation theory.

The shift towards globalisation as a new framing device for understanding Roman imperialism in the early twenty-first century reflects, in part, a desire to adjust the point of contact between the modern world and the past onto more contemporary terrain – transcending the 'Romanisation' debate by moving on from empire, or at least into a more current form of empire (Hingley 2005; cf. Hardt and Negri 2000). It also relates to a wider trend around the turn of the millennium in archaeology, building on a broad inter-disciplinary field of globalisation theory (albeit that this flourished somewhat earlier), seeking ancient forms, or roots, of this phenomenon (cf. Hodos 2016). Perhaps less focused on Roman Britain than preceding developments in the theoretical transformation of Roman archaeology, scholars applying globalisation theory – which is as diverse as post-colonialism, if not more so – have tended to focus on the changing, and expanding, interconnectivity of the Roman world, particularly in economic terms, as well as using the concept of 'glocalisation' as a way of exploring local/indigenous responses to – and consumption of – the dynamic materiality of this world (e.g. Witcher 2000; Hitchner 2008; Pitts 2008; Pitts and Versluys 2014; Versluys 2014; cf. Morley 2010). This kind of approach has led to valuable studies which emphasise the real material shift that Roman imperialism ushered in across the whole empire – an important theme in this book, and directly linking to other new approaches to materiality considered below – but it is not without difficulties. Leaving aside the debate about whether 'globalisation' is strictly only a meaningful description of modernity, while there are some strands within globalisation theory that have considered the deep interconnectivity of this process since the fifteenth century with imperialism, and with the aftermath of modern empires (e.g. Hardt and Negri 2000; Krishna 2009), in other areas there was some naivety about the inevitability of progress in a globalising direction (e.g. Urry 2000), and ignorance of some of the political backlash to this which has become more apparent as the twenty-first century has gone on. Inequality and exploitation have hardly been banished by globalisation, and 're-bordering', especially since 2001, has checked visions of a 'borderless world' (see below; Ohmae 1990; cf. Bude and Dürrschmidt 2010). At best, globalisation theory may offer a partial insight into the imperial world of Rome, but needs to be allied with more politically sensitive post-colonial theory. At worst, it seems increasingly dated in a world which is rapidly transforming.

A range of other theoretical trends have framed understandings of the Roman Empire in different ways over the last three decades, which are more-or-less connected to these major currents, and they in turn play a part in shaping where the discipline is at now. A major theme from the later 1990s which spun off from the post-colonial turn, but often drew upon other sources of theory, was the study of identities in the Roman world. Importantly, this topic was able to bridge the gap between 'civilian' and 'military' archaeologies of provinces like Roman Britain which had been widening in the 1970s and 1980s, though there is still some way to go to fully close this gap (cf. Gardner, Chapter 10 this volume). The interaction between imperialism and ethnic, gender, military, religious and a range of other identities has been considered across a wide spectrum of case studies from all over the Empire (e.g. Laurence and Harlow 2002; Scott and Webster 2003; Gardner 2007; Eckardt 2010; Gardner et al. 2013; Revell 2016). While there is debate about whether some of this work really moves beyond the kinds of traditional cultural structures employed in earlier analyses (Pitts 2007), a more challenging issue is how to synthesise studies which by their nature tend to focus on provincial or regional scales of analysis. At the other end of the spectrum, more generalising approaches which parallel aspects of the globalisation turn have developed, comparing Rome to other ancient empires, particularly China, for broad-scale investigation of imperial structures and economies (e.g. Alcock et al. 2001; Bang 2008; Scheidel 2015). Meanwhile, interdisciplinary work in 'Border Studies', which has been engaged with the increasing prevalence of boundary-making in the last two decades, referred to above, has been drawn upon by some scholars of frontier regions (e.g. Boozer 2013; Gardner 2017; Hingley 2018). This work generally seeks to connect an understanding of the transformative social role of boundaries with other insights derived from earlier phases of the theorisation of Roman imperialism. Alongside all of these trends, and as already mentioned, there is a renewed focus on the politics of the practice of Roman archaeology, which has come about through discussion of decolonisation, and its implications for teaching and for the organisation of research into the Roman world (e.g. Kamash 2021; Redfern, Chapter 6 this volume). This promises to have much more impact in the next decade.

This review is incomplete but it is hoped that it gives a flavour of the diversity of approaches to empire in Roman archaeology over the last 30 years or so. It has been a dynamic and highly fruitful period for generating a wide range of approaches, and of course has run alongside significant expansion of the database on which Roman archaeology draws, through commercial and research excavations and many other kinds of projects across the territory of the former empire. Both of these trends do, though, contribute to the fragmentation of the discipline which was referred to at the beginning of this chapter. In many ways there are complementarities in the kinds of perspectives taken in recent years, emphasising different regions of the Empire, different scales of analysis and different degrees of political critique. Such developments have also been taking place in a rapidly transforming contemporary world, with the optimistic period, for many in the West at least, in the 1990s giving way to increasingly troubled times by the mid-2010s. Now, a new episode of imperial (or post-imperial) aggression in Europe, against the backdrop of accelerating climate change, promises even greater challenges ahead. Insofar as much of the politics of the world is still framed by legacies of the empires which began to fall a century ago, understanding of the Roman Empire is as relevant, and as politically charged, as it has ever been. New approaches along the lines outlined above are pushing the discipline in the direction it needs to go to engage with wider debates. One distinctive element which Roman archaeology might bring to these is its analysis of the materiality of imperialism, and indeed this is a key theme at the centre of all recent approaches. In the next section, some of the different ways of understanding that materiality will be considered.

The materiality of empire

To begin with it is worth examining some of the broader trends in material culture theory that have been debated across archaeology in recent years. For all that the dichotomised theory wars of the 1980s have long departed, and fragmentation characterises twenty-first century archaeology in general, not just Roman archaeology, this topic has seen the most intense discussion. Emerging out of the context of symbolic approaches to objects and of developing engagement with theories of structure and agency in the 1990s, the unfolding of a 'material turn' or 'ontological turn' around the beginning of the new millennium drew upon a wide range of influences. Most proximate to archaeology were a number of anthropological approaches to object biographies and the power of objects in shaping human interactions (e.g. Appadurai 1986; Miller 1994; cf. Gardner 2003); perhaps the most influential of these has been the work of Alfred Gell in the domain of art objects (Gell 1998; cf. Gosden 2005; Osborne and Tanner 2007). Another strand is the influence of the Actor-Network Theory school in Science and Technology Studies, most prominently associated with Bruno Latour, whose *We Have Never Been Modern* (1993) has had significant impact in archaeology, with its argument that a strong separation between humans and things is one characteristic of a misleading Modern ontology. This impact has been particularly propelled by Mike Shanks and his students at Stanford University, framing their project as 'symmetrical archaeology' (e.g. Webmoor 2007; Witmore 2007; Webmoor and Witmore 2008). Another key figure in post-processual archaeology, Ian Hodder, synthesised some of these approaches, along with others, in his work on the 'entanglement' of people and things (Hodder 2012), developing the argument that the interaction between human and non-human is not a straightforward division of agents and objects, but rather that there is a co-dependent relationship that places fundamental importance on materiality in the emergence of complex societies (cf. also Thomas 2004; Ingold 2007; Knappett and Malafouris 2008). Recently, a range of other 'post-human' approaches have been cited across a wide literature (Olsen 2010; Alberti et al. 2011; Crellin et al. 2021), drawing on a spectrum of sources including feminist, ecological and indigenous perspectives. The current state of the field is difficult to summarise, with overlapping but distinct positions on several issues (cf. Harris and Cipolla 2017; Crellin and Harris 2021), but is essentially characterised by a decentring of the 'human' and an emphasis on the potency, or the agency, of the non-human and material world.

The relevance of all of this work to the creation and maintenance of one of the most materially impactful societies of the ancient world has not gone unnoticed. It seems self-evident that the materiality of the Roman Empire was distinctive, and that this played a part in the process of imperialism and the shaping of distinctive ways of living for its people. Indeed, ironically, the rich and complex materiality of the Roman world has often acted as something of a brake on theoretical development, with scholarship preoccupied simply with grappling with so many things. Increasingly, though, some Roman archaeologists are engaged with the kinds of theory outlined above, though in quite varied ways and to greater or lesser lengths in terms of some of the more radical propositions of post-humanism (Selsvold and Webb 2019). One of the earliest and most provocative applications of the concept of 'material agency' to Roman studies came from Chris Gosden, in 2005, arguing that 'people crystallize out in the interstices between objects, taking up the space allowed them by the object world' (2005: 197), and exploring this through case studies of Romano-British houses, brooches and pots. Interestingly Gosden did note that there are similarities between this kind of approach and modern Darwinian theory (cf. Hodder 2012: 139), a rather different tradition poorly represented in Roman archaeology (though see Biddulph 2012), but characterised, particularly with the concept of memes, by a high degree of cultural and environmental determinism. Subsequently, the eclectic use of more object-centred theory in Roman studies has had some connection with globalisation, where the new flows of artefacts and their role in changing provincial societies is emphasised (e.g. Pitts and Verluys 2014; Versluys 2014; Pitts 2019). More strongly post-humanist approaches have appeared in investigations of Roman religious and ritual practice, and of domestic life (Mol 2013; 2019; Parker and McKie 2018), with Eva Mol's work in particular emphasising the power of Egyptianising objects in Italian contexts. Astrid Van Oyen has developed related perspectives in the study of Roman pottery, particularly Terra Sigillata and storage vessels (Van Oyen 2016, 2020), emphasising how the latter, for example, have a long-term impact on domestic life (cf. Van Oyen, Chapter 7 this volume). Certainly, the Roman world is rich in examples of material transformations that require approaches to taking things seriously, and which move the discipline far from its origins as mere illustrative material for historical accounts.

However, in the wider field, and indeed within Roman studies, there are a range of views on the coherence, utility and implications of these 'new materialisms', and alternative approaches remain significant across the diversity of current Roman archaeologies. Indeed, some of the critique of the material turn in archaeology echoes earlier critical discussion of the source material in Actor-Network Theory or in post-humanism more broadly. As in other paradigm shifts in archaeology dating back to at least the 1960s, there is typically a lag in the introduction of new concepts into the field, and thus there is also usually an extensive debate which could be – but not always is – taken account of. The theoretical coherence and empirical and political implications of various of the 'new materialist' theories had thus already been challenged in the 1990s (e.g. Jones 1996; Bloor 1999; Elam 1999). In archaeology, what can be seen as a 'dehumanisation' of the past has also provoked an increasingly strong reaction, particularly as the over-determination of human agency by social structures, environments or indeed artefact assemblages as proxies for these phenomena had only recently begun to be challenged (e.g. Johannsen 2012; Barrett 2014; Van Dyke 2015; Ribeiro 2016; Díaz de Liaño and Fernández-Götz 2021; cf. Johnson 2006: 125). This critique has also developed within Roman archaeology, with the potential political consequences of diminishing human agency and responsibility for what was a predatory empire that treated people as objects troubling some scholars (Fernández-Götz et al. 2020; Gardner 2020; 2021). The debates very much continue, particularly over these political implications, and it can only be advantageous to the vitality of Roman archaeology to engage with them.

Meanwhile, a wide range of other approaches to the artefactuality of the Roman Empire and the role of material culture in both reproducing and transforming that empire, and in shaping our understandings of it, continue to be deployed. In recent years, continued detailed work across a number of suites of artefact types and materials has been pursued in relation to multi-dimensional studies of identity across the north-west provinces (Eckardt 2015), while aspects of the object biography approach to tracing life-histories of things and people in Roman Britain have also been linked to different categories of identity (Rogers 2015). Another concept linked to developments in the theory of materiality, of the actions 'afforded' by different elements of artefact design, is explored in studies of objects as diverse as bottles and dice in Swift's recent work (2020), while other approaches situate artefacts in a more mediating role between agency and structure, as elements in the ongoing practice of different activities, shaping historical agency in distinctive ways, but retaining its locus in the human (Gardner 2022). These sorts of hybrid approaches which selectively engage with the hugely varied theoretical toolkit that Roman archaeology can now draw upon are characteristic of the discipline as we move well into the twenty-first century. They have played a big part in transcending the divides between different evidence-bases that was a major issue in Roman studies in the previous generation (cf. Sauer 2004). They also offer the potential to grapple with the complex problem of capturing something of the alterity, or 'otherness', of the Roman world, which is always challenging when we begin from a starting point of such seeming familiarity, as identification with Rome is deeply embedded in Western cultures. A similarly disparate set of approaches is exhibited by the authors in this volume – ranging from those who embrace 'material agency' to a greater or lesser degree, to those who emphasise empire as a pervasive form of political practice materialised in particular ways. This Introduction will conclude with a brief overview of the chapters to follow.

Contributions in this volume, and conclusions

The chapters in this volume deal largely with specific material dimensions of Roman imperialism and its consequences in provincial societies. Each author has been asked to give a thorough overview of their topic, covering key debates, strands of the evidence and overarching trends, but each has been free to approach these topics in their particular way, and emphasising datasets that they feel most appropriately illustrate salient points. The first three contributions tackle the major technologies which, at first glance, appear to be mechnisms of integration across the Roman Empire – roads, writing and coinage. Ray Laurence discusses a variety of ways in which roads were very important in the materialisation of empire, beyond their simple affordance of greater military movement or faster communications, encompassing their symbolic dimensions, relationships to concepts of space, and enabling of other projections of state power in the infrastructure attached to them. At the same time, the importance of local road networks for smaller-scale groups and communities within the interstices of the imperial network is also emphasised. John Pearce surveys the huge diversity of material culture bearing writing, and the roles these objects played in spanning social distances, facilitating the negotiation of identity, and buttressing the institutional reach of the Empire. The complex issue of the estimation of the variable degrees of literacy within different sub-groups of the Roman imperial population is also considered, with an emphasis on the power of writing at a relatively mass scale. One distinctive category of objects bearing writing is, of course, coinage, and Chris Howgego deals with this in the third chapter, exploring the ways in which coins, perhaps more than any other kind of readily portable artefact, communicated imperial political messages – as miniature monuments – while simultaneously serving the institutional and economic needs of the state. Even so, this was a system subject to regular fluctuation as a currency, and to variability in the progress of monetisation across the Empire.

The next chapters deal with some of the major social structures oriented around particular material forms and activities found all over the Roman world. Andrew Wilson's chapter on trade encompasses the major issues in understanding this form of connectivity in the Empire, including the volumes, scales and economic underpinnings of different forms of exchange activity. He highlights the role of the state in key areas, such as in ensuring the supply of olive oil from Spain to Rome, and also the very significant role of cross-frontier trade (cf. Gardner, Chapter 10 this volume). Turning to a characteristic settlement form of Roman imperialism, Louise

Revell looks at urbanism, particularly in the Roman West, in her chapter. The ideology of urbanism and the roles that the institutions of towns and cities played in articulating imperial power are discussed, as materialised in architecure, inscriptions and so forth. Balancing the commonalities of urban lived experience with variability across and within provinces is important, but among the common themes, the relationship of towns to the significant social structure of patronage/clientage is also considered. In the next chapter, Rebecca Redfern addresses another social institution which is frequently under-served in studies of the Roman world: slavery. This chapter emphasises the ominpresence of violence in the Roman Empire, even far from the battlefields of traditional military narratives, and connects the attitudes which allowed slavery to continue with other common Roman – and indeed modern – prejudices. Making use of bioarchaeological data, among other lines of evidence, Redfern shows how we are increasingly understanding the lived experience of slaves and argues that, as we do so, we can draw this material into current debates about the decolonisation of the discipline. In Astrid Van Oyen's chapter, the kind of work performed by slaves, alongside many others, in the Roman world is discussed, in terms of the organisation and location of production of the many kinds of goods which were moved around the Empire, and the relationship of this production with a 'consumer revolution': the intersection of imperial processes which transformed production, and a new world of goods which transformed the Empire, is a key theme.

The two chapters which follow deal with material forms traditionally regarded as related to more esoteric dimensions of the Roman world than craft products, but which we would now see as closely connected to every other dimension of Roman imperial society. Peter Stewart examines the relationship between art and empire, particularly in the Principate (27 BCE–284 CE), where on the one hand there are clear political agendas behind some art forms, and a high degree of consistency in others, while on the other hand there is much hybridity and 'provincialisation' evident across a number of media, in their formal characteristics. Stewart explores the relevance of globalisation frameworks to account for this kind of pattern. Ton Derks, in the next chapter, discusses the materiality of religion in the Roman world, also exploring more centralising and more disparate tendencies in this domain of life. Comparing imperial cult practice with the diversity of other cults, Derks highlights the innovations of the Roman period, for example in rites of passage for elite individuals in the Rhine frontier region. The complex role of frontiers is considered in my chapter, using the variety of frontier types and histories present even just within Roman Britain as case studies for exploring the transformative role of frontiers on provincial, and indeed wider Roman society. This chapter draws upon Border Studies theory (see above) to tackle the complex dual role of frontiers as dividing and connecting different societies, and to understand the nature of frontier communities – dominated by the military – in new ways. Finally, David J. Mattingly concludes the volume with an in-depth discussion of the nature of imperial power, and its limitations, providing a fitting conclusion to the volume which explores the materiality of Roman-period identities and the ways in which, over time, the Empire itself transformed what it meant to be Roman.

Overall, then, the chapters in this volume present both a thorough grounding in the key elements of many aspects of Roman imperial culture, and a series of arguments and debates about the relative consistency and hybridity of different dimensions of life in the Roman world. Applying different approaches from the many options that scholars can currently draw upon, as outlined above, the significant themes remain the dynamics of power and influence, the balance of new opportunities for some people and new forms of oppression for others, and the increasing scale of inter-connections alongside the potential for new social divisions and new community identities to be created. The chapters also speak to the materiality of empire in the Roman world as a process, with a temporal dimension, its contours shifting at the macro-scale through the phases of Roman expansion, consolidation and fragmentation, and at micro-scales as each generation of inhabitants of the Roman Empire had different identities and experiences of being 'Roman' – or something else. In a discipline so long overshadowed not only by a traditional relationship between archaeological evidence and other sources, but also by an implicit identification between present and past – for Western scholars and many of their audiences – to consider this diversity across time and space is revalatory in its significance. If the price of that progress is increasing fragmentation of our approaches, then this may well be a price worth paying if we are to capture the complexity of the Roman world, and its many manifestations in the present – in service of causes both good and ill. In closing, it is important to note that this volume should have had one additional chapter, on the relationships between imperialism and plant cultivation, by Lisa Lodwick, but very sadly Lisa passed away before she could complete her contribution. As an advocate of new approaches to materiality and to the decolonisation of the discipline, her voice would have been a very significant one to include here, but in her absence it is hoped that the diversity and strength of approaches across the discipline which is represented in this volume is a fitting tribute to the kind of work she created and supported.

References

Alberti, Benjamin, Severin Fowles, Martin Holbraad, Yvonne Marshall and Christopher Witmore. 2011. '"Worlds otherwise": archaeology, anthropology, and ontological difference', *Current Anthropology* 52(6): 896–912.

Alcock, Susan E., Terence N. D'Altroy, Kathleen D. Morrison and Carla M. Sinopoli (eds). 2001. *Empires: Perspectives from archaeology and history*. Cambridge: Cambridge University Press.

Alston, Richard. 1996. 'Conquest by text: Juvenal and Plutarch on Egypt'. In *Roman Imperialism: Post-colonial perspectives*, edited by Jane Webster and Nicholas J. Cooper, 99–109. Leicester: School of Archaeological Studies, University of Leicester.

Appadurai, Arjun. 1986. *The Social Life of Things: Commodities in cultural perspective*. Cambridge: Cambridge University Press.

Bang, Peter F. 2008. *The Roman Bazaar: A comparative study of trade and markets in a tributary empire*. Cambridge: Cambridge University Press.

Barrett, John C. 2014. 'The material constitution of humanness', *Archaeological Dialogues* 21(1): 65–74.

Bénabou, Marcel. 1976. *La résistance africaine à la romanisation*. Paris: Maspero.

Biddulph, Edward. 2012. 'On cultural selection: examining the process of cultural evolution through funerary evidence'. In *TRAC 2011: Proceedings of the Twenty First Theoretical Roman Archaeology Conference, Newcastle 2011*, edited by Maria Duggan, Frances McIntosh and Darrell J. Rohl, 76–90. Oxford: Oxbow Books.

Bloor, David. 1999. 'Anti-Latour', *Studies in the History and Philosophy of Science* 30(1): 81–112.

Bude, Heinz and Jörg Dürrschmidt. 2010. 'What's wrong with globalization? Contra 'flow speak' – towards an existential turn in the theory of globalization', *European Journal of Social Theory* 13(4): 481–500.

Boozer, Anna L. 2013. 'Frontiers and borderlands in imperial perspectives: exploring Rome's Egyptian frontier', *American Journal of Archaeology* 117(2): 275–92.

Crellin, Rachel J. and Oliver J. T. Harris. 2021. 'What difference does posthumanism make?', *Cambridge Archaeological Journal* 31(3): 469–75.

Crellin, Rachel J., Craig N. Cipolla, Lindsay M. Montgomery, Oliver J.T. Harris and Sophie V. Moore (eds). 2021. *Archaeological Theory in Dialogue: Situating relationality, ontology, posthumanism, and indigenous paradigms*. Abingdon: Routledge.

Dench, Emma. 2005. *Romulus' Asylum: Roman identities from the age of Alexander to the age of Hadrian*. Oxford: Oxford University Press.

Díaz de Liaño, Guillermo and Manuel Fernández-Götz. 2021. 'Posthumanism, new humanism and beyond'. In 'Debating posthumanism: a special section', edited by Manuel Fernández-Götz, Andrew Gardner, Guillermo Díaz de Liaño and Oliver J.T. Harris, *Cambridge Archaeological Journal* 31(3): 543–9.

Eckardt, Hella (ed.). 2010. *Roman Diasporas: Archaeological approaches to mobility and diversity in the Roman Empire*. Portsmouth, RI: Journal of Roman Archaeology.

Eckardt, Hella. 2015. *Objects and Identities: Roman Britain and the north-west provinces*. Oxford: Oxford University Press.

Elam, Mark. 1999. 'Living dangerously with Bruno Latour in a hybrid world', *Theory, Culture & Society* 16(4): 1–24.

Fernández-Götz, Manuel, Dominik Maschek and Nico Roymans. 2020. 'The dark side of the Empire: Roman expansionism between object agency and predatory regime', *Antiquity* 94 (378): 1630–9.

Forcey, Colin. 1997. 'Beyond "Romanization": technologies of power in Roman Britain'. In *TRAC 96: Proceedings of the Sixth Annual Theoretical Roman Archaeology Conference, Sheffield 1996*, edited by Karen Meadows, Chris Lemke and Jo Heron, 15–21. Oxford: Oxbow Books.

Gardner, Andrew. 2003. 'Seeking a material turn: the artefactuality of the Roman empire'. In *TRAC 2002: Proceedings of the Twelfth Annual Theoretical Roman Archaeology Conference, Canterbury 2002*, edited by Gillian Carr, Ellen Swift and Jake Weekes, 1–13. Oxford: Oxbow Books.

Gardner, Andrew. 2006. 'The future of TRAC'. In *TRAC 2005: Proceedings of the Fifteenth Annual Theoretical Roman Archaeology Conference, Birmingham 2005*, edited by Ben Croxford, Helen Goodchild, Jason Lucas and Nick Ray, 128–37. Oxford: Oxbow Books.

Gardner, Andrew. 2007. *An Archaeology of Identity: Soldiers and society in late Roman Britain*. Walnut Creek, CA: Left Coast Press.

Gardner, Andrew. 2013. 'Thinking about Roman imperialism: postcolonialism, globalisation and beyond?' *Britannia* 44: 1–25.

Gardner, Andrew. 2014. 'Changing materialities'. In *The Oxford Handbook to Roman Britain*, edited by Martin Millett, Alison Moore and Louise Revell, 481–509. Oxford: Oxford University Press.

Gardner, Andrew. 2016. 'Debating Roman imperialism: critique, construct, repeat?' In *TRAC 2015: Proceedings of the Twenty-Fifth Annual Theoretical Roman Archaeology Conference*, edited by Matthew J. Mandich, Thomas J. Derrick, Sergio González Sánchez, Giacomo Savini and Elenora Zampieri, 1–14. Oxford: Oxbow Books.

Gardner, Andrew. 2017. 'Roman Britain from the outside: comparing western and northern frontier cultures'. In *'Romans' and 'Barbarians' beyond the Frontiers: Archaeology, ideology and identities in the North*, edited by Sergio González Sánchez and Alexandra Guglielmi, 34–47. Oxford: Oxbow Books.

Gardner, Andrew. 2020. 'Re-balancing the Romans', *Antiquity* 94 (378): 1640–2.

Gardner, Andrew. 2021. 'Taking the wrong turn? Re-examining the potential for practice approaches in archaeology'. In 'Debating posthumanism: a special section', edited by Manuel Fernández-Götz, Andrew Gardner, Guillermo Díaz de Liaño and Oliver J.T. Harris, *Cambridge Archaeological Journal* 31(3): 503–8.

Gardner, Andrew. 2022. 'Practicing the borders: structure and creativity on the Roman frontiers'. In *Sozialität–Materialität–Praxis/Sociality–Materiality–Practice*, edited by Tobias Kienlin and Richard Bußmann, 321–34. Köln: Kölner Beiträge zu Archäologie und Kulturwissenschaften.

Gardner, Andrew, Herring, Edward and Lomas, Kathryn (eds). 2013. *Creating Ethnicities and Identities in the Roman World*. London: Institute of Classical Studies.

Gell, Alfred. 1998. *Art and Agency: An anthropological theory*. Oxford: Clarendon Press.

Given, Michael. 2004. *The Archaeology of the Colonized*. London: Routledge.

Goff, Barbara E. (ed.). 2005. *Classics and Colonialism*. London: Duckworth.

Gosden, Chris. 2005. 'What do objects want?', *Journal of Archaeological Method and Theory* 12(3): 193–211.

Hardt, Michael and Antonio Negri. 2000. *Empire*. Cambridge, MA: Harvard University Press.

Harris, Oliver J.T. and Craig Cipolla. 2017. *Archaeological Theory in the New Millennium: Introducing current perspectives*. London: Routledge.

Hingley, Richard. 1989. *Rural Settlement in Roman Britain*. London: Seaby.

Hingley, Richard. 2000. *Roman Officers and English Gentlemen: The imperial origins of Roman archaeology*. London: Routledge.

Hingley, Richard. 2005. *Globalizing Roman culture: Unity, diversity and empire*. London: Routledge.

Hingley, Richard. 2018. 'Frontiers and mobilities: the frontiers of the Roman Empire and Europe', *European Journal of Archaeology* 21(1): 78–95.

Hitchner, R. Bruce. 2008. 'Globalization avant la lettre: globalization and the history of the Roman Empire', *New Global Studies* 2(2): article 2 (1–12).

Hodder, Ian. 2012. *Entangled: An archaeology of the relationships between humans and things*. Oxford: Wiley-Blackwell.

Hodos, Tamar (ed.). 2016. *The Routledge Handbook of Archaeology and Globalization*. London: Routledge.

Ingold, Tim. 2007. 'Materials against materiality', *Archaeological Dialogues* 14(1): 1–16.

James, Simon. 2003. 'Roman archaeology: crisis and revolution', *Antiquity* 77(295): 178–84.

Johannsen, Niels. 2012. 'Archaeology and the inanimate agency proposition: a critique and a suggestion'. In *Excavating the Mind: cross-sections through culture, cognition and materiality*, edited by Niels Johannsen, Mads D. Jessen and Helle Juel Jensen, 305–47. Aarhus: Aarhus University Press.

Johnson, Matthew. 2006. 'On the nature of theoretical archaeology and archaeological theory', *Archaeological Dialogues* 13(2): 117–32.

Johnson, Matthew. 2020. *Archaeological Theory: An introduction* (3rd edition). Hoboken: Wiley-Blackwell.

Jones, Mark P. 1996. 'Posthuman agency: between theoretical traditions', *Sociological Theory* 14(3): 290–309.

Kamash, Zena. 2021. 'Rebalancing Roman archaeology: from disciplinary inertia to decolonial and inclusive action', *Theoretical Roman Archaeology Journal* 4(1): 1–41.

Knappett, Carl and Lambros Malafouris (eds). 2008. *Material Agency: Towards a non-anthropocentric approach*. New York: Springer.

Krishna, Sankaran. 2009: *Globalization and Postcolonialism: Hegemony and resistance in the twenty-first century*. Lanham, MD: Rowman and Littlefield.

Laurence, Ray. 1999. 'Theoretical Roman Archaeology', *Britannia* 30: 387–390.

Laurence, Ray. 2006. '21st century TRAC: is the Roman battery flat?' In *TRAC 2005: Proceedings of the Fifteenth Annual Theoretical Roman Archaeology Conference, Birmingham 2005*, edited by Ben Croxford, Helen Goodchild, Jason Lucas and Nick Ray, 116–27. Oxford: Oxbow Books.

Laurence, Ray and Mary Harlow. 2002. *Growing Up and Growing Old in Ancient Rome: A life-course approach*. London: Routledge.

Latour, Bruno. 1993. *We Have Never Been Modern*. Trans. Catherine Porter. Cambridge, MA: Harvard University Press.

Mattingly, David J. (ed.). 1997. *Dialogues in Roman Imperialism*. Portsmouth, RI: Journal of Roman Archaeology.

Mattingly, David J. 2004. 'Being Roman: expressing identity in a provincial setting', *Journal of Roman Archaeology* 17: 5–25.

Mattingly, David J. 2011. *Imperialism, Power and Identity: Experiencing the Roman Empire*. Princeton, NJ: Princeton University Press.

Millett, Martin. 2014. 'Roman Britain since Haverfield'. In *The Oxford Handbook to Roman Britain*, edited by Martin Millett, Alison Moore and Louise Revell, 22–42. Oxford: Oxford University Press.

Miller, Danny. 1994. 'Artefacts and the meaning of things'. In *Companion Encyclopedia of Anthropology: Humanity, culture and social life*, edited by Tim Ingold, 396–419. London: Routledge.

Mizoguchi, Koji. 2015. 'A future of Archaeology', *Antiquity* 89 (343): 12–22.

Mol, Eva M. 2013. 'The perception of Egypt in networks of being and becoming: a Thing Theory approach to Egyptianising objects in Roman domestic contexts'. In *TRAC 2012: Proceedings of the Twenty Second Theoretical Roman Archaeology Conference, Frankfurt 2012*, edited by Annabel Bokern, Marion Bolder-Boos, Stefan Krmnicek, Dominik Maschek and Sven Page, 117–31. Oxford: Oxbow Books.

Mol, Eva M. 2019. 'Roman cyborgs! On significant otherness, material absence and virtual presence in Roman architecture', *Journal of European Archaeology* 23(1): 64–81.

Moreland, John. 2001. *Archaeology and Text*. London: Duckworth.

Morley, Neville. 2010. *The Roman Empire: Roots of imperialism*. London: Pluto Press.

Ohmae, Ken'ichi. 1990. *The Borderless World: Power and strategy in the interlinked economy*. New York: Harper Business.

Olsen, Bjørnar. 2010. *In Defense of Things: Archaeology and the ontology of objects*. Lanham, MD: Rowman and Littlefield.

Osborne, Robin and Jeremy Tanner (eds). 2007. *Art's Agency and Art History*. Oxford: Blackwell.

Parker, Adam and Stuart McKie (eds). 2018. *Material Approaches to Roman Magic: Occult objects and supernatural substances*. Oxford: Oxbow Books.

Pitts, Martin. 2007. 'The Emperor's new clothes? The utility of identity in Roman archaeology', *American Journal of Archaeology* 111(4): 693–713.

Pitts, Martin. 2008. 'Globalizing the local in Roman Britain: an anthropological approach to social change', *Journal of Anthropological Archaeology* 27: 493–506.

Pitts, Martin. 2019. *The Roman Object Revolution: Objectscapes and intra-cultural connectivity in Northwest Europe*. Amsterdam: Amsterdam University Press.

Pitts, Martin and Miguel John Versluys (eds). 2014. *Globalisation and the Roman World: World history, connectivity and material culture*. Cambridge: Cambridge University Press.

Revell, Louise. 2016. *Ways of Being Roman: Discourses of identity in the Roman west*. Oxford: Oxbow Books.

Ribeiro, Artur. 2016. 'Against object agency: a counterreaction to Sorensen's "Hammers and nails"', *Archaeological Dialogues* 23(2): 229–35.

Rogers, Adam. 2015. *The Archaeology of Roman Britain: Biography and identity*. London: Routledge.

Said, Edward. 1978. *Orientalism*. London: Routledge and Kegan Paul.

Sauer, Eberhard (ed.). 2004. *Archaeology and Ancient History: Breaking down the boundaries*. London: Routledge.

Scheidel, Walter (ed.). 2015. *State Power in Ancient China and Rome*. Oxford: Oxford University Press.

Scott, Eleanor (ed.). 1993. *Theoretical Roman Archaeology: First conference proceedings*. London: Avebury.

Scott, Sarah and Jane Webster (eds). 2003. *Roman Imperialism and Provincial Art*. Cambridge: Cambridge University Press.

Selsvold, Irene and Lewis Webb (eds). 2019. *Beyond the Romans: Posthuman perspectives in Roman archaeology*. Oxford: Oxbow Books.

Smith, Alex, Martyn Allen, Tom Brindle and Michael Fulford. 2016. *The Rural Settlement of Roman Britain. (New Visions of the Roman Countryside, vol. 1)*. London: Society for the Promotion of Roman Studies.

Swift, Ellen. 2020. *Roman Artefacts and Society: Design, behaviour, and experience*. Oxford: Oxford University Press.

Thomas, Julian. 2004. *Archaeology and Modernity*. London: Routledge.

Urry, John. 2000. *Sociology Beyond Societies: Mobilities for the twenty-first century*. London: Routledge.

Van Dyke, Ruth M. 2015. 'Materiality in practice: an introduction'. In *Practicing Materiality*, edited by Ruth M. Van Dyke, 3–32. Tucson, AZ: University of Arizona Press.

Van Oyen, Astrid. 2016. *How Things Make History: The Roman Empire and its Terra Sigillata pottery*. Amsterdam: Amsterdam University Press.

Van Oyen, Astrid. 2020. *The Socio-Economics of Roman Storage: Agriculture, trade and family*. Cambridge: Cambridge University Press.

Van Oyen, Astrid and Martin Pitts. 2017. 'What did objects do in the Roman world? Beyond representation'. In *Materialising Roman Histories*, edited by Astrid Van Oyen and Martin Pitts, 3–20. Oxford: Oxbow Books.

Versluys, Miguel John. 2014. 'Understanding objects in motion: an archaeological dialogue on Romanization', *Archaeological Dialogues* 21(1): 1–64.

Webmoor, Timothy. 2007. 'What about "one more turn after the social" in archaeological reasoning? Taking things seriously', *World Archaeology* 39(4): 563–78.

Webmoor, Timothy and Christopher Witmore. 2008. 'Things are us! A commentary on human/thing relations under the banner of a "social" archaeology', *Norwegian Archaeological Review* 41(1): 53–70.

Webster, Jane. 2001. 'Creolizing the Roman provinces', *American Journal of Archaeology* 105: 209–25.

Webster, Jane and Nicholas J. Cooper (eds). 1996. *Roman Imperialism: Post-colonial perspectives*. Leicester: School of Archaeological Studies, University of Leicester.

Witcher, Robert. 2000. 'Globalisation and Roman imperialism: perspectives on identities in Roman Italy'. In *The Emergence of State Identities in Italy in the 1st Millennium BC*, edited by Edward Herring and Kathryn Lomas, 213–25. London: Accordia Research Centre.

Witmore, Christopher L. 2007. 'Symmetrical Archaeology: excerpts of a manifesto', *World Archaeology* 39(4): 546–62.

Woolf, Greg. 2004. 'The present state and future scope of Roman archaeology: a comment', *American Journal of Archaeology* 108: 417–28.

1
Roads and communications

Ray Laurence

Communications across the Roman Empire, whether in the form of a letter sent from the emperor Trajan from Rome to a governor in northern Turkey, or travel by the governor and his staff, or the movement of goods over land, all depended on the construction and maintenance of a system of roads that crossed environments as diverse as snow-covered mountain ranges and arid deserts. It should be said at the outset that the focus in this chapter is on roads, rather than other forms of pathways that might act as transport routes – this difference is articulated in Roman law as a difference between a road – *via*, a track – *actus* and a path – *semita* (*Dig*. 8.1.13; Laurence 1999: 58–9; compare Gates-Foster 2012 on the difference in materiality of some roads in Egypt). The material remains of roads, milestones, inns and the topography of the transport routes has become a specialised area of study (see the work of Richard Talbert, collected essays in Talbert 2023, also papers in Kolb 2019 and Alcock et al. 2012; see review of the latter in Laurence 2016), but these studies seldom influence mainstream histories of the Roman Empire. Indeed, as we will see, land transport, a key characteristic, is often simply dismissed or misunderstood (e.g. from Finley 1973: 126–8; Saller 2002: 254; Morley 2007: 571; Bang 2008: 133–6). Helmuth Schneider (2007: 163–64) carefully identified the intersection between land transport and shipping through his acute observation of the scale involved, identified in Strabo's observation that there were sufficient carts to take away an entire shipload of goods (5.1.8, 5.1.12; compare Plin. *NH* 14.132; Dion. Hal. 3.67.5). The scale and importance of land transportation is revealed by this observation and it is land transport that characterises the Roman Empire and creates a materiality that is distinctive. Of course, much communication was undertaken by sea, and by river, but it is the roads leading to and from rivers and seas or from cities to other cities that can be defined as having a material specificity that enables the explanation of the nature of the Roman Empire. Another major misconception occurs with reference to the *Cursus Publicus*, which has been assumed to have been some form of postal system, rather than a series of stopping places at which imperial officials might change equids – horses, mules or donkeys – and find a place to stay overnight (Corsi 2000; Kolb 2000). Rather than dwell on the misconceptions of the past, this essay will present a view of the network of roads that materially underpinned the development of the empire under the Republic, and was maintained as an integral form of infrastructure, even by Theodoric the Ostrogothic King who took over Italy in the fifth century CE.

The origins of Roman long-distance and local roads

The Roman state began building long-distance roads in 312 BCE with the construction of the Via Appia from Rome to Capua, some 100 Roman miles (*c.*150 km) to the south (Diod. Sic. 20.36; Frontin, *Aq.*1.4; *ILS* 54; Liv. 9.29; *Per.*9; Stat.*Silv.* 2.2.98; see Figure 1.1). The road both took Rome to the south and the major city of Capua and, potentially, brought her enemies to the gates of the city. Not surprisingly, 16 years after its initial construction, fortified colonies of Roman citizens were established on the route of the road at Minturnae and Sinuessa to defend the new routeway to Rome as well as towns to the south in Campania (Liv. 10.21.7–10; on the military role: 27.38.3; 36.3.5–6). The defensive position of Minturnae at the bridge over the river Liris needs further comment. The bridge over the river, like that of the Pons Sublicius, was constructed from wood, rather than stone faced concrete, and like the Pons Sublicius could have been cut down to thwart an enemy (see Roller 2000 for discussion). The building of this road can be seen as a point of origin for imperial road building by Rome, and the Via Appia remained famous into late antiquity, as the 'Queen of Roads'.

The creation of the Via Appia does not seem to have established any principle that the construction of long-distance roads was a desideratum of state policy. On the contrary, almost 100 years passed before the next major long-distance road was built: the Via Flaminia running north-east from Rome to Rimini (Liv. 32.29.6; *Per.*20). An explanation for this gap may be found in the actions of the next censors after Appius Claudius. Roads were created by the censors in 307 BCE through the public lands (*ager publicus*) conquered by Rome and distributed to her citizens (Liv.

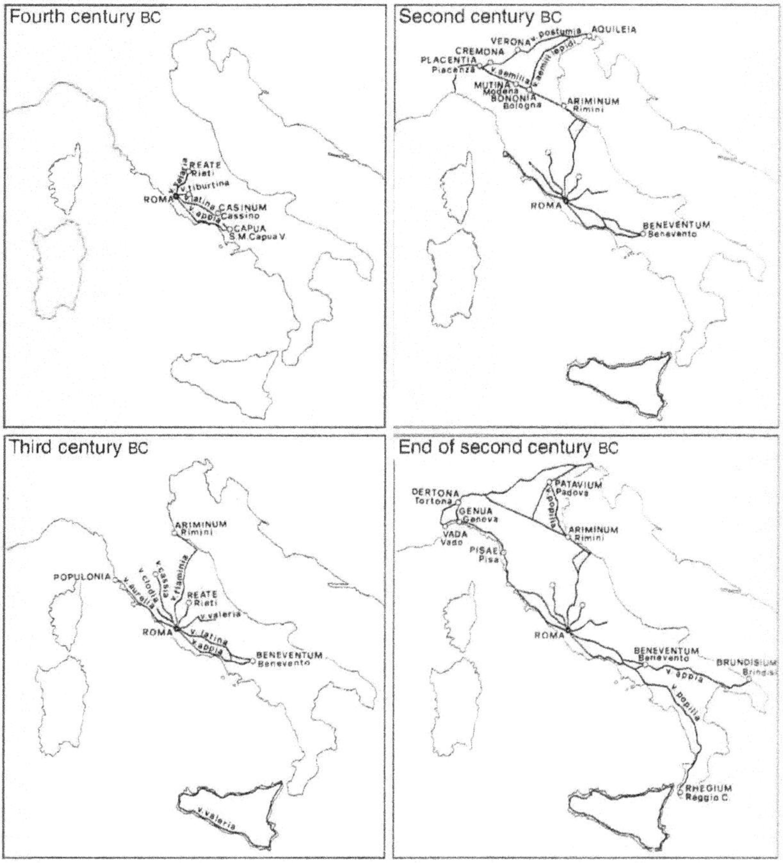

Figure 1.1 The development of the road system in Italy. © Ray Laurence (after Laurence 1999. *Roads of Roman Italy: Mobility and cultural change*, p.14).

9.43.25). Effectively, these were local roads serving Rome's citizens distributed across new territory, just as it has now been shown that the route of the Via Appia engaged with existing inhabitants in the Pontine plain (Attema et al. 2011). It would seem the magistrates elected in 307 BCE may have rejected the need for the construction of a long-distance road. Instead, they chose to construct local roads to make the facility of public roads available to a wider number of citizens. This, incidentally, may be the first instance of a state or funding body choosing local roads over the construction of long-distance highways. Local roads have been found in late twentieth and early twenty-first century development economics to be more effective in creating sustainable agriculture. By contrast, European colonialism from the nineteenth to the mid-twentieth century constructed long-distance highways that extracted commodities and resources from colonies, rather than supporting the local population (see for example Asher and Novosad 2018).

The route of the Via Appia was subject to further improvements. In 295 BCE, the initial stretch from the city gate, Porta Capena, to the Temple of Mars, between the first and second milestone of the road (2 km from the Porta Capena; *CIL* VI.10234) was paved, if only partially. Livy (10.23) uses the word *semita* – a path, rather than *via* – a road. Within this temple by 217 BCE, there were statues of wolves and one of the war god Mars (Liv. 22.1.12). It was the place in 350 BCE at which the army was mustered (Liv. 7.23.3). This section of road leading from the gate at Porta Capena to the temple, just beyond the later Porta Appia in the Aurelian Walls was referred to by the Augustan period as a covered road (*tectae viae* – Ovid *Fasti* 6.191–2). There followed further work to pave the road from the Temple of Mars to the first town on the road at Bovillae in what Livy describes as a hard stone – probably quarried from the local lava flows over which the road ran (Liv. 10.47). Finance for both of these improvements came from fines imposed on pastoralists encroaching on smallholders on the public land (*ager publicus*; App. *B.C.* 1.8.33; Varro *R.R.* 1.2.9; Cornell 1995: 329). The new road surface constructed in 295 BCE clearly became inadequate about a century later and was replaced in 189 BCE by paving in a hard stone (Liv. 38.28), which we might assume was made from stone quarried from the local lava flow. The paving did not cover the whole width of the road, and this seems to have been a pattern repeated in the construction of other roads during the Roman Republic, for example those of Gaius Gracchus (Plut. *C.G.* 7). Sections of excavated paving on, for example, the Via Amerina south of Falerii Novi (central Italy) are 2.4–2.45 m in width (Munzi 1997), which would accommodate a cart with an axle width of *c.* 1.96 m to use the paved section (see Poehler 2017: 110–11 on axle width), but was not wide enough to allow for carts to pass in both directions (see Figure 1.2).

There was a degree of politics involved in road building. Appius Claudius, the censor (a magistrate elected every five years), who let the contract for the building of the Via Appia almost bankrupted Rome and, in so doing, distributed state wealth to contractors and workers on the road. There is an inkling in the sources that Appius Claudius did not just gain considerable support from this policy but may also have been seen as aiming at tyranny (Humm 1996). The road would additionally have been of benefit to those who used it, and that benefit may have led the next censors in 307 BCE to let a contract for roads throughout the public

Figure 1.2 Half-paved road width on the Via Amerina south of Falerii Novi, Italy. © Ray Laurence.

lands of the Roman state. Gaius Gracchus (123–122 BCE), as tribune (an annually elected magistrate), threw himself into the construction of roads (Plut. *C.G.* 7; App. *B.C.* 1.23) and gained considerable support from doing so. It should be stressed that we can see other senators involved in building roads and bridges across the Italian peninsula in the second century BCE, as well as the foundation of towns referred to by the term or place name *Forum* (Laurence 1999: 27–38).

Other towns in Italy, under the governance of Rome's allies till 80 BCE, were building local roads and paving them. In Pompeii, we find inscriptions in the Oscan language referring to the paving of a road from the city gate to a place called the *cisiarii* – the carters (*CIL* X.1064). Eric Poehler's very detailed analysis of the paving of Pompeii and review of excavated sections of the streets of Pompeii has determined a chronology as follows: a master plan of a grid of streets was created in the fourth century BCE (Poehler 2017: 31–2); at least 61 per cent was paved with lava (or *silex*) in 79 CE, when Vesuvius erupted (Poehler 2017: 54–5), with evidence for the paving of these streets in the first century BCE (Poehler 2017: 63–9). The impetus for paving streets in Pompeii occurred after a colony of Roman veterans was settled at the site. This dating horizon may be significant in the development of local roads, which, as can be seen from the *Lex Tarentina* (Crawford 1996: 308), were a responsibility in the hands of annually elected magistrates. Often, roads were built from a city, such as Aquileia, to the major long-distance public road created by the Roman state (*CIL* V.1008) What is clear, though, is that by the end of the first century BCE, the building of local roads was delegated to individual cities, whilst the Roman state had created a network of long-distance routeways that were referred to on the arch constructed to commemorate the emperor Augustus' restoration of the Via Flaminia as 'the famous roads of Italy' (*RG* 20.5; Suet. *Aug.*30; Dio 53.22). Other leading figures, such as Marcus Valerius Messalla and Marcus Agrippa, were expected to pay for the restoration of roads (Tibull. 1.7.57–62; Dio 53.22–23). Interestingly, at the local level, the *Augustales* (priests of the deified emperor Augustus) built local roads (*CIL* V.2116) and donations were given to towns by leading citizens for the purpose of road building (*Dig.* 31.1.30): for example, Publius Decimus Eros Merula, a freed slave, donated 30,000 sesterces for the setting up of statues and also gave a larger sum, 37,000 sesterces, for road building.

The technology of Roman roads

Roman roads were designed to be all-weather surfaces to be used by foot traffic (humans and animals) and vehicles. The roads were defined structures with a fixed width of eight Roman feet widening to 16 feet on curves or bends in the road from as early as the laws known as the Twelve Tables of *c.*450 BCE (*Dig.* 8.3.8; Varro *LL* 7.15; Festus 508L; Hyg. *Const.*134bh; Laurence 1999: 58–9). The surface is quite critical to any understanding of the technology of roads. It appears that early roads, such as the Via Appia of 312 BCE, were initially unpaved, but at some point paving was added, and it is this paving that has been excavated particularly in Italy. The dating of this upgrade to a paved surface is open to debate, but Statius' poem about the Via Domitiana (*Silvae* 4.4) from the late first century CE provides us with a dating point to see an example of the very best form of road building from the Via Appia to the town of Cumae. The use of lava as the characteristic stone for the major roads leading from Rome is probably a relatively late innovation. There is clear evidence at Terracina for the Via Appia being paved at an earlier date in limestone (Blake and Bishop 1973: 281). The paved surface of the roads, whether using lava or limestone, was particularly suitable for driving carriages (Fronto *Ad M. Caes.* 5.40). The difference in quality between limestone and lava for paving was known, certainly by the first century CE (Pliny *N.H.*36.168–70; Laurence 2004). The presence of lava flows from the volcanoes of the Alban Hills to the south of Rome and the Monte Sabatini to the north of Rome provided a ready supply of stone (Worthing et al. 2017, 2018).

The quality of a road's surface was seen by Cicero (*Letters to Quintus* 3.1) to vary according to whether it was a state road or a local/private road. He comments that a section of road leading to his brother's villa was of the same quality as that of a public road. This may be related to the governance and finance available for road building, and the fact that the state could spend considerably more money on roads than private individuals. Public roads were paid for by the state with the addition of a contribution from the land-holders along the route (Siculus Flaccus 146L). This can most easily be seen in practice in the building of the road from the port of Rusicade on the coast of North Africa to Cirta, in which the funding is paid for by Hadrian, but the *possessores* of Cirta are also named in one inscription (*CIL* VIII.10296, 10322, 22370). The cost of road building can be seen in relationship to the restoration of the Via Appia under Hadrian, in which the emperor paid 1,147,000 sesterces, whereas the *possessores* contributed 569,000 sesterces to restore a section of the road over 15¾ miles in 123 CE (*CIL* IX.6075). This contrasts with the governance and finance of local roads (*viae vicinales*), which were paid for by the local towns or villages and were maintained by the work of landowners or possessors of the land (Siculus Flaccus 146L; Ulpian *Dig.* 43.8.21–33). Importantly, public roads were seen to have very definite end points: the seashore, cities, public rivers or another road; whereas local roads may trail off at a point that was not defined (Ulpian *Dig.* 43.7).

The surface of the road was just one factor in the development of Roman technologies of travel. Another important factor was the improvement or breeding of animals to enable the movement of people and goods. The cross-breeding of male donkeys with female horses produced a stronger, but sexually neuter, animal – the mule (Laurence 1999: 123–35). The mule is found represented in mosaics and on coins as the traction animal of choice to pull carts and carriages. However, we need to be conscious that as pack-animals both mules and donkeys could have been utilised equally effectively to haul loads in sacks or liquids in amphorae.

The proliferation of the use of camels in the second half of the first millennium BCE in Egypt and North Africa extended the range of mobility in desert regions, but this extension of communications was not based on the construction of roads as such (Mattingly et al. 2021). The not infrequent finds of camel bones from sites in Italy and Europe, as well as North Africa and the Middle-East, point to the introduction of the

Figure 1.3 Surviving arch from the bridge of the Via Flaminia at Narni, Italy. © Ray Laurence.

new breed of transport animal to facilitate the movement of goods (De Grossi Mazzorin 2010) and is referred directly to in an epitaph from Ostia associating the deceased with some form of camel trade (*AE* 1955: 181, but see Adams 2007: 49–56 on camels in temperate climates). There is also a frieze in the National Archaeological Museum at Chieti showing a man leading a pack-camel (see De Grossi Mazzorin 2010: 100 for image and discussion). This gave rise to a perception of the camel as a pack animal that seems to have survived in Europe down to the sixteenth century. There would appear to have been both a breeding programme to increase the strength of equids and camels (hybridisation by crossing dromedaries with Bactrian camels), alongside the importation of camels from across the Mediterranean to enhance the efficiency of land transportation.

Bridge technology was a further factor in the development of effective land-based communications across the Roman Empire. Rivers posed a major hindrance to the transportation of goods on the backs of animals or in carts, as well as to the journeys of travellers. The possibility for goods to become wet and animals or humans to be swept away by rivers was avoided by the construction of bridges. It was these structures that Plutarch (*C.G.*7) saw as having a beautiful and symmetrical appearance. Indeed, few today cannot be moved by the sheer scale of the bridge of the Via Flaminia at Narni (Figure 1.3) that crosses a valley

Figure 1.4 Viaduct (Muro del Peccato, Italy) carrying the Via Flaminia from a bridge across the river Treia, raising the level of the road by 45 metres to the top of the valley. Courtesy of BSR Photographic Archive, Robert Gardner Collection, rg-1524.

180 m wide and presents a flat roadway a full 33 m above the valley floor, being supported by four arches varying in width: 19.6 m, 32.1 m, 17 m and 16 m (Quilici 2008: 571). Where valleys were wider than this, viaducts were constructed to allow the road to gradually drop down to the river: the Muro del Peccato (Figure 1.4) that crosses the Treia river close to its confluence with the Tiber provides us with an excellent example. The viaduct moves the road a full 45 m in height over a causeway some 250–300 m in length. This is not a gentle slope by any means, producing a gradient of 1:5.5 m or 1:6.6 m (Quilici 2008: 569; Ashby and Fell 1921). The scale of these undertakings is impressive, but what is perhaps more impressive is the diffusion of bridge technology across the Roman Empire, with more than a thousand bridges surviving from antiquity (Gazzola 1963; Galliazzo 1994: for catalogues).

Roads across the mountains

The Via Appia was a particular type of Roman road, combining the practical benefit of the drainage of marshland with a Pythagorean devotion to geometry to create a very straight road aligned precisely on the Temple of Diana in Rome and the colony at Terracina on the coast (see

Humm 1996 on Pythagorean influence). The road was underwritten by a technology that placed an emphasis on straightness – initially being built on the Capo di Bove lava flow as it climbed up to Bovillae to cross the Alban Hills (950 m above sea level). The construction of the Via Flaminia in 220 BCE, crossing the Apennine range of mountains, involved a very different approach to that of the Via Appia. The road rises to 572 m above sea level at Bevagna, but used passes through mountains to traverse ranges as high as 976 m above sea level (Quilici 2008: 561). It also crossed numerous river valleys but is aligned along a route that reduces the number of river valleys to be crossed (Ashby and Fell 1921).

Along the roads were stopping places (*mansiones* and *mutationes*), at which travellers on state business could stay or use animals and wagons at a fixed cost. These places are listed in the travel routes known as the *Antonine Itineraries* and on the map known as the Peutinger Table, alongside towns at which people could also stop. The average spacing between possible stopping places in the Antonine Itineraries on the Via Appia was every 15 Roman miles and on the Via Flaminia every 18 miles (Laurence 1999: 88–90). The distance between stopping places was easily achieved within one day. Some of the routes across the mountain range of the Alps had longer stages as far as 60 miles between stopping places, but on the route from Aquileia to Veldidena we find stopping places ranging from 22 to 36 miles, with an average spacing of 26 miles. Thus, even in the mountains, distances were achievable within a single day between places, at which travellers could rest on the road.

The road surface would have guided travellers including soldiers across the mountains, with their itinerary of places and milestones setting out the distance between stopping places. The milestones were also a means to establish how much of a journey had been undertaken and how much further it was to the next stopping place. An edict of Hadrian makes it clear that, if the road was covered by snow, soldiers were permitted to hire a guide to find the way between the milestones (see Hauken and Malay 2009 for text, translation and discussion). This is a sign that whatever the weather and whatever terrain was to be travelled, soldiers were expected to complete their journeys.

The Alps are a feature written into the *Itinerarium Burdigalense* and encapsulate a boundary between provinces and a form of geography to be crossed. The wording is indicative of this dual meaning of crossing mountains (e.g. *inde incipiunt Alpes Cottiae*), and in entering into a new territory or jurisdiction (*inde incipit Italiae*), but also included *fines* or the boundary between Italy and Noricum and between Pannonia and Misia, and between Dacia and Thrace, as well as between the Italian regions of Apulia and Campania (Elsner 2000: 186–90; Talbert 2005). Journeys across such boundaries were associated with the paying of customs duties (see Campbell 2012: 297 for customs duties on rivers). It is not our concern here to discuss the historical development of customs duties (see De Laet 1949) or the detailed record keeping at these places (e.g. Gallazzi and Sijpesteijn 1989; Sijpesteijn 1989), but it is worth bearing in mind that the creation of an imperial road network facilitated these fiscal practices of the state.

Boundaries and taxation

Within the Antonine Itineraries, the place name associated with a stopping point, *Fines* or *Ad Fines* on the boundaries (Calzolari 1996: 416–17; Cuntz 1929: 232.2, 238.1, 274.6, 285.3, 341.2, 343.4, 356.13, 364.4, 379.7, 387.2, 398.5, 460.1, 461.6, 462.1, 555.5, 559.2, 574.4), was sometimes specifically associated with a *mansio* (556.7) or a *mutatio* (555.5, 559.2, 574.4). The *fines* of a province were clearly boundaries at which customs could be exacted. According to the Customs' Law of Asia, the *statio* neeeded to be provisioned with a building for the collection of taxes and was to be no more than 30 feet by 30 feet (ll. 32–6, Mitchell 2008: 173, 183–8). This text also points to the exaction of customs at the port of a city and at the boundaries of a city (ll. 103–4: *portorium importationis exportationisque terra marique intra fines portusque*). These boundaries or points of tax collection can also be found in other sources. The Vicarello goblets record a journey from Cadiz to Rome and we find a place name *Ad Fines* mentioned (*CIL* XI.3284; Heurgon 1952: 47), which is an abbreviation for the *statio ad Fines Cottii*, at which the collection of the tax on goods known as the *Quadragesima Galliarum* at 2.5 per cent was levied (De Laet 1949: 125–74; France 2001: 81–90; Scuderi 2001). Epigraphy associated with the *Quadragesima Galliarum* indicates the presence of a procurator (*CIL* X.6668; *AE* 1915: 58) and of a staff that included *tabularii* (accountants), a *vilicus* (a bailiff) and *vernae* (homebred slaves) at individual *stationes* (*CIL* XIII.1817; *AE* 1945: 99). Just as the *stationes* of the *beneficarii* included the dedication of altars to Jupiter or to the genius of the *statio* as a place, so also at the *stationes* of the *Quadragesima Galliarum* we can identify altars dedicated to Jupiter Optimus Maximus (*CIL* V.7209 and 7214; Pellizari 2007). What we see is an overall pattern of *stationes* of the *Quadragesima Galliarum* found in ports, on key mountain routes and also in Rome (*CIL* VI.8592). We might also assume a level of movement of the customs dues collected to the central *statio* in Rome. Peter Bang (2008: 202–38) has set out the transaction costs of transporting goods in relation to the payment of customs duties and suggests that travellers could have been subjected to extortion at the *statio*, where they paid their dues. At Zarai (Algeria), we find an inscription dated to 202 CE (*CIL* VIII.4508) that, to circumvent over-charging, sets out the charges for slaves, horses, mules (a denarius and a quinarius each), donkeys and oxen (a quinarius each), plus various charges for pigs, piglets, sheep, goats and lambs. There were also listed charges for items of clothing, shoes, sponge, amphorae containing wine and garum, figs, as well as various minerals such as alum (see Trousset 2005 for discussion).

Space and territory

The road as a linear route across an area of territory became a means to define geographical space and envision the control of the territorial areas which constituted the empire. This may be derived from the practice within ancient geography of describing first the coastline, enumerating all the places along the coast in order, and then progressing to describe the places that were inland (Janni 1984; Nicolet 1991: 95–122; Laurence 1999: 162–76). This can be seen most clearly in Strabo's treatment of Italy in book 5 of the *Geography*. What becomes more interesting and relevant to the relationship between roads as linear forms and space as an area is when Strabo describes Umbria – an inland region, with no coastline, in central Italy. He describes this inland region of Italy using the Via Flaminia as the means of description (*Geography* 5.2.10).

First, he describes the length of Umbria from Rimini to Ocriculum on the river Tiber as 1350 stadia along the Via Flaminia. This is what he gives as the length of Umbria based on the measured distance of the road with its milestones, but he cannot describe its breadth as that varies. He then moves on to name the cities of Umbria with those on the Via Flaminia named as: Ocriculum on the Tiber, Narnia upstream but only navigable by small boats; then Carsulae and Mevania (Bevagna) on a tributary of the Tiber and navigable by small boats; Forum Flaminium, Nuceria and Forum Sempronium.

Subsequently, he names the towns on the other branch of the Via Flaminia again moving north from Ocriculum to Rimini: Interamna, Spoletium, Aesium and Camerinum. Having named all the towns on the road, he then adds in places not on the Via Flaminia: Ameria, Tuder, Hispellum and Iguvium. What we see here is how the road adapts to the geography of cities, needing two routes leading from Ocriculum to Rimini, and that just four of the 15 towns of Umbria were not located on the road itself. Moreover, Strabo takes the trouble to mention that three towns (Forum Flaminium, Nuceria and Forum Sempronium) had become established due to the presence of the road and, presumably, the need to supply travellers.

Strabo takes note of where the road meets rivers and it is relevant in this context to consider the relationship between road and river transport. Gnaeus Piso returned to Rome from the province of Syria, via the port of Ancona (20 CE). He travelled from Ancona across Picenum and then took the Via Flaminia towards Rome (Tacitus *Annals* 3.9). However, finding a legion marching to Rome from its province of Noricum, en route to its final destination in the province of Africa, he chose to divert from the road at Narnia and complete his journey to Rome by boat. The episode allows us to see a preference for road transport over river transport, but also that the river was well supplied with boats for the large retinue that travelled with Piso.

The format found in Strabo that links the Via Flaminia and Umbria together is replicated in the naming of magistrates for this region, notably the *iuridici* as having jurisdiction over the Flaminia and Umbria (*CIL* II.2634, III.6154, VI.1509, XIV.3586) with the region of Picenum added also (*CIL* XI.376). Thus, the transport route defines the area of authority and we may interpret that authority being maintained through the cities of Umbria that were for the most part located on the road itself.

This phenomenon can also be located through an examination of road building in the provinces. The construction of the Via Nova from the boundary of Syria to the Red Sea by Trajan resulted in the erection of numerous milestones that make clear the action as 'redacta in formam provinciae Arabiae viam novam a finibus Syriae usque ad mare rubrum aperuit et stravit' – 'defining the form of the province of Arabia, he paved and opened a new road from the boundary with Syria to the Red Sea' (e.g. *AE* 1897. 65; Graf 1995; Humbert and Desreumaux 1998; Talbert 2005: 29–30). The road followed the Nabatean King's Highway (Bowersock 1983: 91–2). The milestones mark the road, not as a restoration but new and paved – even though it overlies or overwrites an existing caravan route (Graf 1995). The milestones clarify the form or definition of the province as a territory connected to the building of the new road (note that coins also appear at same date to establish a conception of Arabia, Bowersock 1983: 83–4; *BM Coins Roman Empire* III: 185, no. 877). Effectively, Rome overwrote the previous culture through issuing new coins and ensuring the main route/s through the province were clearly marked with milestones and new paving. This was not a new phenomenon: when Rome took over the Attalid kingdom, in the second century BCE, Manlius Aquillius overwrote the existing road network with a series of bilingual Latin and Greek milestones that specifically referred to the restoration of the roads (French 2012: 7).

The conception of territory in the definition of Arabia was from the boundary of Syria to the Red Sea – in other words from a known point to a less-known point. Other milestones express the conception of boundaries differently with the boundary of a province as the destination. For example, the restoration of a road from Carthage in 237 CE was described as to the *Fines Numidiae* – or boundary of Numidia (*CIL* VIII 22020, 22056, 22073, 22123). It was the road that took you from Carthage to the edge of the governor's jurisdiction – across the boundary lay a description of space on the milestones with reference to points within the province of Numidia. This format measuring from the major city of Carthage to an edge of a territory should be seen as a hierarchical description of space: wherever you were on the road, the milestones informed you consistently that you were between Carthage – a city – and the edge of Numidia. The road was represented to take you right across the province – the cities or places along its route are simply not mentioned.

The state and the road

One of the greatest misconceptions in the modern literature on Roman roads is that the state had a postal system. This is not the case and we need to unpick the evidence to explain the purpose of the *Cursus Publicus*. The discovery of inscriptions referring to the regulation of abuses of the system provide us with an understanding of the role of the state in relation to the use of these minor roadside settlements (Mitchell 1976). An edict of the governor of Galatia – Sex. Sotidius Strabo Libuscidianus – in the reign of the emperor Tiberius (14–37 CE) regulated who might use the *mansio* or inn as part of the *Cursus Publicus* (compare Adams 2007: 24–25 for the Oxyrhynchite *mansio* in Egypt; *P.Oxy.* LX 4087–8 discussed by Adams 2001: 142–4). The legate or governor of the province and members of his staff, military personnel from other provinces, and slaves and freedmen of the emperor were all permitted to use the inn at a fixed price. Effectively, the *mansio* was for the use of those who held power or were agents of the state: the governor with his staff, the military, and imperial slaves and former slaves. The inscription also defines who might be provided with mules or donkeys and wagons at a fixed price: the imperial procurator and his son, military personnel with a diploma, senators, *equites* on imperial service, and centurions on military service. All types of personnel mentioned were effectively agents of the state and, thus, needed to be mobile to enforce the will of the state. Hence, a public road was constituted by the road itself and the stopping places provided for the agents of the state, which other road-users, who were not seen as a priority, might use at higher prices. Both the road and the *mansiones* were regulated by edicts of governors and emperors to ensure that transport was facilitated for agents of the state, without the exploitation of the locals providing the resources to enable the transport needed to carry out the state's will.

The mobility of military personnel tends to be underplayed in favour of viewing the archaeology of forts as the places of the military (e.g. Farnum 2005). However, as Hadrian made clear in his address to the legion at Lambaesis, soldiers were frequently assigned to *stationes* across the province of Africa (*CIL* VIII.2532; Tert.*Apol*.2.8). Nelis-Clément (2006) suggests that the stationing of the military along the route-ways of Italy and the provinces from the time of Augustus (Suet. *Aug*.32.1, *Tib*.37.1) formed 'micro-cells' or 'antennae of power' that mediated the power of the emperor at a local level. The publication of the excavation of a *statio* at Obernburg am Main provided further information for our understanding of the use of these local military outposts. The building, as published by the excavators, was in the form of a Mediterranean style courtyard house (47 m by 27 m) located on a road leading to a major fort. To the rear of this structure, 160 altars were found, with each one dedicated to the god/genius of the place in January or July, dating from 144 to 224 CE (Steidl 2005). The density of inscriptions, although only partially published, suggests that the military personnel – *beneficiarii* – moved from *statio to statio* every six months. Another *statio* of the *beneficiarii* has been excavated at Sirmium, again associated with a series of dedicatory altars, dating from 157 to 231 CE (Popović 1989; Mirković 1994; Nelis-Clément 2000: 141–8). The full corpus of evidence has been published, as far as is possible, by Nelis-Clément (2000) and shows the ubiquity of the *beneficiarii* across all parts of the Roman Empire. Placing these *stationes* into sharper focus, allows us to view the roads of the state as much more than functional infrastructure – they were rather a means by which state power was delivered at a local level (France and Nelis-Clément 2014a), even stretching into the highest reaches of the Alps at between 2,200 and 2,400 metres above sea level (Leveau 2014). Indeed, it has been shown recently (papers in France and Nelis-Clément 2014b) that the *stationes* were a key feature of state power and through them we might expect all travellers on the roads to experience contact with the military.

Marking the beginning of the road

Robert Étienne (1992: 362; compare Frothingham 1915: 160–1) draws attention to milestones on the Via Augusta in Spain that include the mention of an arch marking the beginning of the Via Augusta at the river Baetis (Sillières 1990: nos 26, 28, 42, 45, 48, 49, 53: *a Baete et Iano August(o) ad Oceanum* – a formula that was maintained until the reign of Vespasian) that focuses attention on the river Baetis and a Janus Augustus as a terminus for the Via Augusta built in 2 BCE (Haley 2003: 34–5). Later milestones of Domitian refer to this point as having an arch and being at the beginning of Baetica (Sillières 1990: nos 35, 36, 41: *ab arcu unde incipit Baetica viam Augustam militarem vetustate corruptam restituit*). Étienne connects this arch to the coinage of Mérida featuring a gateway (Burnett et al. 1992: nos 10, 12, 20–7, 30–3, 38, 41–5) that would have faced the surviving bridge that crosses the river Guidana, utilising 62 arches with a length of 755 metres (Leather 2006: 84–91), whereas its end point was the ocean itself.

Arches also appear on the coinage of the first emperor Augustus, indeed even before his change of name in 27 BCE from Octavian to Augustus (Figure 1.5). These coins need some discussion to elucidate the combination of bridges and arches which display the representation of the action of road making on issues from mints both in Italy and in Spain. These coins, issued in the reign of Octavian/Augustus bore the legend *QUOD VIAE MUN SUNT* (*RIC* 315–17; *RIC*² 140–4; Mattingly 1965: 75, nos 432–5; Giard 1976: nos 1252, 1254, 1257–63; Wiegels 2016: 115–51), and feature either a bridge with a 'triumphal' arch at its centre or 'triumphal' arches at either end of the bridge. The latter depiction features on a coin issue connected to the much earlier restoration by Augustus of the Via Flaminia from the Mulvian Bridge (Rome) to Rimini (Ballance 1951; Ashby and Fell 1921: 80; Dio 53.22; *RG* 20.5; Cooley 2009: 195–7; see Figure 1.6), where an arch commemorated this action (Mansuelli 1960), dating to 27 BCE with archaeological evidence that the road was raised by *c.*1.1 metres at this time (Mansuelli 1941: 78).

Statius (*Silv.* 4.3.67–94), in his poem on the building of the Via Domitia linking the Via Appia to Cumae and the Bay of Naples, spends many lines presenting the arch that formed an entry point from the Via Appia onto the Via Domitia (*Silv.* 4.3.95–100; on the text see Håkanson 1969: 117–18; Coleman 1988: 126–9; Liberman 2010: 338). He identifies the arch as being located at the *Ianua* (doorway) and at the *limen* (sacred threshold) of the road (*Silv.*4.3) – thus, utilising the language associated

Figure 1.5 Coin commemorating the road building of Augustus using the image of a 'triumphal' arch and a bridge, alongside the inscription 'because the roads were repaired'. © Lloyd Bosworth.

Figure 1.6 Arch of Augustus at Rimini: entrance point onto the Via Flaminia and the road to Rome. © Ray Laurence.

Figure 1.7 The Arch of Trajan at Beneventum, which marks the beginning of the Via Traiana to Brindisi. Courtesy of BSR Photographic Archive, John Bryan Ward-Perkins Collection, wpset-1904.17.

with the Roman house (Lauritsen 2014, but for *limen* see e.g. Mart. *Ep.*8.44; Sen. *De Brev.Vit.*14). We should see this *arcus* through the lens of the earlier language of it as a *Ianus* or arch, but taking its name from the god of beginnings – Janus. Drawing on Jason Banta's (2007) linkage between Janus and agriculture, we might regard the arch as marking the start, both in time and space, of not just the road but the bringing of agriculture to the region – including the river valley of Volturnus (Kleiner 1991; Smolenaars 2006). After all, in Statius' poem the river Volturnus speaks of Domitian's new road with its bridge that included the definition of the banks and confines the river (see Newlands 2012: 52–61 on Statius' focus on fluid boundaries). The entry point to this new road was an *arcus* in marble, commemorating Domitian's victories (Kleiner 1991).

This structure presented in poetry closely parallels the existing Arch of Trajan (Figure 1.7) constructed to mark the Via Traiana that led from Beneventum (a town on the Via Appia) to Brindisi. The imagery on the arch focuses on the military achievements of Trajan in ensuring peace through warfare (for description and images, see Hassel 1966; Rotili 1972). The scenes on the arch include a plough and children – a clear reference to town foundation and the rearing of children to become future soldiers (Figure 1.8; see Hölscher 2002: 143). Michael Spiedel (2005/2006: 202–5) suggests what is represented in the programme of the sculptures is the life course of the military from childhood through

Figure 1.8 The Arch of Beneventum, showing detail of the sculpture on the arch that includes Trajan, Italia, a plough and children. © Camster2, CC BY-SA 3.0, https://www.wikiwand.com/en/Arch_of_Trajan_(Benevento)#Media/File:Benevento_arco_di_Traiano.JPG

to recruitment and, then, to discharge and old age. The arch marked an entry/exit point onto the landscape of the new Via Traiana – in the same way as the arch at the beginning of Statius' Via Domitiana. The landscape of the traveller was marked by new milestones and new bridges (Ashby and Gardner 1916; Silvestrini 1983; Mertens 1994; Ceraudo 2008;) to create an engineered space, similar to that represented by Plutarch (*CG* 7), with the milestones informing the traveller that Trajan had built the road (*VIAM A BENEVENTO BRUNDISIUM*), and inscriptions on bridges (*VIAM ET PONTES A BENEVENTO BRUNDISIUM*) (Chelotti et al. 1985: nos 246–80; Ceraudo 2012).

Travellers to Britain, landing at Richborough, were greeted by a monumental arch, dated by coins to the late Flavian period, but completed under Trajan (Bushe-Fox 1926: 6, 1928: 10–13, 1932: 17–20; Strong 1968; compare examples from Egypt in Talbert 2005: 30–1). A road paved in tufa was built to enable the construction to take place (Cunliffe 1968: 5). The result was a *quadrifons* arch clad in Luni marble with bronze statuary. The foundations of this structure were about nine metres in depth (Bushe-Fox 1949: 38–48) with the *quadrifons* gateway or

Ianus rising to 26 metres in height. It was inscribed and had bronze letters incorporated into some of the inscriptions and the bronze fragments of sculpture suggest that the subject matter was the actions of the emperor Trajan (Strong 1968: 69-70). For Strong (1968: 72–3), this was a classic territorial arch similar to others on the Macedonian–Illyricum border at Ossigi and Bara or in Cilicia, but it was also similar to the Arch of Trajan at his newly constructed harbour at Ancona. This monument at Richborough expressed a conception of geography that can be found elsewhere in the empire – even across the ocean. A *Ianus* could mark the beginning of a journey and a concept of mobility that was familiar: marked by milestones, associated with bridges, in other words a mobility that was similar to everywhere else in the empire (Laurence 2001). For those leaving Britain, the arch marked their arrival at the ocean and at the end of their journey by road.

Time, distance and repairs

The discussion so far has focused on the construction and development of the material form of roads with defined routeways and monumental arches at the start of a routeway. There is another side to the thousands of miles of roads located by archaeologists across the Roman Empire: the exercise of power through the measurement of distance. The Antonine Itineraries list the distances between places on routes across the Roman Empire, just as the Peutinger Table does in pictorial format (see essays in Talbert 2010). These allow for the planning of journeys, something Roman emperors did when going on campaign with each stopping place carefully identified (SHA *Sev.Alex.* 45). Journeys were planned in advance and the time taken to cover a set distance between stopping places was predicted.

The anticipation of journeys and the time taken to cover a distance was not a knowledge reserved for the emperor, but was a form of knowledge widely available. On a journey, communications between individuals by letter was facilitated by the prediction of when they would arrive at a particular place. The correspondence between Cicero and Atticus (e.g. *ad Att.* 5.2 and 5.3) points to the prediction of when Cicero will arrive and the ability of Atticus to send letters in advance of Cicero's arrival to that place. He left Pompeii on 10 May 51 BCE, sending a letter to Atticus as he left, and arrived the same day at Trebula, where two letters from Atticus awaited him that were sent three days earlier; on 12 May we find Cicero at Beneventum, on the 15th at Venusia and by the 19th at Tarentum (Cic. *Att.*5.4–8). Cicero's speed of travel seems ponderous and slow, but this may have been a necessity, if letters were to catch-up with him. Hence, speed may have been sacrificed to enable effective communication by letter on this journey.

Julius Caesar was remarked on as travelling the considerable distance of 100 Roman miles in a day, using a hired carriage (Suet. *Jul.*57); whilst the fastest journey in 24 hours recorded by Pliny (*N.H.* 7.84) was 182 miles. These are certainly exceptional. More realistic might be the 58 miles per day on a 4-day journey from Luni to Rome (Liv. 39.21.5). On foot, a man would cover 35 miles in a day (Pliny *N.H.* 3.100), similar to the speed at which an army travelled per day (Polyb. 2.25; Liv. 24.13.9–11; 22.11.5). If summoned to court, an allowance of 20 miles per day was given for the journey (*Dig.* 11.1.11, 38.15.2.3, 50.16.3). The variation in travel time per day indicates the possibilities for speedy travel as an exceptional action, whereas a normal speed of travel can be seen as 35 to 50 miles per day.

However, these speeds may assume that the road was in a good condition, whereas the much lower speed given by the legal sources in the *Digest of Justinian* of just 20 miles per day accounts for poor road conditions. This was a subject raised in the senate even in the first century CE, with the suggestion that the curators of the roads and the contractors for the repair of the roads had defrauded the state, resulting in the poor condition of the roads (Tac. *Ann.* 3.33; Dio 59.15, 60.17). As indicated by more than 200 inscriptions from across the Roman Empire, roads simply became old and dilapidated, or were damaged by natural phenomena such as earthquakes, landslides and floods (as detailed by Kissel 2002: 132). The roads needed to be restored and it is the restoration of the roads that frequently appears on the milestones along their route. Papyri from Egypt also point to the disruption of the roads (*P.Oxy.* I 118 verso; Adams 2007: 20). Interestingly, Dio Chrysostom (*Oration* 3.127) places the prompt and effective action of a ruler in bridging rivers and building roads, alongside more obviously (to us) imperial achievements such as military success and town foundation. The medical writer, Galen (10.632–3; see Nutton 1978: 218–19 for discussion) lauds Trajan's road-building activities which created stone causeways across marshes, hacking through scrubland, bridging dangerous rivers, shortening the route or making it easier, with the result that once lonely roads infested with wild beasts became broad highways. Galen compares his own achievement in medicine with that of the emperor in road building: Hippocrates discovered and planned the road, but it was Galen – like Trajan – 'who swept aside the tangled confusion, repairing and realigning the old ways of Hippocrates; and his implicit claim was that the Galenic system of medicine would be as impressive and enduring as the road system of Trajan' (Nutton 1978: 219). The emperor had to deal with the ageing roads of the Roman Empire; not to do so would open the emperor up for criticism. Thus, the condition of the roads became a measure for the performance of rulers. It may come as no surprise that many milestones appear at times of political instability, for example in the third century CE, as well as at times of political stability, for example in the reign of Trajan.

Conclusion

By the time of the first emperor, Augustus (27 BCE to 14 CE), Italy had become famous for its roads, which were admired by Greek writers in particular. These were expanded to the provinces of the empire to create a transport infrastructure that was to shape the settlement patterns of cities and transport systems in Europe in particular. However, in terms of material culture, there was considerable investment in the transport system – which can be seen in surviving sections of paved roads, viaducts, bridges and milestones. The power of the state was embedded within the transport system: symbolically arches at the beginning of roads celebrated an emperor's achievements and milestones recalled the emperor's achievement in maintaining the road. Practically, the power of the state depended on the ability of the transport system to support the travel of state officials or agents of the state. This was achieved through the stationing of supplies and animals at inns to support state officials. It is notable also that transport animals increased in size through the breeding of mules. This system of major routes characterised travel across the empire, but within it – for example, in central Italy – a dense system of local roads was developed. The latter have been found to be more effective in the development of regions economically by modern authorities such as the World Bank. Hence, if we are to look for an economic benefit of the system of roads, we need to look to these local initiatives, rather than the major roads associated with the Roman emperors. However, for the state, the major roads were also associated with taxation on the movement of goods across boundaries and borders between provinces. Well-maintained roads were to become a key symbol of good government by the emperor, whereas poorly maintained roads were symbolic of an ageing empire in decline. This caused the material well-being of the roads to be a metaphor for the well-being of the state, thus underlining the importance of travel and communications by land within the Roman Empire.

References

Adams, Colin. 2001. '"There and back again": getting around in Roman Egypt'. In *Travel and Geography in the Roman Empire*, edited by C. Adams and R. Laurence, 138–66. Abingdon: Routledge.

Adams, Colin. 2007. *Land Transport in Roman Egypt: A study of economics and administration in a Roman province.* Oxford: Oxford University Press.

Alcock, Susan E., John Bodel and Richard J. A. Talbert (eds). 2012. *Highways, Byways, and Road Systems in the Pre-Modern World, Ancient World Comparative Histories.* Malden: Wiley-Blackwell.

Ashby, Thomas and Roland Fell. 1921. 'The Via Flaminia', *Journal of Roman Studies* 11: 125–91.

Ashby, Thomas and Robert Gardner. 1916. 'The Via Traiana', *Papers of the British School at Rome* 8: 104–71.

Asher, Samuel and Paul Novosad. 2018. 'Rural roads and local economic development', *World Bank Policy Research Working Paper* 8466.

Attema, Peter, Tymon De Haas and Gijls Tol. 2011. *Between Satricum and Antium: Settlement dynamics in Latium Vetus.* Leuven: Peeters Publishers.

Ballance, M. H. "The Roman Bridges of the Via Flaminia." *Papers of the British School at Rome*, vol. 19, 1951, pp. 78–117. JSTOR, http://www.jstor.org/stable/40310491. Accessed 3 Dec. 2023.

Bang, Peter. 2008. *The Roman Bazaar. A comparative study of trade and markets in a tributary empire.* Cambridge: Cambridge University Press.

Banta, Jason. 2007. 'The Gates of Janus: Bakhtin and Plutarch's Roman *meta-chronotope*'. In *The Sites of Rome: Time, space and memory*, edited by David Larmour and Diana Spencer, 238–70. Oxford: Oxford Unversity Press.

Blake, Marion and Doris Bishop. 1973. *Roman Construction in Italy from Nerva through the Antonines.* Philadelphia, PA: American Philosophical Society.

Bowersock, Glenn. 1983. *Roman Arabia.* Cambridge, MA: Harvard University Press.

Burnett, Andrew, Michel Amandry and Pere Pau Ripollès. 1992. *Roman Provincial Coinage Volume I: From the death of Caesar to the death of Vitellius (44 BC–AD 69).* London: British Museum Press.

Bushe-Fox, Joscelyn. 1926. *First Report on the Excavation of the Roman Fort at Richborough, Kent.* London: Society of Antiquaries.

Bushe-Fox, J. 1928. *Second Report on the Excavation of the Roman Fort at Richborough, Kent.* London: Society of Antiquaries.

Bushe-Fox, Jocelyn, P. 1932. *Third Report on the Excavations of the Roman Fort of Richborough, Kent.* London: Society of Antiquaries.

Bushe-Fox, Jocelyn, P. 1949. *Fourth Report on the Excavations of the Roman Fort of Richborough, Kent.* London: Society of Antiquaries.

Calzolari, Mauro. 1996. *Introduzione allo studio della rete stradale dell'Italia romana: L'*Itinerarium Antonini. Rome: Accademia Nazionale dei Lincei.

Campbell, Brian. 2012. *Rivers and the Power of Ancient Rome.* Chapel Hill: University of North Carolina Press.

Ceraudo, Giuseppe. 2008. *Sulle trace della via Traiana. Indagini aerotopografiche da Aecae a Herdonia.* Foggia: Grenzi.

Ceraudo, Giuseppe. 2012. 'Due nuove lastre iscritte dei ponti della Via Traiana', *ZPE* 183: 255–58.

Chelotti, Marcella. 1985. *Le epigrafi romane di Canosa.* Bari: Edipulglia.

Coleman, Kathleen. 1988. *Statius* Silvae *IV.* Oxford: Oxford University Press.

Cooley, Alison. 2009. Res Gestae Divi Augusti. *Text, Translation, and Commentary.* Cambridge: Cambridge University Press.

Cornell, Tim. 1995. *The Beginnings of Rome.* London: Routledge.

Corsi, Cristina. 2000. *Le Strutture di Servizio del* Cursus Publicus *in Italia.* BAR International Series 875. Oxford: BAR.

Crawford, Michael. 1996. *Roman Statutes.* Bulletin of the Institute of Classical Studies Supplementary Series 64. London: Institute of Classical Studies.

Cunliffe, Barry. 1968. *Fifth Report on the Excavation of the Roman Fort at Richborough, Kent.* London: Society of Antiquaries.

Cuntz, Otto. 1929. *Itineraria Romana I: Itineraria Antonini Augusti et Burdigalense.* Leipzig: Teubner.

De Grossi Mazzorin, Jacopo. 2010. 'Presenze di Cammelli nell' Antichità in Italia ed Europa: aggiornamenti'. In *Vie degli animali, vie degli uomini: Trasumanza e altri spostamenti di animali in Europa tardoantica e medievali*, edited by Giuliano Volpe, Antonietta Buglione and Giovanni De Venuto. Bari: Edipuglia. 91–106.

De Laet, Siegfried. 1949. *Portorium. Étude sur l'organisation douanière chez les romains.* Brugge: De Tempel.

Elsner, Jas. 2000. 'The *Itinerarium Burdigalense:* politics and salvation in the geography of Constantine's empire', *JRS* 90: 181–95.

Étienne, Robert. 1992. 'L'horologe de la *Civitas Igaeditanorum* et la creation de la province de Lusitanie', *REA* 94: 355–62.

Farnum, Jérôme. 2005. *The Positioning of the Roman Imperial Legions.* BAR International Series 1458. Oxford: BAR.

Finley, Moses. 1973. *The Ancient Economy.* London: Chatto and Windus.

France, Jérôme. 2001. Quadragesima Galliarum. *L'organisation douanière des provinces Alpestres, Gauloises, et Germaniques de l'empire romain.* Rome: École française de Rome.

France, Jérôme and Jocelyne Nelis-Clément. 2014a. 'Tout en bas de 'l'empire. Les stationes lieux de contrôle et de représentation du pouvoir'. In *La statio: archéologie d'un lieu de pouvoir dans l'Empire romain*, edited by Jérôme France and Jocelyne Nelis-Clément, 117–246. Bordeaux: Ausonius.

France, Jérôme and Jocelyne Nelis-Clément. 2014b. 'Introduction'. In *La statio: archéologie d'un lieu de pouvoir dans l'Empire romain*, edited by Jérôme France and Jocelyne Nelis-Clément, 11–16. Bordeaux: Ausonius.

French, D.H. 2012: Roman Roads and Milestones of Asia Minor Vol. 3: Milestones, Fasc. 3.1: Republican (BIAA Electronic Monograph 1). London. ISBN: 978 1 898249 24 5 | DOI: https://doi.org/10.18866/BIAA/e-01

Frothingham, Arthur. 1915. 'The Roman territorial arch', *AJA* 19: 155–74.

Gallazzi, C. and Sijpesteijn, P.J. 1989. 'Receipts issued to an overseer of a customs station', *ZPE* 78: 119–22.

Galliazzo, Vittorio. 1994. *I Ponti Romani.* Florence: Canova.

Gates-Foster, Jennifer. 2012. 'The well-remembered path: roadways and cultural memory in Ptolemaic and Roman Egypt'. In *Highways, Byways, and Road Systems in the Pre-Modern World, Ancient World Comparative Histories*, edited by S. E. Alcock, J. Bodel and R. J. A. Talbert, 202–21. Malden: Wiley-Blackwell.

Gazzola, Piero. 1963. *Ponti Romani.* Florence: L.S. Olschki.

Giard, Jean-Baptiste. 1976. *Bibliothèque Nationale Catalogue des Monnaies de l'Empire Romain I: Auguste.* Paris: Bibliothèque Nationale.

Graf, David. 1995. 'The *Via Nova Traiana* in Arabia Petraea'. In *The Roman and Byzantine Army in the East*, edited by Edward Dabrowa, 141–67. JRA Supplementary Series 14. Portsmouth, RI: Journal of Roman Archaeology.

Håkanson, Lennart. 1969. *Statius'* Silvae*: Critical and exegetical remarks with some notes on the* Thebaid. Lund: Gleerup.

Haley, Evan. 2003. *Baetica Felix: People and prosperity in southern Spain from Caesar to Septimus Severus.* Austin, TX: University of Texas.

Hassel, Franz. 1966. *Der Trajansbogen in Benevent. Ein Bauwerk des römischen Senates.* Mainz: Franz Josef.

Hauken, Tor and Hasan Malay. 2009. 'A new edict of Hadrian from the province of Asia setting out regulations for requisitioned transport'. In *Selbstdarstellung und Kommunikation: Die Veröffentlichung staatlicher Urkunden auf Stein und Bronze in der römischen Welt*, edited by Rudolf Haensch, 327–48. Munich: C.H. Beck.

Heurgon, Jacques. 1952. 'La date des Goblets de Vicarello', *Revue des Études Anciennes* 54: 39–50.

Hölscher, Tonio. 2002. 'Bilder der Macht und Herrschaft'. In *Traian: ein Kaiser der Superlative am beginn einer Umbruchzeit?*, edited by Annette Nünnerich-Asmus (ed.), 127–44. Mainz: von Zabern.

Humbert, Jean-Baptiste and Alain Desreumaux. 1998. *Fouilles de Khirbet Es-Samra en Jordaine I: La Voie Romaine, Le Cemetière, Les Documents Épigraphiques.* Turnhout: Brepols.

Humm, Michel. 1996. 'Appius Claudius Caecus et la construction de la via Appia', *Mélanges de l'École Française de Rome* 108: 693–746.

Janni, Pietro. 1984. *La mappa e il periplo. Cartografia antica e spazio odologica.* Rome: Bretschneider.

Kissel, Theodor. 2002. 'Road-Building as a *Munus Publicum*'. In *The Roman Army and the Economy*, edited by Paul Erdkamp, 127–60. Amsterdam: Gieben.
Kleiner, Fred. 1991. 'The trophy on the bridge and the Roman triumph over nature', *L'Antiquité Classique* 60: 182–92.
Kolb, Anne. 2000. *Transport und Nachrichtentransfer im Römischen Reich, Klio. Beiträge zur alten Geschichte. Beihefte, neue Folge*. Berlin: Akademie Verlag.
Kolb, Anne. 2019. *Roman Roads: New evidence – new perspectives*. Berlin: De Gruyter.
Laurence, Ray. 1999. *The Roads of Roman Italy: Mobility and cultural change*. London: Routledge.
Laurence, Ray. 2001. 'The creation of geography: an interpretation of Roman Britain'. In *Travel and Geography in the Roman Empire*, edited Colin Adams and Ray Laurence, 67–94. London: Routledge.
Laurence, Ray. 2004. 'The economic exploitation of geological resources in the Tiber Valley: road building'. In *Bridging the Tiber: Approaches to regional archaeology in the middle Tiber Valley*, edited by H. Patterson, 285–95. London: British School at Rome.
Laurence, Ray. 2016. 'Connectivity, roads and transport: essays on Roman roads to speak to other disciplines?', *Journal of Roman Archaeology* 29: 692–5.
Lauritsen, Taylor. 2014. *Ante Ostium Contextualizing Boundaries in the Houses of Pompeii and Herculaneum*, PhD thesis, University of Edinburgh.
Leather, G.M. 2006. *Roman Bridges in Iberia: Roman and other bridges in Spain and Portugal*. Garstang: Sullom Side.
Leveau, Philippe. 2014. 'Stations routières et *stationes viarum*. Une contribution à l'archéologie de la station en Gaule Narbonnaise et dans les provinces alpines voisines'. In *La* statio. *Archéologie d'un lieu de pouvoir dans l'empire romain*, edited by Jerome France and Jocelyne Nelis-Clément, 17–56. Bordeaux: de Boccard.
Liberman, Gauthier. 2010. *Stace* Silves. Paris: Calepinus.
Mansuelli, Giuseppe. 1941. *Ariminum (Rimini)*. Spoleto: Istituto di Studi Romani.
Mansuelli, Giuseppe. 1960. *Il monumento augusteo del 27 a.c. Nuove ricerche sull'Arco di Rimini*. Bologna.
Mattingly, David J., Martin Sterry, Tyr Fothergal, Aurélie Cuénod, Chloë Duckworth and Victoria Leitch 2021. 'Animal traffic in the Sahara'. In *L'Homme et l'Animal au Maghreb de la Préhistoire au Moyen Âge. Explorations d'une relation complexe*, edited by V. Blanc-Bijon, J.-P. Bracco, M.-B. Carre, S. Chaker, X. Lafon and M. Ouerfelli, 175–92. Aix-en-Provence: Presses Universitaires de Provence.
Mattingly, Harold. 1965. *Coins of the Roman Empire in the British Museum Volume I: Augustus to Vitellius*. London: British Museum.
Mertens, Joseph. 1994. 'Les ponts de la Via Traiana dans la traversé du Tavoliere de Foggia'. In *Strade Romane: Percorsi e Infrastrutture*, edited by Lorenzo Quilici and Stefania Quilici Gigli, 7–18. Rome: Bretschneider.
Mirković, Miroslava. 1994. '*Beneficiarii consularis* in Sirmium', *Chiron* 24: 345–404.
Mitchell, Stephen. 1976. 'Requisitioned transport in the Roman Empire: a new inscription from Pisidia', *JRS* 66: 106–38.
Mitchell, Stephen. 2008. 'Geography, politics, and imperialism in the Asian customs law'. In *The Customs Law of Asia*, edited by M. Cottier, M. Crawford, C.V. Crowther, J.-L. Ferrary, B.M. Levick, O. Salomies and M. Wörrle, 165–201. Oxford: Oxford University Press.
Morley, Neville. 2007. 'The early Roman Empire: distribution'. In *The Cambridge Economic History of the Greco-Roman World*, edited by Walter Scheidel, Ian Morris, and Richard Saller, 570–91. Cambridge: Cambridge University Press.
Munzi, Massimiliano. 1997. 'Nuovi dati sulla via Amerina e note prosopografiche sugli Egnatii di Falerii Novi', *Miscellanea Amerina* 1: 48–60.
Nelis-Clément, Jocelyne. 2000. *Les* Beneficiarii: *Militaires et Administrateurs au Service de L'Empire*. Bordeaux: Ausonius.
Nelis-Clément, Jocelyne. 2006. 'Les stations comme espace et transmission du pouvoir'. In *Herrschaftsstrukturen und Herschaftspraxis*, edited by Anne Kolb, 269–98. Berlin: De Gruyter.
Newlands, Carole. 2012. *Statius, Poet between Rome and Naples*. Bristol: Bristol Classical Press.
Nicolet, Claude. 1991. *Space, Geography, and Politics in the Early Roman Empire*. Ann Arbor, MI: University of Michigan Press.
Nutton, Vivian. 1978. 'The beneficial ideology'. In *Imperialism in the Ancient World*, edited by Peter Garnsey and C Whittaker, 209–21. Cambridge: Cambridge University Press.

Pellizari, Andrea. 2007. 'Viabilità e insediamenti nell'area subalpine della Regio XI: *ad Fines* e il suo territorio'. In *Geograpfi et viaggi nell' antichità*, edited by Stefano Conti, Barbara Scardigli and M. Christina Torchi, 185–95. Ancona: Affinità Elettive Edizioni.

Poehler, Eric. 2017. *The Traffic Systems of Pompeii*. Oxford: Oxford University Press.

Popović, Vladislav. 1989. 'Une station de bénéficaires à Sirmium', *CRAI* 1989: 116–22.

Quilici, Lorenzo. 2008. 'Land transport part 1: roads and bridges'. In *The Oxford Handbook of Engineering and Technology in the Classical World*, edited by John Oleson, 551–80. Oxford: Oxford University Press.

Roller, Matthew. 2000. 'Exemplarity in Roman culture: the cases of Horatius Cocles and Cloelia', *Classical Philology* 99: 1–56.

Rotili, Mario. 1972. *L'Arco di Traiano a Benevento*. Rome: Istituto poligrafico dello Stato, Libreria.

Saller, Richard. 2002. 'Framing the debate over growth in the ancient economy'. In *The Ancient Economy*, edited by Walter Scheidel and Sitta von Reden, 251–69. Edinburgh: Edinburgh University Press.

Schneider, Helmuth. 2007. 'Technology'. In *The Cambridge Economic History of the Greco-Roman World*, edited by Walter Scheidel, Ian Morris, and Richard Saller, 144–71. Cambridge: Cambridge University Press.

Scuderi, Rita. 2001. 'Confine amministrativo e confine douganale nelle Alpi occidental durante l'alto impero'. In *Les Anciens et La Montagne*, edited by Silvia Giorcelli Bersani, 167–84. Torino: CELID.

Sijpesteijn, Pieter. 1989. 'A money account of customs duties?', *ZPE* 78: 100–2.

Sillières, Pierre. 1990. *Les voies de communication de l'Hispaniae méridionale*. Paris: de Boccard.

Silvestrini, Marina. 1983. 'Miliari della via Traiana', *Epigrafia e territorio: politica e società I*, Bari: 79–136.

Smolenaars, Johannes 2006. 'Ideology and poetics along the Via Domitiana: Statius *Silvae* 4.3'. In *Flavian Poetry*, edited by Ruut R. Nauta, Harm-Jan van Dam and Johannes J.L. Smolenaars, 223–44. Leiden: Brill.

Spiedel, Michael. (2005/2006) 'Trajan's Column and the Arch of Benevento', *Rom.Mitt.*112: 189–206.

Steidl, Bernd. 2005. 'Die station der *beneficiarii consularis* in Obernburg am Main', *Germania* 83: 67–94.

Strong, Donald. 1968. 'The monument'. In *Fifth Report on the Excavation of the Roman Fort at Richborough, Kent*, Barry Cunliffe, 40–73. London: Society of Antiquaries Cunliffe.

Talbert, Richard. 2005. '*Ubique Fines:* boundaries within the Roman Empire', *Caesardonum* 39: 93–101.

Talbert, Richard (ed.). 2010. *Rome's World: The Peutinger map reconsidered*. Cambridge: Cambridge University Press.

Talbert, Richard. 2023. *World and Hour in Roman Minds. Exploratory Essays*. Oxford: Oxford University Press.

Trousset, Pol. 2005. 'Tarif de Zaraï: Essai sur les circuits commerciaux dans la zone présaharienne', *Antiquités Africaines* 38–39: 355–73.

Wiegels, Rainer. 2016. *Kleine Schriften zur Germanienpolitik in der römishcen Kaiserzeit*. Rahden: Verlag Marie Ledorf.

Worthing, Michael, Lloyd Bosworth, Josie Bannister and Ray Laurence. 2017. 'Geochemical methods for sourcing lava paving stones from the Roman roads of Central Italy', *Archaeometry* 59(6): 1000–17.

Worthing Michael, Ray Laurence and Lloyd Bosworth. 2018. 'Trajan's Forum (hemicycle) and the Via Biberatica (Trajan's Markets): an HHpXRF study of the provenance of lava paving in Ancient Rome (Italy)', *Archaeometry* 60(6): 1202–20.

2

An empire of words? Archaeology and writing in the Roman world

John Pearce

Introduction

On 28 February 2015, archaeologists excavating a cemetery serving Roman *Corinium* lifted a limestone slab re-used as grave cover to find its underside inscribed with a Latin text, an epitaph set up by an unnamed man for his wife (Holbrook et al. 2017: 140–2) (Figure 2.1). One of a handful from this town (modern Cirencester, south-west England), the epitaph exemplifies the spread of writing to the furthest corners of empire. The find's rapid media exposure is due not only to the woman's resonant name, Bodicacia, echoing that of Boudica, the rebel queen of the Iceni (Hingley and Unwin 2006). It also speaks to the power of stone inscriptions to evoke Roman antiquity (cf. Shaw 2015). The contemporary association between writing, especially monumental writing, and the Roman Empire also reflects the privileging of inscriptions as a subject of scholarly attention from the Renaissance onwards. This chapter will characterise writing within its Roman imperial context, presenting the evidence for its diverse manifestations – monumental inscriptions like the terse Cirencester epitaph now being complemented by many other kinds of surviving evidence – and discussing the ways in which writing was both a product and agent of empire. It follows the conventional distinctions in excluding two types of writing from consideration, literary texts, though these circulated (and were written) in the north-west provinces which form the focus of the chapter (Tomlin 2012), and coins (see Howgego, Chapter 3 this volume).

Figure 2.1 Tombstone from Cirencester commemorating Bodicacia (1.34 m long), second century CE. 'To the spirits of the departed, Bodicacia, spouse, lived 27 years.' Reproduced by permission of Cotswold Archaeology.

The first section will briefly review the historiography of the study of writing (Eckardt 2018; Werner 2009). Inscriptions are long established as historical sources of fundamental importance for understanding the Roman world. A significant shift in their study has nonetheless taken place in recent decades, interrogating the habit of monumental (and related) writing in itself as a practice central to empire, both as a 'social symbol and integrative by-product of Roman government, economy and culture' (Hopkins 1991: 144). Subsequent sections will focus on Rome's provinces in north-western Europe, a region in which writing was largely a novelty, to explore the forms it took and the roles it played practically and symbolically. After considering the material changes which furnished the media and skills to enable writing to proliferate, the chapter will examine some functions of writing, including those directly related to imperial institutions and those within wider social and economic life. It is important not to exaggerate the spread of writing – its usage was patchy and varied significantly between contexts. Nonetheless it can also be considered as a continuous phenomenon across its diverse applications. Above all the imperial presence was fundamental; the latter's manifestation in writing will be explored in the final section with a case study of inscriptions commemorating building in Roman military garrisons (all dates given are CE, unless otherwise stated).

Historiography – writing and literacy

Engagement with Roman inscriptions, their texts, decoration and materials has been continuous from antiquity. The commonest fate was re-use, especially in the limekiln or melting pot, but inscriptions have also been read, collected and faked from the European Middle Ages onwards. Scholarly engagement with them accelerated in the Renaissance, when a more formally historical approach developed to document and interpret inscriptions (Cooley 2000; Buonocuore 2015). The nineteenth century saw two related developments: the systematic elaboration of comprehensive corpora, organised on geographical and chronological as well as historical or textual principles, and the establishment of institutions to compile and disseminate critical editions of epigraphic texts and develop their use as historical sources (Bruun 2015). The academic effort expended on these corpora, emerging as its own sub-discipline of epigraphy, reflects the special status of such documents in the exploration of the ancient world. This continues to the present, increasingly exploiting digital techniques to record and disseminate texts (Elliott 2015; Velázquez Soriano and Espinosa 2021). As historical sources, inscriptions have been fundamental to understanding Roman political and military history, geography and toponymy, imperial institutions and government, laws, prosopography, social structures and economic processes, demography, religious practice, language history and so on (Bodel 2001; Cooley and Oliver 2006; Cooley and Salway 2012).

The continued study of inscriptions for such historical purposes remains central to Roman scholarship, albeit with some shifts in emphasis, for example an increasing attention to non-monumental inscriptions (e.g. Cooley and Salway 2012: 177–89). In the later twentieth century, much fuller consideration was also given to writing as a socio-economic and cultural phenomenon in its own right. A key prompt to considering writing for its own sake was Macmullen's (1982) coinage of the phrase 'epigraphic habit' to describe the Roman practice of monumental writing and the sense of audience it implied. Inscriptions were also central to the characterisation of ancient literacy by William Harris (1989), who explored both the direct surviving evidence for what was written (and read), of which inscriptions supplied the major part, and the wider factors which enabled or inhibited literacy. In a Roman setting he identified the key constraints on literacy to be limited knowledge of written languages (above all Latin and Greek), restricted availability of education and high cost of writing materials, absence of an ideological impetus prompting universal literacy, and limited urbanisation or participation in complex economic activity. These led Harris to argue that literacy, defined as the ability to read and write short personal statements with understanding, was a phenomenon limited largely to elites and to non-elite groups closely connected to them, scribes, often of slave status, soldiers, and a small number of artisans. Such non-elite writing was especially limited in Rome's western provinces, where a pre-Roman writing tradition was limited (Harris 1989: 267–73).

Subsequent work, much of it directly in response to these characterisations of the epigraphic habit and literacy, tends to take either a textual or 'metatextual' approach (Bodel 2015: 755). In the former case the focus lies on the content of epigraphic texts, with a particular interest in language history and sociolinguistics, including variation within Latin (e.g. Adams 2007; Clackson 2012; Mullen 2016) and bi-/multilingualism, between Latin and Greek and other ancient languages (e.g. Adams 2003; Bagnall 2011; Mullen and James 2012). In the latter case, responses to Harris foregrounded the power dynamic inherent in writing, both its enablement of the large-scale control of imperial institutions and territories and the opportunities it afforded for individual betterment of circumstances (Humphrey 1991; Bowman and Woolf 1994a). A sociological approach to the epigraphic habit, both as a whole (e.g. Woolf 1996; Meyer 2011) and in specific cases, has focused on its use by groups who were marginalised within Roman society but for whom there were also opportunities for social mobility, for example freed slaves or recruits from 'barbarian' societies into the Roman army (e.g. Mouritsen 2005; Hope 2016). Local elites too have been argued to assert their position and negotiate their relationship to Roman power through monumental inscriptions in Latin and local languages, as Roman hegemony extended across what became the western provinces (Cooley 2002; Häussler and Pearce 2007; Häussler 2008).

A 'material turn' is also widely visible in recent scholarship on ancient writing. This is exemplified by the prominence given to the life cycle of inscriptions – that is, their creation, viewing/reading and modification/destruction – by Alison Cooley (2012: 285–325; 2018). The emphasis on archaeological context in a recent volume on multilingualism (Mullen and James 2012) illustrates the same shift in perspective. This material turn has diverse facets, for example characterisation of writing materials, attention to taphonomic factors (e.g. how do survival conditions impinge on our understanding of what was written) and above all analysis of the spatial dimensions of writing. Attention to this latter aspect has key potential to improve understanding of who wrote and read texts and under what circumstances (Sears et al. 2013; Benefiel and Keegan 2016). Identifying both the writer and the milieu of writing also much enhances the sociolinguistic information to be extrapolated from content (Mullen 2016). The location evidence has been essential, for example, to demonstrate just how widely mural graffiti were written and for showing that their modern associations with subversion do not apply to Roman examples (Baird and Taylor 2011a). Part of the material turn also includes emphasis on the experiential dimension of texts, for example the way in which monumental inscriptions imposed themselves on the viewer in public space by framing, size and material (Graham 2021). Johnson's (2010: 3–31) reconstruction of the experience of reading Greek and Latin literary texts as a collective, aristocratic identity-defining pursuit provides another instance of the utility of considering material setting. The interplay between verbal and non-verbal elements on inscribed monuments has also been shown to enhance the understanding of inscriptions. Hope's analysis of tombstones from Britain, especially from military garrisons, shows how complementarity between funerary portrait and text served to intensify the memorial's role in representing the deceased, for example as the epitome of martial or marital virtue (Hope 2016). Allowing in this way for the 'agency' of the inscription has potential application for non-monumental examples (e.g. Van Oyen 2016).

Whether focused on content or context, these approaches have also been able to exploit significant new data, in particular writing on portable documents. The major recent finds of texts in the western provinces fall into this category. In Britain, for example, document discoveries include ink and stylus writing tablets, lead curse tablets and votive 'leaves' (see below; also Jackson and Burleigh 2018). Another burgeoning dataset, albeit lacking in stratigraphic documentation, comprises texts discovered by metal-detecting, above all military diplomas (Eck 2015), as well as artefacts used for writing (Mullen 2021).

The cumulative effect of recent analysis and discovery is to extend encounters with writing into ever-broadening spheres of ancient life, but this chapter does not directly re-assess the 'minimalist' version of literacy argued for by Harris (see above). In the following sections it draws on these recent approaches to explore the material constraints on writing, the uses to which it was put and the milieu in which writing was created and read, making maximum use where possible of archaeological context. It focuses less on formative periods and more on characterising writing when it was widely established in provincial culture.

Writing in the north-western provinces

To examine writing practices this discussion will focus principally on Rome's north-western provinces – that is, Britain, the Germanies (from the Netherlands up the Rhine to Switzerland) and the Three Gauls (temperate France and adjacent areas). These areas came under Roman control between the mid-first century BCE and the mid-second century CE. As regions in which writing and Latin were mainly novelties of the conquest period and after, they enable a baseline impression of Roman writing to be established for the wider empire (cf. Woolf 2009: 53–6). The existence in these regions of anaerobic burial environments, preserving organic materials on deeply stratified urban and military sites, is especially advantageous for characterising writing on ephemeral materials. On the other hand, the destruction of building superstructures and the recycling of Roman building materials work against the survival of monumental texts and mural graffiti. As for Roman inscriptions in general, it is conventional in these regions to distinguish two major categories of inscriptions based on form, text and context: (i) monumental inscriptions created on media intended to be permanent, especially stone, inscribed in capital letters and set up in public places; and (ii) inscriptions for ephemeral purposes, less visible because of their small scale, portability, and/or occurrence in domestic spaces and written in a cursive script (Beltrán Lloris 2015a). This is a problematic distinction since these criteria do not always coincide (see below) but applying it for the moment enables the surviving writing from north-west Europe to be outlined.

In the first category, surviving examples comprise small numbers of inscriptions from the public spaces of cities and garrisons, mainly recording honours awarded and buildings constructed as well as occasional fragments of letters and decrees, and many more epitaphs and votive texts from cemeteries and sanctuaries respectively, in total *c.*24,000 texts (Beltrán Lloris 2015b: 138–9). Stone is the main surviving medium. Bronzes survive occasionally as honorific documents, records of speeches, calendars and, more frequently, as military diplomas recording citizenship rights for discharged auxiliary soldiers (Eck 2015; Kolb 2015).

Inscriptions in the second category are so diverse as to challenge any sketch of their variety. As noted, opportunities for preservation of mural graffiti are limited in the Roman north, but texts and images scratched on stone and painted plaster documented across Roman Gaul suggest nonetheless the regional importance of this overlooked form of writing. The many inscriptions from column fragments from private and public buildings at Amiens, northern France, and on tiles and painted plaster at the temple at Châteauneuf, Haute-Savoie, demonstrate the intensity of the 'graffiti habit' in some settings at least (Mermet 1993; Barbet and Fuchs 2008; Binet and Hoët-Van Cauwenberghe 2010). Letters and lists written in ink on wooden tablets, above all at Vindolanda in northern Britain, hint at the high volume of everyday writing in the Roman army (Bowman 2003). Circa 40 findspots of stylus tablets are now also documented – that is, wooden tablets carrying a wax layer into which texts can be inscribed with a stylus; letter traces survive where the stylus's point has penetrated the wood beneath the wax (Pearce 2004; Hartmann 2015). Indeed the distribution of styli and related writing equipment provides a proxy indicator of the widespread use of these organic media (Willi 2021; Mullen 2021). Painted texts on ceramics (ostraca) are much rarer, likely not surviving as well in the Roman north as in arid environments because of the solubility of their ink (cf. Bagnall 2011; Speidel 2018). The most numerous surviving inscriptions in this second category, however, are those texts cast, stamped, scratched, branded or painted on objects and on tags attached to objects and commodities during their production, movement or use. These are often grouped under the heading of *instrumentum domesticum* (Cooley 2012: 82–5; Edmondson 2015a). The dies used to stamp such texts or the moulds in which they were cast also occasionally survive (Cooley 2012: 101–3, 202–3). Such texts are attested in many thousands of instances, especially on objects made of inorganic materials, above all pots and bricks (Beltrán Lloris 2015b: 138). For example, 210,916 instances of potters' names stamped on terra sigillata, a widely distributed ceramic tableware, have been documented in north-west Europe (Fulford 2013: 3). Waterlogged conditions sometimes also preserve texts of this kind on organic media, for instance wooden barrels and leather hides (Baratta 2008; Tamerl 2010: 129–34; Hartmann 2012). This proliferation of writing is largely within the empire; although portable objects bearing texts were sometimes carried into Scotland and Ireland, central Europe and Scandinavia, the practice of writing itself is little documented beyond Rome's borders until late Antiquity.

Materials and writing

This expansion of writing is closely linked to the wider Roman economy. Bowman and Wilson (2009: 38–42) note the importance of documents both for the state, enhancing its fiscal procedures and its redistributive networks, and for private producers, enabling their management of complex production and distribution systems. However the proliferation of documents of all kinds, requiring media on which to write (stone, metal, wood and so on) and the tools and skills to do so, also itself depended on wider economic change, including the increased exploitation of relevant raw materials and an improved infrastructure for distributing these and the objects made from them. These changes were partly a product of conquest and of the requirements of the Roman state, especially supplying the city of Rome and the army. They also developed their own momentum, in the context of economic growth enhanced by long-lasting political stability over a large geographical area (Wilson, Chapter 4 this volume). The expanded creation of writing was also enabled by complementary craft specialisation, augmenting the skills of workers in shaping the diverse media which carried texts.

The most visible sign of the dependence of writing on wider economic change is the abundance of monumental inscriptions on stone outlined above. Necessary for their creation were transformations in the scale of the quarrying and movement of freestone suitable for carving fine detail as text or decoration. Inscriptions were made largely by exploiting local and regional stone sources, using water transport (Russell 2013). The stone to commemorate Bodicacia at Cirencester travelled only a few miles from its Cotswold quarry, but Cotswold limestone was otherwise exploited across southern Britain, especially in London along with other limestones shipped from eastern England, northern France and the Moselle valley (Coombe et al. 2016: xxxiv–xliv; Hayward in Holbrook et al. 2017: 76–8). In the middle Rhine valley, inscriptions were also carved on Moselle stone brought by water as well as on coarser-grained local limestones (Stribrny 1987: 99–101; Giljohann and Wenzel 2015). Longer-distance transport of stone media was much rarer. In north-west Europe, for example, Mediterranean marble only rarely served for small inscriptions such as plaques on tombs (e.g. *RIB* III, 3009, London; *ILA Bordeaux* 54) or records of imperial building projects (e.g. *RIB* I, 330; Tomlin 2018: 4.15).

The expanded availability of metals was crucial to the embellishing of carved stone surfaces with inlaid bronze letters or for cutting or casting bronze texts. The 222 kg fragment of a speech of the emperor Claudius, cast on an inscription from Lyon, is especially suggestive of the scale of use of metal for monumental inscriptions (Kolb 2015). The *c.*1000 surviving diplomas documenting acquisition of Roman citizenship by auxiliary soldiers, a tiny fraction of those originally issued (perhaps 0.3–1 per cent), hint at the metal requirements for portable documents in bronze (Eck 2015: 131). The abundance of lead alloy curse tablets in south-west England was fed by availability of the metal as a local by-product of silver extraction and by the local production of pewter objects to exploit this material (*RIB II.*1, 68; Tomlin 2002). Enhanced exploitation of precious metals enabled their use as votive media in their own right (Jackson and Burleigh 2018) as well as to embellish bronze letters through gilding.

Equally crucial to writing was the expanded exploitation of timber. Wooden stylus tablets found in in northern Europe are mostly (where analysed) made of silver fir (*abies alba*). Examination of the Walbrook documents from London has indicated that such tablets were not distributed as blocks of 'blanks', an expensive form of imported stationery. Instead they were likely made from recycling staves from barrels bringing wine from south-eastern Gaul (Tamerl 2010: 36–40; Goodburn, in Tomlin 2016: 8–15). Since stylus tablets are documented from many sites, this has significant implications for the accessibility of the medium (see below). The availability of other writing materials, for example wax for stylus tablets or inks for leaf tablets, depended on scaled-up exploitation of other commodities, such as beeswax, pitch, gum Arabic, red lead and so on (Bagnall 2011: 10; Eckardt 2018: 27–8). While some writing instruments were based on cheap expedients, such as reeds for ink writing, making texts also often demanded more specialised tools (Willi 2021). The ubiquity of the iron and copper-alloy stylus, the writing tool *par excellence* for wax tablets, or of seal boxes – that is, copper-alloy capsules to protect (perhaps) document seals – in towns, garrisons and the countryside illustrates the dependence of writing on large-scale metalworking (Derks and Roymans 2002; Eckardt 2018; Mullen 2021). The use of animal bone for writing equipment, such as styli, pens, handles of sharpening-knives, rulers and so on, was enabled by its widespread exploitation as a raw material in northern Europe following Roman conquest (Deschler-Erb 1998; Willi 2021).

Uses of documents

Examination of some uses for writing illustrates how texts relate both directly to imperial institutions and to broader changes engendered by the existence of empire. The following paragraphs review three types of text, starting with monumental inscriptions, before examining *instrumentum domesticum* and writing tablets.

Monumental inscriptions on stone and bronze

Monumental inscriptions both publicly commemorated the actions of collectivities and individuals in lasting form and were sometimes themselves an integral part of those actions, for example making an honorific statue or a religious dedication (Meyer 2011; Cooley 2012: 220–8). Stone inscriptions are the best-preserved examples, created mainly in military garrisons (see below) and in cities (Revell, Chapter 5 this volume). Taking some examples from a civilian context, we first illustrate texts which related to urban communities as a whole, marking their collective action. The dedications for buildings and (as here) statues show a fundamental role for inscriptions for expressing political relationships at different levels, both within urban communities and between cities and emperors. In the first example, the *civitas* (i.e. the civic community) of the Silvanectes honoured the emperor Claudius in 48 CE with a bronze statue, placed in a prominent sanctuary in Senlis (Oise, France), the urban centre for the *civitas* (Figure 2.2). Into the bronze sheet which sheathed the statue's masonry plinth an inscription was incised, recording the dedication to the emperor (Rosso 2006: 258–60, no. 53). In finely cut text, the genealogy, offices and honours voted to Claudius are set out first, the immediately recognisable part of his name being in the largest letters. Smaller letters then identify the giver of the honour, that is, the city, in a collective and public action. Thirty years later, following a decision of its senate, the colony of Avenches (Vaud, Switzerland) similarly honoured a fellow citizen and magistrate, Caius Iulius Camillus, with a statue, the base of which recorded his civilian and military offices, the latter bringing him imperial recognition. A near identical inscription cut on a second face showed that a bequest by Camillus himself had generously paid for the statue, through the agency of his daughter Julia Festilla (Tomlin 2018: 9–10, 1.6). Whatever the specific actions which prompted the giving of these statues (probably imperial favours and local benefactions),

Figure 2.2 Inscription cut on bronze sheet for a 1.5 m high plinth, recording the gift of a statue to the emperor Claudius by the Silvanectes (Senlis), 48 CE. © Dépôt du Musée des Antiquités Nationales, Saint-Germain-en-Laye au musée d'Art et d'Archéologie de Senlis.

these dedications formed part of the unequal exchange of honours and gifts on which local and imperial hierarchies depended (Meyer 2011: 198–202).

Such texts, however, comprise only a small minority of monumental inscriptions, being massively outnumbered by votive texts (Derks, Chapter 9 this volume) and epitaphs, which will form our second example. In Italy of the late Republic and early empire funerary commemoration with inscribed monuments had extended beyond the aristocracy to other groups, above all formerly enslaved individuals, to whom economic success after manumission had both given resources and a posterity in the form of legally legitimate families and clients (Mouritsen 2005; Carroll 2006). The 'epitaph habit' in north-west Europe grew out of the movement northwards of individuals who reproduced this commemorative behaviour in a new setting. However, its successful proliferation was driven by local circumstances, especially by the social mobility offered either by the army or trade, the latter being closely linked to cities on trunk routes (Woolf 1998). The inscriptions of Roman Bordeaux offer a good example of this new commemorative habit in a city with a nodal place on ways by land and water from the Mediterranean to north-west Europe, and a population whose names and *origines* document their diverse origins. Tombstones comprise 80 per cent of the *c.*400 monumental inscriptions on stone, found during demolition of the late Roman town walls in which they had been re-used (*ILA Bordeaux*). In formulae, portraits and monumental media these markers drew on Roman commemorative norms, but developed local specificities, a common occurrence in provincial settings (Hope 2001). Thus, by the Garonne most memorials take the form of *cippi* (blocks) and stelae. In identifying the dead, the family name (*nomen*) is often abbreviated, following regional practice, and the voting tribe and filiation for citizens are usually omitted. Age at death is expressed in a regionally favoured formula, *defunctus annorum*... (*ILA Bordeaux* 53, 106–7). Occupation or geographical origin are occasionally supplied, but economic success is more conspicuously signalled in funerary portraits. In these the deceased hold attributes indicating either the means of wealth creation, such as tools including writing tablets, or tokens of the hospitality that their wealth enabled, such as drinking vessels. These memorials would have clustered along the approach roads to Bordeaux, directed at passers-by nearing or leaving the city, asserting successful membership of the community in a place where individual and group memory coalesced (Esmonde Cleary 2013).

Instrumentum domesticum

Texts on portable objects created during their manufacture, circulation or use are often referred to under the umbrella term of *instrumentum domesticum*. This use of writing is partly a function of economic complexity, where the production and distribution of objects involved many agents including workers, managers, owners, traders and shippers, sometimes across large geographical spaces. Much of this documentation is better described as specialised numeracy, that is, employing complex alphanumerical notation inscribed onto commodities and objects (Woolf 2015).

Figure 2.3 A lead ingot or 'pig' (52 cm long) from Westbury (UK), carrying an inscription cast in relief, 164–9 CE. 'The property of the two August emperors Antoninus and Verus, conquerors in Armenia'. © Portable Antiquities Scheme, CC BY-4.0, https://finds.org.uk/database/artefacts/record/id/792503.

Among the most striking examples of texts created during production and movement of key commodities for the Roman state in northern Europe are the prominent inscriptions carried on metal ingots, especially of lead, often cast as a by-product of silver winning (Hirt 2010). Examples have been found both close to production centres in the north-west provinces and en route to the Mediterranean, for example the *plumbum Germanicum* found in the Rena Maiore shipwreck off the Sardinian coast (Rothenhöfer et al. 2017). Drawing on conventions established in the Republican period, many carry names cast in the mould when the ingot was made, often in quasi-monumental form, to document ownership (Figure 2.3). Imperial names may indicate payment to the emperor for the concession to mine, others are those of private individuals, *societates* (partnerships) and communities. Metal dies were later used to cold-stamp further names onto ingots, probably those of carriers, while numbers scratched on ingots may record weight checks (*RIB* II.1, 38; Hirt 2010: 101–3, 279–84). Emphasising their utility captures only part of the likely impact of these texts, which were in practice 'speaking objects'. The square capitals and the imperial titulature shared with monumental inscriptions served as a reminder of the authority behind the metal dealing to all those through whose hands the ingot passed.

Inscriptions on metal objects also illustrate the range of *instrumentum* texts created outside the remit of state activity. Like potters, individual metalworkers in north-west Europe sometimes cast their name plus the verb *fecit* ('she/he made') into the things they made, occasionally also naming the place of making (Figure 2.4). It is usually assumed that those named have a supervisory role (manager, owners, stewards, etc.) but the specific purpose of these maker texts is not clear (Gostenĉnik 2002). In some cases, like the scabbards carrying the name

Figure 2.4 Openwork lettering decorating dagger scabbard made in Baden, Switzerland, 178 mm, found at *Epomandurum*/Mandeure (FR), later second century CE. 'At *Aquae Helveticae* Gemellianus made (this)' (Berger 2002: 47, no. 191). Reproduced by permission of the Collection Musées de Montbéliard. Photo: Pierre Guenat.

of the metalworker Gemellianus (Berger 2002), the openwork lettering's elegance and size make it the most visible element of the object. This may indicate a promotional function derived from an artisan's reputation or a talismanic character for such a text. Other texts unequivocally address users, for example on ornaments, dress items and vessels. Made to complement the giving of the object, often enhanced with metal or enamel inlay, these wish a recipient good fortune or health or imply that they are the subject of emotional or erotic attachment (Cooley 2012: 198). By its 'voice' the object extends the agency of the giver into settings in which they were no longer present. Phrases such as *utere felix* ('use this in happiness'), the most common all-purpose motto, were so familiar that they could be reduced to initials.

Working records created during production are occasionally documented on lead (Aliquot and Feugère 2021) but are better attested in non-metal media. Sometimes this likely represents expedient use when normal media of record (e.g. writing tablets, papyrus) were not available, for example building material output itemised on brick or tile (Charlier 2004) or stock inventory at Pompeii scratched in plaster (Mouritsen 2015). The *c.*200 ostraca documented at the workshops for terra sigillata (a bright red ceramic fineware) at La Graufesenque (Aveyron), represent the most sophisticated surviving examples of such documentation. In language drawing on Latin, Gallic and Greek, they list the firing of large batches of table vessels, in entries specifying potters' names, vessel type, size (occasionally colour) and number (Mullen 2013a). In addition to their tally function, the phrasing of the text and the addition of auspicious symbols were intended to mitigate the risks of the firing process and thus ensure successful making of 'good sigillata' (Van Oyen 2016).

Writing tablets

The ephemeral documentation produced in the Roman west by institutions such as garrisons, the offices of governors and procurators, the *tabularia* (record offices) of cities, aristocratic households as well as commercial enterprises is almost entirely lost (Meyer 2004: 176; Woolf 2009: 60–4). The scale and shape of this lost documentation can be estimated, up to a point. For example, of *c*.225 million individual pay records for Roman soldiers which may have been created, only a handful are currently known (Speidel 2018: 183). Aided by documents from the Egyptian desert quarries, Hirt (2010: 253–8) sketches the likely components of archives of procurators overseeing mining operations as an example of government documentation. However, in the north-west provinces we come closest to these administrative texts themselves in the wooden documents (ink and stylus tablets), now attested by excavation in more than 40 military and urban sites, along with occasional papyri and ostraca (Spickermann 1994; Thüry 1996; Hartmann 2015).

The ink tablets now read from Vindolanda (Northumberland, UK) allow the fullest characterisation of documentation produced in a state context in the north-west provinces (Bowman 2003; 2006). They comprise several hundred ink-written texts on postcard-sized pieces of wood, dated to *c*.90–120 CE, found during excavation of an auxiliary fort created before the building of Hadrian's Wall garrisoned in turn by two main units recruited from northern Gaul. The tablets comprise letters, lists of varying purposes and military documents, for example requests for leave. The presence of many tablets associated with the commanders' households illustrates the characteristic overlap between administering personal and institutional business for Roman elites (Woolf 2000: 891–5). Scribes are responsible for some texts, in particular those associated with the commanding officer and his family, but writers and readers, mainly but not exclusively male, include household members, enslaved individuals, soldiers of all ranks as well as families and traders, with many individual 'hands' attested (e.g. *Tab. Vindol.* II. 291). The soldiers were not native Latin speakers but there is limited evidence for interference from their first languages (Adams 2003). The tablets show sophistication in language use and the application of documentary conventions, for example in laying out a letter on a page. They document in detail the condition and availability of men and materials, the latter even when redistributed in minute quantities (Pearce 2002).

Emerging evidence also reveals similar uses of writing in a non-military milieu. Britain again provides the main instance where texts have been read, specifically in the later first century CE group from the Bloomberg excavation and neighbouring sites in central London. Among the 80 tablets so far (sometimes partly) read are letters, financial and legal documents, including records of judgements and loan notes with witness lists associated with a diverse community, comprising traders, soldiers, citizens and non-citizens, the enslaved and those formerly so, many originating in the Roman north-west provinces (Tomlin 2016; Cooley in press). Acting in their own capacity and as agents for others, these (exclusively) male correspondents used letters to maintain social and business networks and Roman legal instruments to defend their economic interests in a way familiar from documents from elsewhere in the Roman world (Meyer 2004). Some uncertainties concerning the use of such documents remain, for example the relative importance of the act of creating them to establishing mutual obligations versus the ability later to consult them to support legal process (Meyer 2004: 295–6). A label on the edge of a stylus tablet from first century *Augustobona Tricassium* (Troyes, north-eastern France) ('the *vadimonium* of Nerta') illustrates the archiving that enabled some documents at least to be retrieved for subsequent referral. In this case, unusually for the Roman north-west, the find illustrates such a practice by or on behalf of the interests of Nerta, a non-citizen woman (Frei-Stolba et al. 2016).

Discontinuities and continuities in writing

Sketching the uses of writing in this way, emphasising their proliferation and reach, risks giving the impression of writing as a universal phenomenon. There were, however, significant limitations to writing and reading in the Roman west (Harris 1989; see above). Among 'writers' lies a huge spectrum of engagement with writing, from the sophisticated command of language and literary knowledge shown in some Vindolanda writing tablets (*Tab. Vindol.* III. 660; *Tab. Vindol.* IV. 853–856) or in the graffiti scratched into villa plaster (Fuchs and Dubois 1997), to the *fecit* inscriptions of smiths and potters (see above) and the myriad owners' names incised on ceramic vessels (Evans 1987). Within this spectrum clusters can be seen of specialised usages such as 'military literacies' or 'commercial literacies' and numeracies (Woolf 2002; 2015), and varying 'epigraphic micro-habits' (Meyer 2011: 208–18).

However, arguments for a continuous spectrum of writing practices, not strongly separated into distinct literacies, have been set out by Woolf (2000; 2009), emphasising the households of the wealthy as the key location for learning to write and applying the skills in different contexts. This continuous character can be demonstrated in various ways. First, as Woolf noted, different types of writing cluster in general in the same periods. For example, both monumental texts and inscriptions on portable objects proliferate from the late first century BCE and, with occasional exceptions such as curse tablets (Woolf 2022), become much rarer after the mid-third century CE, even if details of the timescale are debated (Fulford 1994; Meyer 2011; Beltrán Lloris 2015b). Few of the more than 60 writing tablet assemblages identified by Hartmann (2015) also date later than the third century CE. Notwithstanding the impact of preservation factors, different kinds of writing also occur in greatest numbers in the same spaces – especially towns, garrisons and major sanctuaries – as witnessed, for example, when the distribution of monumental inscriptions is compared with findspots of graffiti on brick and tile in Gaul (Woolf 1998: 82–8; Charlier 2004: 74–5) or of names scratched on ceramics in Britain (Evans 1987; Mattingly 2008).

Another instance of continuity is the predominance in the west of a single written language, Latin, albeit with varying degree of expertise. Writing in other languages was not entirely excluded, but seems to have been directed into specialised purposes, for example 'Roman Greek' as a use of Greek specifically connected to religion as well as to medicine and luxury arts in the western provinces (Mullen 2013b). Composing written Celtic texts after the conquest might express rejection of Rome (Woolf 2000: 896–7). However, the nature of many surviving documents, such as curse tablets, calendars and dedications, heavily influenced by Roman forms, suggests that writing in Celtic occupies a similar ritual niche (Mullen 2016: 579–83). Rather than by texts in other languages, the diversity of provincial languages may be better illustrated by the bilingual characteristics that Latin inscriptions frequently display (Clackson 2012; 2015).

Other characteristics shared across different types of inscriptions include formulae and abbreviations, with common ways of marking time, space and quantity, and above all the same alphabet (Woolf 2009: 56–8). This is used across epigraphic categories in two principal scripts, cursive and monumental capitals, the latter probably learnt first by would-be writers (Bodel 2015: 271). The similarities visible in cursive letter forms from Britain and Egypt vividly illustrate the geographical continuity in writing across the imperial space (Mullen and Bowman 2021). The

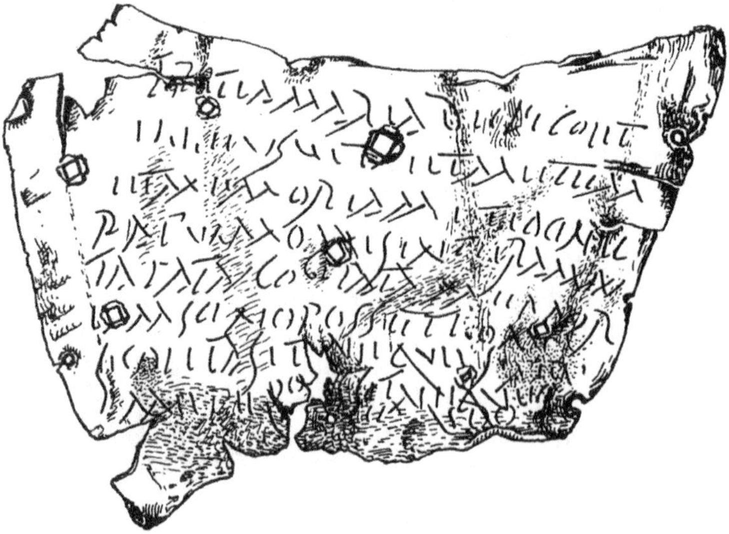

Figure 2.5 Drawing of a lead curse tablet in cursive script, cursing the woman Tertia Maria, with holes from deliberate piercing by nails, first to third century CE (178 × 121 mm, Walbrook, London, *RIB* 7). Reproduced by permission of the Administrators of the Haverfield Bequest.

ability for makers of inscriptions, either as individuals or collaborators, to move between different media and scripts is illustrated by the stages of making a monumental inscription – that is, the drafting, setting out and final cutting of the text (Cooley 2012: 293–8; Edmondson 2015b: 117–26). The occasional occurrence of cursive letters in monumental texts gives away the usually 'silent' movement from a cursive draft to a capital inscription (e.g. a cursive 'b' on a Lincoln tombstone, *RIB* I, 256). Likewise the occasional presence of more fluid letter forms cut in stone, for example the curling serifs on the epitaph for Bodicacia, shows the usual unnoticed translation of a brush-painted form into a chiselled text (unless this is a deliberate stylistic choice) (Figure 2.1) (Tomlin 2015: 384–6, no. 3).

Connections across document categories also reveal the application of skills for writing one type of document in composing others. Curse texts, a form commonly exploited by non-elites, exemplify this permeability. Inherited from a Greek tradition dating back to the sixth century BCE, these texts place the fate of a victim in the hands of a deity asked to punish them by causing their normal mental and physical function to cease (i.e.

the curse victims are 'fixed'). Some others are better described as 'prayers for justice', especially the many British examples which seek retribution against thieves, above all in the assemblages from temples at Bath and Uley, Gloucestershire. Typically incised on lead, some texts are written in monumental capitals, but most are in cursive script, occasionally written retrograde. Their texts draw on different genres, prayers, letters and petitions to patrons and judges, legal formulae and magical invocations, sometimes adding lexical invention (Tomlin 1988; Blänsdorf 2007; Sánchez Natalias 2022) (Figure 2.5). Graffiti, too, draw on different textual genres and their spatial locations do not observe a clear public and private distinction, again illustrating the permeability of categories (Baird and Taylor 2011b). This overlapping quality explains the difficulty of using binary categories to classify writing, for example as monumental, formal and public or informal and private, and the preference expressed by some for defining a spectrum of uses instead (e.g. Bagnall 2011: 3–4; Cooley 2012: 220).

A key linking element across texts is also the power that writing enables, whether through socio-economic benefits, in privileged intercession with the gods, or in the cultural capital that it may demonstrate on the part of the exponent (Bowman and Woolf 1994b). This power is partly that of Roman elites to dominate. For example, whether or not they could read or write, the lives of soldiers at Vindolanda and of their families and associated traders were scrutinised and governed through writing (Bowman 2006). But the observation that use of documents as a control mechanism prompts parallel responses among those it governs is nicely illustrated by examples from Rome's northern provinces (Hopkins 1991). At Vindolanda, ordinary soldiers used letters to negotiate their place within the army and sustain their own economic and social networks (Bowman 2003: 73–6). Likewise, the contemporary Walbrook tablets show traders protecting their own interests by using letters and legal documents whose forms likely originate in the practices of Roman administrators and soldiers with whom they were in close contact (Tomlin 2016: 56). Combining conventions of Latin greeting with Celtic-language terms of affection and esteem, the salutations incised on a distinctive group of spindle whorls from mid-imperial Autun consolidated relationships of solidarity and friendship amongst the city's women spinners (Mullen 2022).

In the absence of many assemblages of documents so far read, other than those from Vindolanda and London, the frequency of funerary portraits showing writing implements, typically a block of writing tablets (*pugillarium*) or papyrus scroll (*volumen*), indicates how widely professional and social advancement and associated empowerment depended on mastery of writing (Eckardt 2018: 149–53). Representations of writing implements are sometimes carved on the tombs of soldiers who have won promotions or privileges, for example on the side of the funerary altar for Quintus Aemilius Rufus at Salona (Eckardt 2018: 141, fig. 8.1). For civilians the symbolism of writing equipment is more fluid. On the stele his parents raised for Thallasius from Metz (France), the young man's scroll, tablets and stylus evoke either his particular erudition acquired from an expensive education or the general economic success which enabled the family's social mobility (*CAG 57.2*: 185). On the memorial commemorating a *faber* (smith) from Bordeaux the writing tablets in his left hand are more likely to allude to the economic transactions in which he was engaged and the wealth which these generated (*ILA Bordeaux* 113). The placing of writing equipment among objects buried with the dead also temporarily displayed the deceased's engagement with writing; unlike monuments, which depict writing equipment with males alone, this practice also reveals female writers (Cresci Marrone and Solinas 2013: 219–20; Eckardt 2018: 158–65).

Power in the imperial name

It is important, however, not to lose sight of perhaps the most obvious connections between writing and power – the omnipresence of the emperor's name as the 'audience and actor' in monumental texts, especially in the public spaces of cities and garrisons (Meyer 2011: 202–5). Even where the emperor was not directly a party to a matter of epigraphic record, his name was inescapable in the processes that generated such records. It might appear, for example, in the exercise of delegated authority by a local agent, in the formulae used to date an action, or as a backdrop to business in the statues and honorific inscriptions of public spaces, like those from Senlis and Avenches. This ubiquity embedded the emperor's position as a source of authority and guarantor of stability (Ando 2000). Sketching occurrences of the term *augustus*, the epithet applied to the first emperor in 27 BCE and inherited by his successors, illustrates this ubiquity in more concrete terms. As well as in those inscriptions directly naming the emperor or imperial property, it occurs in the titles of officials (*legatus Augusti, procurator Augusti*), imperial freed slaves (*libertus Augusti*), in epithets for gods (*Mars Augustus*, etc.), in names for military units (*legio II Augusta, ala Augusta*) or of cities (*colonia Augusta Treverorum* – Trier; *Augustodunum* – Autun), dates (*kalendas augustas*) and so on. Approximately 1700 of the more than 19,000 inscriptions from Britain in the *EDCS* (10 August 2022) contain this imperial epithet and name. Allowing for other related name elements (*Imperator*, *Caesar*, etc.) sees the imperial presence proliferate further, not to mention the amplifying effect of imperial names taken as family names and inscribed on their memorials by innumerable provincials (Iulii, Claudii, Flavii, Aelii, Aurelii, etc.).

The formulation of an emperor's name encapsulated his claims for legitimacy (Hurlet 2015). Beyond Rome, these names were repeatedly given monumental format, especially on the statue bases (see above), building inscriptions and milestones created by myriad local communities, and then adapted in response to news of emperors' achievements (Ando 2000). Among the most visually prominent examples of the emperor's name were those inscriptions commemorating construction or repair of frontier garrison buildings. Since they are closely datable, they have been crucial to dating imperial actions on frontiers and thus for writing military and political narratives (e.g. Tomlin 2018: 177–82). Yet their significance as local translations of imperial presence and expressions of authority to a politically crucial audience is little discussed, perhaps because the inscriptions are less verbose than similar texts created in civilian communities, lacking the acclamations otherwise analysed as evidence for imperial propaganda (e.g. Noreña 2011; Horster 2015).

This translation of authority in a military setting can be illustrated with reference to inscriptions associated with the emperor Septimius Severus (193–211 CE) and his successors. These have received particular attention as legitimising media because of their elaboration and quantity (Saastamoinen 2010: 80–4; Ando 2012: 28–40; Sears 2013). Acclaimed as emperor in 193 CE, Severus consolidated his position by eliminating rival claimants and co-opting his sons as fellow rulers over the next decade (Birley 1999). On the frontiers his authority was translated into the form of reconstruction work put into practice through trusted allies. In northern Britain and the Rhine delta, for example, inscriptions celebrate such work undertaken during his reign under the auspices of Venidius Quietus and Alfenius Senecio, governors respectively in lower Germany (c.205–7 CE) and Britain (207–9 CE) (Birley 1999: 170–2; 2005: 188–92; Haalebos 2001). Whatever the practical purpose of building (enhancing defences, supporting campaigning), the inscriptions served as visible exercises of authority and expressions of loyalty by units of potentially uncertain allegiance.

Two examples, one from Roomburg near Leiden (Netherlands), the other from Risingham, north of Hadrian's Wall, illustrate the characteristics of such inscriptions. Their most striking feature is scale:

Figure 2.6 Severan building inscription (205 CE?), probably from Roomburg (NL) (2.21 × 0.56 m, *CIL* XIII.8825). Reproduced by permission of the National Museum of Antiquities, Leiden.

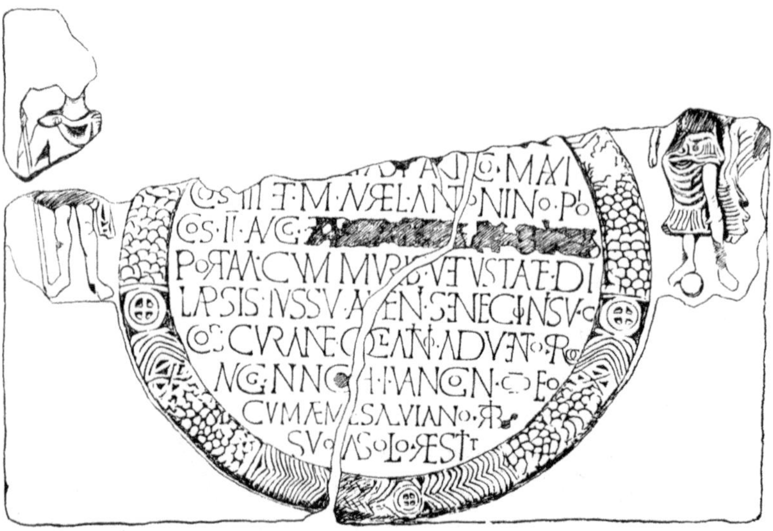

Figure 2.7 Drawing of Severan building inscription, Risingham (UK), 207–9 CE (1.8 × 1.24 m, *RIB* 1234). Reproduced by permission of the Administrators of the Haverfield Bequest.

the Roomburg inscription (Figure 2.6) was close to three metres long in its original form, the Risingham inscription (Figure 2.7) nearly two metres, both being likely set up over fort gates. The texts open with names, including the two senior emperors, Septimius Severus and his older son (Marcus Aurelius Antoninus, whom he co-opted as emperor in 198), both distinguished by the senior imperial title 'Augustus', and of Publius Septimius Geta, the younger son co-opted as a junior emperor ('Caesar') in the same year. There follow the names of the garrison unit and of the emperors' local proxies who supervised the soldiers' building work, the provincial governor at Roomburg and, in order of seniority, the governor, procurator and garrison commander at Risingham.

Emperors' names dominate both texts, comprising the distinctive imperial nomenclature, familial names and other titles. The former is inherited from Augustus, *imperator* as the *praenomen* derived from victory acclamations for successful generals, *Caesar* – the *cognomen* of Julius Caesar which became an imperial family (gentilicial) name – and *Augustus*, a title voted to the first emperor in 27 BCE (Hurlet 2015). The Severan family had no imperial ancestors, but their names embody connections they claimed to their predecessors, including Pertinax, assassinated in 193 CE whom Severus avenged and deified, and Marcus Aurelius, whose name Severus' older son Caracalla took on becoming Augustus in 198 CE (Birley 1999: 130). These connections to forebears instantiated the piety attributed to both Augusti (*pius*). To these names the Risingham text adds the titles Septimius won through victories in 195 and 198 CE, and the consulships held by him and Caracalla. Names thus articulated the bases for the emperors' legitimacy, their distinctive imperial quality, ancestry and piety, their military pre-eminence and their holding of offices inherited from the Roman Republic. Both texts present the building work as the outcome of a negotiated exchange of labour, honour and loyalty between emperors, their delegates and garrisons.

Comparison of these two inscriptions also illustrates the differences which characterised different provincial usage. On the lower Rhine, for example, the emperors are named in the nominative as agents of action, in Britain in the dative – that is, as beneficiaries of work done under their auspices. Contemporary inscriptions from lower Germany record other offices awarded to the emperor by the Senate which are not mentioned here, for example chief priest (*pontifex maximus*) or holder of tribunician power (Haalebos 2001). These varying expressions show the inscriptions as locally derived acknowledgements of imperial authority, creating from the bottom up 'significant resources of shared historical memory and consciousness' (Ando 2012: 40). The visual characteristics of the inscriptions also emphasise this locally generated feel, the fussy framing and recurrent ligaturing of the Risingham text, for example, being typical of northern Britain in the later second and third century CE.

It is easiest perhaps to imagine the inscriptions as attracting their readers' direct attention on the day of their erection, as a condensed counterpart to speeches and acclamations. Likely set high above the gates, with paint peeling and stone weathering, one might wonder how viewers later extracted meaning from them without close attention. Yet the abbreviated names and titles, accessible in a passing glance, perhaps sufficed to identify the emperors concerned, with their claims to rule bolstered by the enduring physicality of the structures to which the texts were fixed. After their erection both inscriptions were modified – the honorific title awarded the Roomburg unit (*Antoniniana*) being squeezed between the second and third line, and the names of Geta chiselled off, following his murder by his older brother in 211 CE. Such modifications, the latter universally practised on inscriptions of this period, suggest the continued potency of inscriptions for use by local actors to align themselves with imperial authority.

Conclusion

Pronouncements on Roman writing risk being overtaken by new data or better understanding of existing evidence. Nearly two decades ago, Meyer (2004: 183) noted 'the 500 heavy wooden *tabulae* surviving from the Roman provinces'; these are now known in equivalent numbers from a single city (Tomlin 2016), while digital imaging promises new readings of documents already known (e.g. Bowman et al. 2009). From new finds of *instrumentum domesticum* will come improved understanding of the role of texts in distribution in relation to commercial literacy (e.g. Hoët-van-Cauwenberghe and Jacques 2010). Future discoveries of media which are known to have existed but are not yet archaeologically attested, for example whitened boards (*alba*), may well extend knowledge of what was written (Kruschwitz 2016). For much writing, we currently remain dependent on extrapolating from single examples to wider practice, for example the Vindolanda tablets for writing in ink, Châteauneuf for votive texts on temple walls, or la Graufesenque for kiln tally lists. The significance of documents not in Latin has only been touched on in discussion above, and new finds continue to modify the picture of other languages written in the imperial period (e.g. Pfahl 2017). The potential for writers' tools to illuminate engagement with texts is only beginning to be realised, for example in Roman administration (Mullen 2021; Olesti 2021) or as gendered practice (Eckardt 2018). New work continues not only to expand the repertoire of surviving artefacts related to writing (e.g. Greep and Rijkelijkhuizen 2019) but also critically to re-assess their function (e.g. Andrews 2012). And even for arguably the best attested survivals of Roman writing, monumental inscriptions, it remains difficult to pin down their original quantities, their relationship to their setting and readers' interactions with them.

Nonetheless writing may be confidently claimed as an imperial phenomenon in multiple ways, at its 'high watermark' in the provinces examined in this chapter. The functioning of Roman power, including the imposition of top-down control and the exploitation of key resources (metals, foodstuffs and humans) and the bottom-up acknowledgement of ultimate authority by governors, garrisons and urban elites, took place through texts of different kinds, the imperial name echoing through them. Yet while encounters with the institutions of government may have contributed to familiarity with writing, the latter's applications nonetheless extended far beyond the relationship of ruler and ruled. Writing was central to the globalised character claimed (by some) for the Roman world, being enabled by and itself enabling the movement of objects, information, money and people. It brought in its train shared standards, for example in measurement of time, space, quantity and so on, which indirectly also contributed to a common imperial culture. The flexibility of alphabetic writing may have lent its own momentum to this dissemination (Woolf 2002). Writing also gave a means to express and to establish socio-economic hierarchies, for example in the economic advantages it gave to its specialised exponents, but also in the opportunities it gave for performative differentiation, especially where orally expressed literary and linguistic sophistication went hand in hand with visible delegation of writing itself to amanuenses. In its likely association with key moments in the lives of communities and individuals, as a visual enhancement of public spaces of objects given as gifts, writing became a widely shared aspect of Roman 'cultural style' (cf. Woolf 2000). The similarities in detail which extend beyond the study area to the wider imperial space provide compelling testimony for this, exemplified in the identity of handwriting, epistolary layout and language in the Vindolanda letters and in contemporary ostraca from Egypt's eastern desert (Bowman 2006).

Arguing for a widespread sensitivity to the power of writing itself, as well as to its content is not the same as arguing for mass literacy; writers whose competence extended beyond writing their own name likely remained uncommon (Harris 1989; 2013). Nonetheless if north-west Europe, with its (near-)absence of pre-Roman literacy, provides a baseline for Roman writing, archaeological evidence continues to prompt that baseline to be nudged higher. Much writing was directed to perpetuating an imperial framework, but its adoption and applications were more open-ended. Above all the ongoing discoveries of writing tablets continue to expand the range of those who made documents, those whose lives were framed by them, and the uses to which documents were put. For Bodicacia's life in *Corinium* only her epitaph survives, but the engagement of ordinary imperial subjects with documents could extend beyond such final lapidary statements. The traces of archival practice from first century Troyes associated with Nerta (see above) suggest that, like her famous near-contemporary Babatha, she too might have deployed her bundle of documents to defend her local interests in relation to family, friends and neighbours (Frei-Stolba et al. 2016).

Acknowledgements

I acknowledge with gratitude the comments on the chapter by conference participants, by Matthew Magee and Claire Millington, and by the editors, especially those of Jeremy Tanner, which have considerably helped in shaping the final written version. Alison Cooley and Alex Mullen kindly made publications available in advance of publication.

Abbreviations

CAG 57.2: Flotté, Pascal. 2005. *Carte archéologique de la Gaule 57.2. Metz*. Paris: Académie des Inscriptions et Belles-Lettres, Maison des Sciences de l'Homme.

CIL XIII: Hirschfeld, Otto and Karl F.W. Zangemeister. 1899–. *Corpus Inscriptionum Latinarum XIII Inscriptiones trium Galliarum et Germaniarum Latinae*. Berlin: G. Reimer.

EDCS: Epigraphik-Datenbank Clauss/Slaby, http://db.edcs.eu/epigr/epi_ergebnis.php

ILA Bordeaux: Maurin, Louis and Milagros Navarro Caballero. 2010. *Inscriptions latines d'Aquitaine. Bordeaux*. Paris: de Boccard.

RIB I: Collingwood, Robin G. and Richard P. Wright. 1995. *The Roman Inscriptions of Britain, vol. I: Inscriptions on stone* (rev. ed.). Stroud: Sutton.

RIB II: Frere, Sheppard S. and Roger S.O. Tomlin. 1990. *The Roman Inscriptions of Britain, vol. II: Instrumentum Domesticum (personal belongings and the like) (fascicules 1–8)*. Gloucester: Sutton.

RIB III: Tomlin, Roger S.O. et al. 2009. *The Roman Inscriptions of Britain, vol. III*. Oxford: Oxbow.

Tab. Vindol. II: Bowman, Alan K. and J. David Thomas. 1994. *The Vindolanda Writing Tablets II*. London: BMP.

Tab. Vindol. III: Bowman, Alan K. and J. David Thomas with John Pearce. 2003. *The Vindolanda Writing Tablets III*. London: BMP.

Tab. Vindol. IV: Bowman, Alan K., J. David Thomas and Roger S.O. Tomlin 2010. 'The Vindolanda writing tablets (*Tabulae Vindolandenses IV*), part 1', *Britannia* 41: 187–224 and Bowman, Alan K., J. David Thomas and Roger S.O. Tomlin. 2011. 'The Vindolanda writing tablets (*Tabulae Vindolandenses IV*), part 2', *Britannia* 42: 113–44.

The inscriptions from Roman Britain are all available from Roman Inscriptions of Britain online: https://romaninscriptionsofbritain.org/.

References

Adams, James N. 2003. *Bilingualism and the Latin Language*. Cambridge: Cambridge University Press.

Adams, James N. 2007. *The Regional Diversification of Latin 200 BC–AD 600*. Cambridge: Cambridge University Press.

Aliquot, Julien and Michel Feugère. 2021. 'Un plomb inscrit de Saint-Couat-d'Aude (Aude): des pérégrins sur le territoire de Narbonne', *Gallia* 78: 219–26.

Ando, Clifford. 2000. *Imperial Ideology and Provincial Loyalty in the Roman Empire*. Berkeley: University of California.

Ando, Clifford. 2012. *Imperial Rome AD 193 to 284: The critical century*. Edinburgh: Edinburgh University Press.

Andrews, Colin. J. 2012. *Roman Seal-Boxes in Britain*. Oxford: Archaeopress.

Bagnall, Roger. 2011. *Everyday Writing in the Graeco-Roman East*. Berkeley: University of California.

Baird, Jennifer and Claire Taylor (eds). 2011a. *Ancient Graffiti in Context*. London: Routledge.

Baird, Jennifer and Claire Taylor. 2011b. 'Ancient graffiti in context: introduction'. In *Ancient Graffiti in Context*, edited by Jennifer Baird and Claire Taylor, 1–19. London: Routledge.

Baratta, Giulia. 2008. '*Pelles scriptae*: Inschriften auf Leder und Lederwaren'. In *Instrumenta inscripta latina, 2, Akten des 2. internationalen Kolloquiums, Klagenfurt, 5.–8. Mai 2005*, edited by Manfred Hainzmann and Reinhold Wedenig, 1–23. Klagenfurt: Geschichtsverein für Kärnten.

Barbet, Alix and Michel Fuchs. 2008. *Les murs murmurent: graffitis gallo-romains: catalogue de l'exposition créée au Musée romain de Lausanne-Vidy, 2008*. Gollion: Infolio.

Beltrán Lloris, Francisco. 2015a. 'Latin epigraphy: the main types of inscriptions'. In *The Oxford Handbook of Roman Epigraphy*, edited by Crister Bruun and Jonathan Edmondson, 89–110. Oxford: Oxford University Press.

Beltrán Lloris, Francisco. 2015b. '"The "epigraphic habit" in the Roman world'. In *The Oxford Handbook of Roman Epigraphy*, edited by Crister Bruun and Jonathan Edmondson, 131–48. Oxford: Oxford University Press.

Benefiel, Rebecca and Peter Keegan (eds). 2016. *Inscriptions in the Private Sphere in the Greco-Roman World*. Leiden: Brill.

Berger, Ludwig. 2002. *Durchbrochene Messerfutteral-Beschläge (Thekenbeschläge) aus Augusta Raurica. Ein Beitrag zur provinzialrömischen Ornamentik*. Augst: Museum Augusta Raurica.

Binet, Eric and Christine Hoët-Van Cauwenberghe. 2010. '*Graffiti* sur éléments architecturaux à *Samarobriva* (Amiens)', *Revue du Nord* 388: 203–24.

Birley, Anthony. 1999. *Septimius Severus. The African Emperor*. London: Routledge.

Birley, Anthony. 2005. *The Fasti of Roman Britain*. Oxford: Oxford University Press.

Blänsdorf, *Jürgen*. 2007. '"Würmer und Krebs sollen ihn befallen": Eine neue Fluchtafel aus Groß Gerau', *Zeitschrift für Papyrologie und Epigrafik* 161: 61–5.

Bodel, John (ed.). 2001. *Epigraphic Evidence: Ancient history from inscriptions*. London: Routledge.

Bodel, John. 2015. 'Inscriptions and literacy'. In *The Oxford Handbook of Roman Epigraphy*, edited by Crister Bruun and Jonathan Edmondson, 745–63. Oxford: Oxford University Press.

Bowman, Alan K. 2003. *Life and Letters on the Roman Frontier* (3rd edn). London: British Museum.

Bowman, Alan K. 2006. 'Outposts of empire: Vindolanda, Egypt and the empire of Rome', *Journal of Roman Archaeology* 19: 75–93.

Bowman, Alan K. and Andrew Wilson. 2009. 'Quantifying the Roman economy: integration, growth, decline?'. In *Quantifying the Roman Economy. Methods and Problems*, edited by Alan K. Bowman and Andrew Wilson, 3–84. Oxford: Oxford University Press.

Bowman, Alan K. and Greg Woolf (eds). 1994a. *Literacy and Power in the Ancient World*. Cambridge: Cambridge University Press.

Bowman, Alan K. and Greg Woolf. 1994b. 'Literacy and power in the ancient world'. In *Literacy and Power in the Ancient World*, edited by Alan K. Bowman and Greg Woolf, 1–16. Cambridge: Cambridge University Press.

Bowman, Alan K., Roger S.O. Tomlin and Klaus A. Worp. 2009. '*Emptio Bovis Frisica*: the 'Frisian ox sale' reconsidered', *Journal of Roman Studies* 99: 156–70.

Bruun, Crister. 2015. 'The major corpora and epigraphic publications'. In *The Oxford Handbook of Roman Epigraphy*, edited by Crister Bruun and Jonathan Edmondson, 66–77. Oxford: Oxford University Press.

Buonocuore, Marco. 2015. 'Epigraphic research from its inception: the contribution of manuscripts'. In *The Oxford Handbook of Roman Epigraphy*, edited by Crister Bruun and Jonathan Edmondson, 21–40. Oxford: Oxford University Press.

Carroll, Maureen. 2006 *Spirits of the Dead: Roman funerary commemoration in western Europe*. Oxford: Oxford University Press.

Charlier, Fabrice. 2004. 'La pratique de l'écriture dans les tuileries gallo-romaines', *Gallia* 61: 67–102.

Clackson, James (ed.). 2012. *Companion to the Latin language*. Oxford: Blackwell.

Clackson, James. 2015. *Language and Society in the Greek and Roman Worlds*. Cambridge: Cambridge University.

Cooley, Alison E. (ed.) 2000. *The Afterlife of Inscriptions: Reusing, rediscovering, reinventing & revitalizing ancient inscriptions*. London: Institute of Classical Studies.

Cooley, Alison E. (ed.). 2002. *Becoming Roman, Writing Latin?* Portsmouth, RI: Journal of Roman Archaeology.

Cooley, Alison E. 2012. *Cambridge Manual of Latin Epigraphy*. Cambridge: Cambridge University Press.

Cooley, Alison E. 2018 'New Approaches to the Epigraphy of the Roman World', *Journal of Epigraphic Studies* 1: 27–46
Cooley, Alison E. (in press) 'The role of the non-elite in spreading Latin in Roman Britain'. In *Social Factors in Latinization*, edited by Alex Mullen. Oxford: Oxford University Press.
Cooley, Alison E. and Graham J. Oliver. 2006. 'Inscriptions'. in *The Edinburgh Companion to Ancient Greece and Rome*, edited by Edward H. Bispham, Thomas Harrison and Brian Sparkes, 262–74. Edinburgh: Edinburgh University Press.
Cooley, Alison E. and R. Benet Salway. 2012. 'Roman inscriptions 2006–2010', *Journal of Roman Studies* 102: 172–286.
Coombe, Penny, Martin Henig, Kevin Hayward and Francis Grew. 2016. *Roman Sculpture from London and the South-East*. Oxford: British Academy.
Cresci Marrone, Giovanella and Patrizia Solinas. 2013. *Microstorie di romanizzazione. Le iscrizioni del sepolcreto rurale di Cerrione*. Venice: Edizioni Ca' Foscari.
Derks, A.(Ton) M.J. and Nico Roymans. 2002. 'Seal boxes and the spread of Latin literacy in the Rhine delta'. In *Becoming Roman, Writing Latin?*, edited by Alison E. Cooley, 87–134. Portsmouth, RI: Journal of Roman Archaeology.
Deschler-Erb, Sabine. 1998. *Römische Beinartefakte aus Augusta Raurica*. Augst: Römermuseum.
Eck, Werner. 2015. 'Documents on bronze: a phenomenon of the Roman west'. In *Ancient Documents and their Contexts. First North American Congress of Greek and Latin Epigraphy (2011)*, edited by John Bodel and Nora Dimitrova, 127–51. Leiden / Boston: Brill.
Eckardt, Hella. 2018. *Writing and Power in the Roman World: Literacies and Material Culture*. Cambridge: Cambridge University Press.
Edmondson, Jonathan. 2015a. 'Economic life in the Roman empire'. In *The Oxford Handbook of Roman Epigraphy*, edited by Crister Bruun and Jonathan Edmondson, 671–95. Oxford: Oxford University Press.
Edmondson, Jonathan. 2015b. 'Inscribing Roman Texts: *officinae*, layout and carving techniques'. In *The Oxford Handbook of Roman Epigraphy*, edited by Crister Bruun and Jonathan Edmondson, 111–30. Oxford: Oxford University Press.
Elliott, Tom. 2015. 'Epigraphy and digital resources'. In *The Oxford Handbook of Roman Epigraphy*, edited by Crister Bruun and Jonathan Edmondson, 78–88. Oxford: Oxford University Press.
Esmonde Cleary, Simon. 2013. 'The city as preferred written space: the case of Aquitania'. In *Written space in the Latin West, 200 BC to AD 300*, edited by Gareth Sears, Peter Keegan and Ray Laurence, 217–30. London, Bloomsbury.
Evans, Jeremy. 1987. 'Graffiti and the evidence of literacy and pottery use in Roman Britain', *Archaeological Journal* 144: 191–204.
Frei-Stolba, Regula, Benjamin Hartmann and Cédric Roms. 2016. '*Vadimonium Nertae.* Zum römischen Privatrecht in den gallischen Provinzen', *Tyche* 31: 149–56.
Fuchs, Michel and Yves Dubois. 1997. 'Peintures et graffiti à la villa romaine de Contigny, Lausanne', *Jahrbuch der Schweizerischen Gesellschaft für Ur- und Frühgeschichte* 80: 173–86.
Fulford, Michael G. 1994. 'The monumental and the mundane: a common epigraphic tradition', *Britannia* 25: 315–18.
Fulford, Michael G. 2013. 'Gallo-Roman sigillata: fresh approaches, fresh challenges, fresh questions'. In *Seeing Red: New economic and social perspectives on Gallo-Roman terra sigillata*, edited by Michael G. Fulford and Emma Durham, 1–17. London: Institute of Classical Studies.
Giljohann, Ricarda and Stefan Wenzel. 2015. 'Verwendung und Verbreitung von Lothringer Kalkstein zwischen Andernach und Mayen in römischer Zeit', *Berichte zur Archäologie in Rheinhessen und Umgebung* 8: 19–40.
Gostenĉnik, Kordula. 2002. 'Agathangelus the bronzesmith: the British finds in their continental context', *Britannia* 33: 227–56.
Graham, Abigail, 2021. 'Reading visual cues on the so-called Archive Wall at Aphrodisias: a cognitive approach to monumental documents', *American Journal of Archaeology* 125.4: 571–601.
Greep, Stephen and Marloes Rijkelijkhuizen. 2019. 'Bone cylinders, discs and terminals-scroll holders from Roman funerary deposits?', *Cuadernos de Prehistoria y Arquelogía de la Universidad de Granada* 29: 219–35.
Haalebos, Jan. K. 2001. 'Eine severische Bauinschrift aus Alphen aan den Rijn-Albaniana'. In *Belgian Archaeology in a European Setting. I*, edited by Marc Lodewijckx, 41–6. Leuven: Leuven University Press.
Harris, William. 1989. *Ancient Literacy*. Cambridge, MA/London: Harvard University Press.

Harris, William. 2013. 'Literacy and epigraphy II'. In *Les affaires de Monsieur Andreau. Economie et Société du monde roman*, edited by Catherine Apicella, Marie-Laurence Haack and François Lerouxel, 289–99. Bordeaux: Ausonius Editions.

Hartmann, Benjamin. 2012. 'Inschriften aus römischen Holzfassern aus dem *Vicus Tasgetium* (Eschenz, CH)', *Zeitschrift für Papyrologie und Epigraphik* 181: 269–88.

Hartmann, Benjamin. 2015. 'Die hölzernen Schreibtafeln im Imperium Romanum – ein Inventar'. In *Lesen und Schreiben in den römischen Provinzen*, edited by Markus Scholz and M. Horster, 43–58. Mainz: RGZM.

Häussler, Ralph (ed.). 2008. *Romanisation et épigraphie*. Études interdisciplinaires sur l'acculturation et l'identité dans l'Empire romain. Montagnac: Mergoil.

Häussler, Ralph and John Pearce. 2007. 'Towards an archaeology of literacy'. In *Literacy and the State in the Ancient Mediterranean*, edited by Kathryn Lomas et al., 219–36. London: Accordia.

Hingley, Richard and Christina Unwin. 2006. *Boudica: Iron Age warrior queen*. London: Bloomsbury.

Hirt, Alfred M. 2010. *Imperial Mines and Quarries in the Roman World: Organizational aspects 27 BC–AD 235*. Oxford: Oxford University Press.

Holbrook, Neil. et al. 2017. *The Western Cemetery of Roman Cirencester: Excavations at the former Bridges garage. Tetbury Road. Cirencester, 2011–2015*. Cirencester: Cotswold Archaeology.

Hoët-van-Cauwenberghe, Christine and Alain Jacques. 2010. 'Artisanat et commerce: l'apport des étiquettes de plomb inscrites découvertes à Arras (*Nemetacum*)', *Revue des Etudes Anciennes* 112: 295–317.

Hope, Valerie. 2001. *Constructing Identity: The Roman funerary monuments of Aquileia, Mainz and Nîmes*. Oxford: Hedges.

Hope, Valerie. 2016. 'Inscriptions and identity'. In *Oxford Handbook of Roman Britain*, edited by Martin Millett, Louise Revell and Alison Moore, 285–302. Oxford: Oxford University Press.

Hopkins, Keith. 1991. 'Conquest by book'. In *Literacy in the Roman World*, edited by John H. Humphrey, 133–58. Ann Arbor, MI: Journal of Roman Archaeology.

Horster, M. 2015. 'Urban infrastructure and euergetism outside the city of Rome'. In *The Oxford Handbook of Roman Epigraphy*, edited by Crister Bruun and Jonathan Edmondson, 515–36. Oxford: Oxford University Press.

Humphrey, John. H. (ed.). 1991. *Literacy in the Roman World*. Ann Arbor, MI: Journal of Roman Archaeology.

Hurlet, Frédéric. 2015. 'The Roman emperor and the imperial family'. In *The Oxford Handbook of Roman Epigraphy*, edited by Crister Bruun and Jonathan Edmondson, 178–201. Oxford: Oxford University Press.

Jackson, Ralph and Gil Burleigh. 2018. *Dea Senuna: Treasure, Cult and Ritual at Ashwell, Hertfordshire*. London: British Museum Press.

Johnson, William A. 2010. *Readers and Reading Culture in the High Roman Empire: A study of elite communities*. Oxford: Oxford University Press.

Kolb, Anne. 2015. 'Bronze in epigraphy'. In *New Research on Ancient Bronzes. Acta of the XVIIIth International Congress on Ancient Bronzes*, edited by Philippe Della Casa and Eckard Deschler-Erb, 342–6. Zürich: Chronos.

Kruschwitz, Peter. 2016. 'Inhabiting a lettered world: exploring the fringes of Roman writing habits', *Bulletin of the Institute of Classical Studies*, 59(1): 26–41.

Macmullen, Ramsay. 1982. 'The epigraphic habit in the Roman empire', *American Journal of Philology* 103: 233–46.

Mattingly, David J. 2008. 'Urbanism, epigraphy and identity in the towns of Britain under Roman rule'. In *A Roman Miscellany: Essays in honour of Anthony R. Birley on his 70th birthday*, edited by Hans M. Schellenberg, Vera-Elisabeth Hirschmann and Andreas Krieckhaus, 53–71. Gdansk: Akanthina.

Mermet, Christian. 1993. 'Le sanctuaire gallo-romain de Châteauneuf (Savoie)', *Gallia* 50: 95–138.

Meyer, Elizabeth A. 2004. *Legitimacy and Law in the Roman World: Tabulae in Roman belief and practice*. Cambridge: Cambridge University Press.

Meyer, Elizabeth A. 2011. 'Epigraphy and communication'. In *The Oxford Handbook of Social Relations in the Roman World*, edited by Mark Peachin, 191–226. Oxford: Oxford University Press.

Mouritsen, Henrik. 2005. 'Freedmen and decurions: epitaphs and social history in imperial Italy', *Journal of Roman Studies* 95: 38–63.

Mouritsen, Henrik. 2015. 'New Pompeian graffiti and the limits of Roman literacy'. In *Antike.Kultur. Geschichte. Festschrift fuer Inge Nielsen zum 65. Geburtstag*, edited by Stefan Faust, Martina Seifert and Leon Ziemer, 201–14. Aachen: Gateways.

Mullen, Alex. 2013a. 'The language of the potteries: communication in the production and trade of terra sigillata'. In *Seeing Red: New economic and social perspectives on Gallo-Roman terra sigillata*, edited by Michael G. Fulford and Emma Durham, 97–110. London: Institute of Classical Studies.

Mullen, Alex. 2013b. *Southern Gaul and the Mediterranean: Multilingualism and multiple identities in the Iron Age and Roman periods*. Cambridge: Cambridge University Press.

Mullen, Alex. 2016. 'Sociolinguistics'. In *Oxford Handbook of Roman Britain*, edited by Martin Millett, Louise Revell and Alison Moore, 573–98. Oxford: Oxford University Press.

Mullen, Alex. 2021. 'Socio-literacy: an interdisciplinary approach to understanding literacy in the Roman north-west'. In *Aprender la escritura, olvidar la escritura*, edited by Noemí Moncunill Martí and Manuel Ramírez-Sánchez, 357–80. Vittoria/Gasteiz: Universidad del País Vasco/ Euskal Herriko Unibertsitatea.

Mullen, Alex. 2022. 'Materializing epigraphy: archaeological and sociolinguistic approaches to Roman inscribed spindle whorls'. In *Dynamic Epigraphy: New approaches to inscriptions*, edited by E. Cousins, 39–64. Oxford: Oxbow.

Mullen, Alex and Patrick James (eds). 2012. *Multilingualism in the Graeco-Roman Worlds*. Cambridge: Cambridge University Press.

Mullen, Alex and Alan Bowman. 2021 *Manual of Roman Everyday Writing, vol. I: Scripts and texts*. Nottingham: LatinNow ePubs.

Noreña, Carlos. 2011. *Imperial Ideals in the Roman West: Representation, circulation, power*. Cambridge: Cambridge University Press.

Olesti Vila, Oriol. 2021. 'Writing instruments for managing provincial resources during the Roman occupation of northeast Hispania (2nd and 1st c. BCE)', *Journal of Roman Archaeology* 34(1), 98–129.

Pearce, John. 2002. 'Food as substance and symbol in the Roman army: a case study from Vindolanda'. In *Limescongress XVIII*, edited by Philip Freeman, Julian Bennett, Zbigniew Fiema and Birgitta Hoffmann, 931–44. Oxford: Archaeopress.

Pearce, John. 2004. 'Archaeology, writing tablets and literacy in Roman Britain', *Gallia* 61: 43–51.

Pfahl, Stefan. 2017. 'A neo-Punic graffito and a Numidic coin from Oberhausen near Augsburg', *Archäologisches Korrespondenzblatt* 47(4): 501–11.

Rosso, Emmanuelle. 2006. *L'image de l'empereur en Gaule romaine. Portraits et inscriptions*. Paris: CTHS.

Rothenhöfer, Peter, Norbert Hanel and Michael Bode. 2017. 'Bleicistae mit Produzenteninschriften aus dem römischen Schiffswrack von Rena Maiore (Sardinien). Arelate/Arles (dép. Bouches-du-Rhône/F) als Umschlagplatz im überregionalen Metallhandel?' *Archäologisches Korrespondenzblatt* 47(2): 217–29.

Russell, Ben. 2013. *The Economics of the Roman Stone Trade*. Oxford: Oxford University Press.

Saastamoinen, Ari. 2010. *The Phraseology of Latin Building Inscriptions in Roman North Africa*. Helsinki: Societas Scientiarum Fennica.

Sánchez Natalias, Celia 2022. *Sylloge of Defixiones from the Roman West: A comprehensive collection of curse tablets from the fourth century BCE to the fifth century CE*. Oxford: British Archaeological Reports

Shaw, Paul. 2015. *The Eternal Letter: Two millennia of the Classical Roman capital*. Cambridge, MA: MIT Press.

Sears, Gareth. 2013. 'A new era? Severan inscriptions in Africa'. In *Written Space in the Latin West, 200 BC to AD 300*, edited by Gareth Sears, Peter Keegan and Ray Laurence, 201–16. London: Bloomsbury.

Sears, Gareth, Peter Keegan and Ray Laurence (eds). 2013. *Written Space in the Latin West, 200 BC to AD 300*. London: Bloomsbury.

Speidel, Michael A. 2018. 'Soldiers and documents: insights from Nubia. The significance of written documents in Roman soldiers' everyday lives'. In *Literacy in Ancient Everyday Life*, edited by Anne Kolb, 179–200. Berlin: de Gruyter.

Spickermann, Wolfgang. 1994. 'Eine Reibschüssel mit griechischer Ritzinschrift aus Frankfurt-Heddernheim', *Germania* 72(2): 597–605.

Stribrny, Claudia. 1987. *Die Herkunft der rômischen Werksteine aus Mainz und Umgebung. Vergleichende petrographische und geochemische Unterschungen an skulptierten Kalksteinen.* CSIR Deutschland II.8, Mainz: Verlag des Römisch-Germanischen Zentralmuseums.

Tamerl, Ingrid. 2010. *Das Holzfass in der Antike*. Innsbruck: Studien-Verlag.

Thüry, Günther E. 1996. 'Ein eingeritzter römischer Brief auf einem Soldatenteller aus Pförring, Ldkr. Eichstatt', *Bayerische Vorgeschichtsblätter* 61: 175–84.

Tomlin, Roger S.O. 1988. 'The curse tablets'. In *The Temple of Sulis Minerva at Bath, vol. 2: The finds from the sacred spring*, edited by Barry Cunliffe, 59–280. Oxford: OUCA.

Tomlin, Roger S.O. 2002. 'Writing to the gods in Britain'. In *Becoming Roman, Writing Latin?* edited by Alison E. Cooley, 165–80. Portsmouth, RI: Journal of Roman Archaeology.

Tomlin, Roger S.O. 2012. 'The book in Roman Britain'. In *The Cambridge History of the Book in Britain I. c.400–1100*, edited by Richard Gameson, 375–88. Cambridge: Cambridge University Press.

Tomlin, Roger S.O. 2015. 'Roman Britain in 2014: III. Inscriptions', *Britannia* 46: 383–420.

Tomlin, Roger S.O. 2016. *Roman London's First Voices: Writing Tablets from the Bloomberg Excavations, 2010–2014*. London: Museum of London Archaeology.

Tomlin, Roger S.O. 2018. *Britannia Romana: Roman inscriptions and Roman Britain*. Oxford: Oxbow.

Van Oyen, Astrid. 2016. *How Things Make History: The Roman Empire and its terra sigillata pottery*. Amsterdam: Amsterdam University Press.

Velázquez Soriano, Isabel and David Espinosa (eds). 2021. *Epigraphy in the Digital Age*. Oxford: Archaeopress.

Werner, Shirley. 2009. 'Literacy studies in Classics: the last twenty years'. In *Ancient Literacies: The culture of reading in Greece and Rome*, edited by William A. Johnson and Holt N. Parker, 333–82. Oxford: Oxford University Press.

Willi, Anna 2021. *Manual of Roman Everyday Writing, vol. II: Writing equipment*. Nottingham: LatinNow ePubs

Woolf, Greg. 1996. 'Monumental writing and the expansion of Roman society in the early empire', *Journal of Roman Studies* 86: 22–39.

Woolf, Greg. 1998. *Becoming Roman: The origins of provincial civilization in Gaul*. Cambridge: Cambridge University Press.

Woolf, Greg. 2000. 'Literacy'. In *The Cambridge Ancient History, vol. XI: The high empire, A.D. 70–192* (2nd edition), edited by Alan K. Bowman, Peter Garnsey and Dominic W. Rathbone, 875–97. Cambridge: Cambridge University Press.

Woolf, Greg. 2002. 'Afterword: how the Latin west was won'. In *Becoming Roman, Writing Latin?*, edited by Alison E. Cooley, 181–88. Portsmouth, RI: Journal of Roman Archaeology.

Woolf, Greg. 2009. 'Literacy or literacies in Rome?' In *Ancient Literacies: The culture of reading in Greece and Rome*, edited by William A. Johnson and Holt N. Parker, 46–58. Oxford: Oxford University Press.

Woolf, Greg. 2015. 'Ancient illiteracy?' *Bulletin of the Institute of Classical Studies* 58(2): 31–42.

Woolf, Greg. 2022. 'Curse tablets: the history of a technology', *Greece & Rome* 69(1): 120–34.

3
Archaeologies of coinage

Chris Howgego

Coinage materialised empire under Rome in many ways. The topic is approached here under four headings. *An empire of coinages* looks at the evolving structure of coinage within the empire and the extent to which imperial forms replaced local or regional forms. *An empire of money* explores how money was used and controlled within the empire. *An empire of monuments* examines the Roman attitude to coins as circulating monuments, how imperial power was presented on the regularly changing coin types, and whether the imperial 'messages' on coins were targeted. Finally, *The archaeology of coinage* outlines some of the current debates about how to interpret coin finds in the archaeological record throughout the empire.

An empire of coinages

Rome expanded into worlds with different kinds of coinage. The Greek-style coinage of much of the Mediterranean was broadly similar to the Roman. By contrast, the coinage of Iron-Age temperate Europe ('Celtic') was originally different in nature, but Roman-style coin use spread there to some extent in advance of conquest (Howgego 2013). The Roman features adopted in the north before conquest include silver coinage (which tended to replace the earlier gold), the development of coinages in multiple metals and structured denominations, and the selective appropriation of Roman iconography and of writing. This early influence from Rome helps to demonstrate Roman 'soft power' in the north-west: the advance of Rome through trade and cultural contact prior to conquest.

Figure 3.1 Iberian denarius (Bolskan, *c.*150–100 BC). Photo: Classical Numismatic Group LLC.

During Rome's first phase of expansion, into Italy and Sicily in the third century BCE, Roman coinage had replaced existing Greek-style civic and royal precious metal coinages (some limited civic bronze coinages continued) (Burnett 2012: 305–8). By contrast, following later phases of expansion beyond Italy and Sicily the penetration of Roman coinage might be slow and it did not necessarily replace local coinages (Crawford 1985). This may be because at least until the mid-first century BCE there was no compelling model of Roman provincial material culture to follow in general (Woolf 1998: 181–5; 238–41; Wallace-Hadrill 2008), so there may have been no perceived pressure from outside or inside local communities to make local coinages 'conform'. Local coinages using local languages might even be introduced after conquest. So Iberian script was used for Iberian and Celtiberian languages on silver and bronze coins produced by peoples in Spain in the process of developing their own discrete identities after conquest, from the first quarter of second century BCE (but in quantity only from *c.*133 BCE) until the 70s BCE (Ripollés 2005) (Figure 3.1).

Local coinages ended much earlier in the West than they did in the East, perhaps because from the mid-first century BCE onwards culture in the West tended to follow the model of Rome. In the East, Greek culture flourished and was valued by the Romans, so the maintenance and development of Greek forms are not surprising (Howgego 1995: 58–9; 2005: 14; Burnett 2005: 171–80). Rome at first manipulated local style coinages in the East, sometimes adding some, often minor, Roman elements (de Callataÿ 2011) (Figure 3.2). Local coinages in bronze and silver (in modern scholarship termed 'Roman provincial

Figure 3.2 Greek-style cistophorus with the name of a Roman governor (proconsul) added in Latin (Asia, Pergamon, 57–55 BC). Photo: Classical Numismatic Group LLC.

Figure 3.3 Roman provincial coin with the local myth of Hero and Leander on the reverse (Abydus, Septimius Severus, 193–211 CE). Photo: Classical Numismatic Group LLC.

coinages') were a vibrant phenomenon in the East until the later third century CE (Howgego et al. 2005). Local civic coinages were increasingly influenced by Roman imperial coinage – their iconography became more varied (like the Roman), their denominations larger (like the Roman) and Roman themes became more prevalent – but their reverses remained predominantly local until the end (Heuchert 2005; Burnett 2011) (Figure 3.3).

The Romans certainly debated imposing a monopoly of imperial coinage, although it is not clear to which period the debate in Dio quoted below applies (it is set in the Augustan period but was written in the third century CE):

> None of the cities should be allowed to have its own separate coinage or system of weights and measures; they should all be required to use ours. (Dio 52.30.9; speech of Maecenas)

The imposition of a monopoly of imperial coinage cannot have been an ideological imperative, however, as the full displacement of local coinages took over five hundred years to be completed. It was only in the 290s CE that the Roman world finally moved to a monopoly of standardised imperial coinage in Latin (Abdy 2012a). The new empire-wide system developed an organisational separation between gold mints (moving with the emperor) and regional small change mints (Hendy 1985: 371–94).

Coinages in the Roman world were state coinages. They were produced by imperial or provincial authorities, cities or client kings. There was no significant minting by or for individuals, by contrast with the western Middle Ages (de Callataÿ 2005). One should not, however, be too categorical about this. At times of shortages of supply of imperial small change, imitative coinages were produced locally (King 1996; Abdy 2012b: 504). It is mostly unclear whether these were public or private, and whether they were official, tolerated or simply illicit.

An empire of money

Roman imperial coinage evolved into a structured system in gold, silver and bronze (Table 3.1). The face value of the most valuable coin (the gold 'aureus') was 1,600 times greater than the smallest (the copper 'quadrans'), allowing considerable flexibility in use (Wolters 2012: 336–40). Civic bronze coinage in the East was also produced in a wide range of denominations, of bewildering variety (Johnston 2007).

The predominant model for coinage entering circulation was by state expenditure, the most important of which was military. The age-structure of hoards in Britain shows that silver denarii were introduced into circulation in military areas rather than at the commercial capital of Londinium (Creighton 2014). The supply of coinage to the military is also evident in large-scale finds of coinage on military sites in the

West (Kemmers 2006). These are mostly of bronze coins, but it is safe to assume that gold and silver was supplied in substantial quantities too (Wolters 2000–1). Precious metal coinages are normally heavily under-represented in site finds (unlike hoards), but disaster sites can be revealing. At the military disaster site of Kalkriese, which gives an idea of the currency with soldiers on the move in 9 CE, 98 per cent by value was in gold and silver (von Kaenel 1999).

Monetisation was galvanised by the military and was spread by urbanisation (Howgego 2013: 38–44). It took longer to penetrate the countryside. The general pattern has been validated by cluster analysis of the relative chronology of coin finds by type of site in Britain (Lockyear 2000). Ancient authors imply that coin use became normative for the Roman world, for example:

> The use of coins is inherent to our existence, it regulates everything in life. Each time we want to buy or sell something, it is done by means of coins. (John Chrysostom, *In Principium Actorum* 4, 3; writing in the Roman East in the fourth century CE)

This general picture is confirmed by documentary sources (Howgego 1992: 16–22) but needs testing in the archaeological evidence, which is also crucial for developing a more variegated and dynamic history of monetisation (see below).

Money became embedded in the structure of the economy (Howgego 1992): it played a role alongside agricultural produce in taxation, rents, wages and credit. It was the normal mode of exchange, at least in cities. Money was critically linked to the Roman state redistributive cycle of taxation and expenditure (Hopkins 1995/6). Taxation and army pay were important drivers of the long-distance movement of coinage around the empire, but we do not really know what proportion of taxation was actually sent to Rome (Millar 1991) or how much army pay was actually delivered to the army camps (possibly as little as one third in some contexts) (Wolters 2000–1). Long-distance movement of coin was also driven by trade, the flow of rents, loans, and the movement of people. There remains a debate about whether we should view the Roman economy as integrated or cellular, but we can at least measure the impressive movement of coin around the empire, including from one side of the empire to the other (Howgego 1994).

High levels of monetisation were enabled by the production of coinage on a massive scale (see below). The supply of metal for coinage was in turn ensured by a high degree of imperial control and oversight of important mining enterprises (Hirt 2010; 2020). For silver, relative production

	Denomination	*Metal*	*Denarii*	*Asses*
	Aureus	Gold	25	400
	Denarius	Silver	1	16
	Sestertius	Brass	0.25	4
	Dupondius	Brass		2
	As	Copper		1

Table 3.1 Early imperial denominations (illustrated with coins of Nero, 64–6 CE). Photos: Classical Numismatic Group LLC. *(cont)*

	Denomination	*Metal*	*Denarii*	*Asses*
	Semis	Brass		0.5
	Quadrans	Copper		0.25

Table 3.1 Early imperial denominations (illustrated with coins of Nero, 64–6 CE). Photos: Classical Numismatic Group LLC.

levels can be traced through sub-annually resolved measurements of lead pollution in Greenland ice (McConnell et al. 2018). The assumption is that European lead emissions largely from mining and smelting of lead-silver sulphide ores (e.g. galena) dominated other sources during antiquity. Emissions reached a sustained maximum during the Roman Empire, at a level not matched again for more than five centuries. Levels plunged in the second century coincident with the Antonine Plague, and remained low. The correlation of the dramatic fall in lead pollution levels with the decline in the fineness of the silver coinage suggests a strong connection between silver mining and refining and the output of silver coinage. It is significant that the recycling of old denarii to make new coin seems to have begun already under Nero, replacing a pattern of sourcing bullion more directly from the mines (Butcher and Ponting 2014: 224–6).

Debasement of the silver coinages (by lowering their silver content and/or decreasing weight standards) was systemic in the imperial period from 64 CE onwards. By the 260s CE the silver coinage fell to only 2 per cent pure (Figure 3.4). The significance of such dramatic debasement is debated: was debasement driven primarily by fiscal inadequacy (not enough precious metal to pay the army) or by a monetary policy seeking

Figure 3.4 Heavily debased silver radiate (Gallienus, 268 CE). Photo: Classical Numismatic Group LLC.

to address the problem of maintaining bimetallism with changing bullion values for gold and silver? Both forces were certainly at play. The sheer scale of the decline makes it hard not to allocate a significant role to fiscal inadequacy (Howgego 1992: 4–8; 1995: 115–21). It is likely that declining supplies of precious metal were a significant factor in that inadequacy, alongside the need for increased military and diplomatic expenditure to meet external threats. On the other hand, a shift of the monetary regime from 64 CE onwards to what has been termed a 'limping bimetallism' (that is, with the value of the gold coinage being more or less fully backed by its metallic content, but the silver coinage only partially) is also plausible. It may be this which opened the way for the progressive debasement of the silver (Butcher and Ponting 2014).

The reconstruction of 'monetary policy', largely in default of contemporary commentary in the ancient sources, remains conjectural, but it is clear that the Romans could control their currency both in theory (legally) and to some extent in practice. The currency was controlled in turn by law, decree of the senate and imperial pronouncement. In terms of practical control, hoard evidence allows us to trace major changes, such as the withdrawal from circulation of earlier and finer denarii in the late first and early second centuries CE (although one cannot formally prove that this was all official rather than partially private) (Duncan-Jones 1994: 194–200). In the fourth century, epigraphic and legal sources show that emperors were able to double or halve the value of coins in circulation, to demonetise coins, and to impose penalties for using obsolete coins (*pecuniae vetitae*) (Erim et al. 1971; Hendy 1985).

Figure 3.5 Republican denarius with iconography relating to the family of the moneyer (135 BCE, descendants paying religious honours to an ancestor by the Columna Minucia). Photo: Classical Numismatic Group LLC.

An empire of monuments

Under the Republic, from the 130s BCE, the Romans abandoned relative uniformity of coinage in favour of annually changing types, which increasingly reflected the family traditions of the yearly board of three in charge of the coinage (Figure 3.5). The practice of regularly changing types is highly unusual in the history of numismatics, where conservatism of types in the interests of maintaining confidence in the currency is more normal. Iconography which reflects individuals who are not heads of state is also highly unusual. This development was part of an aggressive appropriation of the public sphere by private families, which also included the erection of statues and monuments in the city of Rome (Wallace-Hadrill 2008: 218–25). It was part of a broader emphasis on the individual which eventually put an end to the Republic.

At this time the Romans came to regard their coins as little monuments (Meadows and Williams 2001; Clark 2007: 135–41; Rowan 2012: 28–31). Their view of coins as monuments does not imply that the messages on coins were not political, as 'monumentalisation' or 'memorialisation' was a Roman way of doing politics. Family based memory devices were an essential component of the political culture of the Roman Republic at a time when a citizen's vote actually counted (Morstein-Marx 2004: 85; Flower 2006: 51–5). In the same way, 'Roman rhetoric expressed its debates in terms of the past, within culturally determined frameworks of praise or blame of past individuals'

Figure 3.6 Coin of Tiberius (14–37 CE) with an inscription on the reverse stating that it was restored by the emperor Titus (79–81 CE). Photo: Classical Numismatic Group LLC.

(Flower 2006: 60; cf. Morstein-Marx 2004; Wallace-Hadrill 2008: 225–9). The period which saw the invasion of the coinage by private themes also witnessed an explosion of history creation connected with family traditions (Meadows and Williams 2001: 45–8). Alongside the prominence of family ancestry went an increasing emphasis on current politics. It has been estimated that nearly half the post-Sullan denarius coinage referred to contemporary events in some way, however allusive (Hollstein 1993: 388–9; Woytek 2012: 325–9).

Both the practice of frequently changing types and the view of coins as monuments survived the change from Republic to Empire. Emperors even 'restored' older coins when they were being withdrawn, just as they restored old buildings or other edifices (Komnick 2001; Woytek 2022). The restoration of coinage took various forms, but in its purest mode consisted of striking new coins identical in their types and inscriptions with the old coins being restored, but with the addition of an inscription stating that the emperor had restored them (Figure 3.6).

What was being memorialised on the coinage in the imperial period was naturally the achievements and qualities of the emperor as head of state, with some emphasis on his family as ensuring dynastic stability. Comparison of the 'messages' on the coinage with other sources of imperial communication, like the *Res Gestae* of Augustus, shows that the coinage normally reflects imperial self-presentation (Sutherland 1951; 1987; Rowan 2012; Elkins 2017). This need not have been the case in all periods. For example, it has been demonstrated that some of the iconography of the coinage under the 'Gallic Empire' reflected the themes of earlier coinage

Figure 3.7 Even low-value coins could be of amazingly high quality (brass Sestertius of Nero, 66 CE). Photo: Classical Numismatic Group LLC.

and was not all relevant to contemporary concerns (Mairat 2014). This may have been the result of mint workers simply copying old coins brought to the mint for re-striking. The strong impression remains that for most of the time the messages on the coins were carefully considered.

In the imperial period the imagery became less recondite and more standardised, using a well-defined visual language (Hölscher 1984), and with more explanation through the inscriptions on the coins. As the meanings of images and the related inscriptions did not coincide precisely, the combination allowed great flexibility and precision of expression (Hölscher 1980; 1982; Howgego 1995: 75–7). These developments will have aided interpretation, especially beyond the city of Rome itself.

Reception is a notoriously difficult subject, but the quantity, penetration and quality of the coinage suggest a considerable impact on people across the empire. Coins will have been handled routinely by almost everyone. Coin striking uniquely allowed the mass production of high-quality images, rather as printing and digital technologies did later. There might be high-quality sculptural and painted images in civic centres and rich villas (although not all were high quality), but it is important to realise that coins will have been by far the best-made objects which most people ever had in their hands or in their houses (Figure 3.7). Today we have become accustomed to inundation by masses of high-quality images, but the impact of such images in a world without printing and digital media will surely have been greater. It is indicative that the quality of Roman coins surprised scholars in the western Renaissance, who thought they must have been commemorative medals rather than coins (Cunnally 1999: 136–8). In this, Renaissance

Figure 3.8 Jupiter as *Conservator* (IOVI CONSERVATORI, denarius of Macrinus, 217 CE). Photo: Classical Numismatic Group LLC.

scholars were picking up on the commemorative aspect of Roman coinage, which, as we have already seen, the Romans came to regard as monuments in their own right.

Interpretation of the 'messages' on coins will have been cued for Roman audiences, especially for those at Rome itself, by the iteration of the same themes at games, theatrical performances, triumphal processions, public speeches and the like, and by a political life that was lived out in public (Wiseman 1985: 32–4; 1998; 2009: ch. 8; Morstein-Marx 2004, ch. 3). It will have been facilitated by a visual repertoire shared with other monuments (Hölscher 1980; 1982; 1984) and by the shared language of monumental inscriptions (Pearce, Chapter 2 this volume). To some extent, the interpretation of coins will have been cued and facilitated in similar ways for audiences in the cities across the empire. But how most people (mis)interpreted what they saw is largely beyond us.

Coins, as mass-produced objects, allow a quantitative approach to the presentation of Power through the analysis of relative frequency in hoards. For the imperial period quantification demonstrates a greater emphasis on the charismatic qualities of the emperor justifying his rule than on his achievements (Noreña 2001; 2011). Imperial 'virtues' or 'qualities' accounted for 55 per cent of all silver coins between 69 CE and 235 CE (Figure 3.9a). The period from the 180s CE onwards saw a shift from charismatic qualities to divine sanction by particular gods, who were often presented as Preservers (*Conservatores*) (Figure 3.8) or Companions (*Comites*) of emperors (Rowan 2012). This later played out in the emphasis placed on the Sun god by Aurelian and in the eventual emergence of Christianity as a state religion.

Figure 3.9 (a) Liberalitas personified as a woman (denarius of Geta, 211 CE). Photo: Classical Numismatic Group LLC. (b) Liberalitas scene showing the distribution of coins to citizens (sestertius of Hadrian, 118 CE). Photo: Classical Numismatic Group LLC.

There is only a little evidence for the targeting of particular messages on imperial coinage at particular groups of people or places, perhaps because the point was monumentalisation rather than propaganda in the modern sense. Targeting might, in principle, have been accomplished by selecting different types for different denominations, on the assumption that different denominations were intended for different recipients, or by variable distribution geographically of the same denomination(s) with different types. These are discussed in turn.

As an example of targeting by denomination, it has been argued that *Liberalitas* (Liberality, Generosity) was presented differently on precious metal coinages than on base metal because the different metals were targeted at different audiences (Metcalf 1993). On the other hand, it could be that the compact representation of Liberalitas, personified in the form of a woman, tended to be used on the smaller gold and silver coins precisely because they were smaller, and the full scene of the emperor handing out cash to the People tended to be used on larger bronze coins simply because they were larger (Figure 3.9). The iconographies of precious metal and bronze denominations were unquestionably different from each other at certain periods, but patterns are not consistent. Sometimes audience targeting seems a plausible explanation (Marzano 2009; Wolters 2012: 342–6), but often this is not evident (Hekster 2003).

Variable distribution geographically of the same denomination(s) with different types can be measured from site finds or hoards. Again, alternative explanations are possible. For example, a particular batch of existing coinage might be sent from the Mint (or Treasury) to a particular region because of the need for money there, such as a military campaign, without any intention to target the particular iconography on that batch of coins at the region concerned. We detect targeting when the iconography seems appropriate to us: so the identification of 'targeting' is, to some extent, a matter of interpretation.

An assessment of bronze coin distribution in the Western Empire between 81 CE and 192 CE found variation between regions but little evidence for appropriate targeting by iconography, beyond the association of Britannia types with Britain already noted by Walker (Walker 1988; Hobley 1998, esp. 131). This suggests that geographical targeting was not the norm. It is also significant that during the parallel coin production at Rome and Lugdunum under Nero, there was little systematic difference between the two mints in terms of iconography, despite the fact that the two mints supplied different regions (the coins of Lugdunum are not surprisingly mainly found north of the Alps) (Sutherland 1976: 118–19; for limited variation: MacDowall 1979: 130). By contrast, in the Flavian period the iconography of the two mints does vary somewhat (Kemmers 2006: 241–2). This again suggests that concern for geographical targeting was not a dominant or consistent feature, although it may have been a factor at times.

Examples can be cited to support geographical targeting in some contexts, especially from the Flavio-Trajanic period. It has been demonstrated, for example, that bronze in 71 CE tended to have iconography weighted towards military types in military regions (Lower Rhine: Securitas, Victoria, Aequitas; Wales: Aquila [Eagle], Victoria, Securitas) whereas bronze from Italy consisted of a higher proportion of peaceable types (Roma, Aequitas, Pax, Concordia, Judaea) (Kemmers 2006: 219–44; 2014). This analysis is somewhat skewed because comparisons are not like for like, in that the mixed bronze coins in Italy had a higher percentage of the largest denomination (sestertii) and relatively fewer of the lower value asses and dupondii found in substantial quantities in military contexts, so we are not looking at a purely geographical phenomenon. The difference, however, remains significant and interesting, and other cases have been detected (Elkins 2011; 2017).

The topic of targeting is clearly important in helping us to understand the intent behind, and potentially also the effect of, the dissemination of imperial images. A reasonable conclusion would be that geographical targeting was occasional rather than systematic. It is interesting that the majority of plausible examples identified so far belong to the Flavio-Trajanic period. It is notable that this is also the period in which there is most evidence for the mint of Rome producing local-style coinages, sometimes in Greek, for circulation in the East, and for similar centralised production of coinage for other regions at Antioch and Alexandria (*RPC* II: p.11; *RPC* III: p.798; Howgego 1994: 16; Butcher 2004: 34–7, 77–8, 81–92). It has been plausibly suggested, in this connection, that the need to recall and remint silver coinage intensively in this period may have led to a particular concern for, and expertise in, the distribution of coinage (Butcher and Woytek 2018: 272–5). So perhaps the Flavio-Trajanic concern with coin distribution also led to an exceptional level of audience targeting at the same time. Both the extent and chronological development of targeting clearly warrant larger and more systematic investigation.

New coins were mixed with a mass of old coinage in circulation, although whether this resulted in new messages being diluted or being reinforced by being set in a tradition of similar messages is a moot point. Whatever the case, the immense production of coin at the start of reigns clearly suggests a need to publicise the new emperor, presumably in connection with accession donatives. The scale might be staggering. The thousand obverse dies used for the gold and silver coinage of the short-lived emperor Otho suggest that the mint of Rome was able to produce something like 20 million coins in a period no longer than 94 days (Butcher et al. 2009). Calculations for the reign of Victorinus (269–71 CE) suggest a production level for radiates of the order of 48 million a week (Bland 2012: 521).

The archaeology of coinage

Coins stand in the archaeological record for whole systems of doing things, for ways people relate to each other and to things, and for ways of conceptualising the world (Howgego 2013: 19). It is therefore potentially of great interest to explore their archaeology. There are now online databases for hoards (https://chre.ashmus.ox.ac.uk/) for the whole Empire and for single finds for Britain (https://finds.org.uk/) and good explorations in print of how to interpret them (e.g. Walton 2012; Guest 2015; Mairat et al. 2022). Archaeological site finds are another matter.

Archaeological sites mostly produce bronze coins to the extent that archaeological numismatics has been branded 'small change studies' (Butcher 2016: 225). Precious metal coinages are systematically under-represented, owing to the greater care taken not to lose them and the trouble taken to recover them. This is not the case with hoards, which provide the vast majority of surviving gold and silver coins. Disaster sites are also relatively immune (not, of course, wholly immune) from the bias towards bronze coins, revealing the dominance of gold and silver by value. Accordingly, precious metal accounted for 98 per cent by value of the coinage at the military disaster site at Kalkriese in 9 CE, with gold and silver making an equal contribution, and at the volcanic eruption site at Pompeii of 79 CE precious metal accounted for 93 per cent by value, with gold at 61 per cent and silver at 32 per cent (von Kaenel 1999). A disaster site such as Pompeii may also reveal coins in use contexts which are not preserved elsewhere: bodies with purses, strong boxes from villas, tills from shops or inns, and the like (Duncan-Jones 2003; Andreau 2008).

Contextual studies of coin finds are potentially of considerable interest for illuminating coin use, but they face formidable challenges. Some such studies are very helpful. For example, coin finds from the civilian settlement attached to the army camp at Nijmegen, 70–105 CE, reveal an association of coins with houses and with roads, presumably in connection with shops (Kemmers 2006), and the detailed study of one insula at Pompeii demonstrates the heaviest coin loss in areas of commercial transactions (bars, workshops, shops), with coins present, but in smaller numbers, in domestic spaces (Hobbs 2013). This type of study is not unproblematic. It is clear that the process of site formation may be critical, with finds dictated by building and demolition phases (Butcher 2003: 28, 29, 107; Ellis 2016; Stroobants 2017; 2018). Disturbances of various kinds make residuality (coins not found in the original context of deposition) a serious problem. Thus, the potential of contextual archaeology remains unclear. In general, the benefits of such studies are more readily apparent for contexts with mud rather than paved floors, as the coins dropped were more likely to remain *in situ*. This is another area of study which would repay systematic consideration.

Analysis of coin finds by category of site is potentially illuminating for the Roman world, as it has been for the Iron Age (Haselgrove 2005). For example, the Rural Settlement of Roman Britain Project has been able to document a hierarchy of coin use in the countryside (Smith et al. 2016: 12, 397, and e.g. 185–8). Coins were found at 86 per cent of villas, villages and roadside settlements, but at only 42 per cent of farmsteads (small rural settlements without 'villa' architecture). Among farmsteads, coins were more likely to be found at complex farmsteads than at the simpler category of enclosed farm. The degree to which coins were associated with excavated rural sites also varied by region, being much lower to the north and north-west of Britain than in the south. This type of approach allows a more nuanced appreciation of rural monetisation than would be possible from documentary sources alone (Howgego 1992: 20–2).

Finally, it may be worth asking if one could one tell from coins that you were *outside* the empire. The answer is broadly 'Yes'. You would find coins still in use that had long disappeared from circulation within the empire, much less small change, a range of local imitations primarily in silver, and far more coins pierced for use as adornment (Bursche et al. 2008).

Conclusion

The fact that coin profiles are significantly different outside the Roman Empire reinforces the credibility of the attempt, here and elsewhere, to characterise that Empire through its coinage. As a material expression of money, coinage was implicated in everything from the conceptual and symbolic to the practical and behavioural. Four main approaches have been briefly essayed here: the structure of coinage (for much of the time including both imperial and local elements); how money was used and controlled; how imperial power was presented on the coinage; and the significance of coinage in the archaeological record for illuminating variation and change in coin use in different contexts throughout the empire. Together these approaches help to elucidate the multiple ways in which the Roman Empire was materialised through its coinages.

Illustrations

All illustrations of coins are taken from the archives of the Classical Numismatic Group, with their kind permission. Further details can be found in the following permanent links:

Figure 3.1: http://www.coinarchives.com/a/openlink.php?l=517958|929|6|98a8aa29a31de39f132e2e5bdb4a8be6

Figure 3.2: http://www.coinarchives.com/a/openlink.php?l=92521|99|381|321354882c0ad3d627cebd93b031bda0

Figure 3.3: http://www.coinarchives.com/a/openlink.php?l=164708|202|661|4ce88147eccf3e2aa45b66635f764de9

Figure 3.4: http://www.coinarchives.com/a/openlink.php?l=269687|408|135|a2cb7a8294da13dc1959e45bedfb57f9

Figure 3.5: http://www.coinarchives.com/a/openlink.php?l=629772|1147|505|11b1e4abc4b164e30078f0ae0770f4c6

Figure 3.6: http://www.coinarchives.com/a/openlink.php?l=667499|1222|749|fc2a133e35fd1c9099a0d6677563bac9

Figure 3.7: http://www.coinarchives.com/a/openlink.php?l=629921|1147|654|cd49951184ed14c957f55050bc5c7fd2

Figure 3.8: http://www.coinarchives.com/a/openlink.php?l=388047|700|768|9ae2ecad047bf21dee98556fe7c0d313

Figure 3.9a: http://www.coinarchives.com/a/openlink.php?l=729247|1350|266|af220d87f2ac178872921084327b74ca

Figure 3.9b: http://www.coinarchives.com/a/openlink.php?l=151916|181|891|08c0bd0303052ea10aa7a2e30fe03a10

Table 3.1 Aureus: http://www.coinarchives.com/a/openlink.php?l=1160254|2332|577|24a1ba7f15a09a9b79446f30913bcafd

Denarius: http://www.coinarchives.com/a/openlink.php?l=958739|1858|594|42c604f93ae985d777084608896597df

Sestertius: http://www.coinarchives.com/a/openlink.php?l=1382039|2796|367|28934ecd91f21943f20c05c3c3c20aa8

Dupondius: http://www.coinarchives.com/a/openlink.php?l=951482|1839|674|1b83c54dbc709165cce31f879e771e74

As: http://www.coinarchives.com/a/openlink.php?l=846604|1591|498|8e07b77e13aabe6a23723588341f883a

Semis: http://www.coinarchives.com/a/openlink.php?l=48855|52|1247|35bb97f361bcca162714c1c41fcfa775

Quadrans: http://www.coinarchives.com/a/openlink.php?l=397489|719|379|24b8d54851518c1fdba93cc0573a9852

Abbreviations

RPC II: Andrew Burnett, Michel Amandry and Ian Carradice, 1999. *Roman Provincial Coinage, vol. II: From Vespasian to Domitian (AD 69–96)*. London/Paris: The British Museum Press and the Bibliothèque Nationale de France.

RPC III: Michel Amandry and Andrew Burnett. 2015. *Roman Provincial Coinage, vol. III: Nerva, Trajan and Hadrian (AD 96–138)*. London/Paris: The British Museum Press and the Bibliothèque Nationale de France.

References

Abdy, Richard. 2012a. 'Tetrarchy and the House of Constantine'. In *The Oxford Handbook of Greek and Roman Coinage*, edited by William E. Metcalf, 584–600. Oxford: Oxford University Press.

Abdy, Richard. 2012b 'The Severans'. In *The Oxford Handbook of Greek and Roman Coinage*, edited by William E. Metcalf, 499–513. Oxford: Oxford University Press.

Andreau, Jean. 2008. 'The use and survival of coins and of gold and silver in the Vesuvian cities'. In *The Monetary Systems of the Greeks and Romans*, edited by William V. Harris. Oxford: Oxford University Press.

Bland, Roger. 2012. 'From Gordian III to the Gallic empire (AD 238–274)'. In *The Oxford Handbook of Greek and Roman Coinage*, edited by William E. Metcalf, 514–37. Oxford: Oxford University Press.

Burnett, Andrew. 2005. 'The Roman West and the Roman East'. In *Coinage and Identity in the Roman Provinces*, edited by Christopher Howgego, Volker Heuchert and Andrew Burnett, 171–80. Oxford: Oxford University Press.

Burnett, Andrew. 2011. 'The Augustan Revolution seen from the mints of the provinces', *Journal of Roman Studies* 101: 1–30.

Burnett, Andrew. 2012. 'Early Roman coinage and its Italian context'. In *The Oxford Handbook of Greek and Roman Coinage*, edited by William E. Metcalf, 297–314. Oxford: Oxford University Press.

Bursche, Aleksander, Renata Ciołek and Reinhard Wolters (eds). 2008. *Roman Coins outside the Empire: Ways and phases, contexts and functions*. Wetteren: Moneta.

Butcher, Kevin. 2003. *Small Change in Ancient Beirut: Coins from BEY 006 and 045. Berytus* 45–46 (2001–2002). Beirut: American University.

Butcher, Kevin 2004. *Coinage in Roman Syria: Northern Syria, 64 BC–AD 253*. London: Royal Numismatic Society.

Butcher, Kevin and Matthew Ponting. 2014. *The Metallurgy of Roman Silver Coinage: From the reform of Nero to the reform of Trajan*. Cambridge: Cambridge University Press.

Butcher, Kevin. 2016. 'Coin finds and the monetary economy: the good, the bad and the irrelevant'. In *Les monnaies de fouille du monde grec (VIe–Ier siècle a.C.): apports, approches et methods*, edited by Frederique Duyrat and Catherine Grandjean, 225–37. Pessac Gironde: Ausonius.

Butcher, Kevin and Bernhard Woytek. 2018. 'The grand scheme of things: modelling coin production and coin distribution in the Roman Empire in the first and second centuries AD'. In *Infrastructure and Distribution in Ancient Economies: Proceedings of a Conference held at the Austrian Academy of Sciences, 28–31 October 2014*, edited by B. Woytek, 253– 81. Vienna: Austrian Academy of Sciences Press.

Butcher, Kevin, Matthew Ponting and Jyrki Muona. 2009. 'The denarii of Otho: a stylistic and compositional study', *Rivista Italiana di Numismatica* e Scienze Affini 110: 291–310.

Callataÿ, François. de. 2005. 'La frappe libre a-t-elle existé dans l'Antiquité gréco-romaine?' In XIII *Congreso Internacional de Numismática, Madrid, 2003: Actas-proceedings-actes*, edited by Carmen Alfaro, Carmen Marcos and Paloma Otero, 211–18. Madrid.

Callataÿ, François. de. 2011. 'More than it would seem: the use of coinage by the Romans in late Hellenistic Asia Minor (133–63 BC)', *American Journal of Numismatics* 23: 55–86.

Clark, Anna J. 2007. *Divine Qualities: Cult and community in Republican Rome*. Oxford: Oxford University Press.

Crawford, Michael. 1985. *Coinage and Money under the Roman Republic*. London: Methuen.

Creighton, John. 2014. 'The supply and movement of denarii in Roman Britain', *Britannia* 45: 121–63.

Cunnally, John. 1999. *Images of the Illustrious: The numismatic presence in the Renaissance*. Princeton, NJ: Princeton University Press.

Duncan-Jones, Richard. 1994. *Money and Government in the Roman Empire*. Cambridge: Cambridge University Press.

Duncan-Jones, Richard. 2003. 'Roman coin circulation and the cities of Vesuvius'. In *Credito e moneta nel mondo romano: atti degli Incontri capresi di storia dell'economia antica (Capri, 12–14 ottobre 2000)*, edited by Elio Lo Cascio, 161–80. Bari: Edipuglia.

Elkins, Nathan T. 2011. 'Monuments on the move: architectural coin types and audience targeting in the Flavian and Trajanic periods'. In *Proceedings of the XIVth International Numismatic Congress, Glasgow 2009*, edited by Nicholas Holmes, 645–55. Glasgow: The International Numismatic Council.

Elkins, Nathan T. 2017. *The Image of Political Power in the Reign of Nerva, AD 96–98*. New York: Oxford University Press.

Ellis, Steven J.R. 2016. 'Re-evaluating Pompeii's coin finds: monetary transactions and urban waste in the retail economy of an ancient city'. In *The Economy of Pompeii*, edited by Miko Flohr and Andrew Wilson, 294–337. Oxford: Oxford University Press.

Erim, Kenan. T., Joyce Reynolds and Michael Crawford. 1971. 'Diocletian's currency reform; a new inscription', *Journal of Roman Studies* 61: 171–7.

Flower, Harriet I. 2006. *The Art of Forgetting: Disgrace and oblivion in Roman political culture*. Chapel Hill, NC: University of North Carolina Press.

Guest, Peter. 2015. 'The burial, loss and recovery of Roman coin hoards in Britain and beyond: past, present and future'. In *Hoarding and the Deposition of Metalwork from the Bronze Age to the 20th Century: A British perspective*, edited by John Naylor and Roger Bland, 101–16. Oxford: Archaeopress.

Haselgrove, Colin. 2005. 'A new approach to analysing the circulation of Iron Age coinage', *Numismatic Chronicle* 165: 129–74.

Hekster, Olivier. 2003. 'Coins and message: audience targeting on coins of different denominations?'. In *The Representation and Perception of Roman Imperial Power: Proceedings of the Third Workshop of the International Network Impact of Empire (Roman Empire, c. 200 BC–AD 476), Netherlands Institute in Rome, March 20–23, 2002*, edited by Lukas de Blois, 20–35. Amsterdam: J.C. Gieben.

Hendy, Michael F. 1985. *Studies in the Byzantine Monetary Economy c. 300–1450*. Cambridge: Cambridge University Press.

Heuchert, Volker. 2005. 'The chronological development of Roman provincial coin iconography'. In *Coinage and Identity in the Roman Provinces*, edited by Christopher Howgego, Volker Heuchert and Andrew Burnett, 29–56. Oxford: Oxford University Press.

Hirt, Alfred Michael. 2010. *Imperial Mines and Quarries in The Roman World: Organizational aspects, 27 BC–AD 235*. Oxford: Oxford University Press.

Hirt, Alfred Michael. 2020. 'Gold and silver mining in the Roman Empire'. In *Debasement: Manipulation of coin standards in pre-modern monetary systems*, edited by Kevin Butcher, 111–24. Oxford: Oxbow Books.

Hobley, Andrew Stephen. 1998. *An Examination of Roman Bronze Coin Distribution in the Western Empire, A.D. 81–192*. Oxford: Archaeopress.

Hobbs, Richard. 2013. *Currency and Exchange in Ancient Pompeii: Coins from the AAPP excavations at Regio VI, Insula 1*. London: Institute of Classical Studies, School of Advanced Study, University of London.

Hollstein, Wilhelm. 1993. *Die stadtrömische Münzprägung der Jahre 78–50 v. Chr. zwischen politischer Aktualität und Familienthematik: Kommentar und Bibliographie*. München: Tuduv.

Hölscher, Tonio. 1980. 'Die Geschichtsauffassung in der römischen Repräsentationskunst', *JdAI* 95: 265–321.

Hölscher, Tonio. 1982. 'Die Bedeutung der Münzen für das Verstandnis der politischen Repräsentationskunst der späten römischen Republik'. In *Actes du 9ème Congrès International de Numismatique. Berne, Septembre 1979*, edited by Tony Hackens and Raymond Weiller, 269–82. Louvain-La-Neuve, Luxembourg: Association internationale des numismates professionnels.

Hölscher, Tonio. 1984. *Staatsdenkmal und Publikum: vom Untergang der Republik bis zur Festigung des Kaisertums in Rom*. Konstanz: Universitätsverlag Konstanz.

Hopkins, Keith. 1995/6. 'Rome, taxes, rents and trade', *Kodai: Journal of Ancient History* 6/7: 41–75. (Also published in *The Ancient Economy*, edited by Walter Scheidel and Sitta von Reden, 2002, 190–230. Edinburgh: Edinburgh University Press.)

Howgego, Christopher. 1992. 'The supply and use of money in the Roman world 200 BC–AD 300', *Journal of Roman Studies* 82: 1–31.

Howgego, Christopher. 1994. 'Coin circulation and the integration of the Roman economy', *Journal of Roman Archaeology* 7: 5–21.

Howgego, Christopher. 1995. *Ancient History from Coins*. London: Routledge.

Howgego, Christopher. 2005. 'Coinage and identity in the Roman provinces'. In *Coinage and Identity in the Roman Provinces*, edited by Christopher Howgego, Volker Heuchert and Andrew Burnett, 1–17. Oxford: Oxford University Press.

Howgego, Christopher. 2013. 'The monetization of temperate Europe', *Journal of Roman Studies* 103: 16–45.

Howgego, Christopher, Volker Heuchert and Andrew Burnett (eds). 2005. *Coinage and Identity in the Roman Provinces*. Oxford: Oxford University Press, 2005.

Johnston, Ann. 2007. *Greek Imperial Denominations, ca 200–275: A Study of the Roman provincial bronze coinages of Asia Minor*. London: Royal Numismatic Society (Great Britain).

Kemmers, Fleur. 2006. *Coins for a Legion: An analysis of the coin finds from Augustan legionary fortress and Flavian Canabae Legionis at Nijmegen*. Studien zu Fundmünzen der Antike vol. 21. Mainz am Rhein: Von Zabern.

Kemmers, Fleur. 2014. 'Buying loyalty: targeted iconography and the distribution of cash to the legions'. In *De l´or pour les braves! Soldes, armées et circulation monétaire dans le monde romain*, edited by M. Reddé, 229–41. Collection Scripta Antiqua 69. Pessac: Ausonius Publications.

King, Cathy E. 1996. 'Roman copies'. In *Coin Finds and Coin Use in the Roman World*, edited by C.E. King and D.G. Wigg, 237–63. Berlin: Gebr. Mann Verlag.

Komnick, Holger, 2001. *Die Restitutionsmünzen der frühen Kaiserzeit: Aspekte der Kaiserlegitimation*. Berlin: Berlin: De Gruyter.

Lockyear, Kris. 2000. 'Site finds in Roman Britain: a comparison of techniques', *Oxford Journal of Archaeology* 19(4): 397–423.

MacDowall, David W. 1979. *The Western Coinages of Nero*. Numismatic Notes and Monographs no. 161. New York: American Numismatic Society.

Mairat, Jerome. 2014. 'The coinage of the Gallic empire'. Unpublished D.Phil. thesis, University of Oxford.

Mairat, Jerome, Andrew Wilson and Christopher Howgego (eds). 2022. *Coin Hoards and Hoarding in the Roman World*. Oxford: Oxford University Press.

Marzano, Annalisa. 2009. 'Trajanic building projects on base-metal denominations and audience targeting', *Papers of the British School at Rome* 77: 125–58.

McConnell, Joseph R., Andrew I. Wilson, Andreas Stohl, Monica M. Arienzo, Nathan J. Chellman, Sabine Eckhardt, Elizabeth M. Thompson, A. Mark Pollard and Jørgen Peder Steffensen. 2018. 'Lead pollution recorded in Greenland ice indicates European emissions tracked plagues, wars, and imperial expansion during antiquity', *Proceedings of the National Academy of Sciences* 115(22): 5726–31.

Meadows, Andrew and Jonathan Williams. 2001. 'Moneta and the monuments: coinage and politics in Republican Rome', *Journal of Roman Studies* 91: 27–49.

Metcalf, William E. 1993. 'Whose liberalitas? Propaganda and audience in the Early Roman Empire', *Rivista italiana di numismatica* 95: 337–46.

Millar, Fergus. 1991. 'Les congiaires à Rome et la monnaie'. In *Nourrir la plèbe: actes du colloque tenu à Genève les 28/29.ix.1989 en hommage à Denis van Berchem*, edited by A. Giovannini, 143–57. Schweizerische Beiträge zur Altertumswissenschaft 22. Basel: F. Reinhardt.

Morstein-Marx, Robert. 2004. *Mass Oratory and Political Power in the Late Roman Republic*. Cambridge: Cambridge University Press.

Noreña, Carlos F. 2001. 'The communication of the emperor's virtues', *Journal of Roman Studies* 91: 146–68.

Noreña, Carlos F. 2011. *Imperial Ideals in the Roman West: Representation, circulation, power*. Cambridge: Cambridge University Press.

Ripollès, Pere P. 2005. 'Coinage and identity in the Roman provinces: Spain'. In *Coinage and Identity in the Roman Provinces*, edited by Christopher Howgego, Volker Heuchert and Andrew Burnett, 79–93. Oxford: Oxford University Press.

Rowan, Clare. 2012. *Under Divine Auspices: Divine ideology and the visualisation of imperial power in the Severan period*. Cambridge: Cambridge University Press.

Smith, Alexander, Martyn Allen, Tom Brindle and Michael Fulford. 2016. *New Visions of the Countryside of Roman Britain, vol. 1: The rural settlement of Roman Britain*. Britannia monographs series 29. London: The Society for the Promotion of Roman Studies.

Stroobants, Fran. 2017. 'The long-term monetization of Sagalassos: questioning monetary production, circulation and use from a regional perspective'. Unpublished PhD thesis, University of Leuven.

Stroobants, Fran. 2018. 'Daily coin use and the level of monetization at Roman Sagalassos and its territory'. In *Proceedings of the Second International Congress on the History of Money and Numismatics in the Mediterranean World, Antalya, 5–8 January 2017*, edited by Oğuz Tekin. Antalya: AKMED, Koç University, Suna & İnan Kıraç Research Center for Mediterranean Civilization.

Sutherland, C. Humphrey V. 1951. *Coinage in Roman Imperial Policy 31 BC–AD 68*. London: Methuen.

Sutherland, C. Humphrey V. 1976. *The Emperor and the Coinage: Julio-Claudian studies*. London: Spink and Son Ltd.

Sutherland, C. Humphrey V. 1987. *Roman History and Coinage 44 BC–AD 69*. Oxford: Clarendon Press.

von Kaenel, Hans-Markus. 1999. 'Zum Münzumlauf im augusteischen Rom anhand der Funde aus dem Tiber. Mit einem Nachtrag zur geldgeschichtlichen Bedeutung der Münzfunde in Kalkriese'. In *Rom, Germanien und die Ausgrabungen von Kalkriese*, edited by W. Schlüter and R. Wieetgels, 363–79. Osnabrück: Universitätsverlag Rasch.

Walker, David. 1988. *Roman Coins from the Sacred Spring at Bath*. Oxford: Oxford University Committee for Archaeology/Institute of Archaeology.

Wallace-Hadrill, Andrew. 2008. *Rome's Cultural Revolution*. Cambridge: Cambridge University Press.

Walton, Philippa. 2012. *Rethinking Roman Britain: Coinage and archaeology*. Wetteren: Moneta.

Wiseman, Timothy P. 1985. *Catullus and his World: A reappraisal*. Cambridge: Cambridge University Press.

Wiseman, Timothy P. 1998. *Roman Drama and Roman History*. Exeter: University of Exeter Press.

Wiseman, Timothy P. 2009. *Remembering the Roman People: Essays on late-republican politics and literature*. Oxford: Oxford University Press.

Woolf, Greg. 1998. *Becoming Roman: The origins of provincial civilization in Gaul*. Cambridge: Cambridge University Press.

Wolters, Reinhard. 2000–1. 'Bronze, silver or gold? Coin finds and the pay of the Roman army', *Zephyrus* 53–4: 579–88.

Wolters, Reinhard. 2012. 'The Julio-Claudians'. In *The Oxford Handbook of Greek and Roman Coinage*, edited by William E. Metcalf, 335–55. Oxford: Oxford University Press.

Woytek, Bernhard E. 2012. 'The denarius coinage of the Roman Republic'. In *The Oxford Handbook of Greek and Roman Coinage*, edited by William E. Metcalf, 315–34. Oxford: Oxford University Press.

Woytek, Bernhard E. 2022. 'The imperial afterlife of Roman Republican coins and the phenomenon of the restored denarii'. In *Coin Hoards and Hoarding in the Roman World*, edited by Jerome Mairat, Andrew Wilson and Christopher Howgego, 237–72. Oxford: Oxford University Press.

4

Trade in the Roman Empire

Andrew Wilson

Introduction: key debates

Back in the 1970s and 1980s, the debates over Roman trade centred around the question of whether there was much long-distance trade in goods other than luxuries. Sir Moses Finley, in his *The Ancient Economy*, had flatly denied that there was any significant non-luxury trade, basing his opinion on the works of ancient authors, largely members of the aristocratic elite (Finley 1973; 1985). Finley's view was very influential among ancient historians for over two decades (e.g. Whittaker 1985), but others, especially archaeologists, vigorously resisted it, objecting that the material evidence showed that staple goods travelled huge distances in quantities that could only be explained by trade (e.g. Carandini 1983; Pucci 1983; Greene 1986; Peacock and Williams 1986; Fentress and Perkins 1988). At the heart of the debate lay the relative weight that one should assign to textual evidence (which may reflect the biases of particular authorial classes) and to archaeological evidence (which may be skewed because of biases in survival, recovery or publication).

That debate is long over, the growing flood of archaeological publications having demonstrated irrefutably that trade in a wide variety of non-luxury goods was extensive and pervasive (Wilson and Bowman 2018a: 1–6). In parallel, the publication of Horden and Purcell's book *The Corrupting Sea* in 2000 introduced a new and sophisticated environmental conceptual framework explaining the impetus towards long-distance exchange in the Mediterranean. They argued that although the Mediterranean shares an essential similarity of climate and environment at a broad scale, characterised by among other features extreme inter-annual variability of rainfall, it is locally fragmented into a series of micro-regions each with its own micro-climate. The inter-annual variability of rainfall is locally modulated so that different regions might experience a good or a bad harvest in the same year. This uncertainty drove farmers, in Horden and Purcell's words, to 'diversify, store, redistribute'. Diversification of crops spreads risk, and insurance against a bad year could be managed by storing goods that would keep (for either local consumption in a future year, or trade to a region in deficit), or by trading goods that could not keep, in return for cash that could be used to import from elsewhere in a year of shortage locally. Long-distance trade in agricultural staples became essential to manage the uncertainties of yields, and the diversity of micro-regions set up the need for frequent and repeated connections (trading and otherwise) between them – a phenomenon that Horden and Purcell call 'connectivity'. *The Corrupting Sea* has been an extraordinarily influential work, attracting reactions both positive and negative (e.g. Parker 2000; van Dommelen 2000; Fentress and Fentress 2001; Shaw 2001; Malkin 2003; responses in Horden and Purcell 2020), but the basic point about the impetus of Mediterranean 'connectivity' in driving long-distance trade has survived the critiques.

In the place of the debate initiated by *The Ancient Economy* a series of new questions now command attention. To what degree can we trace fluctuations in the volume of trade over time (see e.g. Fentress et al. 2004; Wilson 2009; Wilson and Bowman 2018b)? What was the role of the state? Did the Roman state actively encourage trade, and did it intervene in the market? How significant was trade to the state, in terms of taxes and customs duties? How did the state organise the food supply for the city of Rome, and for the armies on the frontiers – through taxation, through requisitions, or bulk purchase of harvests in advance (Wilson and Bowman 2018b)? And did these flows of goods for a state market stimulate trade in goods for a private market? How integrated was the Roman market economy (for contrasting extreme positions see Bang 2007; Temin 2013)? Did trade form a significant part of elite revenue streams (Wallace-Hadrill 1991; Morley 2000; Tchernia 2016)? Was maritime trade characterised predominantly by 'le grand commerce maritime' – organised repeat flows of bulk shipping between major entrepôts, with local redistribution from them – or by tramping (or 'cabotage'), a smaller-scale pattern of opportunistic coastal trading from port to port, implying much less knowledge or information about conditions in distant markets (Nieto 1997; Horden and Purcell 2000; Morley 2007: 102; Wilson 2011a: 53–54; 2011b; Wilson et al. 2012)?

What was the scale and nature of trade beyond the frontiers of the empire (see e.g.: Silk Roads: McLaughlin 2016; Graf 2018; Red Sea and Indo-Roman trade: Tomber 2008; 2018; McLaughlin 2010; 2014; De Romanis and Maiuri 2015; Cobb 2018a; 2018b; Nappo 2018; Davidde 2018; De Romanis 2020; Saharan trade: Wilson 2012; 2018; Mattingly 2013; Mattingly et al. 2017)?

There is no space here to deal with all of these questions. In this chapter I shall concentrate on the evidence for long-distance trade in pottery, the state's investment in transport infrastructure to support trade, state intervention in the supply of the city of Rome, and the significance of trade beyond the frontiers of the empire.

Tracing trade

Tracing trade in the archaeological record typically relies on being able to identify the region of origin of particular artefacts or materials, and then compare the region of origin with the pattern of distribution of known examples. Such approaches demonstrate an extensive trade in particular types of stone, especially marble for architecture and sculpture (Russell 2013), and timber for construction (Harris 2018; Bernabei et al. 2019).

Pottery is ubiquitous on Roman sites and, for this reason, it is one of the main classes of goods studied by archaeologists. Ceramic petrology allows the identification of source regions of production by matching inclusions in the clay to local geology; assessing the distribution of products of known origin then enables one to gain an idea of trade in those products (Peacock 1974; Tomber and Dore 1998). For the Roman period, the common but not universal practice of stamping many products with the name of the workshop owner or manager can also assist fine-grained analysis of distribution patterns (Oxé et al. 2000; Hartley et al. 2008–11).

Examples of long-distance trade in non-luxuries are provided by the distribution of red gloss table pottery. From about 40 BCE onwards a very popular red gloss tableware, known to modern scholars as Italian Terra Sigillata (ITS), was made at centres in northern Italy, such as Arezzo, Pisa and a number of sites in the upper Tiber Valley north of Rome (Sternini 2019). Its attractive, lustrous red slip and elegant forms assured its popularity, and this pottery was mass-produced in phenomenal quantities. Elegant as it is, it ranks somewhat below metal plates and cups, and possibly below glassware, in terms of status and cost. These are not really luxury goods, yet they achieved very wide distribution. A few *terra sigillata* vessels had closed shapes

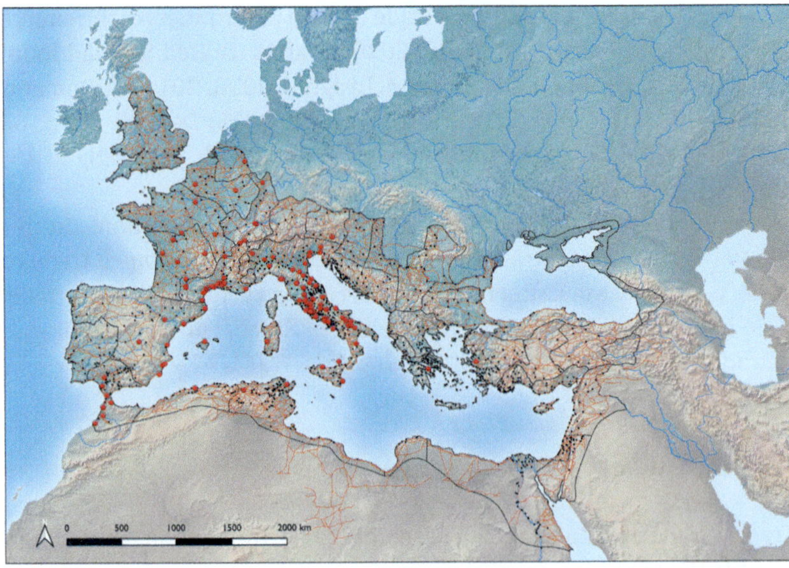

Figure 4.1 Distribution of dated name-stamped *terra sigillata* pottery from the Arezzo workshops, 40 BCE–20/15 BCE. © A. Wilson; pottery data from the Samian Research website by Allard Mees/RGZM: https://www1.rgzm.de/samian/; other data as Fig. 4.5.

and were wheel-thrown, but the majority were open forms (dishes, bowls), which stacked easily for transport, and were mass-produced by mould-forming techniques.

Between 40 and 20/15 BCE, the main centre of production was at Arezzo (ancient Arretium), producing both black and red wares, in non-standardised shapes (Oxé et al. 2000). This 'Arretine Ware' rapidly captured the emerging markets of the central and western Mediterranean (Figure 4.1). It also reached the eastern Mediterranean, and was even exported as far afield as India (Wheeler et al. 1946; Begley 1993; Oxé et al. 2000). From about 20 BCE to 15 CE the production of Arretine ware peaked, with the highest level of output, in standardised shapes; it appears in large quantities at the forts of the Rhine frontier (Figure 4.2). Other workshops making similar pottery were established elsewhere, in the Po Valley and in Campania, some of which were producing pottery stamped ARRETINVM as though it was in fact made at Arezzo. Workshops were also established at Lyon in Gaul in this period. From about 15 CE to 50 CE the workshops of the Po Valley became dominant, again producing standard shapes.

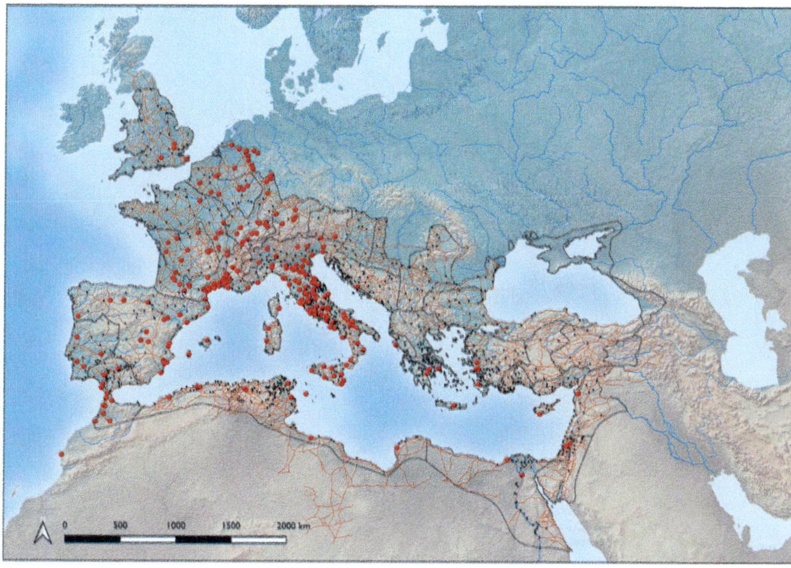

Figure 4.2 Distribution of dated name-stamped *terra sigillata* pottery from the Arezzo workshops, 20 BCE–15 CE. © A. Wilson; pottery data from the Samian Research website by Allard Mees/RGZM: https://www1.rgzm.de/samian/; other data as Fig. 4.5.

But already from the late first century BCE Arretine ware was being imitated in France, first at Lyon and then at the large pottery production centre of La Graufesenque in southern France. Many of these vessels are stamped with the name of their producer, and this enables us to see that some of the key producers from northern Italy were involved. There is still unresolved debate as to whether this means that Italian producers were setting up branch workshops in Gaul, to be nearer those markets, or whether the producers were actually migrating from Italy to Gaul. What is clear is that within a matter of years the Gaulish production captured the north-western European market formerly dominated by the Italian products (Figures 4.3 and 4.4). Over the course of the first century CE the significance and market share of the Italian pottery production declined and was largely replaced by the Gaulish wares.

The pattern of establishing new production centres closer to developing markets continued, and other large centres of pottery production grew up in southern Gaul at Montans (Augustan to late Antonine period), whose products were traded throughout western Gaul and into northern Spain; and in central Gaul at Les Martres-de-Veyre, exporting mainly in the first half of the second century CE, and Lézoux

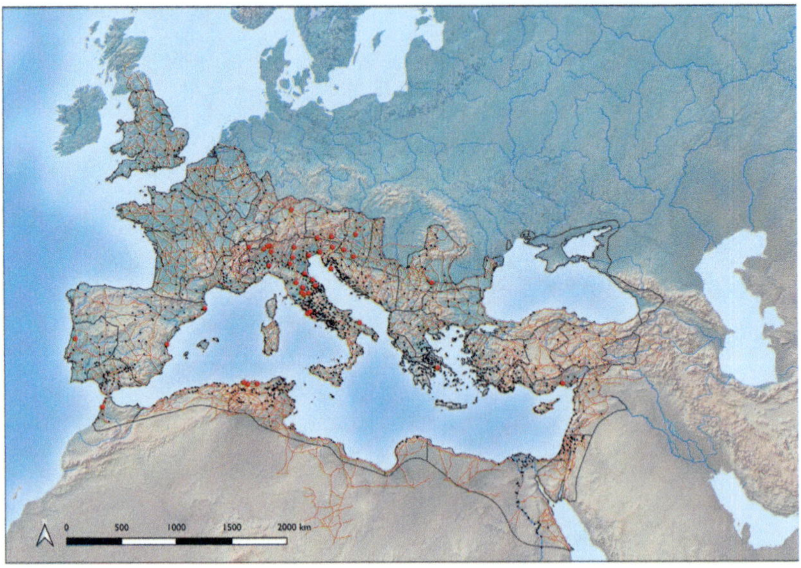

Figure 4.3 Distribution of dated name-stamped *terra sigillata* pottery from the Arezzo workshops, 20–60 CE. © A. Wilson; pottery data from the Samian Research website by Allard Mees/RGZM: https://www1.rgzm.de/samian/; other data as Fig. 4.5.

(Augustan to late second century). Their products were distributed throughout northern and eastern Gaul and reached Britain, the Rhineland and the Danube provinces. Sites in eastern Gaul and the Rhineland – Rheinzabern, Trier and the Argonne – supplied not only their own regions but also Britain and the Danube provinces, particularly in the second century and until a little after the middle of the third (Bémont and Jacob 1986). In Spain, *terra sigillata hispánica*, produced at Tritium Magallum (Tricio) in La Rioja in the upper Ebro valley, is widely distributed through much of the Iberian peninsula, but not often found outside it.

In the eastern Mediterranean, four main fineware types have been identified: Eastern Sigillata A, B, C and D (abbreviated ESA, ESB, ESC and ESD). Of these, production centres have been definitively identified only for ESC, in the region of Pergamon and at Çandarli on the Aegean coast. ESA was made somewhere in the Maeander valley of western Turkey, perhaps at Tralles (modern Aydın); ESB somewhere in the Levantine coastal region between Tarsos and Latakia; and ESD probably in western Cyprus (Hayes 1994; Bes 2015). All these wares were exported across the eastern Mediterranean (Carrignon et al. 2022), but those produced near larger urban centres were more widely and effectively distributed

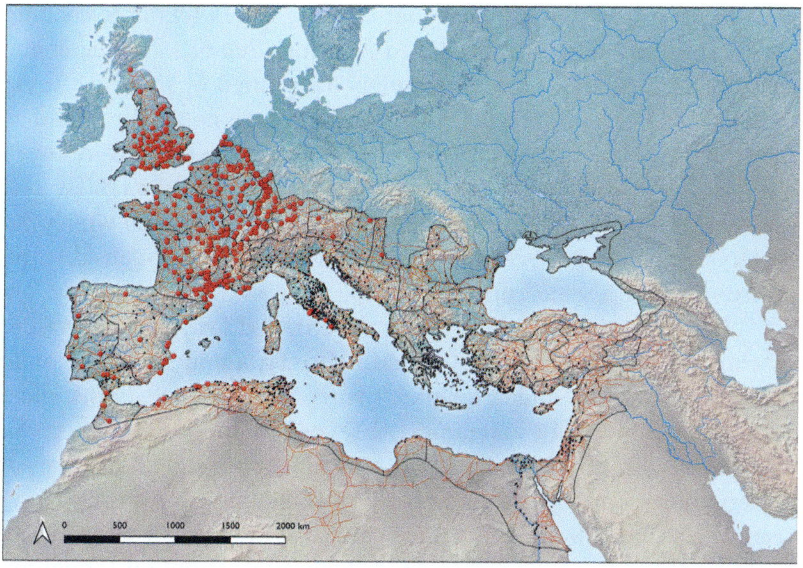

Figure 4.4 Distribution of dated name-stamped *terra sigillata* pottery from La Graufesenque, 20–60 CE. © A. Wilson; pottery data from the Samian Research website by Allard Mees/RGZM: https://www1.rgzm.de/samian/; other data as Fig. 4.5.

(Hanson et al. 2022). But the Gaulish and other western productions began to face competition in their turn from products made in what is now Tunisia, Africa Red Slip ware (ARS), which began to be exported from North Africa around 90 CE, and is found in large quantities at sites throughout the western Mediterranean in the second and third centuries, and across the whole of the Mediterranean from the fourth century onwards (Hayes 1972; Bonifay 2018; 2022). The extraordinary success of ARS is thought to be explained by its travelling from Africa with grain cargoes to Portus, and its wider distribution was then assisted by travelling as return cargoes on ships heading back to other parts of the Mediterranean (Fentress and Perkins 1988). Its distribution to the eastern Mediterranean really occurs only after the foundation of Constantinople, and may be due to the gravitational pull of the new capital.

The significance of the distribution of different tablewares such as ITS, Gaulish sigillata and ARS is not that they were valuable items in themselves (they were not, particularly), but that they show how large trade flows in relatively low-value, common items were possible on an interprovincial scale, and how major production centres might compete with each other for geographical markets. The point is made even more strongly by the fact that cooking wares (ceramic cooking pots, pans and casseroles) produced in certain regions – for example, coastal North Africa – were also widely distributed by maritime trade to the coastal regions of other provinces, although not so far inland as the tablewares (Leitch 2011). This suggests that the cooking wares were cheaper and less resilient to the costs of transport than the tablewares, but that nevertheless the flows in bulk maritime goods, on which the pottery cargoes piggy-backed, were considerable enough to subsidise the transport of the ceramic cargoes.

Tablewares and cooking wares were traded for their own value; by contrast, another common class of pottery, amphorae or ceramic transport jars, were traded for their contents – principally wine, olive oil or fish products, but sometimes other commodities too (alum, pitch, salt, even grain). The distribution of both amphorae and other forms of pottery shows a coastal concentration and, sometimes, a clustering along river valleys, illustrating how the cheaper costs of maritime and riverine trade, compared to road transport, influenced distribution (Loughton 2003). Importantly, however, distribution was not limited to riverine and coastal areas, and the distribution of Arretine pottery in Gaul, and La Graufesenque pottery throughout Gaul and Britain, even well away from the main navigable rivers, shows that road transport was therefore *not* prohibitively expensive. The facile assumption that it must have been, common in scholarship of the 1980s and 1990s (e.g. Finley 1985: 32, 126) and even persisting later in some quarters, ignores fundamental technological issues to which I now turn.

The role of the state: investment in infrastructure

The Roman period saw considerable improvements in overland trade, with developments in wheeled transport (suspension, movable front axles for steering: Greene 1986: 38–9); and roads, bridges and communications infrastructure. This latter factor is especially important; the Roman Empire built thousands of kilometres of roads (Figure 4.5), as part of a state policy that while militarily driven nonetheless also recognised the economic benefits (cf. also Pliny *Letters* 10.41, 42, 61 and 62, on the economic benefits of cutting a transport canal in Bithynia).

Roman roads were usually paved or metalled, with lateral drainage ditches, in contrast to later, medieval, roads that were unpaved tracks covering wide swathes of ground so that livestock could be driven along them and riders and carts had ample opportunity to meander around the

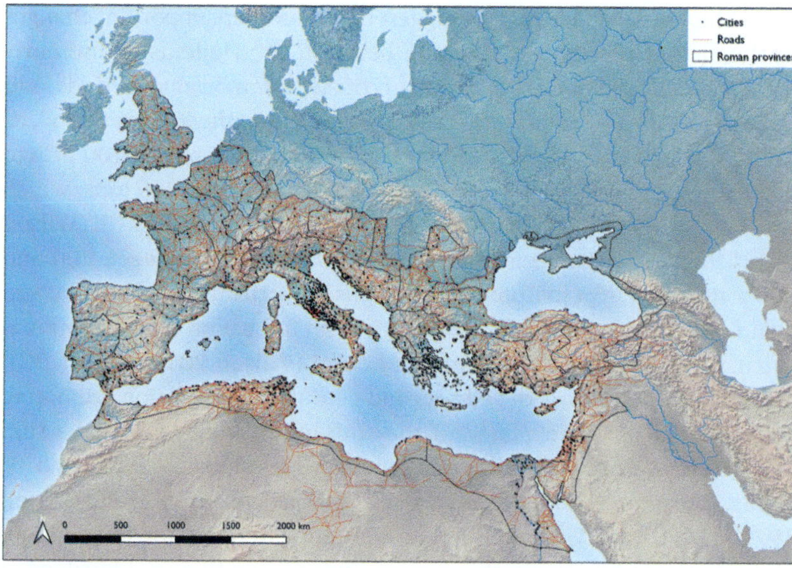

Figure 4.5 Cities and the road network of the Roman Empire. © A. Wilson; cities: Jack Hanson; roads: Ancient World Mapping Centre; provincial boundaries: Andrei Nacu.

worst of the mud. In the Roman world, conditions of security enabled greater capital investment in built road infrastructure to facilitate the physical progress of travel by wheeled traffic (Hitchner 2012; cf. Laurence, Chapter 1 this volume). The point is underlined by the difference between Roman and medieval bridges: the vast majority of Roman bridges were wide enough for two vehicles to pass; many medieval bridges, by contrast, at least in northern Europe, were narrow and steep humpbacked affairs intended for packhorses rather than wheeled transport. Put simply, the transport infrastructure of the Roman Empire was vastly superior to that of medieval Europe.

Effective long-distance trade networks required considerable infrastructure. For maritime trade this was made possible by improvements in shipping technology (greater capacity, improved bilge pumping equipment, faster sailing times), harbour construction (with concrete that could set under water) and harbour infrastructure such as cranes and dredging vessels (three were found at the port of Marseille) (Wilson 2011a; 2011b). It has been proposed that a dramatic reduction between the first and second centuries CE in the number of known shipwrecks may be in part the result of increased harbour construction, particularly along the Italian and Gaulish coasts (Robinson et al. 2020).

Shipwreck evidence does suggest that there were important changes in the size of the largest shipping between the Hellenistic and early medieval periods. Small ships were, of course, common at all periods, and ships of less than 75 tons were common throughout the Roman period, as they were both before and afterwards. But during the period 100 BCE to 300 CE we find wrecks of well over 200 tons, even over 350 tons, which we do not before about 100 BCE or between 400 CE and 1000 CE (Wilson 2011b: 212–17). The transport of obelisks weighing between 200 and 500 tons from Egypt to Rome in the reigns of Augustus and Caligula, and again under Constantine in 337 CE, gives an indication of the minimum capacity of the ships needed to carry them (Wilson 2011a: 40, n. 33). Most telling, perhaps, is the late-second-century CE regulation exempting shipowners from civic *munera* if they put at the state's disposal a ship of *c*.340 tons, or several ships of *c*.70 tons (Suetonius, *Claudius* 18.3–4; Gaius, *Institutes* 1.32C; Scaevola, *apud Digestam* 50.5.3; cf. Casson 1971: 171, n. 23). This implies that such ships were not too uncommon, and affordable by private shipowners. Indeed, the financial burdens of *munera* were so heavy that elite landowners were thus encouraged to invest in large shipping to escape them.

Large ships required more effective propulsion. The addition of a foremast is seen already on some ships of the sixth century BCE (Casson 1971: 70, 240), and became a regular feature of larger Roman merchantmen, as on an early third-century CE mosaic from the frigidarium of the baths at the small port of Themetra near Sousse – the foremast sharply raked forward and carrying a square sail (Foucher 1958; 1967). In combination, the evidence for improved shipbuilding technology, larger ships and harbour construction in the Roman period supports the view that large-scale maritime trade flows directed between major ports ('le grand commerce maritime'), rather than opportunistic tramping, explains the widespread distribution of goods visible (chiefly in the form of ceramics and amphorae) in the archaeological record (Nieto 1997; Wilson 2011a: 53–54; 2011b; Wilson et al. 2012).

The role of the state: supplying Rome

The *annona*

When considering the involvement of the Roman state in the economy, it is impossible to ignore the *annona*. The handout of free or subsidised grain at Rome was an important aspect of Roman politics from 123 BCE onwards, and imperial attempts to secure and safeguard the grain supply to prevent political unrest resulted in the creation of first the Claudian and then the Trajanic harbours at Portus. The emperor Claudius began construction of the first harbour in 42 CE after a bread riot in Rome, when the crowd pelted him with stale crusts, because the grain fleet from Alexandria had not been able to dock and supply grain in the quantities required, and there was a grain shortage (Suetonius, *Claudius* 20). In 100–112 CE Trajan built the inner, landlocked hexagonal harbour, which increased capacity and provided a safer and more sheltered anchorage than the Claudian harbour, whose basin was so big that it did not prevent ships at anchor being wrecked within it, during a large storm only a few years after it had been built (Tacitus, *Annals* 15.18; on the harbour at Portus, see Keay and Paroli 2011; Keay 2012).

But, although we have the impressive harbour remains, the perishability of grain makes tracing the *annona* institutions at Rome through the material record almost impossible. Instead, I want to focus on what I see as an analogous initiative for another foodstuff, olive oil.

The supply of olive oil to the city of Rome

Near the Tiber in Rome is the large roughly triangular hill of Monte Testaccio – 'potsherd mountain', covering an area of 20,000 m^2 at its base and 35 m high, but probably once considerably higher (Figure 4.6) (Blázquez Martínez and Remesal Rodríguez 1999; 2014; Funari 2001). It is entirely artificial, composed of fragments of amphorae which have been deliberately smashed *in situ*. They are all olive oil amphorae, and over 80 per cent are the so-called Dressel 20 type from Baetica in south-west Spain. The total quantity is estimated at 24.75 million amphorae accumulated over nearly 300 years.

The exclusive composition of olive oil amphorae suggests that this is something other than simply an oversized urban waste dump, and study of the composition of the hill confirms this. Discard was not haphazard but done in an organised way; the amphorae were carried up whole and smashed on the spot (excavation has shown that they can be completely reconstructed), and as the dump grew it was raised in level terraces with retaining walls built of amphora sherds. The formation goes back much earlier than 138 CE and probably to Augustus or Claudius. The coarse layers composed of thick fragments of Spanish Dressel 20 amphorae were stabilised by packing them with the smaller debris from the lighter, thinner-walled African amphorae. Then everything was carefully sprinkled with powdered lime to neutralise the rancid smell. All

Figure 4.6 Monte Testaccio, an artificial mound 100 feet high, composed of broken olive oil amphorae. © A. Wilson.

this points to a centralised and highly organised discard of the packaging containers for olive oil coming into Rome, the scale of which immediately suggests some form of state involvement.

This idea is confirmed by a study of the amphorae, especially the Dressel 20s – a globular Spanish olive oil amphora produced in the Guadalcuivir valley in south-west Spain. This type is common around the western and central Mediterranean, but is distributed mainly in north-west Europe (especially in Britain and on the Rhine frontier; military sites especially), and is also found in large numbers at Rome. Production started in the first century CE, and continued until the third quarter of the third century – it is last attested in 267 CE.

Particularly important for an interpretation of the purpose and function of Monte Testaccio is the fact that the Dressel 20 olive oil amphorae found there all seem to have carried inscriptions – *tituli picti* – written in black ink on the body of the amphorae just below the neck. Since these were written after firing, they must relate to the contents rather than to the production of the amphorae, and detailed analysis shows that they followed a highly organised schema.

Five main classes of inscription have been recognised, referred to as alpha through epsilon, of which the first three are always present on the Dressel 20s from Monte Testaccio, and the last two may be present:

α = empty weight of amphora, in Roman pounds.

β = name, in capitals, of the *navicularius* or shipper; from the third century on, after confiscation of estates in the civil war of 192–3 CE, it is replaced by the formula *Fisci rationis patrimoni(i) provinciae Baeticae* ('belonging to the treasury of the province of Baetica').

γ = weight of contents, in Roman pounds.

δ = up to five lines of cursive script; the mark of the authorities controlling export. May contain some or all of: date (by consular year), names of officers performing the export check, estate where the product is from, and the town where control was carried out (usually Hispalis, Seville).

ε = a numeral, whose significance is uncertain, but which may relate to loading or storage.

As different *tituli* on the same amphorae are often in different scripts, several people were involved in adding these records to the amphorae, at different times.

The nature of these *tituli picti* differs radically from those on amphorae of wine or fish products, which are usually more concerned to advertise the contents; here the emphasis is on checking quantity and, sometimes by reference to estates, quality. The emphasis on control confirms a state involvement, which can also be linked to the epigraphic attestation of an *adiutor praefecti annonae ad oleum Afrum et Hispanum recensendu* ('assistant to the prefect of the *annona* for assessing African and Spanish oil') at Rome in the mid-second century CE (*CIL* II.1180). The combination of centralised discard and the rigorous checking of contents indicates a highly organised system in which the state intervened to check the quantity and quality of product for which it has contracted. The Roman state did not hand out olive oil free as part of the *annona* until the reign of Septimius Severus, yet Monte Testaccio began much earlier than that. What, then, is going on?

The most plausible answer seems to be that, since olive oil was in vast demand in the ancient world – as a foodstuff, as lamp fuel, as massage oil and mechanical lubricant – it was a staple product, and since the demand generated by a city the size of Rome was enormous, the state intervened to ensure that it reached Rome in sufficient quantities. Shortages, for whatever reason, would cause price spikes and this could provoke unrest, just as disruptions to the grain supply did. The quantities involved are too great to be seen simply as taxation in kind, and it must be presumed that the state contracted with producers in Baetica to purchase oil at a price agreed beforehand. The producers gained the security of knowing that they had sold perhaps their entire harvest while it was still on the tree, while the state had obtained an assured price and contracted for a fixed quantity. (The advance sale of grain, wine and olive oil was not uncommon in the Roman world: see Erdkamp 2005: 120–34.) On this hypothesis, the state must then have sold the oil at Rome, since it was not handing it out free; but this would provide a context for decanting the oil from the 66-litre amphorae, which were optimised for maritime transport, into smaller vessels more convenient for retail throughout the city. At this point the amphorae needed to be disposed of – and since they carried state control marks, it was all the more desirable to smash them and ensure they could not circulate further for fraudulent reuse. This reconstruction, while hypothetical, has the merit of accounting for all the observed evidence in a way that I think alternatives cannot. It also supports the view that the other main concentration of Dressel 20 olive oil amphorae, on the north-western frontiers, is the result of state contracts for military supply. Note, though, that this is the state intervening in the market primarily as a large customer with the negotiating power for a bulk discount; it does not exclude private activity, and indeed the merchants handling the shipments were not retained by the state but seem to have interacted with it on a private basis.

Since excavations at Monte Testaccio have not got below the levels of 138 CE, we do not know when this phenomenon starts, although it has been suggested that the formation of Monte Testaccio may have originated in the reign of Claudius or even Augustus. At the other end of the scale, none of the *tituli picti* is later than 267 CE; and there are no amphorae of the form Dressel 23, the late and smaller replacement of the Dressel 20, first attested on the Port Vendres wreck alongside Dressel 20s in 267 CE. This period, the sole reign of Gallienus, saw the collapse of the silver currency and a temporary massive drop in the fineness of gold coinage. The conclusion seems inescapable that the fiscal difficulties faced by the state in 267 CE, and the loss of Spain to the Gallic Empire, which was in revolt from the centre, rendered the operation unfeasible and brought it to an end. Even when the later Dressel 23 olive oil amphorae from Baetica are found on other sites, they are never inscribed with *tituli picti* as the Dressel 20s are, showing that the system requiring the imperial checks and record-keeping had ended.

The area where the majority of the amphorae from Monte Testaccio – the Dressel 20s – originated was the province of Baetica in south-west Spain, and especially the valleys of the Guadalcuivir and the Genil (Mattingly 1988: 38–44). Baetican olive oil had a reputation for quality – African olive oil by contrast had a poorer reputation, although it was still in demand, especially for lamp fuel. The lower plain of the Guadalcuivir valley was devoid of villas and associated olive presses and may have been used for growing cereals. Across the higher ground, though, which would have favoured intensive oil cultivation, there is an even scatter of villas, farms and oil press sites – some farms have two, three or four presses. The kiln sites for the Dressel 20 amphorae, however, are concentrated along the rivers of the Guadalcuivir and the Genil, arguing for overland transport of the oil from the farms in skins, to specialised bottling plants on the rivers which bottled the produce of multiple estates. Over 70 different kiln sites are known to have produced Dressel 20s, some with batteries of multiple kilns (Mattingly 1988: 38–44). Here we can see large-scale investment in processing plant for export production, and vertical specialisation within the industry, and we can argue that in part this was stimulated by the security of the guaranteed market for the oil which the state constituted. In essence, if the state was regularly contracting with the same landowners to purchase large quantities of their olive oil, there was a considerable incentive to invest in processing machinery, which enabled producers to maximise their production and sell more to a reliable buyer whose demand was enormous.

The significance of external trade to the Roman state

Rome's external trade has been the subject of a growing amount of research in recent years, and it is increasingly clear that trade with the Indian subcontinent was not merely a small-scale trade in exotic luxuries, but a phenomenon of great significance both fiscally and culturally: pepper and incense have been found on civilian sites in the northern provinces (e.g. Tomber 2008; McLaughlin 2010; 2014; 2016; Sidebotham 2011; De Romanis and Maiuri 2015; Cobb 2018a; 2018b; Wilson and Bowman 2018b). The annexation of Egypt after the defeat of Antony and Cleopatra at Actium in 31 BCE gave Rome a gateway to the Red Sea and Indian Ocean trade routes (Figure 4.7). This enabled capitalisation on the relatively recent discovery of the monsoon winds, which facilitated a direct passage to and from India, rather than coast-hopping around the Arabian peninsula (Casson 1980; Tchernia 2005); and the introduction of Mediterranean shipbuilding technologies to the Red Sea ports allowed the construction of large ships, of several hundred tons' burden, that could ride out the sea conditions created by the monsoons, so that those direct routes could now be exploited on a regular basis. Finally, the development of the road infrastructure between the Nile and the Red Sea, begun by the Ptolemies, was improved to service caravans, so that goods could be offloaded at Berenike or Myos Hormos and carried across the

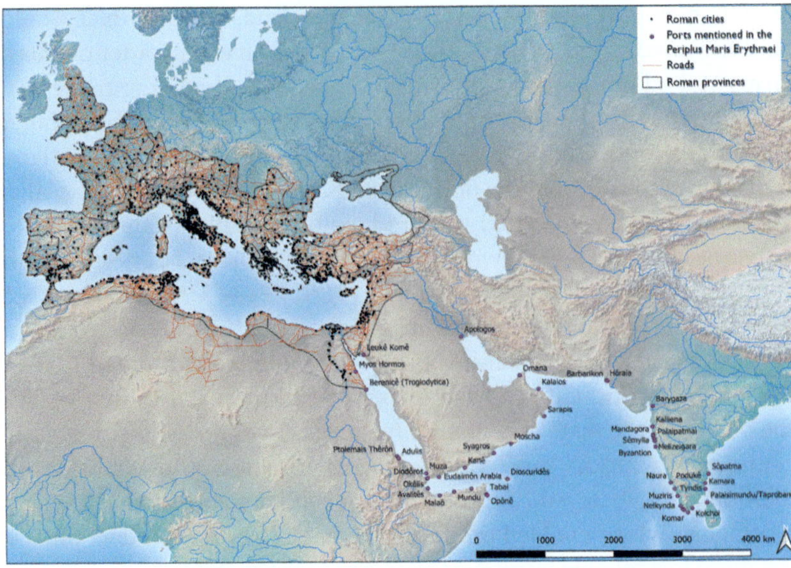

Figure 4.7 The Roman Empire and the ports mentioned in the *Periplus Maris Erythraei*. © A. Wilson/Oxford Roman Economy Project, with the assistance of Giada Manzinali.

desert to the Nile, avoiding the need for ships to beat up the Red Sea to Suez against the prevailing northerly winds which made sailing difficult in the northern Red Sea (on Red Sea sailing conditions, see Cooper 2011).

In the first century CE the Roman state established fortified watering points or *hydreumata* along the roads from Koptos on the Nile to the Red Sea ports at Myos Hormos and Berenike (Figure 4.8). Perhaps as early as the reign of Augustus, cisterns were built at the forts of Apollonos Hydreuma, Compasi and Berenike (*ILS* 2483; Kennedy 1985; De Romanis 1996: 219–24; Bagnall et al. 2001: 330), and more fortified wells and cisterns were built at other sites in 76/77 CE, at the direction of the prefect of Egypt, as attested by inscriptions from the forts at Didymoi and Aphrodites, and at Wadi Sikayt near Berenike (Plin. *HN* 6.102–3; see Sidebotham 2011: 125–74 for the most recent synthesis on the routes across the Eastern Desert in the Roman period). Caravans using these routes across the desert had to pay a tax, which defrayed the costs of maintaining the transport infrastructure, and were provided with armed escorts for protection against nomadic desert tribes (Sidebotham 1986: 80–81; *OGIS* 674, the Koptos Tariff of 90 CE, sets out the charges for these travel permits). The main motive for the creation and upkeep

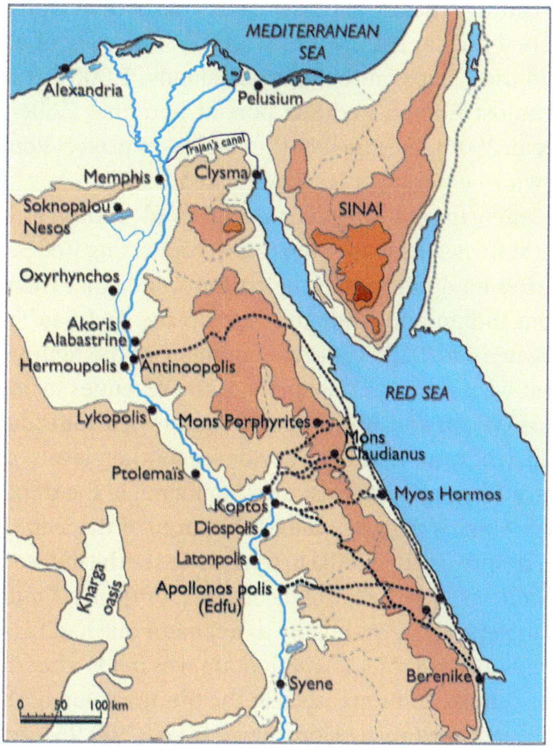

Figure 4.8 Roman Egypt: routes between the Nile and the Red Sea. © M. Anastasi/A. Wilson, based on a map by J.-P. Brun.

of the Koptos–Berenike and Myos Hormos routes and their associated water-supply infrastructure was clearly to support the Red Sea and Indian Ocean trade and the transfer of those cargoes to the Nile Valley.

This state policy was continued and even extended in the first half of the second century CE: Trajan had a road built between Aila on the Red Sea and Bosra in southern Syria, the Via Nova; he also dredged and revived the old canal linking Clysma (Suez) with the Nile at Babylon (Old Cairo), where he built a new river port at the junction of the canal and the Nile. He is also said to have stationed a fleet in the Red Sea; all of these measures seem connected with the annexation of the Nabatean kingdom in or just after 106 CE, and demonstrate the consolidation of Roman control over trading interests in the area. His successor Hadrian built a road from Antinoopolis to Berenike along the Red Sea coast, linking the various smaller harbours en route, apparently for surveillance and to facilitate regional communications and supplies between the Rea Sea ports. In the mid-second century the naval presence established by Trajan in the Red Sea was pushed further southward, with the stationing of a detachment of troops and their ships on the Farasan Islands, 1,000 km south-east of the southernmost Roman Red Sea port at Berenike (Villeneuve 2004; Villeneuve et al. 2004). Presumably, the aim was to protect Roman shipping from piracy whilst entering or leaving the Red Sea.

These measures – infrastructural and military – represent considerable state investment in the routes supporting Red Sea trade, and the explanation no doubt lies in the customs dues that the Roman state received from Indian and Arabian trade up the Red Sea (Young 2001: 207–12; McLaughlin 2010: 164–72 – but many of the figures he gives are for the revenues of Egypt as a whole, not the revenues on eastern trade; Wilson 2015; Wilson and Bowman 2018a: 14). Customs dues on cross-frontier trade, where we have direct evidence for their levels on the eastern frontiers, were 25 per cent at least until sometime in the third century CE. The so-called 'Muziris papyrus' values the cargo of the ship *Hermapollon*, which sailed from Muziris in India to the Red Sea in the mid-second century CE, at 1,151 *talents*, 5,852 *drachmae* of silver, or nearly 7 million *sestertii*. (To put this in perspective, to qualify as a senator one had to own property of at least 1 million *sestertii*.) This valuation was made after the deduction of the 25 per cent customs tax, so that the pre-tax value of the cargo was 9,215,803 *sestertii*, and the customs dues were 2,303,951 *sestertii* on this cargo alone (Morelli 2011; De Romanis 2012; 2020; Wilson 2015). We do not know whether the *Hermapollon* was typical or exceptional, though statistical probability is in favour of the former; but over a hundred years earlier Strabo (*Geography*, 2.5.12) says that 120 ships per year left Myos Hormos for India, and if we imagine just 100 such cargoes each year, then the customs revenues on imports from India alone would total *c*.230 million *sestertii*, one-third of Rome's estimated annual military budget of 643–704 million *sestertii* (Duncan-Jones 1994: 36, table 3.3 for the military budget). One needs to also add the customs dues on merchandise from the coast of Africa and the Arabian Peninsula, and also the export dues (also at 25 per cent) on cargoes leaving the Red Sea ports for the African coast, Arabia and India. Moreover, most of the goods imported via the Red Sea to Egypt will have been exported again through Alexandria, with further inter-provincial customs dues of (usually) 2.5 per cent. Also to be added are the revenues on overland Silk Routes trade, ultimately to China, via Palmyra and other centres, whose importance is increasingly being recognised (McLaughlin 2016; 2018; Meyer and Seland 2016; Graf 2018). The total revenues on external trade must have been several hundred million *sestertii* per annum in the first and second centuries CE, an important share of total state revenues and a key enabling factor in supporting the army and the state's expenditure on transport and urban development (Wilson 2015; McLaughlin 2018).

Conclusion

The unification of the Mediterranean world under the hegemony of Rome significantly reduced transaction costs across a pan-Mediterranean market through the use of common laws, a common currency (except for Egypt), two *linguae francae* (Latin and Greek) — at least one of which would be (largely) understood anywhere in the empire — the establishment of peace, and the virtual eradication of piracy in the mid-first century BCE. Technological developments in shipping, and the state's investment in roads and harbours, all reduced the costs of trade. These created favourable conditions for long-distance trade in agricultural produce, pottery, glass, timber and a host of other goods. This contributed to a partial homogenisation of Roman culture, with certain goods widely available across the empire, although there were still of course regional differences in consumption patterns. Growing urban populations provided concentrated markets, and agricultural production was increasingly organised around villa estate centres engaged in market-oriented cash crop agriculture. As we have seen with the olive oil supply for Rome, sometimes the state would intervene in the market as a powerful actor, thus stimulating large-scale production further (as in the Guadalcuivir valley). Trade with the east, both across the Syrian desert to the Silk Routes to central Asia, and, with the acquisition of Egypt, via the Red Sea to the Indian Ocean, brought in flows of goods, the customs duties on which were a source of considerable revenue to the Roman state. These conditions depended on the political unity and stability of the empire, and when in late antiquity these collapsed and the empire fissured, both internal and external trading networks fell apart and were radically reconfigured under the empire's successor states.

Abbreviations

CIL: *Corpus Inscriptionum Latinarum*. Berlin: Berlin-Brandenburg Academy of Sciences and Humanities, 1863–.

OGIS: Dittenberger, W. 1903, 1905. *Orientis Graeci Inscriptiones Selectae. Supplementum Sylloges inscriptionum graecarum*, 2 vols. Leipzig: S. Hirzel.

References

Bagnall, Roger S., Adam Bülow-Jacobsen and Hélène Cuvigny. 2001. 'Security and water on the eastern desert roads: the Prefect Iulius Ursus and the construction of *praesidia* under Vespasian', *Journal of Roman Archaeology* 14(1): 325–33.

Bang, Peter Fibiger. 2007. 'Trade and empire – in search of organizing concepts for the Roman economy', *Past and Present* 195: 3–54.

Begley, Vimala. 1993. 'New investigations at the Port of Arikamedu', *Journal of Roman Archaeology* 6: 93–108.

Bémont, Colette and Jean-Paul Jacob (eds). 1986. *La terre sigillée gallo-romaine: Lieux de production du Haut Empire: implantations, produits, relations*. Documents d'archéologie française. Paris: Éditions de la Maison des sciences de l'homme.

Bernabei, Mauro, Jarno Bontadi, Rossella Rea, Ulf Büntgen and Willy Tegel. 2019. 'Dendrochronological evidence for long-distance timber trading in the Roman Empire', *PLoS One* 14(12): e0224077. https:/doi.org/10.1371/journal.pone.0224077.

Bes, Philip. 2015. *Once Upon a Time in the East: The chronological and geographical distribution of terra sigillata and red slip ware in the Roman east*. Roman and Late Antique Mediterranean Pottery. Oxford: Archaeopress Publishing Ltd.

Blázquez Martínez, José María and José Remesal Rodríguez (eds). 1999. *Estudios sobre el Monte Testaccio (Roma)*, vol. 1. Barcelona: Universitat de Barcelona.

Blázquez Martínez, José María and José Remesal Rodríguez (eds). 2014. *Estudios sobre el monte Testaccio (Roma) VI*. Instrumenta 47. Barcelona: Universitat de Barcelona.

Bonifay, Michel. 2018. 'The Distribution of African Pottery under the Roman Empire'. In *Trade, Commerce, and the State in the Roman World*, edited by A. Wilson and A. Bowman, 327–51. Oxford Studies on the Roman Economy. Oxford: Oxford University Press.

Bonifay, Michel. 2022. 'The African economy: the ceramic evidence'. In *A Companion to North Africa in Antiquity*, edited by R. Bruce Hitchner, 220–32. Blackwell Companions to the Ancient World 126. Hoboken, NJ: John Wiley & Sons, Inc.

Carandini, Andrea. 1983. 'Pottery and the African economy'. In *Trade in the Ancient Economy*, edited by P. Garnsey, K. Hopkins and C.R. Whittaker, 145–62. London: Chatto and Windus.

Carrignon, Simon, Tom Brughmans, and Iza Romanowska. 2022. 'Copying of economic strategies in Eastern Mediterranean inter-regional tableware trade'. In *Simulating Roman Economies: Theories, methods, and computational models*, edited by T. Brughmans and A.I. Wilson, 144–66. Oxford Studies on the Roman Economy. Oxford: Oxford University Press.

Casson, Lionel. 1971. *Ships and Seamanship in the Ancient World*. Princeton, NJ: Princeton University Press.

Casson, Lionel. 1980. 'Rome's trade with the East: the sea voyage to Africa and India', *Transactions of the American Philological Association* 110: 21–36.

Cobb, Matthew Adam. 2018a. *Rome and the Indian Ocean Trade from Augustus to the Early Third Century CE*. Mnemosyne, Supplements 418. Leiden: Brill.

Cobb, Matthew Adam (ed.). 2018b. *The Indian Ocean Trade in Antiquity: Political, cultural and economic impacts*. London: Routledge.

Cooper, John P. 2011. 'No easy option: Nile versus Red Sea in ancient and mediaeval North-South navigation'. In *Maritime Technology in the Ancient Economy: Ship-design and navigation*, edited by W.V. Harris and K. Iara, 189–210. JRA Supplementary Series 84. Portsmouth, RI: Journal of Roman Archaeology.

Davidde, Barbara. 2018. 'The Port of Qana', a junction between the Indian Ocean and the Mediterranean Sea: the underwater evidence'. In *Trade, Commerce, and the State in the Roman World*, edited by A.I. Wilson and A.K. Bowman, 579–97. Oxford Studies on the Roman Economy. Oxford: Oxford University Press.

De Romanis, Federico. 1996. *Cassia, cinnamomo, ossidiana : uomini e merci tra Oceano indiano e Mediterraneo*. Roma: 'L'Erma' di Bretschneider.

De Romanis, Federico. 2012. 'Playing Sudoku on the verso of the 'Muziris Papyrus': pepper, malabathron and tortoise shell in the cargo of the Hermapollon', *Journal of Ancient Indian History* 27: 75–101.

De Romanis, Federico. 2020. *The Indo-Roman Pepper Trade and the Muziris Papyrus*. Oxford Studies on the Roman Economy. Oxford: Oxford University Press.

De Romanis, Federico and Marco Maiuri (eds). 2015. *Across the Ocean: Nine essays on Indo-Mediterranean trade*. Columbia Studies in the Classical Tradition. Leiden: E. J. Brill.

Duncan-Jones, Richard P. 1994. *Money and Government in the Roman Empire*. Cambridge: Cambridge University Press.

Erdkamp, Paul. 2005. *The Grain Market in the Roman Empire: A social, political and economic study*. Cambridge: Cambridge University Press.

Fentress, James and Elizabeth W. B. Fentress. 2001. 'Review article: The hole in the doughnut', *Past and Present*, 173: 203–19.

Fentress, Elizabeth W.B. and Philip Perkins. 1988. 'Counting African red slip ware'. In *L'Africa romana. Atti del Ve Convegno di studio*, edited by A. Mastino, 205–14. Sassari: Edizioni Gallizzi.

Fentress, Elizabeth W. B., Sergio Fontana, R. Bruce Hitchner, and Philip Perkins. 2004. 'Accounting for ARS: fineware and sites in Sicily and Africa'. In *Side-by-side Survey*, edited by S. E. Alcock and J. F. Cherry, 147–62. Oxford: Oxbow Books.

Finley, Moses I. 1973. *The Ancient Economy*. Sather Classical Lectures. London: Chatto and Windus.

Finley, Moses I. 1985. *The Ancient Economy* (2nd edition). Berkeley and Los Angeles: University of California Press.

Foucher, Louis. 1958. *Thermes romains des environs d'Hadrumète*. Notes et documents, nouvelle série 1. Tunis: Institut National d'Archéologie et d'Arts.

Foucher, Louis. 1967. 'Un voilier antique', *Antiquités Africaines* 1: 83–98.

Funari, Pedro Paulo. 2001. 'Monte Testaccio and the Roman economy', *Journal of Roman Archaeology* 14(2): 585–8.

Graf, David F. 2018. 'The Silk Road between Syria and China'. In *Trade, Commerce, and the State in the Roman World*, edited by A.I. Wilson and A.K. Bowman, 443–529. Oxford Studies on the Roman Economy. Oxford: Oxford University Press.

Greene, Kevin. 1986. *The Archaeology of the Roman Economy*. London: Batsford.

Hanson, John W., Tom Brughmans and Iza Romanowska. 2022. 'Settlement scale and economic networks in the Roman empire'. In *Simulating Roman Economies: Theories, methods, and computational models*, edited by T. Brughmans and A.I. Wilson, 109–43. Oxford Studies on the Roman Economy. Oxford: Oxford University Press.

Harris, William V. 2018. 'The indispensable commodity. Notes on the economy of wood in the Roman Mediterranean'. In *Trade, Commerce, and the State in the Roman World*, edited by A.I. Wilson and A.K. Bowman, 211–36. Oxford Studies on the Roman Economy. Oxford: Oxford University Press.

Hartley, Brian R., Brenda M. Dickinson, Geoffrey B. Dannell, Michael G. Fulford, Allard W. Mees, Paul A. Tyers and Rosemary H. Wilkinson. 2008–11. *Names on Terra Sigillata: An index of makers' stamps & signatures on Gallo-Roman terra sigillata (Samian ware)*, 9 vols. Bulletin of the Institute of Classical Studies Supplement 102. London: University of London, Institute of Classical Studies.

Hayes, John W. 1972. *Late Roman Pottery*. London: The British School at Rome.

Hayes, John W. 1994. 'Eastern Terra Sigillata wares – late Roman red-slip wares and their competitors: filling in the Mediterranean Picture', *PACT: Journal of the European Study Group on Physical, Chemical and Mathematical Techniques applied to Archaeology*, 40(8): 107–16.

Hitchner, R. Bruce. 2012. 'Roads, integration, connectivity and economic performance in the Roman empire'. In *Highways, Byways and Road Systems in the Pre-Modern World*, edited by S.E. Alcock, J. Bodel, and R.J.A. Talbert, 222–33. Malden, MA, and Oxford: John Wiley & Sons.

Horden, Peregrine and Nicholas Purcell. 2000. *The Corrupting Sea: A study of Mediterranean history*. Oxford: Blackwell.

Horden, Peregrine and Nicholas Purcell. 2020. *The Boundless Sea: Writing Mediterranean history*. Variorum Collected Studies. Abingdon; New York: Routledge.

Keay, Simon J. (ed.) 2012. *Rome, Portus and the Mediterranean*. Archaeological Monographs of the British School at Rome 21. London: British School at Rome.

Keay, Simon J. and Lidia Paroli (eds). 2011. *Portus and its Hinterland: Recent archaeological research*. Archaeological Monographs of the British School at Rome 18. London: British School at Rome.

Kennedy, David. 1985. 'The composition of a military work party in Roman Egypt (ILS 2483: Coptos)', *Journal of Egyptian Archaeology* 71: 156–60.

Leitch, Victoria. 2011. 'Location, location, location: characterizing coastal and inland production and distribution of Roman African cooking wares'. In *Maritime Archaeology and Ancient Trade in the Mediterranean*, edited by D. Robinson and A. Wilson, 169–95. Oxford Centre for Maritime Archaeology Monograph 6. Oxford: Oxford Centre for Maritime Archaeology.

Loughton, Matthew E. 2003. 'The distribution of Republican amphorae in France', *Oxford Journal of Archaeology* 22.2: 177–207.
Malkin, Irad (ed.) 2003. *Mediterranean Paradigms and Classical Antiquity*. Special issue of *Mediterranean Historical Review* 18(2).
Mattingly, David J. 1988. 'Oil for export? A comparison of Libyan, Spanish and Tunisian olive oil production in the Roman empire', *Journal of Roman Archaeology* 1: 33–56.
Mattingly, David J. 2013. 'To South and North: Saharan trade in antiquity'. In *Living and Working in the Roman World: Essays in honour of Michael Fulford on his 65th birthday*, edited by H. Eckardt and S. Rippon, 169–90. JRA Supplementary Series 95. Portsmouth, RI: Journal of Roman Archaeology.
Mattingly, David J., Victoria Leitch, Chloe N. Duckworth, Aurélie Cuenod, Martin Sterry and Franca Cole (eds). 2017. *Trade in the Ancient Sahara and Beyond*. Trans-Saharan Archaeology 1. Cambridge: Cambridge University Press and The Society for Libyan Studies.
McLaughlin, Raoul. 2010. *Rome and the Distant East: Trade routes to the ancient lands of Arabia, India and China*. London and New York: Continuum.
McLaughlin, Raoul. 2014. *The Roman Empire and the Indian Ocean: The ancient world economy and the kingdoms of Africa, Arabia and India*. Barnsley: Pen and Sword.
McLaughlin, Raoul. 2016. *The Roman Empire and the Silk Routes: The ancient world economy and the empires of Parthia, Central Asia and Han China*. Barnsley: Pen and Sword.
McLaughlin, Raoul. 2018. 'Indian Ocean commerce in context. The economic and revenue significance of eastern trade in the ancient world'. In *The Indian Ocean Trade in Antiquity: Political, cultural and economic impacts*, edited by M.A. Cobb, London: Routledge.
Meyer, Jørgen Christian and Eivind Heldaas Seland. 2016. 'Palmyra and the trade route to the Euphrates', *Aram* 28(1–2): 497–523.
Morelli, Federico. 2011. 'Dal Mar Rosso ad Alessandria. Il verso (ma anche il recto) del "papiro di Muziris" (SB XVIII 13167)', *Tyche* 26: 199–233.
Morley, Neville. 2000. 'Markets, marketing and the Roman élite'. In *Mercati permanenti e mercati periodici nel mondo romano*, edited by E. Lo Cascio, 211–21. Pragmateiai. Bari: Edipuglia.
Morley, Neville. 2007. *Trade in Classical Antiquity*. Key Themes in Ancient History. Cambridge: Cambridge University Press.
Nappo, Dario. 2018. 'Money and flows of coinage in the Red Sea trade'. In *Trade, Commerce, and the State in the Roman World*, edited by A.I. Wilson and A.K. Bowman, 557–78. Oxford Studies on the Roman Economy. Oxford: Oxford University Press.
Nieto, Xavier. 1997. 'Le commerce de cabotage et de redistribution'. In *La navigation dans l'antiquité*, edited by P. Pomey, 146–59. Aix-en-Provence: Édisud.
Oxé, August, Howard Comfort and Philip Kenrick. 2000. *Corpus Vasorum Arretinorum* (2nd edition). Bonn: Dr Rudolf Habelt GmbH.
Parker, Grant. 2000. 'The Mediterranean and the Mediterranean world of Horden and Purcell', *Journal of Mediterranean Archaeology*, 13(2): 226–30.
Peacock, David P.S. 1974. 'Amphorae and the Baetican fish industry', *Antiquaries Journal* 54: 232–43.
Peacock, David P.S. and David F. Williams. 1986. *Amphorae and the Roman Economy: An introductory guide*. Longman Archaeology Series. London and New York: Longman.
Pucci, Giuseppe. 1983. 'Pottery and trade in the Roman period'. In *Trade in the Ancient Economy*, edited by P. Garnsey, K. Hopkins and C.R. Whittaker, 105–17. London: Chatto and Windus.
Russell, Ben. 2013. *The Economics of the Roman Stone Trade*. Oxford Studies on the Roman Economy. Oxford: Oxford University Press.
Robinson, Damian J., Katia Schörle and Candace Rice. 2020. 'Ship losses and the growth of Roman harbour infrastructure', *Journal of Mediteranean Archaeology* 33(1): 102–25.
Shaw, B.D. 2001. 'Challenging Braudel: a new vision of the Mediterranean', *Journal of Roman Archaeology*, 14(2): 419–53.
Sidebotham, Steven E. 1986. *Roman Economic Policy in the Erythra Thalassa 30 B.C.-A.D. 217*. Leiden: E. J. Brill.
Sidebotham, Steven E. 2011. *Berenike and the Ancient Maritime Spice Route*. Berkeley, Los Angeles and London: University of California Press.
Sternini, Mara. 2019. 'The production centres and river network of Italian terra sigillata between the Arno and Tiber valleys: a geographical point of view', *Journal of Roman Archaeology* 32: 485–94.

Tchernia, André. 2005. 'Winds and coins: from the supposed discovery of the monsoon to the *denarii* of Tiberius'. In *Crossings: Early Mediterranean contacts with India*, edited by F. De Romanis and A. Tchernia, 250–76. New Delhi: Manohar.

Tchernia, André. 2016. *The Romans and Trade*. Translated by J. Grieve and E. Minchin. Oxford Studies on the Roman Economy. Oxford: Oxford University Press.

Temin, Peter. 2013. *The Roman Market Economy*. The Princeton Economic History of the Western world. Princeton, NJ: Princeton University Press.

Tomber, Roberta. 2008. *Indo-Roman Trade: From pots to pepper*. London: Gerald Duckworth & Co. Ltd.

Tomber, Roberta. 2018. 'Egypt and eastern commerce during the second century AD and Later'. In *Trade, Commerce, and the State in the Roman World*, edited by A.I. Wilson and A.K. Bowman, 531–55. Oxford Studies on the Roman Economy. Oxford: Oxford University Press.

Tomber, Roberta and John N. Dore. 1998. *The National Roman Fabric Reference Collection: A handbook*. MoLAS Monograph 2. London: Museum of London Archaeology Service.

van Dommelen, Peter. 2000. 'Writing ancient Mediterranean landscapes', *Journal of Mediterranean Archaeology*, 13(2): 230–6.

Villeneuve, François. 2004. 'Une inscription latine sur l'archipel Farasan, Arabie Séoudite, sud de la Mer Rouge', *Comptes rendus de l'Académie des inscriptions et belles-lettres*: 419–29.

Villeneuve, François, Carl Philipps and William Facey. 2004. 'Une inscription latine de l'archipel Farasan (sud de la mer Rouge) et son contexte archéologique et historique', *Arabia* 2: 143–90.

Wallace-Hadrill, Andrew. 1991. 'Elites and trade in the Roman town'. In *City and Country in the Ancient World*, edited by J. Rich and A. Wallace-Hadrill, 241–72. Leicester-Nottingham Studies in Ancient Society. London and New York: Routledge.

Wheeler, Robert Eric Mortimer, A. Ghosh and Krishna Deva. 1946. 'Arikamedu: an Indo-Roman Trading Station on the East Coast of India', *Ancient India* 2: 17–124.

Whittaker, C. Richard 1985. 'Trade and the aristocracy in the Roman empire', *Opus* 4: 49–75.

Wilson, Andrew I. 2009. 'Approaches to quantifying Roman trade'. In *Quantifying the Roman Economy: Methods and problems*, edited by A.K. Bowman and A.I. Wilson, 213–49. Oxford Studies on the Roman Economy Oxford: Oxford University Press.

Wilson, Andrew I. 2011a. 'Developments in Mediterranean shipping and maritime trade from the Hellenistic period to AD 1000'. In *Maritime Archaeology and Ancient Trade in the Mediterranean*, edited by D. Robinson and A. Wilson, 33–59. Oxford: Oxford Centre for Maritime Archaeology.

Wilson, Andrew I. 2011b. 'The economic influence of developments in maritime technology in antiquity'. In *Maritime Technology in the Ancient Economy: Ship-design and navigation*, edited by W.V. Harris and K. Iara, 211–33. JRA Supplementary Series 84. Portsmouth, RI: Journal of Roman Archaeology.

Wilson, Andrew I. 2012. 'Saharan trade in the Roman period: short-, medium- and long-distance trade networks', *Azania: Archaeological Research in Africa* 47(4): 409–49, https://doi.org/10.1080/0067270X.2012.727614.

Wilson, Andrew I. 2015. 'Red Sea trade and the state'. In *Across the Ocean: Nine essays on Indo-Mediterranean trade*, edited by F. De Romanis and M. Maiuri, 13–32. Columbia Studies in the Classical Tradition. Leiden: E. J. Brill.

Wilson, Andrew I. 2018. 'Trade across Rome's southern frontier: the Sahara and the Garamantes'. In *Trade, Commerce, and the State in the Roman World*, edited by A.I. Wilson and A.K. Bowman, 599–624. Oxford Studies on the Roman Economy. Oxford: Oxford University Press.

Wilson, Andrew I. and Alan K. Bowman. 2018a. 'Introduction: trade, commerce, and the state'. In *Trade, Commerce, and the State in the Roman World*, edited by A.I. Wilson and A.K. Bowman, 1–24. Oxford Studies on the Roman Economy. Oxford: Oxford University Press.

Wilson, Andrew I. and Alan K. Bowman (eds). 2018b. *Trade, Commerce, and the State in the Roman World*. Oxford Studies on the Roman Economy. Oxford: Oxford University Press.

Wilson, Andrew Ian, Katia Schörle and Candace M. Rice. 2012. 'Roman ports and Mediterranean connectivity'. In *Rome, Portus and the Mediterranean*, edited by S. Keay, 367–91. Archaeological Monographs of the British School at Rome. London: British School at Rome.

Young, Gary K. 2001. *Rome's Eastern Trade: International commerce and imperial policy 31 BC–AD 305*. London and New York: Routledge.

5
Empire and urbanism in ancient Rome

Louise Revell

Introduction

Urbanism is one of the defining characteristics of Roman imperialism: the rapid appearance of Roman-style towns from the late first century BCE onwards marked a dramatic change in settlement patterns, particularly notable in areas with a limited pre-existing tradition of urbanism, such as the western provinces. For a twenty-first century inhabitant of today's global culture, towns, cities and now megacities seem an inevitable consequence of modernity and capitalism, and the architectural competitions for the next statement skyscraper have led to a new form of global rivalry. The presence and form of urban centres becomes one way to distinguish between 'developed' and 'developing' countries. However, it is this familiarity with the specific twenty-first century city which has the danger of obscuring the significance of cities in the past. Urbanism is not a universal phenomenon: its social, political and cultural roles are specific to its social context, and the architectural form the physical environment takes is a reflection of that role. The materiality of urbanism both reflects and constructs the priorities and concerns of the people who built cities.

If urbanism is a culturally specific phenomenon rather than an inevitable step in cultural evolution models, then this reorientates the types of questions we want to consider in relation to the Roman Empire. It is no longer enough to describe the archaeological remains of the town, to reconstruct its ancient cityscape and provide a chronology of its development and decline, although this remains a necessary part. More recent approaches to the built environment have stressed the ways in which they are inhabited, and a neutral space is turned into a meaningful place (Rykwert 1976; Lefebvre 1991; Ingold 2011). The urban place is the product of the social knowledge of the people who built it, but in turn it is the arena for an individual's repeated (everyday or occasional) encounters with both their immediate community and with the wider structures of power and imperialism (Revell 2009). In this chapter, I will explore the relationship between the urban place, the reproduction of imperial authority and the lived experience of Roman rule. I will focus on the towns within the Iberian peninsula as a means of investigating both the common features and the variability within the urbanisation of Rome's provinces.

The town in imperial thought

Within the western provinces, urbanism was an imperial phenomenon, both an imposition by the imperial powers, but also their way to deal with the administrative complexity of a large empire. In some ways this contrasts with the already urbanised eastern provinces, but even here, the analysis of how imperial power was made manifest in the urban fabric still applies. In thinking about this relationship between urbanism and imperialism, we need to cast aside modernising assumptions about the inevitability of urban centres and consider why the Roman imperial authorities might have considered urbanism the best way to rule an empire. To build a town, in Roman thought, was to foster a community, organised through a series of rules based on the idea of the group of citizens and their dependent families. For the Romans, as for many other societies, the adoption of an urban centre brought with it the social and cultural structures which they considered 'civilisation'.

This idea is clearly expressed in a passage from Cicero, in which he gives his thoughts on the development of the state (Cic. *Inv. Rhet.* 1.2). He describes a time before urbanism, when people lived like animals, without agriculture or settlements. As well as towns, these people lacked other aspects of an ordered society: religion, social organisation such as marriage, and legal codes. Once the Romans started to dwell in a town, all these ways of organising a society were also developed. Therefore, for the Romans, towns equated to good social, political and religious order – their definition of civilisation. This focus on urbanism as the medium for political organisation can also be traced in the archaeological record of Rome and the material form the city took (Davies 2017). The evidence for its earliest monumentalisation shows an emphasis on public spaces which allowed for large-scale activities, involving the community of citizens coming together and participating in the political and religious life of the state. Political space, as represented by the Forum Romanum with the *comitium* and the senate house, formed the conceptual heart of the city (Coarelli 1983). Public space also included religious space, designed for communal religious worship, and spaces for spectacles such as the Circus Maximus. Urban life for the citizens of Rome involved a regular series of shared experiences located in these core spaces, including the annual elections on the Campus Martius (Varro *de Agr*. 3; discussed in Patterson 2000: 15–17), religious festivals such the Ludi Romani (Dion. Hal. *Rom. Ant.* 72–3) and triumphal processions for the victorious general (Beard 2007; Popkin 2016). The change from Republic to the monarchy of the Principate instituted a new political system, but from its inception under Augustus, part of being an emperor was the provision of public spaces for the citizens, whether it was the imperial fora of the first centuries BCE and CE or the large bathing complexes of the second and third centuries CE. Political activity might have been curtailed, but the idea of the citizen body remained. Throughout the Republic and Principate, the fundamental idea was of the people of Rome interacting as a group and, in turn, the consequence of such activities was to reinforce this group identity.

Nevertheless, at the same time as urban living created the idea of the urban community, it also reinforced specific social divisions, particularly between the elite and the non-elite. During the Republic, the dividing of the citizen body according to wealth during the census, the physical act of voting by census group in the Comitia Centuriata, and the mustering in the Campus Martius prior to war all created a hierarchy of citizens (Nicolet 1980). Participation in elections, assemblies, religious *ludi* and triumphs all provided an opportunity for the senatorial elite to take centre stage, and to set themselves apart from the ordinary citizen. Furthermore, paying for the construction of these public spaces also became a way for the elite to compete between themselves, such as the funding of temples from the spoils of increasingly lucrative wars during the mid to late Republic (Ziolkowski 1992; Popkin 2016). These and other acts of benefaction provided a means to legitimise these inequalities, creating a dependent relationship through the system of formal and informal patronage (Saller 1992). This creation of hierarchies went beyond rank and encompassed other forms of social identity: as the rules for citizenship excluded women, the young and the unfree, it created multiple axes of social differentiation. In this way, the physical city brought with it a form of political organisation which defined the social community and created social differences. More than this, it became the stage on which these identities were performed.

This very brief exploration of urbanism in Roman thought is important because this mentality of the primacy of the town and a performative urban citizenship underpinned Rome's means of ruling its empire, particularly from the time of Augustus. A series of changes in the organisation and administration of the provinces was instituted, and then solidified over the course of the first century CE. Whilst the detail is beyond the scope of this chapter, broadly speaking these changes created a more formalised series of provinces within an organised framework of governorship, taxation and legal codes (summarised in Garnsey and Saller 2014: 35–54; see also Lintott 1993). As part of this, we see an explosion in town building, particularly in regions where there had been limited urbanisation prior to conquest. This should be seen as part of a change in the concept of imperialism, and a new approach to the relationship between Rome and its provinces (Woolf 1995; Richardson 2008).

Urbanism in the Iberian provinces

The Iberian provinces have the highest density of Roman towns within the western provinces, although this is offset by regions, particularly in the north and west, which have a much sparser distribution of towns. This complex distribution coupled with the long period of rule by Rome make these provinces an ideal case study for exploring the significance of Roman urbanism, and raising issues which are pertinent to the wider empire. The peninsula had a diverse pre-conquest cultural history (Bendala Galán 2000), consisting of indigenous tribal groups loosely classified by modern scholars as Tartessian, Iberian or Celtiberian. External influences include colonisation by Phoenicians in the south and Greeks in the north-east, and then growing Carthaginian power, particularly after its defeat in the First Punic War. Rome's first substantive incursion into Iberia came as a result of the Second Punic War (Richardson 1996). After expelling the Carthaginians in 206 BCE, the Romans became rulers of a substantial area, although it took until the Augustan period to finally subdue the whole peninsula, with fierce rebellions and warfare throughout the intervening two centuries. However, that Iberia was considered part of Rome's *imperium* can be seen from the 190s BCE, when the territory was divided into two provinces: Hispania Citerior and Hispania Ulterior. The latter was later divided into two provinces by Augustus: Baetica and Lusitania.

Even in the regions that came under Rome's rule after the Second Punic War, there is limited evidence for the construction of new towns before the 50s BCE (Keay 1995; 1998). There were some *coloniae* formed from Roman citizens, such as Cordoba, Emporion and Carteia, but these were very few in number. In contrast, whether dated by textual or archaeological evidence, a large number of towns see their first Roman-style buildings constructed during the late first century BCE or early first century CE. To account for this delay in urbanisation, we need to consider the administrative role of these towns. For the first three centuries CE, the Roman Empire functioned with a small specialist bureaucracy, comprising the provincial governor, accompanied by other appointed officials and their immediate entourages (Lintott 1993). Other duties might be carried out by slaves and freedmen of the imperial household, and soldiers and their officers might also have had administrative duties. At a local level, the running of the provincial communities was usually carried out through the institutions of the local town, and in particular, by the local elites. This raises the question of what constituted a provincial Roman town in administrative and political terms. Its legal status rested on the grant of a charter by Rome, defining its relationship with Rome and specifying a new mode of internal governance. As demonstrated above, the Roman ideology of urbanism involved specific ideas of social and political organisation and participation. Extant charters show limited respect for previous, local political practice, and instead are based on the political system of Rome, revolving around popular participation and a wealthy elite from whom the local magistrates were elected on an annual basis.

The partial survival of such charters from the Iberian Peninsula allows us to reconstruct something of the role of these towns within the imperial administration. Two slightly different forms of urban charter have been found (*municipium* and *colonia*), but here I shall focus on the charters of the *municipium*, found in particularly large numbers following the grant of the Latin right to the peninsula by Vespasian (González 1986; Richardson 1996: 190–210; Caballos Rufino 2009b). A detailed analysis of the bronze plaques from a number of towns has demonstrated that they were based upon a single master-document, allowing a composite charter to be assembled. The language of these charters emphasises the idea that each town was made up of a group of citizens – freeborn, male and adult. These were local citizens who might also hold citizenship of Rome, but in this context, it is their local citizenship which is more important. Through a system of magistrates, elected by the local citizens and who held office for one year, the town was responsible for organising its own justice (below a certain level), finances and infrastructure. This system relied on democratic participation and an elected oligarchic magistracy, all based on a community defined by membership of the urban citizen-body.

The core political institutions were the elected magistrates, the council of decurions and the citizen body (all adult men). They were then responsible for the local administration of the town. The adjudication of trials, for example, was in the hands of the leading magistrates, the duumviri, or the aediles, depending on the value of the case (González 1986: chapters 19, 84; see also Rodger 1990). Similarly, the decision to construct new roads, or alter existing ones, was taken by the duumviri (González 1986: chapter 82), whilst their ongoing maintenance was the responsibility of the aediles (chapter 19). Financial matters were the preserve of the quaestors (chapter 20). The town councils, drawn from the wealthiest and most powerful men in the town, voted on certain matters put to them by the magistrates, such as taking out loans (chapter 80), and sending out ambassadors on behalf of the town (chapters G, I). They themselves could take on such matters, for example acting as an ambassador.

As well as defining the roles for the political elite, these charters placed certain obligations on the citizen body, which integrated the non-elite into the administration of the town as active participants (Revell 2023). They voted in the annual election of the magistrates, a large-scale event involving all citizens, whether resident in the town or the countryside. Voting only took place in one location, and this was within the town itself, probably the forum. The citizens were grouped into sub-sections (*curiae*), with each *curia* voting in a separate enclosure (González 1986: chapter 55). As each magistracy was filled, the successful candidate then swore an oath in front of the citizens that he would act in accordance with the statute (chapter 59). The municipal charters not only created an urban community of citizens, but mandated an annual event in which they exercised their collective political power. This was not the only such event: the charter refers to religious sacrifices, banquets and games which would involve community participation (chapter 77). Other activities were more mundane, such as the registration of property and the settling of land disputes, or the census. These all confirmed the individual's role within the civic community and made the town a key place in their mental landscapes.

A very similar picture can be traced in the one colonial charter from Iberia, the *lex Colonia Genetivae Iuliae* (Crawford 1996). Therefore, in both types of urban charter we see the influence of the Roman ideology of urbanism in two aspects. The first is organisational: of an urban community, defined by participation primarily in politics, but also in religion and legal activity (Revell 2023). The second is that these activities rely on specific urban facilities accessible to the whole citizen body, most notably the forum, but also temples and theatres or amphitheatres. These promote a specific mentalité of what physical form the town should take. As Claude Nicolet argues in relation to citizenship at Rome, 'A striking feature is the importance of the monumental setting which the Roman city ... came to create as a framework for its collective activity' (Nicolet 1980: 11). Since he wrote these words, work on buildings and space across multiple disciplines has taken this further. The activities regularly performed in buildings and constructed spaces, and consequently the buildings and spaces themselves, not only reflect or evidence specific social structures, but also play a role in their creation and perpetuation. Furthermore, they also create different types of social agents, as they differentiate between groups through the differential experiences. In this way, buildings are tied up in the creation and maintenance of communities and power at a local, regional and empire-wide level. It is this that we observe in the archaeology of the western provinces.

The development of Roman towns

As outlined in the previous section, although the urban charters did not stipulate that the town should take a particular physical form, they contained the assumption that it would possess similar types of public buildings to those of Rome and other Italian cities. It is this form of urban configuration that we see emerging in the three Iberian provinces, particularly from the end of the first century BCE onwards. The town of Baelo Claudia in the southern province of Baetica, for example, developed the public facilities necessary for this Roman concept of urban living (Sillières 1995). During the second and first centuries BCE, it seems to have been primarily commercially orientated, with building limited to facilities for fish processing (Arévalo and Bernal 2007). Strabo (3.1.8) describes this as a fishing town and producer of fish products, as well as becoming a major crossing point from Iberia to Mauretania. It is likely that this new urban population relocated from the hilltop settlement of la Silla del Papa, a substantial pre-Roman settlement on the main summit of la Sierra de la Plata, overlooking Baelo Claudia. This hilltop site continued to be occupied post-conquest (as the town was developing), but went out of use in the second half of the first century BCE (Sillières 1995: 67–70).

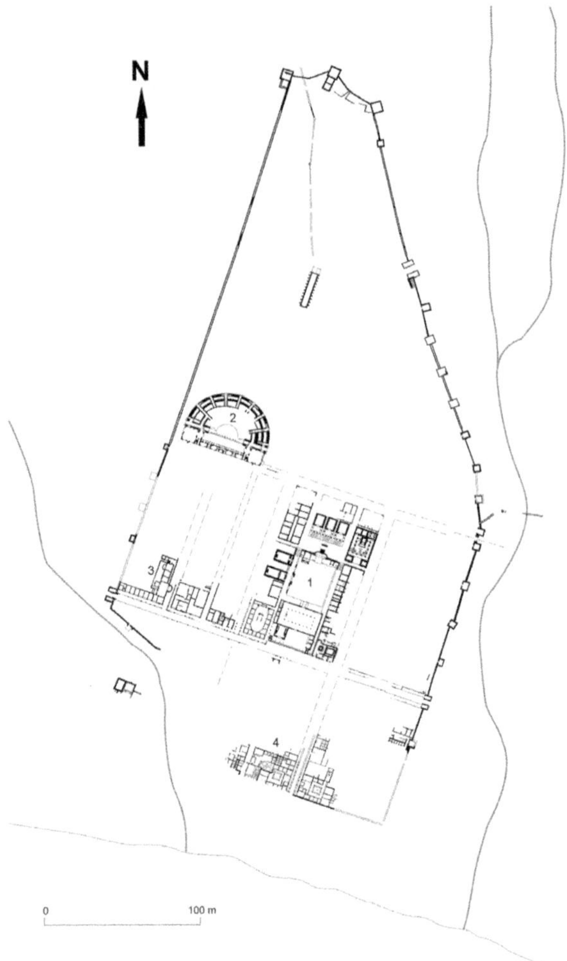

Figure 5.1 Plan of Baelo Claudia: 1 – forum complex; 2 – theatre; 3 – public baths; 4 – industrial zone. Adapted from Caballos Rufino, Rodríguez Gutiérrez et al. (2018), fig. 1. © Louise Revell.

It was only from the Augustan period onwards, around the time Silla del Papa was going out of use, that Baelo Claudia acquired Roman forms of public architecture with the construction of a forum. This required the terracing of the area, and the demolition of pre-existing industrial structures (Sillières 1995) (Figure 5.1). The forum complex dominated the new layout, prominently sited on the main east–west road through the town, running from Carteia to Gades. Originally the forum square opened directly onto the road, although this was later blocked by the construction

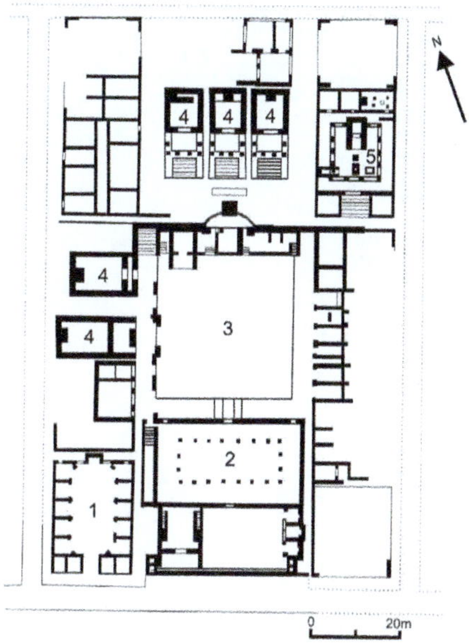

Figure 5.2 Detailed plan of forum of Baelo Claudia: 1 – market hall; 2 – basilica; 3 – forum square; 4 – temples; 5 – temple to Isis. Adapted from Sillieres (1995), fig. 33. © Louise Revell.

of the large basilica in the third quarter of the first century CE (Figures 5.2 and 5.3). The forum square was flanked by porticoes on its east and west sides, which led into temples and other rooms. Following this same axis, a terrace stood above, surrounded on three sides with buildings of unknown function. The terrace originally housed three freestanding podium temples overlooking the forum square. In the final quarter of the first century CE, the eastern side building was demolished and replaced with a temple to Isis. The function of the various rooms associated with the forum is uncertain, but by reference to the urban charters and analogy with other towns, we might expect them to comprise a council chamber, record offices, and perhaps a treasury, all essential for the various administrative functions of the town. The basilica would be used for judicial trials and suchlike, and seems to have held a small shrine to the imperial cult. We can imagine the large open space of the forum courtyard being used for elections, with the presiding magistrate announcing the results from the tribunal on the north side of the square. The three podium temples on the terrace as well as the three on the lower level, opening onto the main courtyard, all point to the interconnectedness of religion and politics, whilst the spacious courtyard could also be used for

Figure 5.3 View of the forum at Baelo Claudia, looking north across the forum courtyard towards the upper terrace with the temples. © Louise Revell.

large religious festivals, revolving around sacrifices and offerings. This complex provided the facilities for many of the activities associated with urban citizenship: political, administrative and religious.

A further stage of monumentalisation took place during the third quarter of the first century CE. As well as the basilica already mentioned, a theatre was constructed to the north of the forum. Whilst this would have an entertainment element, games (*ludi*) were also part of the religious calendar, associated with the urban festivals. Prior to the construction of this monumental facility, it is possible that such games would have taken place in the forum or in a temporary wooden structure. A little later, a market hall (*macellum*) was built beside the basilica, and a small set of baths beside the forum, probably in the early second century. It is possible that there was a second, larger set of public baths to the north of the theatre. One thing to note is the comparatively sparse evidence for housing, outside of the industrial quarter at the south of the town. Although the area within the walls has not been completely excavated, and excavation has tended to focus on the monumental buildings, nevertheless, a large proportion of the interior of the town was taken up by these public buildings, leaving limited available space for housing. Instead, a settlement whose original function seems to have been economic and industrial was transformed into a centre for the practice

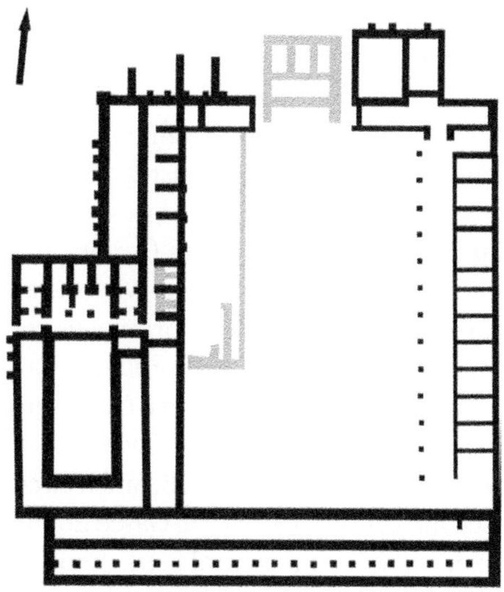

Figure 5.4 Plan of the forum area at Saguntum; the Republican temple is shown in grey and the Augustan structures of the forum in black. Adapted from Aranegui Gascó (1992), fig. 3. © Louise Revell.

of citizenship and imperial administration. The economic activity in the town continued with the fish processing centre in the south of the town, but the urban fabric primarily facilitated the activities through which the citizen community was created, and the administration of the empire maintained.

The urban form of Baelo Claudia can be taken as comprising the typical elements of the Roman town, with political space, religious space and spaces for public spectacles, and although the typology of the particular buildings might vary regionally, these elements are repeated throughout the western provinces (Gros 1996; Laurence et al. 2011). It also illustrates one of the two ways in which Roman urbanism developed: the transformation of pre-existing settlements into Roman style towns. This can also be seen at Saguntum, in Tarraconensis (Aranegui Gascó 1992; 2006). From the fifth century BCE, this was a hill-top settlement, exploiting its access to the coast to tie into both the western Mediterranean trade-routes and connections with the Greek world. Monumental architecture seems to have been confined to the walls and gateways, and a small sanctuary site. Following its incorporation into the growing Roman Empire at the end of the third century BCE, at the end of the second Punic War, there was some rebuilding, necessitated in part by the sack of the town by the Carthaginian forces. However, this seems to have focused on the religious sanctuary, and the construction of a new set of town walls (Aranegui Gascó 2006). The architectural style of the temple seems to have followed Roman Republican styles, but continuing the Iberian tradition of monumentalising its religious role (Figure 5.4). The major redevelopment was during the Augustan period, when the hillside was transformed by the construction of a series of terraces to create the platforms for a number of public buildings (Aranegui Gascó 2004). The epigraphic evidence suggests that this was when the city was granted chartered status as a *municipium*. A new forum was constructed around the existing temple, with the temple and probably basilica forming the north side, and porticoes the remaining three (Aranegui Gascó 1992). As well as the forum and the temple, a theatre was constructed on a lower terrace in the middle of the first century CE, and a circus outside the city walls in the mid-second century (Aranegui Gascó 2004). It is at this point that we see the Iberian idea of a central settlement transformed into a Roman one.

The alternative to the transformation of a pre-existing settlement was a completely new site with a non-local population. The foundation of new towns with a population of veteran soldiers discharged from the legions was an important factor in this process of urbanisation. One example is Augusta Emerita, the provincial capital of Lusitania. This was founded in the 20s BCE, probably between 25 and 23 BCE, with soldiers from the legions who had fought in Augustus' wars against the Cantabrians and Asturians (Arce 2004), and became the capital of the new province of Lusitania at some point after 19 BCE. There is no trace of a pre-existing settlement nearby, and epigraphic evidence suggests a population drawn from elsewhere in Iberia, as well as other parts of the empire. The gridded layout and the town walls seem to have been Augustan. As was the case with all three provincial capitals in Iberia, there seem to have been two fora, one for the townspeople and the other for the provincial council, both of which contained a substantial podium temple, although it is not clear to whom they were dedicated (Mateos Cruz 2004). There were three buildings for spectacles: a theatre and amphitheatre, which were initially extra mural but brought within the city walls during the Flavian period, and a stadium approximately 500 m outside the walls (Durán Cabello 2004). Construction of all three seems to have been in stages over time: the theatre and amphitheatre are both dated epigraphically to the late first century BCE, but work continued through to the mid-first century CE.

In spite of their different settlement histories and the different roles they played in the imperial system, all three examples of Baelo Claudia,

Saguntum and Augusta Emerita shared an idea of urbanism. The physical form of these towns was remarkably similar, with places for communal participation in politics, religion and entertainments, and these traits are replicated across the Iberian provinces. However, it is not enough to produce a checklist of the physical characteristics of a town. Although a frequently used method for synthesising patterns of urban characteristics, it is in reality a short-hand which assumes the use of these buildings and the way they communicated particular social and political values. To take the forum as an example, its constituent elements allowed for the practice of politics and administration. It generally contained a large open space, suitable for activities such as voting. There was usually a basilica, with or without a raised area, which may have been used for trials. Often it contained individual rooms. Identifying the function of specific rooms is difficult, although we can expect a chamber for the town council (Balty 1991) and another for the archives mentioned in the urban charters and inscriptions. The citizens of the town used the forum, perhaps to vote (if eligible), perhaps to register their property, or they may have been called as a witness in a trial. These activities were based on their knowledge of appropriate behaviours according to their rights and responsibilities as urban citizens. A similar equation between a building and the behaviours and ideas it engenders can be applied to other forms of public building, such as temples and theatres, and in a similar way, move the focus on the analysis from a checklist of buildings to the people who used these buildings.

As the materiality of the town promoted the urban community, it simultaneously formed part of the process of creating social hierarchies through who could and who could not participate. The charters promoted a social system based on that at Rome, incorporating distinctions between social classes based on wealth and legal status, and between genders and age groups. The use and experience of public buildings was differentiated according to social category, particular experiences were privileged and endowed with greater authority, which led to the maintenance of social hierarchies. Reconstructing these patterns of differential use can be problematic, but a careful analysis of the buildings themselves demonstrates how the layout and decoration divided the occupiers of these spaces and privileged certain experiences. To go through this for all public building is beyond the scope of this chapter (see Revell 2009: chapter 5 for a fuller discussion), but this may have included access to specific spaces, which were then accentuated through being elevated, or closed off, or through their decoration. For example, in the theatre at Italica, a detailed analysis of the fabric reveals how social groups were segregated, and different levels of comfort created (Rodríguez Gutiérrez 2004). The different tiers (*caveae*) were separated by corridors or low walls, with their own access routes. The lowest tier was reserved for the local elite and any visiting dignitaries, and this area was marked out by the use of marble, wider seats with armrests, and individual seats reserved for a specific person with an inscription. Through these methods, the elite had a more comfortable day at the theatre, and seated as a single block, were also marked out as a single social group. The flipside of this creation of a privileged experience was the way social inferiors were rendered invisible, whether squashed into the narrower seats at the rear of the theatre, or via other means such as the creation of service areas to hide the work necessary for the smooth running of these events.

Reconstructing these patterns is a two-stage process. The first is the close analysis of the buildings themselves, relocating the remains of the decoration and reconstructing patterns of access and visibility. Recent work has added sensory perception to this, not only seeing but also smell and hearing (Betts 2011; 2017). From this analysis it is possible to reconstruct patterns of use and therefore how different experiences of the building were created. The second stage is the allocation of particular social groups to these experiences, and this is more difficult to do from the archaeological evidence alone. The identification of who used which spaces and in what ways relies on the integration of the material evidence with the textual, and here there is the issue of the applicability of the available evidence to the western provinces. There are very limited literary works which deal directly with daily life in these provincial communities (unlike North Africa and the eastern provinces). Authors whose families came from the Iberian Peninsula (such as Martial or the Seneca family) primarily wrote when based in Rome and for an audience at Rome. Descriptions of religious festivals or a visit to the baths can be used as an analogy, but come with the question of how far they are applicable to a specific provincial context (Allison 2001). More relevant are the legal charters and epigraphic evidence from the region or province being examined. However, these are largely produced by a restricted number of the community and are a public display of their values and aims. They are not without value, but they need to be used with care.

One aspect we can identify is the use of the public spaces of the town by the elite to reinforce and legitimise their social position. Under the Roman system, the social elite were drawn from the wealthiest members of the citizen body, and the political and religious magistracies formed the means through which their authority and power was maintained. The forum was an important place where this authority was acted out in public, such as during their election or the meetings and trials they might preside over. It was also a place to memorialise their power through the dedication of honorific statues, its frequent use by the urban community enhancing the visibility of the display (Trifiló 2008). The forum of Singilia Barba demonstrates the careful selection of place for maximum impact. Although it has only been partially excavated, the complex comprised a large open courtyard, with three staircases leading to upper levels (Serrano Ramos 1988). At the foot of one of these staircases stood an inscription to the town's *duovir* Marcus Valerius Proculinus (*CIL* II.5.789), which formed the base for a bronze statue, creating a public monument that was probably over three metres tall. This was dedicated by the town community, both the citizens and the non-citizens who dwelt in the town (*incolae*) in thanks for his sound administration of the town during his time in office, and also the acts of benefaction he had bestowed on the townspeople. Proculinus was granted permission to choose the position for this statue, and so he chose one of the most prominent places within the forum. This was an official monument, not only paid for by the local community, but also sanctioned by a decree of the town council (Roux 1987). The other two staircases in the forum were also appropriated by other members of the elite. A pair of statues with dedicatory inscriptions, one to a father and the other to his son, stood either side of one staircase (*CIL* II.5.786, 799), and another statue stood beside the third staircase, in this case dedicated by the recipient's parents after his death (*CIL* II.5.797). Such public honours, set in the political heart of the town, reinforced the significance of this new socio-political system and the criteria for social authority: administrating the community with integrity, acting as a benefactor for the population, and carrying out public duties.

In this way, we can begin to build up a picture of how the ideology of urbanism, which was a fundamental part of Roman thought, led to the development of both physical towns and a political system based on communities of urban citizens. Whilst there is a tendency to focus on the privileged position of the elite magistrates, in reality this idea of citizen participation had a wider impact, creating citizens who took part in the urban system through their responsibilities as citizens. Furthermore, the urban system created new categories of people who were excluded from this by their lack of citizenship, in particular women and slaves (Laurence 2006: 167–81; Revell 2023). This urban experience was potentially a disruption to pre-existing socio-political structures, marking a change to the pre-Augustan settlement patterns and modes of living.

A wider system

So far, I have focused on individual towns and the creation of citizen bodies. A further element of their significance was that urban centres became an important space for understanding what it was to be part of the wider networks of the Roman Empire. For the peoples of the Iberian Peninsula, as with the western provinces more widely, conquest meant a shift from being part of an autonomous tribal community, with a limited geographical spread and local power structures, to being part of a much larger political community, both in terms of geography and in layers of political authority. Although there was some earlier urbanisation by Phoenicians and Carthaginians (e.g. Gadir, modern Cadiz) or Greeks (Emporion, modern Empuriés), and some quasi-urban indigenous settlements (Ullastret, Numantia), this was of limited extent and appears to have taken a different form to Roman urbanism. Part of this difference was a shift from local, face-to-face interaction between subject and ruler to something encountered through representations and symbols. One example was the urban charters themselves: they not only detailed the new constitution, but also monumentalised the new external authority.

A fundamental question is how Roman authority and power were manifested in the daily lives of its subjects. Arguably the most important element was the figure of the emperor, who came to be a uniting force within the empire (Millar 1977; Hopkins 1978: 197–242; Price 1984; Revell 2009: 80–109). Whilst he might never be seen in person, he and the imperial family became part of the political landscape of their Iberian subjects through dedications to them, statues depicting them, and their worship as gods after death. The emperor was both a shared cultural symbol, and a shared political authority. Whilst the details of these feature in other chapters in this volume (see Chapter 2 by Pearce and Chapter 8 by Stewart), here I want to stress the way in which they were preferentially located in the public spaces of the town. At Italica, the epigraphic and sculptural evidence both point to the public spaces of the town being dominated by images of the emperors and their families (León 1995). These cluster in four major zones: the area that was probably the forum, the theatre, the terrace above the theatre, and the area of the Los Palacios baths (León 1995: 18–24; Revell 2009: 82–9; see Figure 5.5). Whilst the numbers from Italica are exceptional outside of the provincial capitals, presumably due to its connection to Trajan and Hadrian, the adornment of public space with imperial statues was not unusual, in particular fora and theatres. In some towns, dynastic programmes have

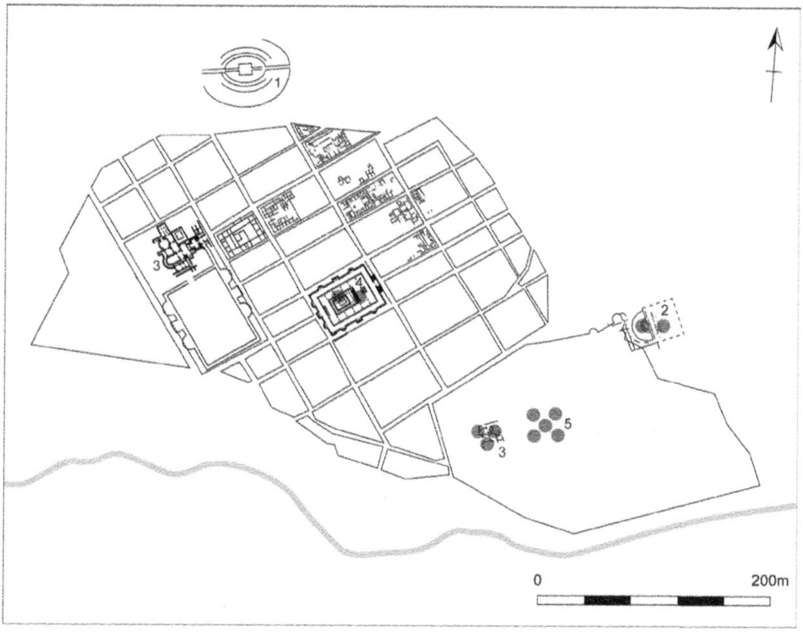

Figure 5.5 Plan of Italica showing the known location of statues of the imperial family: 1 – amphitheatre; 2 – theatre; 3 – baths; 4 – temple to the Imperial Cult; 5 – probable location of the forum. Source: P. Copeland; adapted from Rodríguez Hidalgo and Keay (1995), fig. 4. © Louise Revell

been identified, where a series of statues of a particular family were set up as a single group (Garriguet 2004). These statues and other dedications to the emperors were preferentially located in the towns as opposed to more rural contexts – and consequently to move through the town was to be reminded of the authority of the emperor and ultimately rule by Rome.

The second way in which urbanism formed a means of tying the town into the wider imperial structures was through the graded layers of administration, and the personal ties which linked these various levels. Each province had its own capital which was the centre for the provincial council and the provincial cult. In the case of the Iberian Peninsula, the three provinces were Baetica, Tarraconensis and Lusitania, and their capitals Cordoba, Tarraco and Augusta Emerita respectively. Towns sent representatives to the provincial council, and supplied the priests for the provincial cult, drawn from the same group who served as their own magistrates and priests. Consequently, the provincial administrative systems were not separate from the local towns, but depended on them to function. For some members of the elite, their role within the local towns gave them the ability to serve on a wider stage.

The town was also the means through which an individual interacted with the networks of patronage and influence which acted to integrate the discrete parts of the empire (Mackie 1983: 133–40; Saller 1992: 168–87). The town could adopt official patrons, members of the equestrian and senatorial elite who might act favourably towards the community, whether representing it at Rome, or acting as benefactor through the construction of new buildings or the provision of alimentary schemes. A bronze plaque found in the forum at Munigua formalised the relationship of *hospitium* and clientship between Sextus Curvius Silvinus, a questor with praetorian authority, and the council and people of Munigua (*CILA* II.1053). The agreement was expected to pass down to their descendants, suggesting the multi-generational possibilities of these relationships. The town was also one medium through which the population could express their grievances to the emperor. Again from Munigua we have a letter from the emperor Titus concerning an appeal in the townspeople's dispute with the provincial governor (*CILA* II.1052; Millar 1977: 441–2). This was a collective grievance as a town, and again it was commemorated through its display on a bronze plaque in the forum.

Through all of these elements, we see a system which linked the lowest with the highest, at least in theory. The common factor in this was the town: as a (male) citizen of a town, an individual was linked into a political body which then fed through to the provincial capital and ultimately Rome itself. This was not a direct link, but operated through chains of influence and patronage: the local magistrates he elected also served on the provincial council. They might then come into contact with provincial governors and other officials who might prove helpful to the town, and the nature of such relationships meant that even once such officials moved on to other provinces, or back to Rome, such links were maintained. The urban framework provided the means for such networks to be created, and also the stage on which they were monumentalised through dedications and statues. Urbanism in this way was an integral part of the connectivity and complexity of a large-scale empire.

Urban variability

While there was a common ideology underpinning Roman urbanism within the provinces, this does not create a series of identical towns or urban experiences (Woolf 1997; Hanson 2016; de Ligt and Bintliff 2020). There are differences within the physical characteristics of the town, whether by individual building or by the town as a whole. Another factor is the relationship between the towns and the multiple levels of imperial administration outlined in the previous section. Finally, the individual histories of each town and the way in which they were remembered or forgotten would also impact on the development of each town.

The most visible variable is the lack of uniformity within urban architecture and, in particular, the regional differences in the layout and components of specific building types. For example, there are differences between the Iberian provinces and Gaul and Britain in terms of the layout of fora, temples and theatres (Gros 1996; Laurence et al. 2011). However, the significance of this needs to be thought through. It points to the way in which the adoption of new forms of material culture might be subject to multiple factors, one of which is human creativity, and another is imitation of regional exemplars, such as Britain adopting the Romano-Celtic temple from Gaul (Lewis 1966). Perhaps more important is whether these buildings facilitate the same activities and also embody the same socio-political structures and ideologies (Revell 2013). For example, in Britain and the Gallic and German provinces we find a variant on the classical Roman style theatre (Gros 1996: 294–8; Sear 2006: 98–100). These had the same constituent elements, but the seating extended beyond the usual semicircle, the stage was smaller than the diameter of the *cavea*, and there was no *scaenae frons*. Although different in form, these theatres fulfilled the same urban and civic function, providing a venue for communal games and religious festivals, whilst differentiating the different social groups according to rank.

More important for the urban experience is the variability in the size and density of these provincial towns. A larger town might have more public buildings, such as multiple temples, bath-houses, and perhaps an amphitheatre or stadium as well as a theatre. However, this might not have related to a larger urban community: we should be careful about the significance ascribed to the absolute numbers of houses within a town, given the agricultural base of the economy and the possibility of a high percentage of the citizens living outside the city walls. As well as the size of the town, there was also variability in the density of towns, both between provinces, and within provinces (Keay and Earl 2011). In the Iberian provinces, for example, there was a heavy density of towns in the province of Baetica and on the eastern coast of Tarraconensis, whereas in Lusitania and north-western Tarraconensis, there was a lower density. These differing densities may reflect a difference in the size of the territory governed by the town, and therefore how far away the most distant citizen lived. In areas of high density, citizens might have been able to travel to their local town in under a day, whereas in towns with a larger territory, this might have taken several days. This difference would have impacted on ease of participating in civic duties such as voting or access to justice, as well as participation in religious festivals and games. In areas with a sparser density, the development of unchartered centres might provide some of the facilities such as markets, baths and temples, but not the same political role (Woolf 1998: 129–32).

Another level of variability was how closely each town was tied into the empire-wide links of patronage and influence, and the impact this might have on the development of the town. This could be entirely an accident of history, as in the case of Italica, the birthplace of the Spanish-born Emperor Hadrian. The early imperial town (the Vetus Urbs) was small in size, but under Hadrian almost tripled its size with the construction of a large extension (the Nova Urbs), comprising a suite of monumental buildings, including a large temple to the emperor Trajan, an amphitheatre and a substantial baths complex (Boatwright 1997; Rodríguez Hidalgo 1997: fig 4). Whilst this is a somewhat unusual case, other towns might be tied in at a lesser level through families who joined the elite in Rome itself, but who did not necessarily lose their ties to their home town. Even in the case of those raised to senatorial rank, who were required to renounce their local citizenship, they may have retained their connection through patronage and hospitality. Not all towns boasted such social climbers, and analysis of the known origins of senators and equestrians from the Iberian provinces has demonstrated that a small number of towns produced more examples, such as Cordoba, Tarraco, Gades, Italica, Barcino and Evora (Caballos Rufino 2009a). This created an informal hierarchy, with some towns possessing a closer connection to the imperial centre than others.

This heterogeneity of Roman towns in Iberia, replicated across the empire, should be seen as an important characteristic of Roman urbanism. Explaining it within a simplistic pre-Roman/Roman binary opposition is inadequate: it ignores the complexity of imperial rule and provincial cultures. Part of this was the historical and cultural context within which Roman rule was imposed, but other factors which impact on urban development include Roman attitudes to the conquered peoples, the demands of the imperial authorities on the region, pre-existing or developing contacts with other regions of the empire, and finally, the agency and responses of the provincial communities in adapting to their new imperial context. Within an empire as vast and as diverse as that of the Roman Empire, we should expect urban development to include similar features, but also elements of variability.

Conclusion

Urbanism was an important part of Roman imperialism, both in ideological and practical terms. The Romans had a commitment to a concept of urbanism based on communal participation as fundamentally connected with civilisation. From the time of the emperor Augustus, Rome instituted a more organised system of organising its provinces, and this depended upon the formation of networks of towns. These were chartered, with a political and administrative law code based on that of Rome, including the transformation of the pre-existing populations into bodies of urban citizens. This was based on a hybrid political system of partial democracy and an oligarchy of magistrates. This much we can reconstruct from the textual evidence. However, in order to understand the development and form of towns as experienced by Rome's subjects, we need to turn to the archaeological record, where we see a change in settlement pattern, with the foundation ex novo of Roman-style towns, or the transformation of existing settlements. This did not produce uniform towns, and so we need to be careful about how we use heuristic templates of a 'typical' Roman town. Rather, the people of each town responded to their place within these new networks to develop distinctive physical forms. This might depend on their administrative role within a province, their pre-existing cultural traditions, their own unique histories, the development of regional architectural styles, or even other factors not considered here.

One consequence of this was to bring these provincial populations into the imperial system as active participants through institutions such as elections and the more privileged role of magistrates. They were now organised through towns, and came to self-identify through their towns and town names. A second consequence was that they were now part of a much larger political system of empire-wide connections, a factor which also applies to areas with a pre-existing tradition of urbanism. In many cases, the towns were the conduit through which an individual came to be part of these connections. Thus towns not only stand as evidence for the spread of imperial authority, but they were also an important instrument through which these provincial populations experienced what it was to be a subject of Roman power and a member of a new form of local community.

Abbreviation

CILA: *Corpus de Inscripciones Latinas de Andalucía*. Seville: Consejería de Cultura y Medio Ambiente, Junta de Andalucía, 1989–2002.

References

Allison, P. 2001. 'Using the material and written sources: turn of the millennium approaches to Roman domestic space', *American Journal of Archaeology*, 105: 181–208.

Aranegui Gascó, C. 1992. 'Evolución del área cívica saguntina', *Journal of Roman Archaeology* 5: 56–68.

Aranegui Gascó, C. 2004. 'El foro y los edificios de espectáculos'. In *Opulentissima Saguntum*, edited by P. P. Ripollés Alegre, 101–11. Sagunto: Fundación Bracaja.

Aranegui Gascó, C. 2006. 'From Arse to Saguntum'. In *Early Roman Towns in Hispania Tarraconensis*, edited by L. Abad Casal, S. Keay and S. Ramallo Asensio, 63–74. JRA Supplementary Series 62. Portsmouth, RI: Journal of Roman Archaeology.

Arce, J. 2004. 'Introducción histórica'. In *Mérida: Colonia Augusta Emerita*, edited by X. Dupré Raventós, 7–13. Rome: L'Erma di Bretschneider.

Arévalo, A. and D. Bernal. 2007. *Las cetariae de Baelo Claudia: avance de las investigaciones arqueológicas en el barrio meridional (2000–2004)*. Seville: Junta de Andalucia, Consejería de Cultura.

Balty, J.C. 1991. *Curia ordinis: Recherches d'architecture et d'urbanisme antiques sur les curies provinciales du monde romain*. Brussels: Académie royale de Belgique.

Beard, Mary. 2007. *The Roman Triumph*. Cambridge, MA: Harvard University Press.

Bendala Galán, M. 2000. *Tartesios, iberos y celtas: pueblos, culturas y colonizadores de la Hispania antigua*. Madrid: Temas de Hoy.

Betts, E. 2011. 'Towards a multisensory experience of movement in the city of Rome'. In *Rome, Ostia and Pompeii: Movement and space*, edited by R. Laurence and D.J. Newsome, 118–32. Oxford: Oxford University Press

Betts, E. (ed.). 2017. *Senses of Empire: Multisensory approaches to Roman culture*, London: Routledge.

Boatwright, M.T. 1997. 'Italica and Hadrian's urban benefactions'. In *Itálica MMCC. Actas de las jornadas del 2.200 aniversario de la fundación de Itálica*, edited by A. Caballos Rufino and P. León, 115–35. Seville: Consejería de Cultura.

Caballos Rufino, A. 2009a. 'La extracción de hispanos para formar parte de la aristocracia imperial: senadores y caballeros'. In *Hispaniae: Las provincias hispanas en el mundo romano*, edited by J. Andreu Pintado, J. Cabrero Piquero and I. Rodà de Llanza, 264–281. Tarragona: Institut Català d'Arqueologia Clàssica.

Caballos Rufino, A.F. 2009b. 'Publicación de documentos públicos en las ciudades del Occidente romano: el ejemplo de la Bética'. In *Selbstdarstellung und Kommunikation. Die Veröffentlichung staatlicher Urkunden auf Stein und Bronze in der Römischen Welt*, edited by R. Haensch, 131–72. Munich: Verlag C. H. Beck.

Caballos Rufino, A., O. Rodríguez Gutiérrez and L. Brassous. 2018. '*Aes collectanus*: fragmentos de bronces jurídicos procedentes del foro de Baelo Claudia', *Archivo Español De Arqueología* 91: 39–54.

Coarelli, F. 1983. *Il foro romano. 1 Periodo arcaico*. Rome: Quasar.

Crawford, M. 1996. *Roman Statutes*. London: Bulletin of the Institute of Classical Studies Supplement 64.

Davies, P.J. 2017. *Architecture and Politics in Republican Rome*. Cambridge: Cambridge University Press.

de Ligt, L. and J. Bintliff (eds). 2020. *Regional Urban Systems in the Roman World, 150 BCE–250 CE*. Mnemosyne Supplements 431. Leiden & Boston, MA: Brlll.

Durán Cabello, R.-M. 2004. 'Edificios de espectáculo'. In *Mérida: Colonia Augusta Merita*, edited by X. Dupré Raventós, 55–65. Rome: L'Erma di Bretschneider.

Garnsey, P. and R. Saller. 2014. *The Roman Empire: Economy, society and culture*. London: Bloomsbury.

Garriguet, J. 2004. 'Grupos estatuarios imperiales de la Bética: la evidencia escultórica y epigráfica'. In *IV Reunión sobre escultura romana en Hispania, Madrid*, edited by T. N. Bassarate and L.J. Gonçalves, 67–101. Madrid: Ministerio de Cultura.

González, J. 1986. 'The lex Irnitana: a new copy of the Flavian municipal law', *Journal of Roman Studies* 76: 147–243.

Gros, P. 1996. *L'architecture romaine du début du IIIe siècle av. J.-C. à la fin du Haut-Empire. 1 Les monuments publiques*. Paris: Picard.

Hanson, J.S. 2016. *An Urban Geography of the Roman World: 100 BC–AD 300*. Archaeopress Roman Archaeology 18. Oxford: Archeopress.

Hopkins, K. 1978. *Conquerors and Slaves*. Cambridge: Cambridge University Press.

Ingold, T. 2011. *The Perception of the Environment: Essays on livelihood, dwelling and skill*. London: Routledge.

Keay, S.J. 1995. 'Innovation and adaptation the contribution of Rome to urbanism in Iberia'. In *Social Complexity and the Development of Towns in Iberia*, edited by B.W. Cunliffe and S.J. Keay, 291–337. London: Proceedings of the British Academy.

Keay, S.J. 1998. 'The development of towns in early Roman Baetica'. In *The Archaeology of Early Roman Baetica*, edited by S.J. Keay, 55–86. JRA Supplementary Series 29. Portsmouth, RI: Journal of Roman Archaeology.

Keay, S. and G. Earl. 2011. 'Towns and Territories in Roman Baetica'. In *Settlement, Urbanization, and Population,* edited by A. Bowman and A. Wilson. Oxford: Oxford University Press.

Laurence, R. 2006. *Roman Pompeii: Space and society*. London: Routledge.

Laurence, R., S. Esmonde Cleary and G. Sears. 2011. *The City in the Roman West c 250 BC– AD 250*. Cambridge: Cambridge University Press.

Lefebvre, H. 1991. *The Production of Space*. Oxford: Blackwell.

León, P. 1995. *Escultura de Itálica*. Seville: Consejería de Cultura, Junta de Andalucía.

Lewis, M.J.T. 1966. *Temples in Roman Britain*. Cambridge: Cambridge University Press.

Lintott, A. 1993. *Imperium Romanum: Politics and administration*. London: Routledge.

Mackie, N. 1983. *Local Administration in Roman Spain, AD14–212*. Oxford: British Archaeological Reports International Series 172

Mateos Cruz, P. 2004. 'Arquitectura oficial'. In *Mérida: Colonia Augusta Emerita*, edited by X. Dupré Raventós, 41–53. Rome: L'Erma di Bretschneider.

Millar, F. 1977. *The Emperor in the Roman world*. London: Duckworth.

Nicolet, C. 1980. *The World of the Citizen in Republican Rome*. London: Batsford.

Patterson, J. 2000. *Political Life in the City of Rome*. Bristol: Bristol Classical Press.

Popkin, M.L. 2016. *The Architecture of the Roman Triumph: Monuments, memory, and identity*. Cambridge: Cambridge University Press.

Price, S. 1984. *Rituals and Power: The Roman imperial cult in Asia Minor*. Cambridge: Cambridge University Press.

Revell, L. 2009. *Roman Imperialism and Local Identities*. Cambridge: Cambridge University Press.

Revell, L. 2013. 'Romanization'. In *The Blackwell Companion to Roman Architecture*, edited by C. Quenemoen and R. Ulrich, 381–98. Oxford: Wiley-Blackwell.

Revell, L. 2023. 'Local citizenship and non-elite integration in Roman Iberia'. In *Understanding Integration in the Roman World*, edited by E.M. Grijalvo and R.M. Soldevila, 104–22. Leiden: Brill. https://doi.org/10.1163/9789004545632_008.

Richardson, J.S. 1996. *The Romans in Spain*. Oxford: Blackwell.

Richardson, J. 2008. *The Language of Empire: Rome and the idea of empire from the third century BC to the second century AD*. Cambridge: Cambridge University Press.

Rodger, A. 1990. 'The jurisdiction of local magistrates: chapter 84 of the Lex Irnitana', *Zeitschrift für Papyrologie und Epigraphik* 84: 147–61.

Rodríguez Gutiérrez, O. 2004. *El teatro romano de Itálica: estudio arqueoarquitectónico*. Madrid: Servicio de Publicaciones de la Universidad Autónoma de Madrid, Fundación Pastor de Estudios Clásicos, Diputación de Sevilla.

Rodríguez Hidalgo, J.M. 1997. 'La nueva imagen de la Itálica de Adriano'. In *Itálica MMCC. Actas de las jornadas del 2.200 aniversario de la fundación de Itálica*, edited by A. Caballos Rufino and P. León, 87–113. Seville: Consejería de Cultura.

Rodríguez Hidalgo, J.M. and S.J. Keay. 1995. 'Recent work in Italica'. In *Social Complexity and the Development of Towns in Iberia from the Copper Age to the Second Century AD*, edited by B.W. Cunliffe and S.J. Keay, 395–420. Oxford: Oxford University Press.

Roux, P.l. 1987. 'Cité et culture municipale en Bétique sous Trajan', *Ktema* 12: 271–84.

Rykwert, J. 1976. *The Idea of a Town: The anthropology of urban form in Rome, Italy and the ancient world*. London: Faber.

Saller, R.P. 1992. *Personal Patronage Under the Early Empire*. Cambridge: Cambridge University Press.

Sear, F. 2006. *Roman Theatres: An architectural study*. Oxford: Oxford University Press.

Serrano Ramos, E. 1988. 'Singilia Barba, una ciudad de la Baetica'. In *Actas del Congreso Internacional 'El Estrecho de Gibraltar'*, edited by E. Ripoll Perelló, 821–31. Madrid: Universidad Nacional de Educación a Distancia.

Sillières, P. 1995. *Baelo Claudia: une cité romaine de Bétique*. Madrid: Casa de Velázquez.

Trifiló, F. 2008. 'Power, architecture and community in the distribution of honorary statues in Roman public spaces'. In *TRAC 2007. Proceedings of the Seventeenth Theoretical Roman Archaeology Conference, London 2007*, edited by C. Fenwick, M. Wiggins and D. Wythe, 109–20. Oxford: Oxbow Books.

Woolf, G. 1995. 'The formation of Roman provincial cultures'. In *Integration in the Early Roman West: The role of culture and ideology*, edited by J. Metzler, M. Millett, N. Roymans and J. Slofstra, 9–18. Luxembourg: Dossiers d'Archeologie du Musee National d'Histoire et d'Art IV.

Woolf, G. 1997. 'The Roman urbanization of the East'. In *The Early Roman Empire in the East*, edited by S.E. Alcock, Oxford: Oxbow Books.

Woolf, G. 1998. *Becoming Roman: The origins of provincial civilization in Gaul*. Cambridge: Cambridge University Press.

Ziolkowski, A. 1992. *The Temples of the Mid-Republican Rome and their Historical and Topographical Context*. Rome: L'Erma di Bretschneider.

6
'Becoming darkness' and the invisible slave economy: archaeological approaches to the study of enslavement in the Roman world

Rebecca Redfern

Introduction

Interest in and study of the Roman world has always included slavery, ranging from the collecting of slave collars by Antiquarians (Thurmond 1994: 5) to material culture analyses seeking to find evidence for this 'invisible' economy (Webster 2005). The perspectives, methodologies and techniques vary between the disciplines which study the Roman world – ancient history, classics, classical archaeology, bioarchaeology and Roman archaeology – and this has not only shaped our understanding of this economy, but also created a false hierarchy of the reliability or robustness of evidence, with written sources elevated above all others (Terrenato 2002; Webster 2008; 2010a). The situation is compounded by a lingering reticence within and between these disciplines to use multi-field and/or comparative approaches, with Mattingly's (2008) observation that we are better at delineating Roman archaeology than we are at interpreting it, still feeling as relevant today as it did 14 years ago.

Jane Webster (2001; 2005; 2008; 2010b) has been notable in advocating for a change in approach to the Roman world, and through her work has proven the benefits of drawing on methods and approaches of historical archaeology concerned with the Trans-Atlantic slave trade (sixteenth to nineteenth centuries CE), and stepping away from hierarchies of knowledge. This latter approach is exemplified by Joshel and Petersen's (2014: 8) stance: 'the material world we observe ... words translate into objects, objects into words. At other points, as misfit of words and things shows what the sources ... say about one another and about slavery.' Over the years, a range of publications have used novel ways to re-examine the evidence for enslavement, and investigated the intersections with issues of identity and agency (Joshel and Murnaghan 2005; Kamen 2010; George 2013; Joshel 2013; Baird 2015; Trimble 2016). Nevertheless, Webster's (2008: 122) observation still rings true, and unconsciously (or not), still shadows research: 'Archaeologists want to believe that the experience of slaves in the Classical world was somehow "better" than that of their Atlantic counterparts'.

This attitude could be viewed as a response to the perceived 'threat' (rather than benefit) to a system which benefits and prioritises white European, typically male, perspectives on the past – mirroring the overwhelming dominance of elite Roman male voices (Webster 2008; Joshel and Petersen 2014: 5). Work to decolonise and decentre whiteness in the study of the ancient world has exposed the extent to which the naivete or reluctance on the part of modern scholars to accept the realities of captive-taking and enslavement in the Roman world is a result of the manipulation of Greco-Roman history by imperial and colonial powers from the seventeenth century CE onwards, as a model and rationale for their own military and trading expansionism, which in turn has influenced the study and teaching of the ancient world (Hingley 2000; Kamash 2021; The Roman Society 2021). Archaeology is used by states and political groups to shape their narratives and to stoke culture wars, emphasising that we must be mindful about our studies and how we disseminate the findings, as they have power and resonance beyond academic publication (Bonacchi et al. 2018; Hingley et al. 2018; MacSweeney et al. 2019; Bonacchi and Krzyzanska 2021).

As there is extensive literature concerned with captive-taking and enslavement in the Roman world, this chapter is not exhaustive. Instead, it endeavours to provide an overview of the key types of evidence and current debates. The evidence reviewed will span many disciplines. It draws on and is embedded in the following theoretical frameworks: Black Feminist archaeology (Franklin 2001; Battle-Baptiste 2016; Watkins 2020), web of violence (Turpin and Kurtz 1997; Hamby and Grych 2013), embodiment (Csordas 1990; Geller and Suri 2014) and archaeologies of the heart (Supernant et al. 2021). It is also written with care, recognising that ancient slavery cannot be untangled from later periods of enslavement, and all contribute to trauma experienced by survivors and descendants (Gill et al. 2019; Parry 2021). This makes it different to other overviews, as does its foundation: 'the material traces of slavery are inscribed into everything so captivity is not a spatially or socially isolable phenomenon reflected simply in unique material patterns of goods' (Mullins 2008: 126–7).

Roman worldview and web of violence

Several key points about how Romans understood and categorised the world, particularly human bodies, need to be briefly summarised, as they intersect with captive-taking and enslavement. In their worldview, male bodies were the norm and all other bodies – female or intersex – were deviations from this ideal, which in itself varied according to status (Foxhall and Salmon 1998; Robb and Harris 2013; Goldberg 2021). These notions underpinned Roman sexual relationships, with the active role (with same/opposite genders) being preferable for adult men, as it signalled their virility (*vir* = man/male), and the passive role being taken by others, including children and the enslaved (Hubbard 2013; Skinner 2013; Ivleva and Collins 2020; Roth 2021). This misogyny also extended into how non-male and lower-status people were treated in law, and the political and economy autonomy available to them (Peachin 2011), forming part of the web of violence that was physically present in people's lives (Fagan 2020).

The presence of racism in the Roman world is now more openly acknowledged and discussed than ever before, but because racism is a social construct (Spillers 2003; Weheliye 2014; McKittrick 2015), it must be understood that it operated differently to the contemporary world. The Roman world has been described as proto-racist (Snowden 1970; 1983; Thompson 1989; Yamauchi 2001; Isaac 2006; 2013; McCoskey and Talbot 2006; McCoskey 2012) and the racism present in that world was different to ours, because although variations in skin colour and colourism held racial meanings in the Roman world, they were not the basis of political, social and economic discrimination and inequality (Snowden 1970; McCoskey 2012: 24–7). Instead, race intersected with ethnicity and gender to create a complex system of social acceptance (McCoskey 2012).

Fernández-Götz and colleagues (2020) do not shy away from identifying the empire as a predatory system, which embedded exploitation and asymmetries of power, much of which was enacted and achieved through physical violence. Importantly, they assert the need for scholars not to gloss over or explain away this web of violence by invoking the 'greater good' argument and minimising 'the dimensions of hard power' (Fernández-Götz 2020: 1654), the realities of which were included in public art (e.g. Trajan's Column) and embodied in human remains (Redfern 2018) (cf. Gardner 2020).

The web of violence was not confined to state-level military activities, law and justice. It was present within the communities which made up the Roman world, throughout their lived experience of state-level interventions, including, amongst others: colonisation; forced relocation; the disenfranchisement of women and the elderly; use as predatory landscapes for exploitation; and the continuation of local ritualised violence (e.g. Mays and Steele 1996; Cokayne 2003; Parkin 2003; Bodel 2005; Heather 2017; Phang 2022). The web of violence also operated at the interpersonal level, with infanticide, child and elder abuse, and intimate partner assault all being socially acceptable forms of violence. For women, from conception to death, their lives were shaped by violence (Redfern 2019; forthcoming). For the enslaved, the web of violence also allowed them to be used for non-consensual sex, and they could be beaten, maimed, impaired, tortured and executed (Saller 1991; Clark 1998; Lenski 2016; Kamen and Marshall 2021). We must also not forget that they were used by owners to commit violence on their behalf, acting as bodyguards or enforcers (Lenski 2016).

One legal case from fourth-century CE Egypt exemplifies the almost lethal levels of violence that could be perpetrated within a household but were socially acceptable within wider society. An affidavit, given by a Christian wife against her husband, details the violence he committed against her, their enslaved, her foster-daughters, and his agent and son: being locked in a cellar for a week; beating the enslaved; stripping and torturing the foster-daughters with fire; verbal abuse; imprisonment and threatening infidelity (*P.Oxy*. 6 903; Kruschwitz 2015). We can only imagine the earlier episodes of intimate terrorism (Johnson 2008) which preceded this event (Bent-Goodley 2007; Abramsky et al. 2011).

Why did the Romans need slaves?

The slave trade is believed to have been present in Bronze Age Europe and the Near East, if not earlier (Taylor 2021; Vlassopoulos 2021). Consequently, the Romans did not always introduce enslavement to the communities they conquered, and there are examples where communities outside of the empire took captives from Roman territories (Lenski 2008; 2014). Rather, the conquered communities saw an expansion in the number of people enslaved, and greater variation in their occupations (Morley 2011; Mata 2019). The enslaved were present in all areas of the economy and household in the Roman Empire, and although many people were born into slavery (*vernae*), Scheidel (2005; 2007; 2011) estimates that, every year, 250–400,000 captives would be required to maintain the likely 5–8 million enslaved people present in Italy, and the entire system was totally dependent on the balance between labour supply and demand, with prices for slaves fluctuating over time and between locales.

It is also clear, from literary sources and inscriptions, that the labour and other economic activities of lower-status freeborn and freed people was hugely important in the Roman world, and their experiences overlapped and intersected with the enslaved (Garnsey 1976; Bradley 1985; Whittaker 1987; Mouritsen 2011; Bell and Ramsby 2012). Although, beyond the remit of this chapter, it is important to note that although they had been freed, they continued to experience various legal and social unfreedoms (Gardner 2011). For example, many freedwomen continued to be trapped in coercive and asymmetrical relationships (Phang 2004; Phang et al. 2005). For example, the actions of freedwoman Acte's against her husband and former owner included poisoning, adultery and running away with his slaves, all of which led to Acte being removed from her child's funerary altar inscription (Carroll 2011; *CIL* VI.20905) – her actions could be viewed as resistance against her situation.

The enslaved: origins, *natio* and racism

Broadly speaking, the paths to enslavement can be divided into those external or internal to the empire. Externally, the people who were taken captive and enslaved were not geographically defined, and neither was the practice targeted towards a particular population or community. Instead the geographies of enslavement at any time reflected where territories were being conquered, the predatory landscapes bordering the empire, and the extensive trade networks with south Asia, Africa and the Near East, where the military activities of those empires were producing huge numbers of captives (Scheidel 1997; Lenski, 2008; 2016; Webster 2010a; Cameron 2011; Woolf 2016). The Roman literary sources reveal that captives were acquired by raiding, kidnapping and warfare, with the military playing an influential role (Scheidel 1997). These sources, in addition to funerary monuments (e.g. *CIL* XIII.8348), reveal that the lucrative practice of slave trading was undertaken by freedmen, mercantile families, and individual men and women, often alongside the purchase and transport of other commodities (Bodel 2005; Roymans and Zandstra 2011; George 2013).

Although an enslaved status was not directly connected to a person's origin or physical appearance, it does not mean that racism did not play a role in their experience of being enslaved. Nevertheless, the situation was complex because of how racism intersected with prejudices held against people of different ethnicities and origins within and without the empire. It has been suggested that there was an absence of physical differences between the enslaved and enslavers (amongst others, Morley 2011), a statement which requires some scrutiny. It reveals the extent to which whiteness is embedded in Roman studies: that enslavers were what many readers might regard as white European populations (see M'charek et al. 2014; M'charek and Schramm 2020; M'charek 2021); that the majority of the enslaved came from within Europe and the Mediterranean world and therefore, were not (or unlikely to be) people of colour; and perceived baselines about population homogeneity, compounding the paucity of research concerning colourism in the Roman world. Although these baselines have been challenged for several decades (e.g. Snowden 1970; 1983), and increasingly through the use of ancient DNA, isotopes and forensic-based methods (e.g. Eckardt 2010; Antonio et al. 2019; Salesse et al. 2021), they remain firmly embedded. We must shift to accepting that, as a given, the Roman world was inhabited by people of diverse heritages, and reject that a birthplace or residency during a lifetime equated to a form or type of physical appearance.

Literary sources from Italy suggest that captive and enslaved individuals of African and south Asian heritage and/or origin were more valuable, representing prestigious acquisitions, and sometimes even believed to hold apotropaic power (Thurmond 1994; Scheidel 1997). Some authors go so far as to suggest that the purchase of figurines, lamps or glassware (amongst other objects) shaped to look like people of African heritage, represented a proxy form of ownership (George 2003; 2013: 4). Whether real people or as representations of a prestigious acquisition, these behaviours signal the Romans' racist views.

Certain ethnicities and origins were deemed as entirely appropriate for enslavement and were believed to be innately suitable for certain tasks, such as Gaulish men being naturally suited to animal herding (Varro *De Re Rustica*; Scheidel 1997; Kahlos 2022). Legally, an individual's '*natio*' (ethnic origin) had to be given at the point of sale, so that buyers could avoid disruption within their household by ensuring that their human property remained disparate and alienated from their original ethnic identities (Scheidel 1997; Webster 2010b; Patterson 2018: 5), although that was not a barrier to the enslaved creating families or having camaraderie with one another (Joshel and Petersen 2014: 208). In reality, the depth of this alienation was probably variable, because individuals who were captured as older children or adults may have remembered and held onto aspects of their natal identity (e.g. *RIB* 1065). It seems that the majority of the enslaved across the Empire were given new names. This should be understood as trauma because it erased their previous identity. For the most part these new names were Greek (e.g. Eros). Inscriptions suggest that some people kept their original name or perhaps gave themselves one from their own culture, and, in some circumstances, managed to retain a part of their natal identity, such as 'Ibu', a man believed to be of African origin whose funerary inscription was found in Rome (Solin 1996; Bodel 2003; Webster 2010a); but again, keeping his natal name or a version of it may have increased his value.

Valuing the enslaved

The value of an enslaved person can be explored in a number of ways, as it was not based just on their monetary worth. Literary sources show that physical appearance could potentially increase a person's price, whether this was because of their attractiveness, often enhanced by the slave trader (Bodel 2005), or the shape of their body, as people with growth restrictions and congenital anomalies were sold at the 'market of monsters' in Rome (Plutarch *Moralia* 520c). It is worth noting that in the oral histories of freed African-American people, those who had had enslaved childhoods remembered their monetary value and this became an important part of their identity (Sánchez-Eppler 2017: 43).

A range of archaeological evidence informs us about these non-monetary values, but it should be remembered that such evidence is often heavily shaped by socially prescribed patterns of behaviour or expression, and reflect asymmetries of power, so that implied personal connections may not be all that they seem. One famous example is a gold bracelet worn by a young woman who died during the eruption of Vesuvius (Italy) in 79 CE (Guzzo 2003: 178; SAP 81580). On the inner surface, the inscription reads 'the master to his very own slave-girl'. Edmondson (2011: 352–3) interprets this as a gift between lovers, and cites other authors who conclude that it was a decoration to enhance the charms of a prostitute. Baird (2015) has heavily criticised these interpretations, noting that it is reductive to assume the woman was enslaved or a (free) sex worker, and reminds us that she was found carrying a bag of jewellery, wearing other jewellery, and died alongside a woman and three children, which suggests a more complex scenario.

One key group to examine alternative values are *vernae* – homeborn enslaved. The work of Duane (2017a) raises two points for re-centring and critically examining how we think and write about this group of people in the Roman world: focusing on them compels us to look at relationships of power and dependence, and their enslavement demonstrates how people become property. Joining these concepts with Johnson's (1999: 22) observation that in the southern United States during the Antebellum period (1812–61 CE), 'children were taught to experience their bodies twice at once, to move through the world as both child and slave, person and property'. These observations allow us to explore the duality *vernae* embody, and which is seen in the literary and the archaeological evidence. The sources strongly suggest that many *vernae*, despite being homeborn, experienced natal alienation, as their biological parents may or may not have been resident and, unless the male parent was the enslaver, they did not legally belong to their biological relatives (Sigismund-Nielsen 2013). They were fed by wet nurses and cared for by childminders, with the impression that every effort was made to ensure they were not cared for by a biological parent (Bradley 1987; *CIL* VI.21151). It is also worth noting that despite there being no word to differentiate the male owner's formal family from the enslaved people that he owned, these distinctions were socially important (Saller 1987; *CIL*.29436).

Vernae did receive better treatment than other enslaved children, with some becoming substitutes for the owner's recognised children who had died (Bradley 1984; Sigismund-Nielsen 2013; Pudsey and Vuolanto 2022). This was in contrast to children who had passed into slavery through captive-taking or exposure – some of whom were literally named 'small basket', such as the well-behaved six-year-old girl 'Passia' commemorated in Thrace (Sigismund-Nielsen 2013: 286). Several authors have addressed shared play and skill learning with freeborn children within a household, and highlighted that slaves' dual embodiment could have negatively impacted their physical brain development and emotional attachments (Dolansky 2016; Laurence 2016; Duane 2017b; Vuolanto and Laes 2017).

Their preferential treatment reflects the Roman perception that they were more loyal, trustworthy and worked harder (Perry 2021) – as the fear of violence against and murder of owners was ever-present

(Hopkins 1993; Joshel 2010; *CIL* XIII.7070). Their commemorations and presence in the funerary inscriptions of others also marks out the complex sexual and emotional paths that the enslaved navigated because of their embodied duality (Laes 2008; 2011; Rawson 2010; Bruun 2013). For example, a funerary inscription found in Turcoaia (Romania), commemorating the death of one Euticus was set up by his enslaver, a tribune of the Fifth Macedonian legion. Mihailescu-Bîrliba (2015) acknowledges that the tribune may not have been his biological parent, but the presence of bath utensils implies that Euticus was responsible for his intimate care, which suggests that relationship was far from simple and may have involved what we would frame as coercive sexual labour by Euticus (contra, Alexandrescu 2021). Sánchez-Eppler (2017) reminds us of the trauma that such asymmetrical relationships can produce because of sexual abuse, emotional detachment and poor care. For example, we can only imagine the emotional world of a young Egyptian child called Narcissus, who was resold after the death of his biological mother (Laes 2008: 243).

Resistance, punishment and becoming darkness

The web of violence which operated in the Roman world and ensnared the bodies of captive and enslaved people, often provoked them to acts of resistance, sometimes captured in public art, such as on Trajan's Column (Speidel 1971; Duran 2021) (Figure 6.1). These acts of resistance to captivity and enslavement were often drastic. Literary sources record that to avoid being sold by the Roman army, Germanic women killed their children and then themselves (Dio Cassius 14.2). Resistance took many forms, from the slave wars in Italy (Shaw 2001), to running away or shirking responsibility; truancy had to be listed at sale (Joshel and Petersen 2014: 95–7). De Haas (2011) also suggests that enslaved women, whose value was greatest during their fertile years, practised reproductive resistance.

Resistance is also recorded in graffiti, with people scoring their name into walls or vessels, and in the case of some made at Pompeii, a record of their escape: 'Polucarpus fled' (*CIL* IV.2351). One case of resistance was recorded on the reverse of a Lydion brick tile found in London (Figure 6.2), whose elegant rhyming couplet neatly expresses the frustration or resignation of the writer, 'Every day for thirteen days Austalis has been wandering by himself' (*RIB* 2491.147).

Figure 6.1 Part of the relief on Trajan's Column, showing the suicide of Decebalus, a Dacian leader. © Roger B. Ulrich.

In many houses and villas across the Roman world, cosmological symbols or magical designs have been found, which are believed to have been created by the enslaved (Keegan 2014). Webster (2005) makes parallels with similar drawings made by the African diaspora in the Caribbean, where the merging of various Atlantic world cultures created new cosmologies, and suggests that a similar situation could have arisen in the Roman world.

Magic was also used by the enslaved, often to cope with the reality of their situation or as an aid to running away: the superstitious slave is a common stereotype (Webster 2010b; McKeown 2012). They used it to resist the will of their owners, to enable their transformation into animals or inanimate objects (Bradley 2000), to prevent their recapture, or wearing amulets to invoke 'darkness' so they would become invisible (de Haas 2011; McKeown 2012). The need to supress superstition in order to maintain discipline was recognised by owners, with the author Columella (*De Re Rustica* 1.8.7) urging villa owners to stop witches and seers entering an estate.

The surveillance of slaves' lives extended outside of their owner's dwellings, with runaways being reported by neighbours – such information was financially rewarded – and even those not truanting or escaping might run the risk of being mistaken for one and get punished

Figure 6.2 The reverse of a Lydion brick tile found in London with the graffiti '*Austalis dibus tredecim, vagatur sibi cotidim*' ('every day for thirteen days Austalis has been wandering by himself') (*RIB* 2491.147). © Museum of London

(Joshel and Petersen 2014). Runaways often took the owner's children with them – with one such case recorded in Roman Egypt, where Prima took the 5-month-old daughter of her owner (de Haas 2011). When enslaved women took children, it should make us ask whether the act would be understood today as a maternal-desire or emotion-based abduction (Boudreaux et al. 2000).

A number of riveted and inscribed metal collars (some of which held inscribed tags) have been found, dating to the late fourth century CE, sometimes still around the neck of the enslaved. One has a tag that states, 'I have run away; hold me. When you have brought me back to my master Zoninus, you will receive a gold coin' (Thurmond 1994; George 2013; Trimble 2016). It is thought that with the change to Christianity, the collars replaced facial tattoos, which had previously been used to identify runaways or truants (Thurmond 1994); Trimble (2016) is one of the few to consider how restrictive and uncomfortable wearing such a collar would be.

The enslaved were frequently punished, often at the whim of the owner, who for four sesterces (roughly equivalent to just over US$7) could pay to have their slave crucified. The owner's right to execute

Figure 6.3 Manacle and attached chain (3563) found at the National Safe Deposit site. © Museum of London.

their enslaved lasted until the fourth century CE (Parkin and Pomeroy 2007; Lenski 2016; Venters 2019). A recent case has been found in rural Britain (Grierson 2021). Ancient literary sources such as Galen (*Passions and Errors of the Soul* 1.4, 1.8) show that a frequent form of punishment was beating and whipping, but the enslaved (and criminals) were often placed in stocks, chained-up and/or placed in restraints – examples of stocks, chains, fetters and shackles survive in a variety of contexts, including burials and an individual who died at Pompeii (Thompson 1993; Joshel 2011; Morley 2011; Czarnecka 2013; cf. Roth 2011) (Figure 6.3). Secure holding spaces, or prisons, have been suggested as being present at numerous villas (e.g. El Munts, Spain) and buildings across the Roman world (Morley 2011; Roymans and Zandstra 2011; George 2013; Joshel and Petersen 2014). The imagery of restrained captives, often chained or tied at the neck, was also common, with depictions existing in a wide variety of materials and spaces: public art, funerary monuments and figurines (Ferris 2000; Jackson 2005; Webster 2005; Roymans and Zandstra 2011; e.g. *RIB* 2193 and 3507). Restrained individuals have been found in cemeteries, and in clandestine and atypical funerary contexts, including near a tufa mine in Germany (Thompson 1993; 2003; Chinnock and Marshall 2021). It should be noted that sometimes the burials of individuals wearing large, heavy iron, leg rings have been found, but these are not always linked by a chain nor do all appear to have had a chain attached to them. Therefore, many authors urge caution about seeing these as restraints (Harward et al. 2015).

Punishments also included being relocated to another property belonging to the owner, usually from urban to rural, thereby removing the enslaved from their social network and, typically, compelling them to do manual labour. Thinking empathetically about this emphasises how devasting this could be, because literary sources show that the enslaved had mental maps of their residences and neighbourhoods, and formed strong personal connections with each other (Joshel and Petersen 2014). Being relocated and starting over would be a source of anxiety and stress (Hansen and Oliver-Smith 2019). One unusual case is recorded in the Justinian *Digest* (49.xv.6) and details how an enslaved woman in Britain, convicted of a crime, was sentenced to hard labour at a salt-works in Scotland, where she was captured by bandits and sold in 'the course of lawful trade'. She was repurchased by her enslaver (Marcus Cocceius Firmus), an army centurion from Lower Moesia, who claimed that he should be refunded by the imperial treasury (Birley 1936; Evans Grubbs 2013). These few sentences reveal the web of violence, clearly showing the links between the imperial state, the military, activities in predatory landscapes and the engagement by non-conquered peoples with Roman enslavers. Throughout, the nameless woman victim was subjected to violence for which she could never expect to receive justice (for the experiences and health outcomes for modern trafficked women, see amongst others, Zimmerman et al. 2006; 2008).

The enslaved also committed acts of physical violence against their owners, with the proverb 'you have as many enemies as you have slaves' being a real source of fear for owners (Seneca *Epistles* 47.5; Lenski 2016). Accounts from the Atlantic World provide some pointers and suggest caution about some of the literary evidence from antiquity (Rodriguez 2007). For example, Escott (1979) found that from a total of 826 freed African-American slave narratives which spoke about resistance, only 16 per cent recalled being violent against their owners. A handful of Roman funerary inscriptions record the murder of owners (e.g. *CIL* XIII.7070). There were also legal cases, including one where the consul Lucius Pedanius Secundus was murdered by one of his male enslaved, either due to jealousy or because the owner had reneged on a deal to manumit him (Tacitus *Annals* xiv.42). The law stated that, as punishment, all of the Lucius' enslaved should be crucified and in this case the senate upheld the law, despite it resulting in the execution of many women and children (Hopkins 1993; Tacitus *Annals* xiv.42). Only very rarely in the discussion of this violence is attention paid to the causes and provocations, with most authors taking a steer from the primary sources, such as sexual jealousy, but as Hopkins (1993) reminds us, stories like Tacitus' are important, because they were so often repeated. Lenski (2016) suggests that one reason why the slave system lasted for so long was the use of physical violence and executions against those who had been violent to their owner.

De Haas (2011) suggests funerary commemoration could also be another act of resistance, which is a very empathetic way to view these often very brief lines recording a person's existence. The importance attached to such memorialisation shows the enslaved pushing back against the erasure of their identity (Hope 1997; 2009; Carroll 2006). The acts of commemoration undertaken by slaves' own social network, rather than their owner (e.g. Treggiari 1973), are particularly evocative, as exemplified by an inscription from Rome for two freedmen: 'we were sold into slavery together, we were freed together from the same household, and no day could have separated us, apart from this fateful one' (*CIL* VI.22355A; *ILS* 8432). In contrast, the funerary monuments of gladiators can be read as a continuation of the reflected glory of their owner (Hope 2000; 2001), and often when owners commemorated their enslaved, as with the example of Euticus, it is not always entirely clear whether coercion played a role in their relationship or not (Ivleva 2020).

Embodying enslavement

It is clear from Roman literature and personal letters that slave-traders and enslavers sought to transform and modify the bodies of the enslaved, ranging from castration to depilation (Joshel and Petersen 2014: 9). This control extended to the behaviours and bodily functions of the enslaved, such as preventing them from coughing and sneezing at inappropriate moments, and controlling how they spoke and made gestures. Joshel and Petersen (2014: 9, 220) explain that the owners wanted to transform the enslaved's identity and body, because 'they were participants in their master's narratives'. Joshel (2011: 215) makes the important point that the enslaved could be 'turned to any use', and this can be illustrated in the writings of Seneca (*Epistles* 47):

> another, who serves the wine, must dress like a woman and wrestle with his advancing years; he cannot get away from his boyhood; he is dragged back to it; and though he has already acquired a soldier's figure, he is kept beardless by having his hair smoothed away or

> plucked out by the roots, and he must remain awake throughout the night, dividing his time between his master's drunkenness and his lust; in the chamber he must be a man, at the feast a boy.

There is extensive literature about the depictions and presence of the enslaved in material culture and domestic space/architecture, with interesting explorations about the representation of and engagement with people of colour, the reduced body size of the enslaved compared to freeborn people, and the use of striped patterns on walls to signify routes that the enslaved should use to move discretely around an elite home (Snowden 1970, 1983; Webster 2005; 2008; Joshel 2010; George 2013; Joshel and Petersen 2014). Research on graffiti in Italian houses has also provided insights into the experiences of the enslaved, with clusters found in kitchen, service and portico areas, where children seemingly spent a lot of time in hidden and marginalised spaces (Baldwin et al. 2013; Huntley 2013).

Considerable attention has also been paid to the horrific working conditions of enslaved adults and children who worked in mines across the empire (Diodorus Siculus 3.12.1–4; Laes 2008: 250–1; Hirt 2010; Odochiciuc and Mihailescu-Bîrliba 2014). Chemical analyses of the bones of miners (criminals/enslaved) from Wadi Faynan (Jordan) found that mining and smelting copper was so toxic that the heavy metal loads in their skeletons were much higher than normal (Grattan et al. 2002; Pyatt et al. 2005). Research has also looked at the work and responsibilities of the enslaved owned by the military, not just individual soldiers (Phang 2004; Phang et al., 2005; Silver 2016). Inscription evidence for these roles demonstrates the long-distance mobility experienced by the enslaved (e.g. Carroll 2006: 228).

Many decades of bioarchaeological research on enslaved people and racialised minorities in North America and elsewhere in the Atlantic world have contributed to identifying patterns of disease, trauma, congenital anomalies, dental health and age-at-death (amongst many, Mack and Blakey 2004; Pearson et al. 2011; Shuler 2011; Harrod and Martin 2014; 2015; Isable 2021; Maass 2022), which can be used in the analysis of Roman populations (data summarised in Redfern 2018; 2020a). However, this is not a simple exercise, because Roman enslavement was highly variable with respect to life course, gender, occupations, and the existence of food insecurities and insufficiencies. Furthermore, these patterns are frequently observed in populations from other locales and periods who have experienced poverty and food insecurity (Geber 2015; Mant and Holland 2019), as well as in those who have been colonised or forced to migrate because of climate change (Baker and Tsuda 2015; Klaus et al. 2017). Therefore, it is the wider context which must be used to inform and guide osteobiographies or the interpretation of groups of individuals.

It is clear from many bioarchaeological studies across the Roman world that the inequalities embedded in the socio-political organisation of the empire are captured in human remains, with children, women and the elderly bearing the brunt of this violence (Sperduti 1997; Gowland and Redfern 2010; Redfern and DeWitte 2011a; 2011b; Redfern and Gowland 2011; Redfern 2013; 2020b; forthcoming; Brandt et al. 2016; Gowland 2017; Killgrove 2017; 2018; Bourbou 2018; Marklein 2020; Marklein and Fox 2020; Avery et al. 2021; Moore et al. 2021a; 2021b). Nevertheless, the presence or absence of certain conditions (e.g. rickets), or stable isotope evidence for dietary insufficiencies (Redfern et al. 2019), cannot simply be read as evidence for someone being born to an enslaved person or into unfreedom (e.g. Lockau et al. 2019). However, when taken as part of an osteobiography (Hosek and Robb 2019), they may be able to help point in that direction.

The impact and consequences of enslavement can be traced back to a person's prenatal development. Gowland and other scholars (Gowland 2015; Gowland and Halcrow 2020; Gamble and Bentley 2022) have demonstrated the importance of the Developmental Origins of Health and Disease (DoHAD) or Barker hypothesis in bioarchaeology. Whereby, the effects of poor health, socio-economic status and risk of disease all have the potential to play out across generations, reminding us that an individual's osteobiography also tells us about other lives (Gowland 2015; Hodson and Gowland 2020).

Gowland and Halcrow's (2020) research also emphasises the importance of the first 1000 days after conception, as this is where many long-term health outcomes and mortality risks are created. It is now possible to explore health during the early stages of an individual's life through stable isotope analyses, which have revealed childhood stress/disease events that lead to a premature death (Leskovar et al. 2019; Kendall et al. 2020). Peacock et al.'s (2019) study of mobility and vitamin D deficiency in individuals from Roman Switzerland found that three adults who died between the ages of 25–35 years old were migrants from Central and Eastern Europe. All three had suffered from rickets as young children and two had also experienced it again during puberty – potentially from enforced movement because of enslavement (Peacock et al. 2019).

Macroscopic observations continue to provide crucial insights, such as Hodson's (2017) analysis of the pre-term (<40 weeks gestation) and full-term (>40 weeks gestation) individuals from Piddington villa (Britain), which found that their skeletal development had been compromised by poor health. This suggests that the deceased had been born to mothers with poor health and adverse living conditions. A clay tablet discovered at Villafranca de los Barros (Spain) records the precarity of what Gowland (2015) calls 'entangled lives': 'the girl, who was already pregnant, whom you had sent, to such labour that the master's slave-offspring perished, who was made for great work' (*EE* IX, 176). Again, this correspondence shows the erasure of the enslaved's identity, and it is the loss of a future worker, which is cause of upset, rather than the miscarriage and subsequent trauma for the mother (cf. Gowland 2020).

Many bioarchaeological and stable isotope studies have proven that growing up in the Roman world resulted in a higher burden of disease, pollution and risk of death (Cucina et al. 2006; FitzGerald et al. 2006; Gowland and Redfern 2010; Redfern and DeWitte 2011b; Redfern and Gowland 2011; Redfern et al. 2015; Mays et al. 2018; Lockau et al. 2019; Minozzi et al. 2020; Moore et al. 2021a; 2021b). As outlined above, unpicking whether the evidence for disease and early death results from poverty, enslavement or other forms of adversity may not always be possible (e.g. Cardoso et al. 2019). Rohnbogner's (2017; 2018; 2022; Rohnbogner and Lewis 2016) reviews of subadult (<18 years old) bioarchaeological data from rural sites in Britain strongly argues for the presence of poverty and enslavement in the rural population. They observe a decline in overall health from the age of 6.5 years old, and the presence of vitamin C and D deficiencies (scurvy and rickets), evidence for episodes of stress, alongside evidence for respiratory disease and accidental fractures, the latter two highlighting the involvement of children in agricultural and rural-based industries from an early age. Of course, the Roman life course varied temporally and spatially (Harlow and Laurence 2002; Revell 2005; Moore 2009). We must be open to the possibility that the decline in health, accompanied by dietary insufficiencies, could have arisen through enslavement, as the literary sources show that enslaved children began working from as young as five years old (Bradley 1985; Laes 2008). The remains of children involved in manual labour have been identified in Italy (Bisel and Bisel 2002; Scuibba et al. 2013; Rossi et al. 2020) and elsewhere in the Roman world (Laes 2008).

As many aspects of childhood are recorded within an adult body (e.g. diet, trauma, disease), it is possible to use adult remains to explore an individual's earlier life experience (Humphrey and King 2000; Lewis 2007; Reitsema and McIlvaine 2014). However, we must ask ourselves where this childhood took place. Being mindful of the highly mobile lives of people within the Roman world (De Ligt and Tacoma 2016; Prowse 2016; Woolf 2016), forces us to challenge the assumption that evidence for an adverse childhood reflects the location/community where a person was buried. This is important when researching women and children, who were especially vulnerable to captive-taking and for whom stable isotope and inscriptions signal their often long-distance mobility (Bradley 1987; Shaw et al. 2016; Stark et al. 2020; 2022). Neither must we underestimate the complexities of Roman lives, as it was entirely possible for families in poverty to sell their children into slavery (Bradley 1985). In this case, it could mean that multiple layers of adversity are recorded by a person's skeleton, and it may not be possible to separate out the causes.

At Narbonne (France), a freedman created a funerary monument whose inscription contains the words 'my whole being changed' (Knapp 2011: 139–40; *CIL* XII.5026). That tremendously powerful statement perfectly captures the bodily changes wrought by enslavement, and reflects the bioarchaeological evidence suggestive of enslavement, particularly for roles involving physical risk and manual labour. That said, we must be cautious in our inferences, bearing in mind the overlap in activities/occupations with tenured labour (Roymans and Zandstra 2011). Two case studies can be used to explore the embodiment of enslavement from a bioarchaeological approach, which draws on wider funerary and archaeological contexts (Martin et al. 2014). In the town of Saintes (France), excavations revealed the graves of 100 individuals, dating to the first and second centuries CE, with seven individuals buried wearing iron restraints (Méténier et al. 2017) (Figure 6.4). One of these individuals, a male over 30 years old (*SEP* 2084), was found with an iron ring restraint on his right ankle; another ring restraint was found in the grave fill (Figure 6.5). His right shoulder joint was dislocated and the joint had fused. He also had a small depressed cranial fracture (Méténier et al. 2017). Dislocations are rare in the bioarchaeological record: acromioclavicular ones are usually produced by a fall onto the shoulder; the small cranial fractures, from a blow to the head, are often produced accidentally (Redfern 2016). The lack of reduction suggests a lack of or inadequate medical treatment, with the infection indicating a compromised health status. The injuries are suggestive of accidents happening during manual work and limited access to medical treatment, which points to this individual having a lower status, but the presence of restraints puts these accidental causes in a new light. Did his shoulder fail

Figure 6.4 A male aged >30 years old excavated from Saintes (France), who was found with a restraint on their left lower leg (SEP 2055). © INRAP.

Figure 6.5 A young adult male excavated from Saintes (France), who was buried wearing restraints around his neck and right lower leg (SEP 2073). © INRAP.

to heal properly because he wasn't given sufficient time to recover? Could they have been caused by intentional violence against him? It is being open to these possibilities that provides the opportunity to re-evaluate our perceptions of the Roman world.

The funerary context and remains of one adult male excavated from a first- to fourth-century CE rural cemetery in Suffolk (Britain) is also highly suggestive of an enslaved life (Archaeological Solutions Ltd, unpublished manuscript).[1] In total, the remains of 68 individuals were found, many of whom were buried in a non-normative fashion, including several decapitated adults and a child. The majority of adults have evidence for extensive osteoarthritis, poor dental health and injuries caused by falls and excess loading, and one child may have been branded on the head (Archaeological Solutions Ltd, unpublished manuscript). Overall, the bioarchaeological and funerary data strongly suggest that this burial ground was used for enslaved or indentured agricultural workers (Redfern 2018).

One adult male (skeleton 24) had osteoarthritis to his ankle, knee and hip joints, his finger, wrist, elbow and shoulder joints, and also in his spine and jaw. He also had osseous changes indicative of ischial bursitis, soft-tissue injuries to his left foot, non-specific infection on his lower legs, congenital spinal anomalies, Schmorl's nodes in his spine, and poor dental health. A series of healed fractures were also observed to the spine, right and left lower legs, right foot, multiple left ribs and the left forearm; two possible hand fractures and a possible fracture to the left portion of the pelvis were also reported. Healing fractures were also seen on the sacrum and two ribs (Archaeological Solutions Ltd, unpublished manuscript). He had been decapitated and buried apart, in an area previously used for quarrying. The osteoarthritis, Schmorl's nodes and bursitis have multifactorial aetiologies, but can be caused by physical labour (see Schrader 2019). Multiple left rib fractures are mostly commonly produced by a fall, but the fact that they were fractured mid-body means it is more likely that they were broken by blows to the chest. Given that the mid-shaft of the left ulna had a healed fracture, together these trauma suggest one or multiple assaults (Wedel and Galloway 2014: 189–92, 226–8). Fractures of the pubic ramus (part of the pelvis) is typically caused by falls, often from standing height (Wedel and Galloway 2014: 52), with the fractures to the spine and sacrum also caused by falls or from repeatedly carrying heavy loads (Wedel and Galloway 2014: 178–9, 185–7). The fractures to the joint surfaces of the right leg and foot, and proximal left fibula, suggest activity-related trauma (Wedel and Galloway 2014: 273–5, 288, 307). Combined with the other diseases and conditions observed in his skeleton, his remains strongly suggest that he endured intense manual labour over many years, and survived multiple episodes of accidental and intentional violence. At least one episode occurred only a few months before his death and may have contributed to it. Sacral fractures are serious and frequently cause neurological trauma, which can result in impairment and caring needs (Gibbons et al. 1990; Tilley and Cameron 2014). The manner of his death is more difficult to understand, as decapitation appears to be a wide-spread burial rite in Roman Britain (Crerar 2015). However, owners could execute their enslaved and that may well be the case here (Lenski 2016). Speith (2015) makes the case that individuals like skeleton 24, who had compromised physical health and required care, may have been released from their pain by a mercy killing.

Conclusion

The experience of captivity and enslavement in the Roman world was not 'better' than the Trans-Atlantic slave trade (Webster 2008: 122). Although many people may have had 'light duties', the erasure of their identity and, for some, their dual embodiment all contributed to them existing as a 'socially dead' person (Patterson 2018: 38). The inscription and graffiti evidence point to further complexities, particularly for women and children, where their unfreedoms and risk of sexual violence are attested (e.g. Phang 2004; Roth 2021). We must also recognise that enslavement, part of the web of violence that existed in the Roman world, intersected with proto-racism and xenophobia to embed additional inequalities.

Bioarchaeology offers a unique dataset to contribute to these research endeavours, because inequalities and violence become embodied and can be investigated by looking at osteological evidence for disease and trauma (Gravlee 2009; Kuzawa and Gravlee 2016). Human remains, particularly those of children and babies, offer the possibility to see 'entangled lives' (Gowland 2015), where the outcomes of enslavement resonate across the generations. These independent data are able to reveal evidence at the individual and group level, and show variation between locales and time periods, reflecting how conquest and colonisation varied across the Mediterranean and northern Europe. Above all, it is the evidence for physical violence found in the remains of both children and adults, which is most immediate and often profoundly shocking. Their remains bear witness to the cruelty and accepted levels of violence that existed, and are a challenge to those who would down-play that aspect of the Roman world.

Over the past three years, in response to wider social changes and activism, Roman scholarship has begun to be more open about the challenges it faces, especially embedded whiteness. Such shifts in power, and the raising-up of alternative voices and perspectives will continue to change how we excavate, research and interpret the Roman world. This transformation will benefit the study of enslavement, which for many years has shied away from addressing issues such as racism, child sexual exploitation and coercive relationships. It is also pleasing to see how enslavement is now being written about with more empathy, and majority population scholars in the Global North are being more open about their privileges and questioning their practice: who and what are we not seeing, and whose voices are we excluding from researching the Roman world (Liebow and Glazer 2019; The Roman Society 2021)? It seems we are finally achieving the aims set out by Webster (2005) almost two decades ago. It is a challenging process that has consequences not only for how we create new insights into the Roman world, but also for today, as the majority of Roman scholars live and work in Global North countries and institutions, which are being confronted by their colonial pasts and involvement in the Trans-Atlantic slave trade, and because many political bodies are employing our content to engage in culture wars (Bonacchi 2018; MacSweeney et al. 2019).

Acknowledgements

I am indebted to two generous colleagues at INRAP, Tristan Tocqueville for sending me a copy of the Saintes site report, and Valerie Bureau for arranging image use; Archaeological Solutions Ltd for allowing me to use their unpublished site report; The Hellenic and Roman Library; John Pearce for all his help with the inscription evidence; Jane Webster for her advice and guidance about this chapter, and enslavement more generally; Sara Phang and Ulrike Roth for their correspondence about Roman women, children and the enslaved which has informed this work. Thanks are also given to Richard Stroud and John Chase for the photography, and Meriel Jeater for making the time to let me look at the shackle and for the discussion we had about our emotional responses to it.

The chapter is dedicated to the memory of Dr Ross Thomas, a fellow Sandown High student and archaeologist from Brading, Isle of Wight.

Note

1 Archaeological Solutions Ltd. *Fentons Farm: Mid and late Roman quarrying, high status feasting, and burial at Great Whelnetham, Suffolk*. Unpublished manuscript.

Abbreviations

CIL: *Corpus Inscriptionum Latinarum*. Berlin: Berlin-Brandenburg Academy of Sciences and Humanities, 1863–.

EE: Zangemeister, K. (ed.). 1884. *Ephemeris Epigraphica, Corporis Inscriptionum Latinarum Supplementum*. Deutsches Archäologisches Institut, Instituti Archaeologici Romani.
ILS: H. Dessau. 1892–1916. *Inscriptiones Latinae Selectae*. Berlin: Weidmann.
RIB: *Roman Inscriptions of Britain*, https://romaninscriptionsofbritain.org/.

References

Abramsky, Tanya, Charlotte H. Watts, Claudia Garcia-Moreno, Karen Devries, Ligia Kiss, Mary Ellsberg, Henrica A.F.M. Jansen and Lori Heise. 2011. 'What factors are associated with recent intimate partner violence? Findings from the WHO multi-country study on women's health and domestic violence', *BMC Public Health* 11: 109.

Alexandrescu, Cristina-Georgeta. 2021. 'The extraordinary funerary stele of the verna of an eques Romanus from Troesmis'. In *Studii de arheologie și istorie antică în onoarea lui Victor Henrich Baumann cu ocazia celei de a 80-a aniversări*, edited by Sorin-Cristian Ailincăi, George Nuțu, Christian Micu, Marion Mocanu and Aurel-Daniel Stănică, 191–220. Cluj-Napoca: Editura Mega.

Antonio, Margaret L., Ziyue Gao, Hannah M. Moots, Michaela Lucci, Francesca Candilio, Susanna Sawyer, Victoria Oberreiter, Diego Calderon, Katharina Devitofranceschi, Rachael C. Aikens, Serena Aneli, Fulvio Bartoli, Alessandro Bedini, Olivia Cheronet, Daniel J. Cotter, Daniel M. Fernandes, Gabriella Gasperetti, Renata Grifoni, Alessandro Guidi, Francesco La Pastina, Ersilia Loreti, Daniele Manacorda, Giuseppe Matullo, Simona Morretta, Alessia Nava, Vincenzo Fiocchi Nicolai, Federico Nomi, Carlo Pavolini, Massimo Pentiricci, Philippe Pergola, Marina Piranomonte, Ryan Schmidt, Giandomenico Spinola, Alessandra Sperduti, Mauro Rubini, Luca Bondioli, Alfredo Coppa, Ron Pinhasi and Jonathan K. Pritchard. 2019. 'Ancient Rome: a genetic crossroads of Europe and the Mediterranean', *Science* 366: 708–14.

Avery, L. Creighton, Megan B. Brickley, Sheri Findlay, Cécile Chapelain De Seréville-Niel and Tracy L. Prowse. 2021. 'Child and adolescent diet in Late Roman Gaul: an investigation of incremental dietary stable isotopes in tooth dentine', *International Journal of Osteoarchaeology* 31: 1226–36.

Baird, Jennifer A. 2015. 'On reading the material culture of ancient sexual labor', *Helios* 42: 163–75.

Baker, Brenda J. and Takeyuki Tsuda (eds). 2015. *Migration and Disruptions: Toward a unifying theory of ancient and contemporary migrations*. Gainesville, FL: University of Florida Press.

Baldwin, Eamonn, Helen Moulden and Ray Laurence. 2013. 'Slaves and children in a Roman villa: writing and space in the villa San Marco at Stabiae'. In *Written Space in the Latin West*, edited by Gareth Sears, Paul Keegan and Ray Laurence, 153–66. London: Bloomsbury.

Battle-Baptiste, Whitney. 2016. *Black Feminist Archaeology*. London: Routledge.

Bell, Sinclair and Teresa Ramsby (eds). 2012. *Free at Last! The impact of freed slaves on the Roman Empire*. London: Bloomsbury.

Bent-Goodley, Tricia B. 2007. 'Health disparities and violence against women: why and how cultural and societal influences matter', *Trauma Violence Abuse* 8: 90–104.

Birley, Eric. 1936. 'Marcus Cocceius Firmus: an epigraphic study', *Proceedings of the Society of Antiquaries of Scotland* 70: 363–77.

Bisel, Sara and Jane E. Bisel. 2002. 'Health and nutrition at Herculaneum: an examination of skeletal remains'. In *The Natural History of Pompeii*, edited by Wilhelmina Feemster Jashemski and Frederick G. Meyer, 451–75. Cambridge: Cambridge University Press.

Bodel, John. 2003. Review of Solin, H. 1996. 'Die stadtrömischen Sklavennamen. Ein Namenbuch IIII (Stuttgart)', *Bryn Mawr Classical Review* 1.

Bodel, John. 2005. 'Caveat emptor: towards a study of Roman slave-traders', *Journal of Roman Archaeology* 18: 181–95.

Bonacchi, Chiara. 2018. 'Public archaeology cannot just "fly at dusk": the reality and complexities of generating public impact', *Antiquity* 92: 1659–61.

Bonacchi, Chiara and Marta Krzyzanska. 2021. 'Heritage-based tribalism in Big Data ecologies: deploying origin myths for antagonistic othering', *Big Data & Society* 8: 20539517211003310.

Bonacchi, Chiara, Mark Altaweel and Marta Krzyzanska. 2018. 'The heritage of Brexit: roles of the past in the construction of political identities through social media', *Journal of Social Archaeology* 18: 174–92.

Boudreaux, Monique C., Wayne D. Lord and Stephen E. Etter. 2000. 'Child abduction: an overview of current and historical perspectives', *Child Maltreatment* 5: 63–71.

Bourbou, Chryssi. 2018. 'Life and death at the "The Land of Three Lakes": revisiting the non-adults from Roman Aventicum, Switzerland (1st–3rd century CE) ', *International Journal of Paleopathology* 22: 121–34.

Bradley, Keith. 1984. *Slavery and Society at Rome*. Cambridge: Cambridge University Press.

Bradley, Keith R. 1985. 'Child labour in the Roman world', *Réflexions Historiques* 12: 311–30.

Bradley, Keith R. 1987. 'On the Roman slave supply and slavebreeding'. In *Classical Slavery*, edited by Moses I. Finley, 53–81. London: Routledge.

Bradley, Keith. 2000. 'Animalizing the slave: the truth of fiction', *The Journal of Roman Studies* 90: 110–25.

Brandt, J. Ramus, Erika Hagelberg, Gro Bjørnstad and Sven Ahrens (eds). 2016. *Life and Death in Asia Minor in Hellenistic, Roman and Byzantine Times: Studies in archaeology and bioarchaeology*. Oxford: Oxbow Books Limited.

Bruun, Christer. 2013. 'Greek or Latin? The owner's choice of names for vernae in Rome'. In *Roman Slavery and Roman Material Culture*, edited by Michele George, 19–42. London: University of Toronto Press.

Cameron, Catherine M. 2011. 'Captives and culture change: implications for archaeology', *Current Anthropology* 52: 169–209.

Cardoso, Hugo, Laure Spake, Sofia Wasterlain and Marie Ferreira. 2019. 'The impact of social experiences of physical and structural violence on the growth of African enslaved children recovered from Lagos, Portugal (15th–17th centuries)', *American Journal of Physical Anthropology* 168: 209–21.

Carroll, Maureen. 2006. *Spirits of the Dead: Roman funerary commemoration in Western Europe*. Oxford: Oxford University Press.

Carroll, Maureen, P. 2011. 'Memoria and damnatio memoriae: preserving and erasing identities in Roman funerary commemoration'. In *Living Through the Dead: Burial and commemoration in the Classical world*, edited by Maureen P. Carroll and Jane Rempel, 65–90. Studies in Funerary Archaeology 5. Oxford: Oxbow Books.

Chinnock, Christopher and Michael Marshall. 2021. 'An unusual Roman fettered burial from Great Casterton, Rutland', *Britannia* 52: 1–31.

Clark, Patricia. 1998. 'Women, slaves, and the hierarchies of domestic violence: the family of St Augustine'. In *Women and Slaves in Greco-Roman Culture: Differential equations*, edited by Sandra R. Joshel and Sheila Murnaghan, 109–29. London: Routledge.

Cokayne, Karen. 2003. *Experiencing Old Age in Ancient Rome*. London: Routledge.

Columella. *De Re Rustica, vol. 1: Books 1–4*. Translated by Harrison Boyd Ash. 1941. Loeb Classical Library 361. Cambridge, MA: Harvard University Press.

Crerar, Belinda. 2015. 'Deviancy in late Romano-British burial'. In *The Oxford Handbook of Roman Britain*, edited by Martin Millett, Louise Revell and Alison Moore. Oxford: Oxford University Press. https://doi.org/10.1093/oxfordhb/9780199697731.013.023.

Csordas, Thomas J. 1990. 'Embodiment as a paradigm for anthropology', *Ethos* 18: 5–47.

Cucina, Andrea, Vargiu, Rita, Domenico Mancinelli, Riccardo Ricci, E. Santandrea, Paola Catalano and Alfredo Coppa. 2006. 'The necropolis of Vallerano (Rome, 2nd–3rd century AD): an anthropological perspective on the ancient Romans in the Suburbium', *International Journal of Osteoarchaeology* 16: 104–17.

Czarnecka, Katarzyna. 2013. 'Das Grab eines Sklavenhändlers? Zum Fund eines Vorhängeschlosses aus dem baltischen Gräberfeld von Mojtyny (pow. mrągowski) in Masuren', *Archäologisches Korrespondenzblatt* 43: 397–407.

De Haas, Ingrid I. 2011. 'Female slave resistance in the Roman Empire: first–fourth centuries CE'. PhD thesis, University of California, Riverside.

De Ligt, Luuk and Laurens E. Tacoma (eds). 2016. *Migration and Mobility in the Early Roman Empire*. Leiden: Brill.

Dio Cassius. *Roman History*. Translated by Ernest Cary. 1914–1927. Loeb Classical Library. Cambridge, MA: Harvard University Press.

Diodorus Siculus. *The Library of History*. Translated by C.H. Oldfather. 1933. Loeb Classical Library. Cambridge, MA: Harvard University Press.

Dolansky, Fanny. 2016. 'Roman girls and boys at play'. In *Children and Everyday Life in the Roman and Late Antique World*, edited by Christian Laes and Ville Vuolanto, 116–36. London: Routledge.

Duane, Anna M. 2017a. 'The child as gift: the logic of the peculium in perpetuating logics of enslavement'. In *Child Slavery Before and After Emancipation: An argument for child-centered slavery studies*, edited by Anna M. Duane, 23–6. Cambridge: Cambridge University Press.
Duane, Anna M. 2017b. 'Introduction'. In *Child Slavery Before and After Emancipation: An argument for child-centered slavery studies*, edited by Anna M. Duane, 1–22. Cambridge: Cambridge University Press.
Duran, Adrian R. 2021. 'Art history and human suffering: pasts, pedagogies, and possibilities'. In *Artistic Representation of Suffering: Rights, resistance, and remembrance*, edited by Mark Celinsca and Curtis Hutt, 21–36. London: Rowman & Littlefield.
Eckardt, Hella (ed.). 2010. *Roman Diasporas: Archaeological approaches to mobility and diversity in the Roman Empire*. JRA Supplementary Series 78. Portsmouth, RI: Journal of Roman Archaeology.
Edmondson, Jonathan. 2011. 'Slavery and the Roman family'. In *The Cambridge World History of Slavery, vol. 1: The ancient Mediterranean world*, edited by Keith Bradley and Paul Cartledge, 337–61. Cambridge: Cambridge University Press.
Escott, Paul D. 1979. *Slavery Remembered: A record of twentieth-century slave narratives*. Chapel Hill, NC: University of North Carolina Press.
Evans Grubbs, Judith. 2013. 'Between slavery and freedom: disputes over status and the Codex Justinianus', *Roman Legal Tradition* 9: 31–93.
Fagan, Garrett G. 2020. 'Roman violence: attitudes and practice'. In *The Cambridge World History of Violence: vol. 1: The prehistoric and ancient worlds*, edited by Garrett G. Fagan, Linda Fibiger, Mark Hudson and Matthew Trundle, 550–71. Cambridge: Cambridge University Press.
Fernández-Götz, Manuel. 2020. 'Migrations in Iron Age Europe: a comparative view'. In *The Arras Culture of Eastern Yorkshire: Celebrating the Iron Age*, edited by Peter Halkon, 179–99. Oxford: Oxbow Books.
Fernández-Götz, Manuel, Dominik Maschek and Nico Roymans. 2020. 'Power, asymmetries and how to view the Roman world', *Antiquity* 94: 1653–6.
Ferris, Iain M. 2000. *Enemies of Rome: Barbarians through Roman eyes*. Stroud: Sutton Publishing Ltd.
Fitzgerald, Charles, Shelly Saunders, Luca Bondioli and Roberto Macchiarelli. 2006. 'Health of infants in an imperial Roman skeletal sample: perspective from dental microstructure', *American Journal of Physical Anthropology* 130: 179–89.
Foxhall, Lin and John Salmon (eds). 1998. *When Men were Men: Masculinity, power and identity in Classical antiquity*. London: Routledge.
Franklin, Maria. 2001. 'A Black feminist-inspired archaeology?', *Journal of Social Archaeology* 1: 108–25.
Gamble, Julia and Gillian Bentley. 2022. 'Developmental origins of health and disease (DOHaD): perspectives from bioarchaeology'. In *Palaeopathology and Evolutionary Medicine: An integrated approach*, edited by Kimberley A. Plomp, Charlotte A. Roberts, Sarah Elton and Gillian R. Bentley, 17–41. Oxford: Oxford University Press.
Gardner, Andrew. 2020. 'Re-balancing the Romans', *Antiquity* 94: 1640–2.
Gardner, Jane F. 2011. 'Slavery and Roman law'. In *The Cambridge World History of Slavery, vol. 1: The ancient Mediterranean world*, edited by Keith Bradley and Paul Cartledge, 414–37. Cambridge: Cambridge University Press.
Garnsey, Peter. 1976. 'Peasants in ancient Roman society', *The Journal of Peasant Studies* 3: 221–35.
Geber, Jonny. 2015. *Victims of Ireland's Great Famine: The bioarchaeology of mass burials at Kilkenny Union Workhouse*. Gainesville, FL: University Press of Florida.
Geller, Pamela L. and Miranda S. Suri. 2014. 'Relationality, corporeality and bioarchaeology: bodies qua bodies, bodies in context', *Cambridge Archaeological Journal* 24: 499–512.
George, Michele. 2003. 'Images of Black slaves in the Roman Empire', *Syllecta Classica* 14: 161–85.
George, Michele (ed.). 2013. *Roman Slavery and Roman Material Culture*. Toronto: University of Toronto Press.
Gibbons, K.J., D.S. Soloniuk and N. Razack. 1990. 'Neurological injury and patterns of sacral fractures', *Journal of Neurosurgery* 72: 889–93.
Gill, Josie, Catriona Mckenzie and Emma Lightfoot. 2019. '"Handle with care": literature, archaeology, slavery', *Interdisciplinary Science Reviews* 44: 21–37.
Goldberg, Charles. 2021. *Roman Masculinity and Politics, From Republic to Empire*. London: Routledge.

Gowland, Rebecca L. 2015. 'Entangled lives: implications of the developmental origins of health and disease hypothesis for bioarchaeology and the life course', *American Journal of Physical Anthropology* 158: 530–40.

Gowland, Rebecca L. 2017. 'That "tattered coat upon a stick" the ageing body: evidence for elder marginalisation and abuse in Roman Britain'. In *Care in the Past: Archaeological and interdisciplinary perspective*, edited by Lindsay Powell, William Southwell-Wright and Rebecca Gowland, 71–92. Oxford: Oxbow Books.

Gowland, Rebecca. 2020. 'Ruptured: reproductive loss, bodily boundaries, time and the life course in archaeology'. In *The Mother-Infant Nexus in Anthropology: Small beginnings, significant outcomes*, edited by Rebecca Gowland and Sîan Halcrow, 257–74. Switzerland: Springer.

Gowland, Rebecca and Sîan Halcrow (eds). 2020. *The Mother-Infant Nexus in Anthropology: Small beginnings, significant outcomes*. Switzerland: Springer.

Gowland, Rebecca L. and Rebecca C. Redfern 2010. 'Childhood health in the Roman World: perspectives from the centre and margin of the Empire', *Childhood in the Past: An International Journal* 3: 15–42.

Grattan, John, Steven Huxley, Lotus A. Karaki, Harry Toland, David Gilbertson, Brian Pyatt and Ziad al Saad. 2002. '"Death... more desirable than life"? The human skeletal record and toxicological implications of ancient copper mining and smelting in Wadi Faynan, southwestern Jordan', *Toxicology and Industrial Health* 18: 297–307.

Gravlee, Clarence C. 2009. 'How race becomes biology: embodiment of social inequality', *American Journal of Physical Anthropology* 139: 47–57.

Grierson, Jamie. 2021. 'Best physical evidence of Roman crucifixion found in Cambridgeshire', *Guardian*, 8 December.

Guzzo, Pier G (ed.). 2003. *Tales From an Eruption: Pompeii, Herculaneum, Oplontis. Guide to the exhibition*. Italy: Electa.

Hamby, Sherry and John Grych. 2013. *The Web of Violence: Exploring connections among different forms of interpersonal violence and abuse*. Amsterdam: Springer.

Hansen, Art and Anthony Oliver-Smith (eds). 2019. *Involuntary Migration and Resettlement: The problems and responses of dislocated people*. London: Routledge.

Harlow, Mary and Ray Laurence. 2002. *Growing Up and Growing Old in Ancient Rome: A life course approach*. London: Routledge.

Harrod, Ryan P. and Debra L. Martin. 2014. 'Signatures of captivity and suborbdination of skeletonized human remains: a bioarchaeological case study from the ancient Southwest'. In *Bioarchaeological and Forensic Perspectives on Violence: How violent death is interpreted from skeletal remains*, edited by Debra L. Martin and Cheryl P. Anderson, 103–19. Cambridge: Cambridge University Press.

Harrod, Ryan P. and Debra L. Martin. 2015. 'Bioarchaeological case studies of slavery, captivity, and other forms of exploitation'. In *The Archaeology of Slavery. A comparative approach to captivity and coercion*, edited by Lydia Wilson Marshall, 41–63. Center for Archaeological Investigations Occasional Paper No. 41. Carbondale, IL: Southern Illnois University.

Harward, Barney, Natasha Powers and Sadie Watson (eds). 2015. *The Upper Walbrook Valley Cemetery of Roman London: Excavations at Finsbury Circus, City of London, 1987–2007*. MoLA Monograph Series 69. London: Museum of London.

Heather, Peter J. 2017. 'Refugees and the Roman Empire', *Journal of Refugee Studies* 30(2): 220–42.

Hingley, Richard. 2000. *Roman Officers and English Gentlemen*. London: Routledge.

Hingley, Richard, Bonacchi, Chiara and Kate Sharpe. 2018. '"Are you local?" Indigenous Iron Age and mobile Roman and post-Roman populations: then, now and in-between', *Britannia* 49: 283–302.

Hirt, Alfred M. 2010. *Imperial Mines and Quarries in the Roman World: Organizational aspects 27 BC–AD 235*. Oxford: Oxford University Press.

Hodson, Claire M. 2017. 'Between roundhouse and villa: assessing perinatal and infant burials from Piddington, Northamptonshire', *Britannia* 48: 195–219.

Hodson, Claire M. and Rebecca Gowland. 2020. 'Like mother, like child: investigating perinatal and maternal health stress in post-medieval London'. In *The Mother-Infant Nexus in Anthropology: Small beginnings, significant outcomes*, edited by Rebecca Gowland and Sîan Halcrow, 39–64. Switzerland: Springer.

Hope, Valerie M. 1997. 'Constructing Roman identity: funerary monuments and social structure in the Roman world', *Mortality* 2: 103–21.

Hope, Valerie. 2000. 'Fighting for identity: the funerary commemoration of Italian gladiators', *Bulletin of the Institute of Classical Studies* 44(S73): 93–113.

Hope, Valerie M. 2001. 'Negotiating identity and status: the gladiators of Roman Nîmes'. In *Cultural Identity in the Roman Empire*, edited by Ray Laurence and Joanne Berry, 179–95. London: Routledge.

Hope, Valerie. 2009. *Roman Death. The dying and the dead in ancient Rome.* London: Continuum.

Hopkins, Keith. 1993. Novel evidence for Roman slavery. *Past and Present* 138: 3–27.

Hosek, Lauren and John Robb. 2019. 'Osteobiography: a platform for bioarchaeological research', *Bioarchaeology International* 3: 1–15.

Hubbard, Thomas K. (ed.). 2013. *A Companion to Greek and Roman Sexualities.* Oxford: Wiley-Blackwells.

Humphrey, Louise T. and Tania King. 2000. 'Childhood stress: a lifetime legacy', *Anthropologie* 38: 33–49.

Huntley, Katherine V. 2013. 'Identifying children's graffiti in Roman Campania: a developmental psychological approach. In *Ancient Graffiti in Context*, edited by Jennifer Baird and Claire Taylor, 17–35. London: Routledge.

Isaac, Benjamin. 2006. 'Proto-racism in Graeco-Roman antiquity', *World Archaeology* 38: 32–47.

Isaac, Benjamin. 2013. *The invention of racism in classical antiquity*. Princeton, NJ: Princeton University Press.

Isable, Kendal B. 2021. 'Contributing to the discussion: the health of enslaved Africans through the lens of bioarchaeology'. MA thesis California State University, Northridge, CA. http://hdl.handle.net/10211.3/221562.

Ivleva, Tatiana. 2020. 'Coming out of the provincial closet: masculinity, sexuality, and same-sex sexual relations amongst Roman soldiers in the European north-west, first-third centuries A.D'. In *Un-Roman Sex: Gender, sexuality, and lovemaking in the Roman provinces and frontiers,* edited by Tatiana Ivleva and Rob Collins, 241–73. London: Routledge.

Ivleva, Tatiana and Rob Collins (eds). 2020. *Un-Roman Sex: Gender, sexuality, and lovemaking in the Roman provinces and frontiers*. London: Routledge.

Jackson, Ralph. 2005. 'Roman bound captives: symbols of slavery?' In *Image, Craft and the Classical World. Essays in honour of Donald Bailey and Catherine Johns*, edited by Nina Crummy, 143–56. Monograph Instrumentum 29. Montgnac: M. Mergoil.

Johnson, Michael P. 2008. *A Typology of Domestic Violence: Intimate terrorism, violent resistance, and situational couple violence.* London: University Press of New England.

Johnson, Walter. 1999. *Soul by Soul: Life inside the antebellum slave market*. Harvard: Harvard University Press.

Joshel, Sandra R. 2010. *Slavery in the Roman World.* Cambridge: Cambridge University Press.

Joshel, Sandra. 2011. 'Slavery and Roman literary culture'. In *The Cambridge World History of Slavery, vol. 1: The ancient Mediterranean world*, edited by Keith Bradley and Paul Cartledge, 214–40. Cambridge: Cambridge University Press.

Joshel, Sandra R. 2013. Geographies of slave containment and movement. In *Roman Slavery and Roman Material Culture*, edited by Michele George, 99–128. Toronto: University of Toronto Press.

Joshel, Sandra R. and Sheila Murnaghan. 2005. *Women and Slaves in Greco-Roman Culture: Differential equations*. London: Routledge.

Joshel, Sandra R. and Lauren H. Petersen. 2014. *The Material Life of Roman Slaves*. Cambridge: Cambridge University Press.

Kahlos, Maijastina. 2022. 'Late Roman ideas of ethnicity and enslavement'. In *Slavery in the Late Antique world, 150–700 CE*, edited by Chris L. De Wet, Maijastina Kahlos and Ville Vuolanto, 87–106. Cambridge: Cambridge University Press.

Kamash, Zena. 2021. 'Rebalancing Roman archaeology: from disciplinary inertia to decolonial and inclusive action', *Theoretical Roman Archaeology Journal* 4: 1–41.

Kamen, Deborah. 2010. 'A corpus of inscriptions: representing slave marks in antiquity', *Memoirs of the American Academy in Rome* 55: 95–110.

Kamen, Deborah and C.W. Marshall (eds). 2021. *Slavery and Sexuality in Classical Antiquity*. Madison, WI: University of Wisconsin Press.

Keegan, Paul. 2014. *Graffiti in Antiquity.* London: Routledge.

Kendall, Ellen J., Andrew Millard, Julia Beaumont, Rebecca Gowland, Marise Gorton and Andrew Gledhill. 2020. 'What doesn't kill you: early life health and nutrition in early Anglo-Saxon East Anglia'. In *The Mother-Infant Nexus in Anthropology: Small beginnings, significant outcomes*, edited by Rebecca Gowland and Sîan Halcrow, 103–23. Switzerland: Springer.

Killgrove, Kristina. 2017. 'Imperialism and physiological stress in Rome, first to third centuries A.D'. In *Colonized Bodies, Worlds Transformed: Toward a global bioarchaeology of contact and colonialism*, edited by Melissa S. Murphy and Hagen D. Klaus, 247–280. Gainesville, FL: University Press of Florida.

Killgrove, Kristina. 2018. 'Using skeletal remains as a proxy for Roman lifestyles: the potential and problems with osteological reconstructions of health, diet, and stature in Imperial Rome'. In *The Routledge Handbook of Diet and Nutrition in the Roman World* edited by Paul Erdkamp and Claire Holleran, 245–58. London: Routledge.

Klaus, Hagen D., Amanda R. Harvey and Mark N. Cohen (eds). 2017. *Bones of Complexity: Bioarchaeological case studies of social organization and skeletal biology*. Gainesville, FL: University Press of Florida.

Knapp, Robert C. 2011. *Invisible Romans: Prostitutes, outlaws, slaves, gladiators, ordinary men and women… the Romans that history forgot*. London: Profile Books Ltd.

Kruschwitz, Peter. 2015. 'Lapidary poetics of roman domestic violence'. The Petrified Muse, 26 April. https://thepetrifiedmuse.blog/page/13/?archives-list=1 [accessed 1 October 2022].

Kuzawa, Christopher W. and Clarence C. Gravlee. 2016. 'Beyond genetic race: biocultural insights into the causes of racial health disparities'. In *New Directions in Biocultural Anthropology*, edited by Molly K. Zuckerman and Debra L. Martin, 89–105. New York: Wiley Blackwell.

Laes, Christian. 2008. 'Child slaves at work in Roman Antiquity', *Ancient Society* 38: 235–83.

Laes, Christian. 2011. *Children in the Roman Empire: Outsiders within*. Cambridge: Cambridge University Press.

Laurence, Ray. 2016. 'Children and the urban environment: agency in Pompeii'. In *Children and Everyday Life in the Roman and Late Antique World*, edited by Christian Laes and Ville Vuolanto, 235–83. London: Routledge.

Lenski, Noel. 2008. 'Captivity, slavery, and cultural exchange between Rome and the Germans from the first to the seventh century CE'. In *Invisible Citizens: Captives and their consequences*, edited by Catherine M. Cameron, 80–109. Salt Lake City, UT: The University of Utah Press.

Lenski, Noel. 2014. 'Captivity among the Barbarians and its impact on the fate of the Roman Empire'. In *The Cambridge Companion to the Age of Attila* edited by Michael Maas, 230–46. Cambridge: Cambridge University Press.

Lenski, Noel. 2016. 'Violence and the Roman slave'. In *The Topography of Violence in the Greco-Roman World*, edited by Werner Reiss and Garrett Fagan, 275–98. Ann Arbor, MI: University of Michigan Press.

Leskovar, Tania, Julia Beaumont, Nidia Lisić and Suzanne McGalliard. 2019. 'Auditory ossicles: a potential biomarker for maternal and infant health in utero', *Annals of Human Biology* 46: 367–77.

Lewis, Mary E. 2007. *The Bioarchaeology of Children*. Cambridge: Cambridge University Press.

Liebow, Nabina and Trip Glazer. 2019. 'White tears: emotion regulation and white fragility', *Inquiry* 66(1): 122–42, https://doi.org/10.1080/0020174X.2019.1610048.

Lockau Laura, Stephanie Atkinson, Simon Mays, Tracy Prowse, Michele George, Alessandra Sperduti, Luca Bondioli, Carolan Wood, Marissa Ledger and Megan Brickley. 2019. 'Vitamin D deficiency and the ancient city: skeletal evidence across the life course from the Roman period site of Isola Sacra, Italy', *Journal of Anthropological Archaeology* 55: 10169.

M'charek, Amade. 2021. 'Traces of race, roots of gender: a genetic history'. In *The Routledge Companion to Black Women's Cultural Histories*, edited by Janell Hobson. London: Routledge. https://doi.org/10.4324/9780429243578-35.

M'charek, Amade and Katharina Schramm. 2020. 'Encountering the face—unraveling race', *American Anthropologist* 122: 321–6.

M'charek, Amade, Katharina Schramm and David Skinner. 2014. 'Topologies of race: doing territory, population and identity in Europe', *Science, Technology, & Human Values* 39: 468–87.

Maass, Claire. 2022. 'Childhood in captivity: bioarchaeological evidence from a late colonial sugar plantation in Central Peru', *Latin American Antiquity* 34(1): 194–211. https://doi.org/10.1017/laq.2022.35.

Mack, Mark E. and Michael L. Blakey. 2004. 'The New York African burial ground project: past biases, current dilemmas, and future research opportunities', *Historical Archaeology* 38: 10–17.

MacSweeney, Naoíse, Samuel Agbamu, Rosa Andújar, Michael Okyere Asante, Juliana Bastos Marques, Gwladys Bernard, Chiara Bonacchi, Curtis Dozier, Güneş Duru, Barbara Goff, Rebecca Futo Kennedy, Elif Koparal, Damjan Krsmanovic, Denise McCoskey, Neville Morley, Julia Müller, Jan Nelis, Anne-Sophie Noel, Grant Parker, Konstantinos Poulis, Catherine Psilakis, Helen Roche, Elizabeth Sawyer, Netta Schramm and Michael Scott. 2019. 'Claiming the classical: the Greco-Roman world in contemporary political discourse', *Council of University Classical Departments Bulletin*, 48. https://www.cucd.blogs.sas.ac.uk/files/201902/MAC-SWEENEY-ET-AL-Claiming-the-Classical.pdf.

Mant, Madeleine L. and Allison J. Holland (eds). 2019. *Bioarchaeology of Marginalized People*. London: Academic Press.

Marklein, Kathryn E. 2020. 'East of Rome: exploring potential impacts of Roman imperialism on northeastern Mediterranean populations through a bioarchaeological perspective', *Journal of Archaeological Science: Reports* 34: 102590.

Marklein, Kathryn E. and Sherry C. Fox. 2020. 'The bioarchaeology of children in Greco-Roman antiquity'. In *Children in Antiquity*, edited by Lesley A. Beaumont, Matthew Dillon and Nicola Harrington, 567–80. London: Routledge.

Martin, Debra L., Ryan P. Harrod and Ventura R. Pérez. 2014. *Bioarchaeology: An integrated approach to working with human remains*. Amsterdam, Springer.

Mata, Karim. 2019. *Iron Age Slaving and Enslavement in Northwest Europe*. Oxford: Archaeopress.

Mattingly, David. 2008. 'Comparative advantages: Roman slavery and imperialism', *Archaeological Dialogues* 15: 135–9.

Mays, Simon and James Steele. 1996. 'A mutilated human skull from Roman St Albans, Hertfordshire, England', *Antiquity* 70: 155–61.

Mays, Simon, Tracy Prowse, Michele George and Megan Brickley. 2018. 'Latitude, urbanization, age, and sex as risk factors for vitamin D deficiency disease in the Roman Empire', *American Journal of Physical Anthropology* 167: 484–96.

McCoskey, Denise E. 2012. *Race: Antiquity and its legacy*. London: I.B. Tauris.

McCoskey, Denise E. and James Talbot. 2006. 'Naming the fault in question: theorizing racism among the Greeks and Romans', *International Journal of the Classical Tradition* 13: 243–80.

McKeown, Niall. 2012. 'Magic, religion, and the Roman slave: resistance, control and community'. In *Slaves and Religions in Graeco-Roman Antiquity and Modern Brazil*, edited by Stephen Hodkinson and Dick Geary, 279–308. Newcastle upon Tyne: Cambridge Scholars Publishing.

McKittrick, Katherine. 2015. *Sylvia Wynter: On being human as praxis*. Durham, NC, Duke University Press.

Méténier, Frédérick, Pierre Caillat, Pauline Duneufjardin, Vincent Geneviève, David Guitton, Laure Simon and Jenny Kaurin. 2017. *7 rue de l'Alma, contribution à l'étude des espaces funéraires en périphérie ouest de Saintes antique*. 2 vols. Poitiers: INRAP Grand-Sud-Ouest.

Mihailescu-Bîrliba, Lucrețiu. 2015. 'An eques romanus and his slave in a new funerary inscription from Troesmis'. In *Homines, Funera, Astra 2: Life beyond death in ancient times (Romanian case studies)*, edited by Raluca Kogălniceanu, Mihai Gligor, Roxana-Gabriela Curcă and Susan Stratton, 121–4. Oxford: Archaeopress.

Minozzi, Simona, Carla Caldarini, Walter Pantano, Stefania Di Giannantonio, Paola Catalano and Valentina Giuffra. 2020. 'Enamel hypoplasia and health conditions through social status in the Roman imperial age (first to third centuries, Rome, Italy)', *International Journal of Osteoarchaeology* 30: 53–64.

Moore, Alison. 2009. 'Young and old in Roman Britain: aspects of age identity and life-course transitions in regional burial practice'. PhD thesis, University of Southampton. http://eprints.soton.ac.uk/id/eprint/360559.

Moore, Joanna, Kori Filipek, Vana Kalenderian, Rebecca Gowland, Elliott Hamilton, Jane Evans and Janet Montgomery. 2021a. 'Death metal: evidence for the impact of lead poisoning on childhood health within the Roman Empire', *International Journal of Osteoarchaeology* 31: 846–58.

Moore, Joanna, Michelle Williams-Ward, Kori L. Filipek, Rebecca L. Gowland and Janet Montgomery. 2021b. 'Poisoned pregnancies: consequences of prenatal lead exposure in relation to infant mortality in the Roman Empire'. In *The Family in Past Perspective*, edited by Ellen J. Kendall and Ross Kendall, 137–58. London: Routledge.

Morley, Neville D.G. 2011. 'Slavery under the principate'. In *The Cambridge World History of Slavery, vol. 1: The ancient Mediterranean world*, edited by Keith Bradley and Paul Cartledge, 265–86. Cambridge: Cambridge University Press.

Mouritsen, Hendrik. 2011. *The Freedman in the Roman World.* Cambridge: Cambridge University Press.

Mullins, Paul R. 2008. 'The politics of an archaeology of global captivity', *Archaeological Dialogues* 15: 123–7.

Odochiciuc, Ana and Lucrețiu Mihailescu-Bîrliba. 2014. 'Occupations of private slaves in Roman Dacia', *Studia Antiqua et Archaeologica* 20: 231–47.

Parkin, Tim G. 2003. *Old Age in the Roman world: A cultural and social history.* London: The John Hopkins University Press.

Parkin, Tim and Amanda Pomeroy (eds). 2007. *Roman Social History: A sourcebook.* London: Routledge.

Parry, Tyler D. 2021. '"How much more must I suffer?": post-traumatic stress and the lingering impact of violence upon enslaved people', *Slavery & Abolition* 42: 184–200.

Patterson, Orlando. 2018. *Slavery and Social Death: A comparative study, with a new preface.* Cambridge, MA: Harvard University Press.

Peachin, Michael (ed.). 2011. *The Oxford Handbook of Social Relations in the Roman World.* Oxford: Oxford University Press.

Peacock, Taylor, Chryssi Bourbou, Lori D'Ortenzio, Bonnie Kahlon, Tracy Prowse and Megan B. Brickley. 2019. 'Mobility and rickets: investigating Vitamin D deficiency and regional mobility in *Aventicum*, Roman Switzerland (first to third century CE)', *International Journal of Osteoarchaeology* 29: 654–64.

Pearson, Andrew, Ben Jeffs, Ann-Sofie Witkin and Helen MacQuarrie (eds). 2011. *Infernal Traffic: Excavation of a liberated African graveyard in Rupert's valley, St Helena.* CBA Research Report 169. London: Council for British Archaeology.

Perry, Matthew J. 2021. 'Control of Roman slave sexuality: authority, profit and resistance'. In *Slavery and Sexuality in Classical Antiquity*, edited by Deborah Kamen and C.W. Marshall, 254–70. Madison, WI: University of Wisconsin Press.

Phang, Sara E. 2004. 'Intimate conquests: Roman soldiers' slave women and freedwomen', *The Ancient World* 15: 207–17.

Phang, Sara E. 2022. *Daily Life of Women in Ancient Rome.* New York: Greenwood.

Phang, Sara E., Jean-Jacques Aubert and Várhelyi, Zsuzsanna. 2005. 'Soldiers' slaves, "dirty work", and the social status of Roman soldiers'. In *A Tall Order: Writing the social history of the ancient world. Essays in honor of William V. Harris*, edited by Jean-Jacques Aubert and Zsuzsanna Várhelyi, 203–25. München: K.G. Saur Verlag.

Plutarch. *De Curiositate* 10/*Moralia* 520c. Translated Frank Cole Babbitt. 1914–1927. Loeb Classical Library. Cambridge, MA: Harvard University Press.

Prowse, Tracy L. 2016. 'Isotopes and mobility in the ancient Roman world'. In *Migration and Mobility in the Early Roman Empire*, edited by Luuk De Ligt and Laurens E. Tacoma, 204–33. Leiden: Brill.

Pudsey, April and Ville Vuolanto. 2022. 'Enslaved children in Roman Egypt: experiences from the Papyri'. In *Slavery in the Late Antique World, 150–700 CE*, edited by Chris De Wet, Maijastina Kahls and Ville Vuolanto, 210–23. Cambridge: Cambridge University Press.

Pyatt, F.B., A.J. Pyatt, C. Walker, T. Sheen and J.P. Grattan. 2005. 'The heavy metal content of skeletons from an ancient metalliferous polluted area in southern Jordan with particular reference to bioaccumulation and human health', *Ecotoxicology and Environmental Safety* 60: 295–300.

Rawson, Beryl. 2010. 'Degrees of freedom: Vernae and Junian Latins in the Roman familia'. In *Children, Memory, and Family Identity in Roman Culture*, edited by Veronique Dasen and Thomas Späth, 195–221. Oxford: Oxford University Press.

Redfern, Rebecca C. 2013. 'Violence in the Roman world'. In: *A History of Human Conflict: Osteology and "traumatized bodies" from earliest prehistory to the present*, edited by Christopher Knüsel and Martin Smith, 203–12. London: Routledge.

Redfern, Rebecca C. 2016. *Injury and Trauma in Bioarchaeology: Interpreting violence in past lives.* Cambridge: Cambridge University Press.

Redfern, Rebecca C. 2018. 'Blind to chains? The potential of bioarchaeology for identifying the enslaved of Roman Britain', *Britannia* 49: 251–82.

Redfern, Rebecca C. 2019. 'Gendered violence in late Iron Age and Roman Britain'. In *The Cambridge World History of Violence*, edited by Garrett G. Fagan, Linda Fibiger, Mark Hudson and Matthew Trundle, 320–41. Cambridge: Cambridge University Press.

Redfern, Rebecca C. 2020a. 'Iron Age "predatory landscapes": a bioarchaeological and funerary exploration of captivity and enslavement in Britain', *Cambridge Archaeological Journal* 30: 531–54.

Redfern, Rebecca C. 2020b. 'Changing people, changing settlements? A perspective on urbanism from Roman Britain'. In *The Bioarchaeology of Urbanization*, edited by Sharon N. DeWitte and Tracy K. Betsinger, 25–47. New York: Springer-Link.

Redfern, Rebecca C. forthcoming. 'Assaults and abuse in Roman Britain: an attempt to untangle the web of violence experienced by women (1st to early 5th centuries CE)'. In *Poetics of Violence in the Eastern Hemisphere*, edited by Rose Campbell and Anna Osterholtz. Philadelphia, PA: University of Pennsylvania Press.

Redfern, Rebecca C. and Sharon N. DeWitte. 2011a. 'A new approach to the study of Romanization in Britain: a regional perspective of cultural change in late Iron Age and Roman Dorset using the Siler and Gompertz-Makeham models of mortality', *American Journal of Physical Anthropology* 144: 269–85.

Redfern, Rebecca C. and Sharon N. DeWitte. 2011b. 'Status and health in Roman Dorset: the effect of status on risk of mortality in post-Conquest populations', *American Journal of Physical Anthropology* 146: 197–208.

Redfern, Rebecca C. and Rebecca L. Gowland. 2011. 'A bioarchaeological perspective on the pre-adult stages of the life course: implications for the care and health of children in the Roman Empire'. In *Families in the Roman and Late Antique Roman World*, edited by Mary L. Harlow and Lena L. Lovén, 111–40. London: Continuum International Publishing Group.

Redfern, Rebecca C., Sharon N. DeWitte, John Pearce, Christine Hamlin and Kirsten Egging Dinwiddy. 2015. 'Urban-rural differences in Roman Dorset, England: a bioarchaeological perspective on Roman settlements', *American Journal of Physical Anthropology* 157: 107–20.

Redfern, Rebecca, Sharon DeWitte, Julia Beaumont, Andrew Millard and Christine Hamlin. 2019. 'A new method for investigating the relationship between diet and mortality: hazard analysis using dietary isotopes', *Annals of Human Biology* 46: 378–87.

Reitsema, Laurie J. and Britney K. McIlvaine. 2014. 'Reconciling "stress"' and "health" in physical anthropology: what can bioarchaeologists learn from the other subdisciplines?', *American Journal of Physical Anthropology* 155: 181–85.

Revell, Louise. 2005. 'The Roman life course: a view from the inscriptions', *European Journal of Archaeology* 8: 43–63.

Robb, John and Oliver J.T. Harris (eds). 2013. *The Body in History: Europe from the Palaeolithic to the future.* Cambridge: Cambridge University Press.

Rodriguez, Junius, P. (ed.). 2007. *Encyclopedia of Slave Resistance and Rebellion. Vols 1 and 2.* London: Greenwood Press.

Rohnbogner, Anna. 2017. 'Listening to the kids: the value of childhood palaeopathology for the study of rural Roman Britain', *Britannia* 48: 221–52.

Rohnbogner, Anna. 2018. 'The rural population'. In *Life and Death in the Countryside of Roman Britain: New visions of the countryside of Roman Britain, vol. 3,* edited by Alexander Smith, Martyn Allen, Tom Brindle, Michael Fulford, Lisa Lodwick and Anna Rohnbogner, 281–345. Britannia Monograph Series No. 31. London: Society for the Promotion of Roman Studies.

Rohnbogner, Anna. 2022. *Dying Young: A bioarchaeological analysis of child health in Roman Britain.* BAR British Series 673. Archaeology of Roman Britain vol. 7. Oxford: BAR Publishing.

Rohnbogner, Anna and Mary Lewis. 2016. 'Dental caries as a measure of diet, health, and difference in non-adults from urban and rural Roman Britain', *Dental Anthropology* 29: 16–31.

Rossi, María C., Maria S. Busana, Alessandro Canci and Anita Radini. 2020. 'Written on the bones: textile working in Roman Veneto from tools to human remains'. In *Redefining Ancient Textile Handcraft Structures, Tools and Production Processes: Proceedings of the VIIth International Symposium on Textiles and Dyes in the Ancient Mediterranean World (Granada, Spain 2–4 October 2019)*, edited by Elena Sánchez López, Javier Jiménez Ávila and Macarena Bustamante-Álvarez, 311–24. Granada: Universidad de Granada.

Roth, Ulrike. 2011. 'Men without hope', *Papers of the British School at Rome* 79: 71–94.

Roth, Ulrike. 2021. 'Speaking out? Child sexual abuse and the enslaved voice in the Cena Trimalchionis'. In *Slavery and Sexuality in Classical Antiquity*, edited by Deborah Kamen and C.W. Marshall, 209–36. Madison, WI: University of Wisconsin Press.

Roymans, Nico and Marenne Zandstra. 2011. 'Indications for rural slavery in the northern provinces'. In *Villa Landscapes in the Roman North: Economy, culture and lifestyles,* edited by Nico Roymans and Ton Derks, 161–78. Amsterdam: Amsterdam University Press.

Salesse, Kevin, Élise Dufour, Vincent Balter, Robert H. Tykot, Nina Maaranen, Maïté Rivollat, Arwa Kharobi, Marie-France Deguilloux, Marie-Hélène Pemonge, Jaroslav Brůžek and Dominique Castex. 2021. 'Far from home: a multi-analytical approach revealing the journey of an African-born individual to imperial Rome', *Journal of Archaeological Science: Reports* 37: 103011.

Saller, Robert. 1987. 'Slavery and the Roman family'. In *Classical Slavery*, edited by Moses I. Finley, 65–87. London: Routledge.

Saller, Robert. 1991. 'Corporal punishment, authority, and obedience in the Roman household'. In *Marriage, Divorce, and Children in Ancient Rome*, edited by Beryl Rawson, 144–65. Oxford: Clarendon Press.

Sánchez-Eppler, Karen. 2017. 'Remember Dear, when the Yankees came through here, I was only ten years old': valuing the enslaved child of the WPA slave narratives'. In *Child Slavery Before and After Emancipation: An argument for child-centered slavery studies*, edited by Anna M. Duane, 27–49. Cambridge: Cambridge University Press.

Scheidel, Walter. 1997. 'Quantifying the sources of slaves in the early Roman Empire', *The Journal of Roman Studies* 87: 156–69.

Scheidel, Walter. 2005. 'Real slave prices and the relative cost of slave labor in the Greco-Roman world', *Ancient Society* 35: 1–17.

Scheidel, Walter. 2007. 'The Roman slave supply', *Princeton/Stanford Working Papers in Classics*. https://www.princeton.edu/~pswpc/pdfs/scheidel/050704.pdf.

Scheidel, Walter. 2011. 'The Roman slave supply'. In *The Cambridge World History of Slavery, vol. 1: The ancient Mediterranean world*, edited by Keith Bradley and Paul Cartledge, 287–310. Cambridge: Cambridge University Press.

Schrader, Sarah. 2019. *Activity, Diet and Social Practice: Addressing everyday life in human skeletal remains*. Switzerland, Springer.

Scuibba, Mariangela, Assunta Paolucci, Ruggero D'Anastasio and Luigi Capasso. 2013. 'Paleopathology of Herculaneum's population (79 BC)', *Medicina nei Secoli* 25: 85–99.

Seneca. *The Epistles of Seneca, vol. 1: Epistles 1–65*. Translated by Richard M. Gummere. 1917. Loeb Classical Library 75. Cambridge, MA: Harvard University Press.

Shaw, Brent D. 2001. *Spartacus and the Slave Wars: A brief history with documents*. New York: Palgrave Macmillan US.

Shaw, Heidi, Janet Montgomery, Rebecca Redfern, Rebecca Gowland and Jane Evans. 2016. 'Identifying migrants in Roman London using lead and strontium stable isotopes', *Journal of Archaeological Science* 66: 57–68.

Shuler, Kristrina. A. 2011. 'Life and death on a Barbadian sugar plantation: historic and bioarchaeological view of infection and mortality at Newton Plantation', *International Journal of Osteoarchaeology* 21: 66–81.

Sigismund-Nielsen, Hanne. 2013. 'Slave and lower-class Roman children'. In *The Oxford Handbook of Childhood and Education in the Classical World*, edited by Judith Evans Grubbs, Tim Parkin with Roselynne Bell, 286–301. Oxford: Oxford University Press.

Silver, Morris. 2016. 'Public slaves in the Roman army: an exploratory study', *Ancient Society* 46: 203–40.

Skinner, Marilyn B. 2013. *Sexuality in Greek and Roman Culture*. Oxford: Wiley-Blackwell.

Snowden, Frank M. Jr. 1970. *Blacks in Antiquity: Ethiopians in the Greco-Roman experience*. Cambridge, MA: Harvard University Press.

Snowden, Frank M. Jr. 1983. *Before Color Prejudice: The ancient view of blacks*. Cambridge, MA: Harvard University Press.

Solin, Heikki. 1996. *Die stadtrömischen Sklavennamen: Teil. Lateinische Namen*. Wiesbaden: Franz Steiner Verlag.

Speidel, Michael P. 1971. 'The suicide of Decebalus on the tropaeum of Adamklissi', *Revue Archéologique Nouvelle Série* 1: 75–8.

Speith, Nivien. 2015. 'Care for the afterlife? A bioarchaeological investigation of a Romano-British decapitation burial'. In *42nd Annual Paleopathology Association Meeting*, St Louis, Missouri. https://www.researchgate.net/publication/278957746_Care_for_the_afterlife_A_bioarchaeological_investigation_of_a_Romano-British_decapitation_burial.

Sperduti, Alessandra. 1997. 'Life conditions of a Roman Imperial age population: occupational stress markers and working activities in Lucus Feroniae (Rome, 1st–2nd century A.D.)', *Human Evolution* 12: 253–67.

Spillers, Hortense J. 2003. *Black, White and in Color: Essays on American literature and culture*. Chicago, IL: University of Chicago Press.

Stark, Robert J., Matthew V. Emery, Henry Schwarcz, Alessandra Sperduti, Luca Bondioli, Oliver E. Craig and Tracy Prowse. 2020. 'Imperial Roman mobility and migration at Velia (1st to 2nd c. CE) in southern Italy', *Journal of Archaeological Science: Reports,* 30: 102217.

Stark, Robert J., Matthew V. Emery, Henry Schwarcz, Dominique Castex and Tracy Prowse. 2022. 'Assessing Gallo-Roman mobility at the Rue Jacques Brel necropolis site (1st to 3rd c. CE), France', *Journal of Archaeological Science: Reports* 43: 103470.

Supernant, Kisha, Jane E. Baxter, Natasha Lyons and Sonia Atalay (eds). 2021. *Archaeologies of the Heart*. New York: Springer.

Tacitus. *Annals*. Translated by John Jackson. 1934. Loeb Classical Library. Cambridge, MA: Harvard University Press.

Taylor, Timothy. 2021. 'The arrogation of slavery: prehistory, archaeology, and pre-theoretical commitments concerning people as property'. In *The Archaeology of Slavery in Early Medieval Northern Europe: The invisible commodity*, edited by Felix Biermann and Marek Jankowiak, 9–21. New York: Springer.

Terrenato, Nico. 2002. 'The innocents and the sceptics: antiquity and classical archaeology', *Antiquity* 76: 1104–11.

The Roman Society 2021. 'Race: antiquity and its legacy'. A panel discussion with Zena Kamash, Denise McCoskey, and Dan-el Padilla Peralta, chaired by Professor Phiroze Vasunia. Held online, 23 April 2021. https://youtu.be/UuWM0Jq6CwE.

Thompson, Hugh. 1993. 'Iron Age and Roman slave shackles', *The Archaeological Journal* 150: 57–168.

Thompson, F. Hugh. 2003. *The Archaeology of Greek and Roman Slavery*. London, Bloomsbury.

Thompson, Lloyd A. 1989. *Romans and Blacks*. Oklahoma, OH: University of Oklahoma Press.

Thurmond, David L. 1994. 'Some Roman slave collars in CIL', *Athenaeum* 82: 459–93.

Tilley, Lorna and Tony Cameron. 2014. 'Introducing the Index of Care: a web-based application supporting archaeological research into health-related care', *International Journal of Paleopathology* 6: 5–9.

Treggiari, Susan. 1973. 'Domestic staff at Rome in the Julio-Claudian period, 27 BC to AD 68', *Histoire Sociale/Social History,* 6: 241–55.

Trimble, Jennifer. 2016. 'The Zoninus collar and the archaeology of Roman slavery', *American Journal of Archaeology* 120: 447–72.

Turpin, Jennifer and Lester R. Kurtz (eds). 1997. *The Web of Violence: From interpersonal to global*. Chicago, IL: University of Illinois Press.

Varro. *De Re Rustica*. Translated by W.D. Hooper. 1934. Loeb Classical Library 283. Cambridge, MA: Harvard University Press.

Venters, Laurie. 2019. 'Recovering runaways: slave catching in the Roman World'. PhD Thesis, Universiteit Leiden. https://studenttheses.universiteitleiden.nl/access/item%3A2659945/view.

Vlassopoulos, Kostas. 2021. *Historicising Ancient Slavery*. Edinburgh: Edinburgh University Press.

Vuolanto, Ville and Christian Laes (eds). 2017. *Children and Everyday Life in the Roman and Late Antique World*. London: Routledge.

Watkins, Rachel J. 2020. 'An alter(ed)native perspective on historical bioarchaeology', *Historical Archaeology* 54: 17–33.

Webster, Jane. 2001. 'Creolizing the provinces', *American Journal of Archaeology* 105: 209–25.

Webster, Jane. 2005. 'Archaeologies of slavery and servitude: bringing "New World" perspectives to Roman Britain', *Journal of Roman Archaeology* 18: 161–79.

Webster, Jane. 2008. 'Less beloved: Roman archaeology, slavery and the failure to compare', *Archaeological Dialogues* 15: 103–23.

Webster, Jane. 2010a. 'A distant diaspora: thinking comparatively about origins, migrations and Roman slavery', *African Diaspora Archaeology Newsletter* 13: 3.

Webster, Jane. 2010b. 'Routes to slavery in the Roman world: a comparative perspective on the archaeology of forced migration'. In Eckardt 2010: 45–65.

Wedel, Vicki L. and Alison Galloway (eds). 2014. *Broken Bones: Anthropological analysis of blunt force trauma* (2nd edition). Springfield, IL: Charles C. Thomas.

Weheliye, Alexander G. 2014. *Habeas Viscus: Racializing assemblages, biopolitics, and black feminist theories of the human*. Durham, NC: Duke University Press.

Whittaker, C. Richard. 1987. 'Circe's pigs: from slavery to serfdom in the later Roman world', *Slavery and Abolition* 8: 88–122.

Woolf, Greg. 2016. 'Moving peoples in the early Roman Empire'. In *Migration and Mobility in the Early Roman Empire*, edited by Luuk De Ligt and Laurens E. Tacoma, 25–41. Leiden: Brill.

Yamauchi, Edwin M. (ed.). 2001. *Africa and Africans in Antiquity.* East Lansing, MI: University of Michigan Press.

Zimmerman, Cathy, Mazeda Hossain, Kate Yun, Brenda Roche, Linda Morison and Charlotte Watts (eds). 2006. *Stolen Smiles: A summary report on the physical and psychological health consequences of women and adolescents trafficked in Europe.* London: London School of Hygiene and Tropical Medicine. https://www.icmec.org/wp-content/uploads/2015/10/Stolen-Smiles-Physical-and-Psych-Consequences-of-Traffic-Victims-in-Europe-Zimmerman.pdf.

Zimmerman, Cathy, Mazeda Hossain, Kate Yun, Viorel Gajdadziev, Natalia Guzun, Maria Tchomarova, Rosa A. Ciarrocchi, Anna Johansson, Anna Kefurtova, Stefania Scodanibbio, Nenette Motus, Brenda Roche, Linda Morison and Charlotte Watts. 2008. 'The health of trafficked women: a survey of women entering posttrafficking services in Europe', *American Journal of Public Health* 98: 55–9.

7 The Roman Empire and transformations in craft production

Astrid Van Oyen

How did empire shape Roman craft production? The imperial Roman period brought larger and more integrated markets, as well as a rudimentary but solid institutional framework including such mechanisms as taxes, contracts (e.g. *locatio conductio*), professional associations (*collegia*) and so on. To speak of a proper state apparatus would be an exaggeration, but there was undoubtedly a grain of truth in the first Roman emperor Augustus's boasting about having heralded an age of newfound stability. Whether such stability proved the right breeding ground for economic growth, however, is a more contentious issue. Proxy indicators such as shipwrecks, lead pollution, animal bones and human physical stature are variously read to indicate a peak in the rate of growth through the tumultuous late Republican period, flattening out again in the early empire when economic performance was at its maximum (Scheidel 2009: 52–3) or as suggesting more sustained growth throughout the early imperial period (Wilson 2009a). In any case, empire created novel economic conditions in the Mediterranean, whose impact on craft production merits investigation.

But this chapter also seeks to flip the question, considering not only how empire shaped craft production, but also how craft production shaped the Roman Empire. After all, craft products – ceramic pots and amphorae, glass vessels, metal brooches – have long served as proxy evidence for the political, social and economic reach of empire. Where once such products were seen as direct references to a Roman lifestyle or even mindset in older, now-jettisoned 'Romanisation' models, they are now considered as more active contributors to the creation of new settings and practices (Van Oyen 2017). Like the craft products that anchored them, such new settings and practices were at once locally more diverse and globally more homogeneous than what preceded them. Put differently, in any one place a greater diversity of goods encouraged choice, yet across regions and across the empire as a whole, the package of goods became more streamlined.

This chapter discusses these issues in relation to the 'what', 'where' and 'how' of craft production, drawing on a wide range of cases and materials. Threaded throughout the narrative is the example of Podere Marzuolo (Cinigiano, Grosseto), a rural craft site situated in inland Tuscany (Italy) (Van Oyen 2020; Bowes 2021) investigated since 2016 by the Marzuolo Archaeological Project (MAP). Not intended as a full-blown case study, the example of Marzuolo rather provides a mirror that at times confirms, at times distorts long-held assumptions about Roman craft.

Craft production: what?

The kinds of crafts in operation did not undergo drastic change in the transition either from Hellenistic kingdoms (in the east) or from Iron Age tribes (in the west) to empire, and include ceramic production, blacksmithing, working of precious metals, production of architectural materials, glass working, but also a series of crafts that largely remain archaeologically invisible, such as leatherworking, weaving, basketry and so on. (For compendia of Roman crafts and craft products, see the *Instrumentum* consortium, http://www.instrumentum-europe.org; Polfer 2004 (France); Santoro 2004 (northern Italy); Polfer 2005 (Italy and western provinces).) Similarly, craft products tended to conform to the same broad functional categories throughout these periods, such as cooking pots, drinking and dining vessels, perfume bottles, loomweights, needles, coins, jewellery, furniture fittings, and many others. No products were launched that even approached the systemic novelty of modern cars, computers or mobile phones.

What did change, however, was both the scale and the range of these crafts' outputs, as well as the reach of their distribution. Before the advent of glassblowing, for instance, consumption of glass vessels had been socially restricted. Hellenistic glass is noted for its vibrant, deep colours, its dramatic, often angular forms achieved through casting, and its intricate decorative patterns and techniques such as mosaic and network glass. Non-renewable materials and time-consuming production processes restricted glass products to the upper end of the market. Glassblowing, invented probably around the middle of the first century

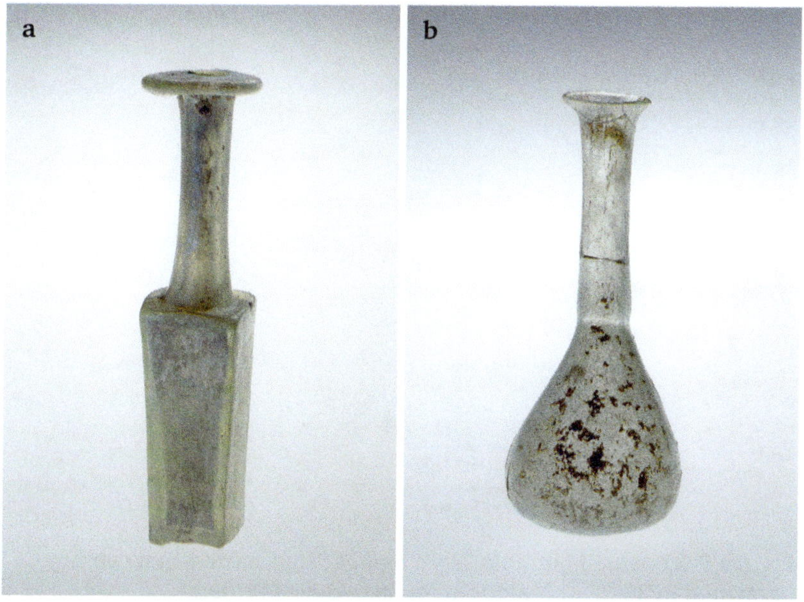

Figure 7.1 Mould-blown glass bottle (a) and free-blown unguentarium (b). (a) Toilet bottle (25–199 CE, CMoG 69.1.18). Gift of New Hampshire Historical Society, by exchange. (b) Bottle (100–299 CE, CMoG 66.1.168). Both images licensed by The Corning Museum of Glass, Corning, NY (https://home.cmog.org/) under CC BY-NC-SA 4.0.

BCE in the Syro-Palestine area (Israeli and Katsnelson 2006) and adopted in Italy during the first century CE (Grose 1977; Stern 1999; Lightfoot 2003; beyond Italy: Amrein and Hochuli-Gysel 2000), radically changed the outlook of glass products and their consumers (Larson 2019). Mould- and especially free-blowing allowed the rapid production of series of small and medium-sized closed containers such as perfume jars. Raw glass wastage was reduced, and, in addition, higher firing temperatures allowed for glass recycling, which became a business in and of itself (Stern 1999: 451, 467). The tandem of recycling and blowing increased the number of glass vessels in circulation, with a majority of repetitive, pale blue or pale green, closed shapes, either globular such as free-blown perfume bottles or angular like mould-blown glass flasks (Figure 7.1). As a result, consumption of glass vessels spread both socially and geographically. A niche for luxury products remained (e.g. cameo glass: Whitehouse 1991), but glass became cheaper and accessible to lower-class households, and to people and sites in previously less connected places, from Roman Britain to inland Roman Italy. Indeed, the early

Figure 7.2 Podere Marzuolo, *terra sigillata* stacks (mid-first century CE) excavated in 2018. © Marzuolo Archaeological Project.

imperial small sites occupying the region around Marzuolo may not all have had much in the way of permanent architecture, but all yielded vessel glass fragments (Bowes 2021).

Ceramic fine ware production saw a similar, albeit less technologically radical evolution. The Hellenistic and late Republican Mediterranean boasted a series of successful fine wares, in particular the black gloss wares of Italy and the western Mediterranean (Morel 1981; Principal 2006; Di Giuseppe 2012). Inspired by more luxurious counterparts in metal, these tablewares were not particularly high end, and adorned many a table, but tended to circulate regionally. In the second half of the first century BCE, a new firing process led to the gradual creation of so-called *terra sigillata* pottery, with a distinct red, glossy surface, and an evolving series of shapes (Ettlinger et al. 1990) (Figure 7.2). Functionally, *terra sigillata* tableware was largely equivalent to its predecessors, but its range of shapes expanded, so that now not one type of dinner plate existed, but a variety of rim shapes and sizes. Consumer choice seemed paramount. Yet paradoxically this variety was highly modular in nature: different size variations cluster neatly (Monteil 2012), and different finishings are so recurrent as to allow the creation of a new 'type'. As a result, sites, assemblages and people were differentiated no longer by whether or not they had access to a certain type of pottery

Figure 7.3 Roman mould-made lamps, provenance unknown. Cornell University. © Astrid Van Oyen.

such as *terra sigillata,* but by their consumption profile, namely the relative proportions of different shapes. As such, for example, Willis (2005) has distinguished the *sigillata* consumption profiles of urban, rural and military sites in Britain. The unit of consumer choice and the means of fostering identities became less the individual object and more the assemblage or the artefact 'suite' (Pitts 2010).

While most new practices, consumer habits and identities revolved around the composition of new kinds of assemblages rather than around functionally novel objects, certain types of objects did spread into regions that had not previously known their use. For example, expanded trade networks made both oil lamps and their fuel source a staple in the north-western provinces (Eckardt 2002). As a portable source of light, and one which users could position to suit their convenience, oil lamps would have profoundly influenced patterns of everyday mobility and activities. Their metal variant, sometimes very ornate indeed, still existed, but the mould-made, mass-produced ceramic oil lamps provided all classes and regions alike with a source of both light and popular imagery (Figure 7.3). In Batavia (Netherlands), sealboxes mark the spread of a writing habit among a population at the very periphery of the Roman Empire (Roymans 2004). The Roman military aggressively recruited among the Batavians, and returning veterans introduced new objects and their associated practices, albeit, again, within a distinctly Batavian assemblage of longhouses, dispersed rural habitation and so on. In Roman Britain, instruments for bodily grooming such as needles, earspoons and tweezers became more prominent and were also more often found in domestic contexts in the Roman period, signalling an increased concern with bodily care which has been read tentatively as the spread of a notion of 'individual' personhood (Hill 1997).

Wider social and geographical accessibility of craft products, combined with a modular expansion of their product range, meant that all consumers became part of a single material and semantic system; a system which, however, also provided ample scope for internal differentiation. This process has been labelled the Roman 'consumer revolution' (Woolf 1998; Wallace-Hadrill 2008; Pitts 2018) and was both product and producer of empire. The consumer revolution, which was very much a revolution in the nature and spread of craft products, enveloped everyone and everything in a material-semiotic system generative of empire and its relative ordering. At the same time, it was a consequence of empire, and more specifically of sustained interregional trade – whether triggered by the army (Middleton 1983), by taxation (Hopkins 1980) or by market forces (Temin 2013) – and of an overall increased buying power indicative of moderate economic growth. The rural, inland area around Marzuolo, for instance, saw increased, yet dispersed, settlement in the Augustan period around the late first century BCE and early first century CE (Ghisleni 2010). The small farmers inhabiting this landscape – whatever their legal status – consumed glass vessels, window glass, oil and wine from across the Mediterranean (Bowes 2021), and created enough of an aggregate demand to warrant an attempt at establishing *terra sigillata* production at Marzuolo (Vaccaro et al. 2017; Van Oyen 2020). The Roman emperor and his court had no monopoly on consumption of certain kinds of craft goods; disparities were a result of greater buying power, not of a sumptuary canon.

Key to this literal and metaphorical *crafting* of empire was the remarkable standardisation of craft products across the Roman Empire. Bricks in different buildings of the early imperial period can be interchangeable (Mogetta 2019: 19–20), as can pots found in places as far apart as southern France and northern Britain. Standardisation of production sequences and of the resulting products is an economic indicator of mass production and expanded markets (Wilson 2009b): it is production's reply to the anonymity of consumers, allowing it to move away from customisation and production to order. 'Need' and 'demand' became abstract parameters. Already in 1981, Marsh's analysis of *terra sigillata* assemblages in Roman London showed a 'push' economy at work, with peaks and dips in supply correlating more with the fate of production centres in southern France than with the economic history of London itself. Similarly, the brick industry around Rome relied not on the construction schedules of any individual building, but on an abstract notion of aggregate demand in the city of Rome (DeLaine 2000). Yet more recent research finds space for customisation, production to order and consumer choice despite – or maybe because of – standardisation: ostraca from the Egyptian quarry of Mons Claudianus, for instance, reveal specific orders for monumental columns (Russell 2013: 211–13).

At the same time, standardised craft products also actively facilitated certain conditions of empire. Elsewhere, for instance, I have explored how standardised products usher in new possibilities of comparison that are fundamental to the creation of competitive markets (Van Oyen 2016). Both producers and consumers can weigh the performance of any two standardised products against a set of desired parameters. What standardisation does is not make everything alike, but generates such a shared set of parameters, for example size, colour, decoration and so on, that provide axes for differentiation. Similarly, in the social and cultural realm, consuming standardised craft objects served to differentiate people as it placed them in a shared realm. While standardised craft objects such as *terra sigillata* pots, brooches or bricks have long been interpreted as the spread of an equally standard 'Roman' identity, it is now recognised, to the contrary, that such objects were culturally underdetermined. Their effectiveness in lubricating an imagined community (*sensu* Anderson 1983) of empire lay not in their communicating a message of 'Romanness', but, instead, in their slotting into a variety of identities, meanings and practices (Van Oyen 2015a). Promising questions for comparative research are how the circulation of craft products contributed to creating a material ecology of empire, and how standardisation mediated between similarity and difference, between homogeneity and variation within imperial populations.

Craft production: where?

The location of craft production has implications for one of the most contentious issues in ancient economic history: the consumer city question. In Finley's appropriation of Weber's concept, ancient cities were consumer cities, operated by rentier elites who drew rents from their landholdings in the countryside (Morley 1996: 20; Finley 1999: 123–49).

The medieval mercantile towns of western Europe are often modelled as the opposite: actively generating wealth through craft production for the market economy (Morley 1996: 19). Epigraphical and archaeological evidence demonstrates that craft production did thrive in Roman urban centres (e.g. Mattingly et al. 2001; Flohr 2013), but a mere distribution map of production centres does not suffice to settle the debate on the consumer city: what is at stake is not so much the location of craft production, but the relative structural importance of agricultural rents and taxes (Erdkamp 2001).

Craft production in the Roman Empire straddled city and countryside. Urban crafts and craftspeople have attracted more investigation, partly because a greater wealth of evidence is available, partly because craft production in cities was often more formalised, with more readily identifiable infrastructure, as it served a larger market. Rural craft production, however, also thrived, from additions to agricultural estates (so-called villas) (Whittaker 1990), to specialised production centres, such as Lezoux in central Gaul, which exported its *terra sigillata* vessels as far as the Rhine frontier (Delage 1998). Peña (2017: 205–8) distinguishes five locational models for craft production in the Roman world: town-based, town-adjacent, rural town-proximate, rural town-remote and mobile. In general terms, the location of craft production was dependent on the nature of the product – including raw materials – on the scale of demand, and on the accessibility of a distribution network (on which I will not dwell, as it is addressed in Chapter 4 in this volume). More contingent factors, however, were also at play, such as the vagaries of landownership – for instance the distribution of property of a particular investor – and pre-existing knowledge traditions and concentrations of skill (Van Oyen 2016).

Some raw materials were claimed by the state, in particular metal mines and stone quarries (Wilson 2012: 133–4; Russell 2013: 38; Hirt 2015; on Han China, see Razeto 2014: 340). Precious and base metals served the Roman army's need for weaponry and armour, and the Roman state's coin supply, which was highly dependent on continued minting (see Howgego, Chapter 3 this volume), whereas stone quarries facilitated the emperor's construction projects and the conspicuous consumption that became a hallmark of his role. The Roman Empire's taxation system merits its own discussion, but while taxes both in kind and in coin were levied in the provinces, and while slave labour operated imperial mines and quarries, there was no tradition of tribute labour of the kind that characterised other world empires in Mesoamerica or China (Barbieri-Low 2007: 9).

Most raw materials, however, were more widely accessible (Wilson 2012), as was, for instance, clay for ceramic production. At Sagalassos, in Roman Pisidia, ceramic tableware production in the Hellenistic period used clays dug up immediately underneath the potters' quarter itself. From the Roman period onwards, however, finer clays, needing less preparation, were transported from the Çanaklı valley 8 km away (Poblome et al. 2002; Degryse et al. 2003). In major Gaulish tableware production sites, such as Lezoux, a similar shift has been observed: when production scaled up and standardisation increased, clay sources often changed and became more specialised, used only and consistently for certain production lines (Van Oyen 2016: 46). Increased efficiency has a role to play, but a more important yet archaeologically elusive factor may well be landownership – put differently: who invested in and who owned the clay sources? As products of landownership – the most respected form of occupation according to Cicero (*De Officiis* I.150–151; Finley 1999: 41–2) – raw materials may well have bypassed a moral disdain for crafts, much as did, for instance, elite ownership of the large brickyards supplying Rome.

Another parameter impacting both the availability of raw materials and the location of craft production was recycling (Duckworth et al. 2020). Recycling could recast centres of consumption, such as villas, into production sites with a ready-made concentration of raw materials (Munro 2012). On a larger scale, glass recycling decreased the dependency of secondary production centres in Italy and the western provinces on the supply of raw glass from primary production centres in the eastern Mediterranean (Stern 2009). Finally, fuel consumption increased for many crafts in the Roman period, both because of the scale and the techniques of production. Glassblowing, for instance, needed higher and more sustained firing temperatures (Stern 1999: 454), as did the oxidising firing necessary to create the bright red glossy finish of *terra sigillata* pottery (see Fernandes et al. 2005 for an experimental study; Janssen et al. 2017 for a contextual calculation for Sagalassos red slip ware production). The downfall of major craft production centres such as Lyon (France) has been attributed to deforestation (Desbat et al. 1996: 241), although craftspeople wielded strategies of wood management such as coppicing (Rackham 1990: 155; Van Oyen 2015b: 287). New research on fuel sources shows even greater ingenuity and flexibility, including the use of charcoal (transportable yet more wasteful of wood), olive pressings and dung (Veal 2019).

The scale, nature and location of demand obviously influence the location of craft production. One can state with some confidence that only a small proportion of the craft products consumed across the empire were made 'at home' (de Ligt 1993: 140 considers the demand side). Initially, in the Late Republic with its dramatic conquests, craft products could be distributed widely, from a few esteemed centres, much as Italian wine in Dressel 1 amphorae. Origin would have lent particular value to craft products, like a patina, as was the case for instance for consumption of 'eastern' products in Italy (Wallace-Hadrill 2008), or of 'Italian' products in Gaul and Britain. In the Early Empire, however, production became more regional (Woolf 1992), with centralisation applying across regions rather than empire-wide. In economic terms, this can be read as a response to the development of new, more sustained markets: both the late first-century BCE attempt at *terra sigillata* production and the first-century CE blacksmithing at Marzuolo, for instance, catered for the demand of a newly developed countryside (Bowes 2021; Van Oyen et al. 2022). The precise parameters defining regionalism – how a region crystallised economically – are not yet fully understood, despite increased attention (see Poblome et al. 2017 on oligopoly – a situation where few suppliers cater for large demand). What is less often considered is that in the process origin became less of a signifier in socio-cultural terms. Truly 'Roman' craft products, then, were not rooted in particular production places: understated origins were part of their universal appeal (cf. Van Oyen 2016: 126).

On a lower scale of analysis, the question of where craft production took place pertains to the nature of workshops, which is at once a segue into the 'how' of craft production. From the point of view of production, it is more difficult to corroborate the above claim that the domestic mode of production diminished. After all, production in a domestic setting is less likely to leave functionally specific traces. Yet, as mentioned above, it is clear that craft products in circulation were more likely to have been made in a specialised workshop, and often beyond the locale. Most craft production of imperial Roman times can be defined as nucleated workshops (Peacock 1982: 9–10). Even Rostovtzeff (1926: 164), the patriarch of the modernising view of the ancient economy, conceded that workshops remained small in size (also Hawkins 2012: 175–6). Some production sites nevertheless attained mind-boggling outputs, such as the 1.5 million *terra sigillata* pots estimated to have left La Graufesenque (France) each year (Hartley 2005: 116). The *terra sigillata* production site of Scoppieto in the Tiber Valley (Italy) has a room (room O) with an ordered sequence of no less than 20 potters' workstations (Bergamini 2013: 90) (Figure 7.4). But generally scaling up amounted to a horizontal multiplication of smaller workshops, not to the development of large concerns or 'firms'. The limits behind vertical integration might betray a general risk aversion on the part of investors, but also reveal significant

Figure 7.4 Scoppieto, Room O with individual potters' workstations. © Astrid Van Oyen.

autonomy of each production unit, which might be the sign of more developed types of craft production. Vertical integration prevails in new industries, where high information costs are absorbed by gathering as many production stages as possible into a single concern (Silver 2009: 172–3). In a more mature industry, instead, as was the case for most types of craft production in the Roman Empire, lesser unknowns reduced information asymmetries and allowed smaller units to settle risks through contracts. Hawkins (2012) relates such horizontal multiplication to the role of *collegia*, loose trade associations, whose network of social relations would have helped channel information and contracts – a reminder that the social and the economic can never be separated in the study of Roman crafts.

What is as yet unclear is the extent to which horizontal multiplication acted as an amplifier of or a limit to specialisation. As far as precious metal production is concerned, for instance, the former scenario seems to hold true: contracts and *collegia* facilitated a highly segmented production chain, with each small workshop or each individual craftsperson specialising in a specific step of the process (Hawkins 2012: 179–80). As for *terra sigillata* production, some degree of specialisation applied – for instance mould-makers and firing masters – but even in a larger production site such as Lezoux (France) most workshops seem to have catered for the entire production sequence, and for the entire product range (Van Oyen 2016: 80, 90). More research is thus needed to understand the underlying differences between crafts, their knowledge traditions and their production organisation.

That knowledge traditions might hold the key to many of the pending questions concerning the location of craft production is suggested by another unresolved riddle: why did *terra sigillata* production never take off in Britain, despite the large demand, the available skills and resources, and its locational advantage over competitors in Gaul? I have elsewhere proposed that the answer should be sought in a more careful investigation of knowledge traditions and practices – in other words, in an inquiry spearheaded by the question of 'how' (Van Oyen 2016: 117). Standardised products can travel widely but their associated production knowledge does not spread so easily.

Craft production: how?

This final section considers the 'how' of craft production: questions of practice, which will at once bring us closer to the craftspeople themselves. And yet all too often such questions are abstracted away, by cultural and economic histories alike. They seem to open up too much descriptive detail, not quite trivial but only of interest to the technical historian, not to socio-economic histories and their goal of explanation.

This unspoken rule hampers even the much-debated question of innovation. Finley (1965) famously maintained that the Roman Empire lacked (or at any case was not conducive to the spread of) innovations, a condition symptomatic of an overriding concern with status, and a reluctance to invest in productivity. According to this paradigm, whatever innovation did occur operated in the elite realm of conspicuous consumption, but did not spur economic growth. The charges against Finley's substantivist position have been empirical in nature, listing examples of innovations, mostly in agriculture (Brun et al. 1998; Wilson 2002), but also in craft production (Greene 2000). Yet without investigating questions of *practice*, debates on innovation risk reduction to a shallow presence/absence game (Pfaffenberger 1992; Knappett and van der Leeuw 2014).

The new firing techniques used in production of *terra sigillata* pottery were developed in Italy around 40 BCE (Ettlinger et al. 1990; Kenrick et al. 2000), strictly speaking before the start of the Imperial Roman period, whereas the real take-off of glassblowing occurred during the first century CE (Grose 1977; Stern 1999). Overall, and especially after the Early Imperial period, craft production techniques saw little change. Combined with the mass output of standardised products facilitated by the few inventions that did occur, the 'how' of imperial Roman craft production can appear rather stagnant. Indeed, the supposedly 'mechanical reproductions' of Roman craft products held less appeal to early modern antiquarian collectors steeped in romantic visions of artisanship than did, for instance, hand-painted Greek vases (Van Oyen 2016: 21). But on the producer's end, the shift to mass production and an expanded product range need not signal a reduction in skill (Murphy and Poblome 2017: 76). After all, glassblowing is every bit as skilful a process as is casting or core forming, it only reduces investment per product. And, as mentioned above, it is unclear whether the division of labour was necessarily greater. The industrial revolution with its mechanised production provides a misleading parallel.

Marzuolo was far from the first *terra sigillata* production site in Italy. Yet already by 30 BCE, only about a decade after *terra sigillata* pottery was developed – presumably in Arezzo – potters at Marzuolo were experimenting with production of tablewares in the same new shapes, and trying to reproduce the same, lustrous red appearance, albeit not without problems. Excavations in 2012 revealed an assemblage of experimental *sigillata* pots of early shapes, which were poorly or not slipped with a discoloured or patchy surface, and partially fired (Vaccaro et al. 2017). This dump was found abutting the back wall of a building with large, open cells (Bowes et al. 2013: 604; Bowes 2021), in whose front yard a rectangular kiln of the same date showed tinkering with the firing atmosphere through the addition of a secondary flue or entrance (Bowes et al. 2014: 496–7). A gap in evidence does not allow us to trace what happened next, but by the middle of the first century CE, Marzuolo was either producing or exporting standardised, glossy red *terra sigillata* pots, as shown by a unique context of stacked pots (Vaccaro et al. 2017) (Figure 7.2). The initial phase's skills, resources and distribution channels may have been predated upon and replaced by a bigger investor, either locally or regionally (Van Oyen 2020). While questions of investment and production organisation at Marzuolo merit further investigation, this evidence highlights the micro-innovation and the work needed to create and sustain the pattern of mass-produced, widespread, standardised craft goods that both reflected and constituted empire.

The case of Marzuolo demonstrates a concern with the development of human capital. This is important to consider within the context of the Roman Empire, a pre-industrial economy with high mortality rates and short lifespans. As Saller (2012: 74) has noted, the Roman demographic reality would have curbed development of human capital – only a limited amount of experience could be had in any one individual lifespan – while also disincentivising investment in training. Marzuolo, instead, shows that even in its environment of small farmers, human capital *was* seen as worth investing in, albeit also curbed by the reigning social, economic and legal structures. Archaeometry – hitherto used predominantly to provenance craft goods – holds particular promise to untangle the process of skills development, by documenting changes and continuities in technological choices, from clay selection and preparation over forming techniques to firing practices.

Archaeometry also has potential to contribute to an emerging concern in the study of Roman craft production: the role of collaboration, cross-craft interaction and knowledge development. Scholarly specialisation and a privileging of finished products over process often entail a mono-craft or mono-product view on craft production (Shimada 2007: 4). While formal crossovers between different categories of new consumer goods in the Roman world (e.g. glass and *terra sigillata* vessels) have long been noted (Löbbing 2015), such parallels have rarely been explored in technical terms (Greene 2007). For the Roman world in particular, a recognition of increased specialisation should not obfuscate the many shared concerns among craftspeople, such as pyrotechnology and distribution networks (Vennarucci et al. 2018; Van Oyen et al. 2022 on blacksmithing and woodworking). Consideration of production sequences and the networks on which these rely can draw out intricate relations between crafts, craftspeople and craft products, an approach practiced by Gosner (2016: 134) for mining communities.

Stamps can give us unique access to the 'who' behind ancient craft production. Yet while relatively many Roman craft products (*instrumentum domesticum*) bore name stamps – tablewares, amphorae, bricks, lamps, glass vessels and so on (e.g. Sternini 1993 for glass; Pucci 1993 for *terra sigillata*) (Figure 7.5) – their meaning is often unclear. Stamps could be measures of quantity and/or quality, in production and/or marketing. They could act as a kind of advertisement towards the consumer. They could function as a surveillance mechanism in production, keeping track

Figure 7.5 Podere Marzuolo, MANNE *terra sigillata* stamp *in planta pedis*, mid-first century CE. © Marzuolo Archaeological Project.

of the output of individual makers. Or they could play some other role in production organisation, for instance by facilitating communal phases of production such as firing. For *terra sigillata* pots, stamps probably fulfilled all of these roles, some at different stages of their production sequence, others at different moments in the ware's production history (cf. Barbieri-Low 2007: 14 for early China). Stamps have in particular been mined for production relations (e.g. on lamps, Auer and Sitz 2014). For instance, Italian *terra sigillata* stamps often include two names, one of which in the genitive, suggesting a relation of dependency (Fülle 1997). Later in Gaul, genitives disappear, and single names are paired either with the qualifier '*officina*' – suggesting a workshop owner – or with '*fecit*' (made by) or '*manu*' (by the hand of) – implying a more tactile, direct involvement in production, at least in spirit. The *Names on Terra Sigillata* project (Hartley and Dickinson 2008–12) and the Mainz dabatase (https://www1.rgzm.de/samian/home/frames.htm) document, and in many cases illustrate, Gaulish *terra sigillata* stamps, including information on different dies, wear and so on – a most useful resource for questions of production organisation.

But more could be done with stamps to trace the structure of knowledge production, for instance through the development of partnerships and apprenticeships (e.g. Fülle 1997). At Marzuolo, vessel fragments from the experimental *terra sigillata* deposit all carried the name stamp Sextilius, in two die varieties (Vaccaro et al. 2017: 239). It is as yet unclear whether Sextilius was a local potter venturing into a new production line, or established a workshop at Marzuolo having acquired *terra sigillata* production knowledge elsewhere. The 'SEX' die is attested at Arezzo and elsewhere, while a 'SEXTILI' die is known from Arezzo too (Kenrick et al. 2000: 407–8, numbers 1958 and 1961) – but Sext(ili)us is not a rare name. What is clear is that Sextilius considered a name stamp to be a crucial aspect of the kind of tableware he intended to produce, even if the small scale of the operations probably did not warrant its use for internal production organisation. In the second, standardised, *sigillata* deposit a series of names are represented on the stamps, dominated by Manneius (Vaccaro et al. 2017: 247; also attested, sparingly, at Torrita di Siena, see Pucci 1992: 113–6 and 143–5) (Figure 7.5). This second deposit may represent local production at Marzuolo or a consignment delivered from a nearby production site such as Torrita di Siena (chemical characterisation of the fabrics and clays is ongoing). In any case, a role of the stamps in production organisation is now more likely. Tracing the connections between stamps within and across sites should yield information about the trajectories of investment and skill development.

In addition, stamps could also generate other types of insights into the 'who' of craft production. As personal names, they reflect a process of objectification and self-identification, whereby the maker comes to understand himself through the act of making and its products (cf. Miller 2005; Sennett 2008). The *manu* and *fecit* formulae are particularly revealing here, even if they betray an ideal rather than actual practice. This type of evidence provides an antidote to the moral prescriptions of elite landowners such as Cicero (cf. Finley 1999: 41–2; see the commemoration and celebration of occupation in funerary inscriptions: Joshel 1992).

As is the case with farmers, the legal status of craftspeople is difficult to pin down. The use of slave labour in particular is almost completely impossible to identify other than through such rare instances as the names and formulae on stamps (Fülle 1997). Traditionally, slave labour is invoked for labour-intensive, low-skilled jobs, such as mining, or brick making and laying. But the institution of slavery was elastic, encompassing domestic slaves who were part of the household and had good prospects of gaining their freedom, as well as chattel slaves considered as 'speaking tools' (Varro *Res Rusticae* I.17) and labouring in dire conditions on estates or in mines (Joshel 2010). This variety of roles for slaves represents a range of investment attitudes on the part of their owners. Slaves identifiable as such on stamps or craft products would have been either acquired or trained with a view to their specialist skills (Saller 2012: 78). A large part of the human capital of the Roman world may well have been quite literally in the hands of slaves.

Slavery came with a peculiar set of transaction costs: especially in the case of high-skilled slaves, the cost of acquisition would have been high, as was the risk of the slave cheating, underperforming, or even running away. The principle of *peculium* alleviated that risk by giving a slave-owner the opportunity to put a slave in charge of managing a business and sharing in the profits, which they could put to their own purposes, including buying their freedom (Frier and Kehoe 2007: 131–2; Scheidel 2012: 100). As such, the interests of slave and owner would be aligned, and the slave would have a strong incentive to perform. For *terra sigillata* production, for instance, it has been suggested that some of the earliest workshops in Gaul were in fact branch workshops launched by dependents, possibly slaves, of the Ateius workshop in Arezzo (Picon and Garmier 1974; Desbat et al. 1996; on possible branch workshops in the production of ceramic lamps, see Auer and Sitz 2014). Fülle (1997: 141–4) casts doubt on the hypothesis of branch workshops for *terra sigillata* production, suggesting instead networks of economically, if not socially, independent craftspeople.

Social and legal status, as well as personal relationships, remained important in all aspects of Roman craft production (as for the Roman economy at large, see Bang 2008), but the Roman Empire created an institutional framework to reduce transaction costs. The concept of *peculium* is one example, but more generally the recognition of property rights and the presence of an empire-wide legal system made possible the use of contracts between any two parties (Frier and Kehoe 2007). Egyptian papyri show the use of a *locatio conductio* contract in the production of amphorae: the landowner put infrastructure and raw materials at the disposal of the potter, in return for a fixed number of vessels of prescribed types (Cockle 1981). As such the landowner had a relatively risk-free, secured return, while the potter did not have to bear the risk of investing, but had every incentive to produce more pots than the specified number, for his own count.

Conclusion

Empire impacted on craft production in the Roman world, in particular by fostering certain macro-economic conditions and through the development of an institutional framework enforcing property rights and enabling contracts. As a result, demand for craft products not only increased in intensity but also expanded in its social and geographical reach. Larger demand triggered mass-production and increased specialisation, which was predominantly managed through horizontal multiplication of production units. In terms of craft production, any differentiation between city and countryside became a matter of degree rather than nature. Similarly, the social reach of mass-produced Roman craft goods was very wide indeed, enveloping consumers in a shared material system through which differences took on relative form. Consumption habits thus became comparable, enabling processes of emulation and differentiation which defined the material ecology of the Roman Empire.

Acknowledgements

I would like to thank my co-directors of the Marzuolo Archaeological Project, Rhodora Vennarucci and Gijs Tol, for sharing unpublished material and for the years of discussion of many of the concepts developed in this chapter. The Marzuolo Archaeological Project has received the generous support of the following institutions: Cotsen Excavation Grant from the Archaeological Institute of America; Cambridge Humanities Research Grant; McDonald Institute for Archaeological Research; Centre for Advanced Spatial Technologies (University of Arkansas); Einaudi Center for International Studies (Cornell University); President's Council for Cornell Women; Loeb Classical Library Foundation.

References

Amrein, Heidi and Anne Hochuli-Gysel. 2000. 'Le soufflage du verre: attestations de la technique à Avenches (Suisse) et à Saintes (France) au Ier siècle ap.J.-C'. In *Annales Du 14e Congrés de l'Association Internationale Pour l'Histoire Du Verre (Venice-Milan 1998)*, 89–98. Lochem: International Association for the History of Glass.

Anderson, Benedict. 1983. *Imagined Communities: Reflections on the origin and spread of nationalism*. London: Verso.

Auer, Martin and Stephanie Sitz. 2014. 'Die Firmalampenproduktion des EVCARPVS – eine Studie zur römischen Keramikproduktion', *Germania* 92: 85–125.

Bang, Peter F. 2008. *The Roman Bazaar: A comparative study of trade and markets in a tributary empire*. Cambridge: Cambridge University Press.

Barbieri-Low, Anthony J. 2007. *Artisans in Early Imperial China*. Seattle, WA and London: University of Washington Press.

Bergamini, Margherita (ed.) 2013. *Scoppieto III: Lo scavo, le strutture, i materiali (coroplastica, marmi)*. Rome: Edizioni Quasar.

Bowes, Kimberly (ed.). 2021. *The Roman Peasant Project 2009–2014: Excavating the Roman rural poor*. Philadelphia, PA: University of Pennsylvania Press.

Bowes, Kimberly, Marielena Ghisleni, Cam Grey and Emanuele Vaccaro. 2013. 'Cinigiano (GR). Il sito di Marzuolo: Quarto anno del Roman Peasant Project', *Notiziario della Soprintendenza per i Beni Archeologici della Toscana* 9: 601–5.

Bowes, Kimberly, Marielena Ghisleni and Emanuele Vaccaro. 2014. 'Cinigiano (GR). Il sito di Marzuolo, seconda campagna di scavo: Quinto anno del Roman Peasant Project', *Notiziario della Soprintendenza per i Beni Archeologici della Toscana* 10: 494–7.

Brun, Jean-Pierre, Marc Borréani and Jean-Louis Guendon. 1998. 'Deux moulins hydrauliques du haut-empire Romain en Narbonnaise: *villae* des Mesclans à La Crau et de Saint-Pierre/Les Laurons aux Arcs (Var)', *Gallia* 55: 279–326.

Cockle, Helen. 1981. 'Pottery manufacture in Roman Egypt: a new papyrus', *Journal of Roman Studies* 71: 87–97.

Degryse, Patrick, Jeroen Poblome, Kristien Donners, Jozef Deckers and Marc Waelkens. 2003. 'Geoarchaeological investigations of the "Potter's Quarter" at Sagalassos, Southwest Turkey', *Geoarchaeology* 18(2): 255–81.

Delage, Richard. 1998. 'Première approche de la diffusion des céramiques sigillées du centre de la Gaule en Occident Romain', *SFECAG Actes du congrès d'Istres*: 271–313.

DeLaine, Janet. 2000. 'Bricks and mortar: exploring the economics of building techniques at Rome and Ostia'. In *Economies beyond Agriculture in the Classical World*, edited by David J. Mattingly and John Salmon, 230–68. London and New York: Routledge.

de Ligt, Luuk. 1993. *Fairs and Markets in the Roman Empire: Economic and social aspects of periodic trade in a pre-industrial society*. Amsterdam: J.C. Gieben.

Desbat, Armand, Martine Genin and Jacques Lasfargues. 1996. 'Les productions des ateliers de potiers antiques de Lyon, 1ère Partie: Les Ateliers Précoces', *Gallia* 53: 1–249.

Di Giuseppe, Helga. 2012. *Black-gloss Ware in Italy: Production management and local histories*. British Archaeological Reports International Series 2335. Oxford: British Archaeological Reports.

Duckworth, Chloe N., Andrew Wilson, Astrid Van Oyen, Catherine Alexander, Jane Evans, Christopher Green and David J. Mattingly. 2020. 'When the statue is both marble and lime'. In *Recycling and the Ancient Economy*, edited by Chloe N. Duckworth and Andrew Wilson, 449–59. Oxford: Oxford University Press.

Eckardt, Hella. 2002. *Illuminating Roman Britain*. Monographies Instrumentum 23. Montagnac: Monique Mergoil.

Erdkamp, Paul. 2001. 'Beyond the limits of the 'consumer city': a model of the urban and rural economy in the Roman world', *Historia* 50(3): 332–56.

Ettlinger, Elisabeth, Bettina Hedinger, Bettina Hoffmann, Philip M. Kenrick, Giuseppe Pucci, Katrin Roth-Rubi, Gerwulf Schneider, Siegmar von Schnurbein, Colin M. Wells and Susanne Zabehlicky-Scheffenegger (eds). 1990. *Conspectus Formarum Terrae Sigillatae Italico Modo Confectae*. Bonn: R. Habelt.

Fernandes, José, Mathias Fernandes and Catherine de Casas. 2005. 'Cuisson de sigillée rouge dans un four à tubulures à la Graufesenque', *SFECAG Actes du congrès de Blois*, 447–50.

Finley, Moses I. 1965. 'Technical innovation and economic progress in the ancient world', *The Economic History Review* 18(1): 29–45.

Finley, Moses I. 1999. *The Ancient Economy* (2nd edition). Berkeley, CA: University of California Press.

Flohr, Miko. *The World of the Fullo: Work, economy, and society in Roman Italy*. Oxford: Oxford University Press, 2013.

Frier, Bruce W. and Dennis B. Kehoe. 2007. 'Law and economic institutions'. In *The Cambridge Economic History of the Greco-Roman* World, edited by Walter Scheidel, Ian Morris and Richard P. Saller, 113–43. Cambridge: Cambridge University Press.

Fülle, Gunnar. 1997. 'The internal organization of the Arretine terra sigillata industry: problems of evidence and interpretation', *Journal of Roman Studies* 87: 111–55.

Ghisleni, Marielena. 2010. 'Carta archeologica della provincia di Grosseto: comune di Cinigiano. Dinamiche insediative e di potere fra V e XI secolo nella bassa val d'Orcia e nella media valle dell'Ombrone'. Unpublished Ph.D. thesis, Università di Siena.

Gosner, Linda. 2016. 'Extraction and empire: multi-scalar approaches to Roman mining communities and industrial landscapes in Southwest Iberia', *Archaeological Review from Cambridge* 31(2): 125–43.

Greene, Kevin. 2000. 'Technological innovation and economic progress in the ancient world: M.I. Finley reconsidered', *The Economic History Review* 53(1): 29–59.

Greene, Kevin. 2007. 'Late Hellenistic and early Roman invention and innovation: the case of lead-glazed pottery', *American Journal of Archaeology* 111(4): 653–71.

Grose, David F. 1977. 'Early blown glass: the Western evidence', *Journal of Glass Studies* 19: 9–29.

Hartley, Brian R. 2005. 'Pots for tables; tables awaiting pots: an exercise in speculative archaeoeconomy', *Journal of Roman Pottery Studies* 12: 112–6.

Hartley, Brian R. and Brenda M. Dickinson (eds). 2008–12. *Names on Terra Sigillata: An index of makers' stamps and signatures on Gallo-Roman terra sigillata (Samian Ware)*, 9 vols. London: Institute of Classical Studies.

Hawkins, Cameron. 2012. 'Manufacturing'. In *The Cambridge Companion to the Roman Economy*, edited by Walter Scheidel, 175–94. Cambridge: Cambridge University Press.

Hill, Jeremy D. 1997. 'The end of one kind of body and the beginning of another kind of body? Toilet instruments and 'Romanization' in Southern England during the first century AD'. In *Reconstructing Iron Age Societies. New approaches to the British Iron Age*, edited by Adam Gwilt and Colin Haselgrove, 96–107. Oxford: Oxbow.

Hirt, Alfred M. 2015. 'Centurions, quarries, and the emperor'. In *Ownership and Exploitation of Land and Natural Resources in the Roman World*, edited by Paul Erdkamp, Koenraad Verboven and Arjan Zuiderhoek, 289–314. Oxford: Oxford University Press.

Hopkins, Keith. 1980. 'Taxes and trade in the Roman empire (200 BC–AD 400)', *Journal of Roman Studies* 70: 101–25.

Israeli, Yael and Natalya Katsnelson. 2006. 'Refuse of a glass workshop of the Second Temple period from Area J'. In *Jewish Quarter Excavations in the Old City of Jerusalem III: Area E and other studies*, edited by Hillel Geva, 411–60. Jerusalem: Israel Exploration Society.

Janssen, Ellen, Jeroen Poblome, Johan Claeys, Vincent Kint, Patrick Degryse, Elena Marinova and Bart Muys. 2017. 'Fuel for debating ancient economies: calculating wood consumption at urban scale in Roman imperial times', *Journal of Archaeological Science. Reports* 11: 592–9.

Joshel, Sandra. 1992. *Work, Identity, and Legal Status at Rome: A study of the occupational inscriptions*. Norman, OK: University of Oklahoma Press.

Joshel, Sandra. 2010. *Slavery in the Roman World*. Cambridge: Cambridge University Press.

Kenrick, Philip M., August Oxé and Howard Comfort. 2000. *Corpus Vasorum Arretinorum: A catalogue of the signatures, shapes and chronology of Italian Sigillata*. Bonn: Habelt.

Knappett, Carl and Sander van der Leeuw. 2014. 'A developmental approach to ancient innovation: The potter's wheel in the Bronze Age East Mediterranean', *Pragmatics and Cognition* 22(1): 64–92.

Larson, Kate. 2019. 'Cheap, fast, good: the Roman glassblowing revolution reconsidered', *Journal of Roman Archaeology* 32: 7–22.

Lightfoot, Christopher S. 2003. 'From East to West: the early Roman glass industry'. In *Échanges et Commerce Du Verre Dans Le Monde Antique*, edited by Danièle Foy and Marie-Dominique Nenna, 341–7. Montagnac: Editions Monique Mergoil.

Löbbing, Jan-Piter. 2015. 'The concept of skeuomorphism and the spread of glass vessels in the Augustan period'. In *Tarraco Biennal. Actes 2 Congrés Internacional d'Arqueologia i Món Antic: August i les províncies occidentals, 2000 aniversari dela mort d'August*, edited by Jordi López Vilar, 105–11. Tarragona: Impremta Torrell.

Marsh, Geoffrey. 1981. 'London's Samian supply and its relationship to the development of the Gallic Samian industry'. In *Roman Pottery Research in Britain and North-West Europe. Papers presented to Graham Webster. Part I*, edited by Anne C. Anderson and Alastair Scott Anderson, 173–238. British Archaeological Reports International Series 123(i). Oxford: British Archaeological Reports.

Mattingly, David J., David Stone, Lea Stirling and Nejib Ben Lazreg. 2001. 'Leptiminus (Tunisia): a 'producer' city?' In *Economies Beyond Agriculture in the Classical World*, edited by David J. Mattingly and John Salmon, 66–89. Leicester-Nottingham Studies in Ancient Society 9. London and New York: Routledge.

Middleton, Paul. 1983. 'The Roman army and long distance trade'. In *Trade and Famine in Classical Antiquity*, edited by Peter Garnsey and C.R. Whittaker, 75–83. Proceedings of the Cambridge Philological Society Supplement 8. Cambridge: Cambridge Philological Society.

Miller, Daniel. 2005. 'Introduction'. In *Materiality*, edited by D. Miller, 1–50. Durham, NC and London: Duke University Press.

Mogetta, Marcello. 2019. *The Origins of Concrete Construction in Roman Architecture: Technology and society in republican Italy*. Cambridge: Cambridge University Press.

Monteil, Gwladys. 2012. 'The sizes of Samian vessels and dining: evidence from Roman London. In *Dating and Interpreting the Past in the Western Roman Empire: Essays in honour of Brenda Dickinson*, edited by David Bird, 330–45. Oxford: Oxbow.

Morel, Jean-Paul. 1981. *Céramique campanienne: Les formes*. Bibliothèque des Écoles françaises d'Athènes et de Rome 244. Rome: École française de Rome.

Morley, Neville. 1996. *Metropolis and Hinterland: The city of Rome and the Italian economy, 200 B.C.–A.D. 200*. Cambridge: Cambridge University Press.

Munro, Beth. 2012. 'Recycling, demand for materials, and landownership at villas in Italy and the Western provinces in Late Antiquity', *Journal of Roman Archaeology* 25: 351–70.

Murphy, Elizabeth A. and Jeroen Poblome. 2017. 'From formal to technical styles: production challenges and economic implications of changing tableware styles in Roman to Late Antique Sagalassos', *American Journal of Archaeology* 121(1): 61–84.

Peacock, David P.S. 1982. *Pottery in the Roman World: An ethnoarchaeological approach*. London and New York: Longman.

Peña, J. Theodore. 2017. 'Issues in the study of rural craft production in Roman Italy'. In *The Economic Integration of Roman Italy: Rural communities in a globalizing world*, edited by Tymon C.A. De Haas and Gijs W. Tol, 203–30. Leiden and Boston, MA: Brill.

Pfaffenberger, Bryan. 1992. 'Social anthropology of technology', *Annual Review of Anthropology* 21: 491–516.

Picon, Maurice and Joëlle Garmier. 1974. 'Un Atelier d'Ateius à Lyon'. Mélanges d'archéologie et d'histoire ancienne à la mémoire d'Adrien Bruhl. *Revue archéologique de l'Est* 25(1): 71–6.

Pitts, Martin. 2010. 'Artefact suites and social practice: an integrated approach to Roman provincial finds assemblages', *Facta* 4: 125–52.

Pitts, Martin. 2018. *The Roman Object Revolution: Objectscapes and intra-cultural connectivity in northwest Europe*. Amsterdam: Amsterdam University Press.

Poblome, Jeroen, Patrick Degryse, Willy Viaene, Raoul Ottenburgs, Marc Waelkens, Roland Degeest and Jean Naud. 2002. 'The concept of a pottery production centre: an archaeometrical contribution from ancient Sagalassos', *Journal of Archaeological Science* 29(2): 873–82.

Poblome, Jeroen, Senem Özden Gerçeker and Maarten Loopmans. 2017. 'Different similarities or similar differences? Thoughts on koine, oligopoly and regionalism'. In *Materialising Roman Histories*, edited by Astrid Van Oyen and Martin Pitts, 85–100. Oxford: Oxbow.

Polfer, Michel. 2004. 'Archéologie de l'artisanat et économie de l'empire Romain: contexte historiographique, méthodologie de travail et perspectives de recherche du projet international CRAFTS'. In *Artigianato e produzione nella Cisalpina. Problemi di metodo e prime applicazioni*, edited by Sara Santoro, 9–17. Florence: All'insegna del Giglio.

Polfer, Michel. 2005. *Artisanat et économie romaine: Italie et provinces occidentales de l'Empire. Actes du 3e Colloque International d'Erpeldange (Lux.) sur l'artisanat romain, 14–16 octobre 2004*. Montagnac: Éditions Monique Mergoil.

Principal, Jordi. 2006. 'Late Hellenistic black-gloss wares in the north-eastern Iberian peninsula: production traditions and social practices'. In *Old Pottery in a New Century: Innovating perspectives on Roman pottery studies. Atti del Convegno Internazionale di Studi. Catania, 22–24 Aprile 2004*, edited by Daniele Malfitana, Jeroen Poblome and John Lund, 41–56. Monografie dell' Istituto per i Beni Archeologici e Monumentali 1. Catania: [s.n.].

Pucci, Giuseppe. 1992. *La fornace di Umbricio Cordo: l'officina di un ceramista romano e il territorio di Torrita di Siena nell'antichità*. Florence: All'insegna del Giglio.

Pucci, Giuseppe. 1993. 'I bolli sulla *terra sigillata: Fra epigrafia e storia economica*'. In *The Inscribed Economy: Production and distribution in the Roman Empire in the light of* Instrumentum Domesticum, edited by William V. Harris, 73–9. JRA Supplementary Series 6. Ann Arbor, MI: Journal of Roman Archaeology.

Rackham, Oliver. 1990. *Trees and Woodland in the British Landscape*. London: J. M. Dent.

Razeto, Anna. 2014. 'Comparing East and West: aspects of urban manufacture and retail in the capitals of the Roman and Han empires'. In *Making Ancient Cities: Space and place in early urban societies*, edited by Andrew T. Creekmore III and Kevin D. Fisher, 337–69. New York: Cambridge University Press.

Rostovtzeff, Michael I. 1926. *The Social and Economic History of the Roman Empire*. Oxford: Clarendon Press.

Roymans, Nico. 2004. *Ethnic Identity and Imperial Power: The Batavians in the early Roman Empire*. Amsterdam: Amsterdam University Press.

Russell, Ben. 2013. *The Economics of the Roman Stone Trade*. Oxford: Oxford University Press.

Saller, Richard. 2012. 'Human capital and economic growth'. In *The Cambridge Companion to the Roman Economy*, edited by Walter Scheidel, 71–86. Cambridge: Cambridge University Press.

Santoro, Sara (ed.). 2004. *Artigianato e produzione nella Cisalpina: Problemi di metodo e prime applicazioni*. Florence: All'insegna del Giglio.

Scheidel, Walter. 2009. 'In search of Roman economic growth', *Journal of Roman Archaeology* 22: 46–70.

Scheidel, Walter. 2012. 'Slavery'. In *The Cambridge Companion to the Roman Economy*, edited by Walter Scheidel, 89–113. Cambridge: Cambridge University Press.

Sennett, Richard. 2008. *The Craftsman*. New Haven, CT: Yale University Press.

Shimada, Izumi. 2007. 'Introduction'. In *Craft Production in Complex Societies: Multicraft and producer perspectives*, edited by Izumi Shimada, 1–21. Salt Lake City, UT: University of Utah Press.

Silver, Morris. 2009. 'Glimpses of vertical integration/disintegration in Ancient Rome', *Ancient Society* 39: 171–84.

Stern, E. Marianne. 1999. 'Roman glassblowing in a cultural context', *American Journal of Archaeology* 103(3): 441–84.

Stern, E. Marianne. 2009. 'Glass production'. In *The Oxford Handbook of Engineering and Technology in the Ancient World*, edited by John Peter Oleson, 520–47. Oxford: Oxford University Press.

Sternini, Mara. 1993. 'I vetri'. In *The Inscribed Economy: Production and distribution in the Roman Empire in the light of* Instrumentum Domesticum, edited by William V. Harris, 82–94. JRA Supplementary Series 6. Ann Arbor, MI: Journal of Roman Archaeology.

Temin, Peter. 2013. *The Roman Market Economy*. Princeton, MA and Oxford: Princeton University Press.

Vaccaro, Emanuele, Claudio Capelli and Marielena Ghisleni. 2017. 'Italic sigillata production and trade in rural central Italy: new data from the project "Excavating the Roman Peasant"'. In *The Economic Integration of Roman Italy: Rural communities in a globalizing world*, edited by Tymon C.A. De Haas and Gijs W. Tol, 231–62. Leiden and Boston, MA: Brill.

Van Oyen, Astrid. 2015a. 'Actor-network theory's take on archaeological types: becoming, material agency, and historical explanation', *Cambridge Archaeological Journal* 25(1): 63–78.

Van Oyen, Astrid. 2015b. 'The Roman city as articulated through *Terra Sigillata*', *Oxford Journal of Archaeology* 34(3): 279–99.

Van Oyen, Astrid. 2016. *How Things Make History: The Roman Empire and its terra sigillata pottery*. Amsterdam: Amsterdam University Press.

Van Oyen, Astrid. 2017. 'Material culture in the Romanization debate'. In *The Diversity of Classical Archaeology* (Studies in Classical Archaeology 1), edited by Achim Lichtenberger and Rubina Raja, 287–300. Turnhout: Brepols.

Van Oyen, Astrid. 2020. 'Innovation and investment in the Roman rural economy through the lens of Marzuolo (Tuscany, Italy)', *Past & Present* 248(1): 3–40.

Van Oyen, Astrid, Gijs W. Tol, Rhodora G. Vennarucci, Alexander Agostini, Vincent Serneels, Anna Maria Mercuri, Eleonora Rattighieri and Alessandra Benatti. 2022. 'Forging the Roman rural economy: a blacksmithing workshop and its toolset at Marzuolo (Tuscany)', *American Journal of Archaeology* 126(1): 53–77.

Veal, Robyn. 2019. 'The history and science of fire and fuel in the Roman Empire'. In *Fuel and Fire in the Ancient Roman World: Towards an integrated economic understanding*, edited by Robyn Veal and Victoria Leitch, 11–24. Cambridge: McDonald Institute for Archaeological Research.

Vennarucci, Rhodora G., Astrid Van Oyen and Gijs W. Tol. 2018. 'Una Comunità Artigianale nella Toscana Rurale: Il Sito di Marzuolo'. In *Volume per i 70 Anni di Giuseppe Pucci*, edited by Antonio Pizzo and Valentino Nizzo, 589–597. Sesto San Giovanni: Mimesis Edizioni.

Wallace-Hadrill, Andrew. 2008. *Rome's Cultural Revolution*. Cambridge: Cambridge University Press.

Whitehouse, David. 1991. 'Cameo glass'. In *Roman Glass: Two centuries of art and invention*, edited by Martine Newby and Kenneth Painter, 19–32. London: The Society of Antiquaries of London.

Whittaker, C.R. 1990. 'The consumer city revisited: the vicus and the city', *Journal of Roman Archaeology* 3: 110–8.

Willis, Steve. 2005. *Samian Pottery, a Resource for the Study of Roman Britain and Beyond: The results of the English Heritage funded Samian Project. An e-monograph*. Internet Archaeology. http://intarch.ac.uk/journal/issue17/1/toc.html [accessed 18 March 2011].

Wilson, Andrew. 2002. 'Machines, power and the ancient economy', *Journal of Roman Studies* 92: 1–32.

Wilson, Andrew. 2009a. 'Indicators for Roman economic growth: a response to Walter Scheidel', *Journal of Roman Archaeology* 22: 71–82.

Wilson, Andrew. 2009b. 'Large-scale manufacturing, standardization, and trade'. In *The Oxford Handbook of Engineering and Technology in the Ancient World*, edited by John Peter Oleson, 393–417. Oxford: Oxford University Press.

Wilson, Andrew. 2012. 'Raw materials and energy'. In *The Cambridge Companion to the Roman Economy*, edited by Walter Scheidel, 133–55. Cambridge: Cambridge University Press.

Woolf, Greg. 1992. 'Imperialism, empire, and the integration of the Roman economy', *World Archaeology* 23(3): 283–93.

Woolf, Greg. 1998. *Becoming Roman: The origins of provincial civilization in Gaul*. Cambridge: Cambridge University Press.

8
Art and empire in the ancient Roman world

Peter Stewart

From Greece to Rome

The artistic traditions of the Roman Empire were deeply rooted in those of the Hellenistic Mediterranean. It was within this context that Rome developed, first as a city-state, then as the dominant political and military force in Italy and Sicily, and finally, in the last two centuries BCE, as the major power in the Greek eastern Mediterranean. Even during the Republican period, before the emergence of monarchical rule, Rome acquired a large empire which included the Greek colonies of southern Italy and Sicily, Greece itself, and the western part of Asia Minor, as well as parts of France, Spain and north Africa.

The Romans and the other communities of ancient Italy had always been neighbours of Greek culture and their art reflects this proximity. But Rome's active military and commercial engagement with the Hellenistic world in the third century BCE radically transformed its exposure and receptivity to Greek art, establishing the latter's stylistic, technical and iconographic repertoires within the Roman west. 'Greek art became the basis of a new visual language', writes Paul Zanker, suggesting that for him 'Roman art begins' with the great Roman victories over the cities of Magna Graecia and mainland Greece between 211 and 168 BCE (Zanker 2010: 1; cf. Hölscher 2004: e.g. 6–7).

Later on, the Romans' own narrative of their indebtedness to Hellenic culture emphasises the impact of these military conquests (Pollitt 1978; Gruen 1992: 84–130), but it is not until the first century BCE that the Roman importation of Greek art, artists and artistic traditions becomes really manifest in the archaeological record. The wreck of a cargo ship excavated off the coast of Mahdia in Tunisia in 1907 offers a glimpse of the demand for Hellenistic luxuries and *objets d'art* in Roman Italy (Hellenkemper Salies et al. 1994; Wallace-Hadrill 2008: 361–71). The ship, which was apparently travelling from Greece to Italy some time around the 70s BCE, was carrying bronze and marble sculptures, furniture, architectural elements and various marble columns. In the same period, Cicero's letters describe his choice of sculptures for the decoration of one of his villas, which he was acquiring through friends and middle-men in Greece (Cicero, *Ad Atticum* 1.1, 1.3–11; *Ad Familiares* 7.23; see Marvin 1993). At Pompeii around 100 BCE we have fine *opus vermiculatum* mosaics ('micro-mosaics') signed by a certain Dioskourides of Samos (Bieber and Rodenwaldt 1911). In this case we are probably dealing with prefabricated imports, but there is also abundant evidence of Greek artists themselves working in Italy for their expanding Roman clientele (Stewart 2008: 11–18, with further references; other aspects of the Roman republican reception of Greek art are addressed in Harris 2015: 401–3).

The evidence above may give the impression that we are concerned here only with fine art objects in the modern sense – with culturally elevated 'high art'. Indeed, in some respects Roman elite attitudes to Greek art resemble our own. Cicero and his contemporaries admired the celebrated artists of the Greek past (if not those of their own day) and they 'collected' works as the cultivated backdrop to their domestic lives. Famous cult images were appropriated from Greek cities and displayed in new settings in the city of Rome, admired as much for their aesthetic qualities as for their sacred function. But the word 'art' in this chapter should be taken more broadly to refer to the visual and material culture of Roman society at large. In the Roman world, as in the Hellenistic Greek world, art was embedded in many aspects of life, including religion, funerary commemoration and the political domain. At an early stage in Rome's imperial expansion, all of these areas were permeated by imagery that had Hellenic roots (see Tanner 2006: 264–76 and Rutledge 2012 on ancient perceptions of 'art' in this period; Beard and Henderson 2001 addressing the Greek inheritance).

Artists from the Greek lands of the eastern Mediterranean continued to cater for Roman customers throughout the period of Roman rule, but the growing demand for their work was met through an expansion of production which did not rely on native Greek manufacture (Harris 2015: esp. 397–401 on the development of this market). By the start of the imperial period in the late first century BCE, works of art drawing upon Greek craft traditions of various kinds were frequently (perhaps usually) produced by slaves or former slaves who are mostly anonymous to us (Calabi Limentani 1958: esp. 34–42; Stewart 2008: 17–28). Such names of these 'Roman' artists that we know are principally Greek names, but this tells us little about their origins since Greek names were customarily given to slaves. What matters is not the ethnic origins of the makers of art, but the extent to which the practice of Roman imperial art emerged from Greek culture. The Romans themselves could be self-conscious about their reliance on Hellenic traditions. Famously, the ghost of Anchises in Virgil's *Aeneid* (*c*.26–19 BCE) prophesies a future of martial domination for the Romans, leaving arts and sciences to the Greeks: '*excudent alii spirantia mollius aera,/ credo equidem, vivos ducent de marmore voltus*' ('Others will beat out more subtly breathing figures in bronze – that I believe – and draw living faces from marble') (Virgil, *Aeneid* 6. 847–53). Horace's comment on Rome's Hellenised literary traditions a few years later could apply equally to art: '*Graecia capta ferum victorem cepit et artes/intulit agresti Latio*' ('Captive Greece took captive her savage conqueror and brought the arts to rustic Latium') (Horace, *Epistulae* 2.1.156).[1]

The functions to which art was put in the Roman world and the art forms themselves were often unchanged. For example, the practice of erecting honorific portrait-statues in public places had occurred both in Rome and the Greek cities for centuries (Stewart 2003: esp. 28–35); the Greek and Roman pantheons were essentially identical and it was easy to adopt the iconography of Greek deities and mythological characters for the same religious purposes, including the cult images in temples or votive dedications. The decorative elements of Roman architecture which have so profoundly influenced the modern world, such as the details of the Corinthian order, were effortlessly assimilated from Hellenic traditions and adorned very similar temples and porticoes.

In some cases, however, Greek stylistic, iconographical or technical conventions were re-charged with new significance in the Roman context. Realistic portraiture is a good example, for the Roman preference for portrait images which more or less plausibly record the physiognomy of specific individuals (sometimes in unflattering detail) has often been regarded in the past as a characteristically Roman trait. Indeed the so-called 'veristic' portraits of the first century BCE, which present a 'warts and all' treatment of their often elderly subjects, probably carried distinctly Roman ethical and ideological values, associating the sitters with the qualities of venerable dignity and *gravitas* thought to befit the elders who were participants in public life. Yet sculptural studies of aged features were already well established in Hellenistic Greek portraiture (in representations of philosophers and intellectuals, for example) and the Roman portraitists, if not actually Greek, were evidently using Greek methods in this new Roman context (Smith 1981; Gruen 1992: 152–82; Tanner 2000).

Another stereotypically Roman art form is so-called 'historical relief' – relief sculpture representing scenes of virtuous imperial activities like sacrifices, distributions of largesse, or triumphal returns from war. The tendentious but apparently realistic, documentary quality of such works of art is manifestly implicated in Roman power politics and the *realia* in their scenes leave no doubt about their setting. But in the imperial period the style of the reliefs, the poses and naturalistic forms of the figures, and the narrative techniques employed are invariably informed by elements of the Greek artistic tradition (cf. Holliday 2002: 195–203 on the earlier process of Hellenisation).

We could continue to isolate particular kinds of art which metamorphose Greek traditions into something Roman without any essential change in their form. In the context of the Roman provinces mosaic-work is an especially clear case, because tessellated floor mosaics were so widely spread across the Roman Empire – and are such a familiar part of the modern encounter with Roman archaeology in the countries that occupy its territory today – that it is easy to forget their origins in third-century BCE Greece (for overview and bibliography see Dunbabin 1999).

Donald Strong (1989: 11–12) sums up the relationship between Roman and Greek art concisely:

> It is generally unprofitable to attempt to isolate specifically Roman elements of style and technique in the study of Roman art. Many supposedly 'Roman' elements are found to have a basis in the earlier Greek tradition and to develop logically from it. Almost all the subject matter of Roman art is derived in some way from the Greek, but the interpretation or the emphasis is genuinely Roman, developing and changing as Roman taste and ideas change.

For generations scholars were very exercised by the lack of originality that this Roman dependence on Greek art seemed to suggest (on this 'problem of Roman art' see Brendel 1979). Nowadays the preoccupation with nationally distinctive art traditions has waned, and there has been much interest in the ways in which the heritage of past Greek styles was internalised by Roman-period artists and their customers, used as a sort

Figure 8.1 Part of a sacrifice scene from the so-called Altar of Domitius Ahenobarbus. From Rome (?), probably *c.* late second century BCE. Paris, Louvre Photo: Jastrow, Public domain, Wikimedia Commons, available at https://bit.ly/3D3VJo4.

Figure 8.2 Part of the marine *thiasos* from reverse of so-called Altar of Domitius Ahenobarbus. Munich, Glyptothek. Photo: Bibi Saint Pol. Public domain, Wikimedia Commons, available at bit.ly/41r4KC6.

of visual language in which particular styles were adapted to appropriate subjects (Hölscher 2004). A famous early example is the 'altar of Domitius Ahenobarbus', probably in fact a statue-base and perhaps erected in the Campus Martius of Rome around the late second century BCE. The 'altar's' four reliefs employ markedly different styles according to their subject matter: on the wide front rather stumpy, awkward-looking Romans paratactically arranged within a religious ceremony before the god Mars (Figure 8.1); on the other sides a fluid and naturalistic Marine *thiasos*, the retinue of the sea-gods Neptune (Poseidon) and Salacia (Amphitrite), a Greek mythological subject rendered in a retrospective style first developed in Greece some three centuries earlier (Figure 8.2; from the large bibliography see e.g. Kleiner 1992: 49–51; Holliday 2002: 161–6; Maschek 2018).

Greek art and the Roman vision of empire

The Roman capacity for internalising the heritage of Greek art traditions comes into sharp focus at the start of the principate, when Octavian became the first Roman emperor and the republican constitution was transformed, after a prolonged period of civil war, into a *de facto* monarchy. Augustus's accession is often dated to 31 BCE, the year in which he defeated his last powerful opponents, Marcus Antonius and the Hellenistic Egyptian client-queen Cleopatra VII. But it should be stressed that Augustus's power resided in his personal authority – the recognition that his will was now beyond challenge – and a succession of constitutional offices and honours decreed by the senate. There was, in fact, no official position of emperor, nor even a word for 'emperor' in the Latin language (even if Augustus's Greek subjects did not hesitate to regard him as a *basileus* – 'king').

In these fluid political circumstances, art had assumed a significant role in constructing an image of imperial power and (literally) giving monarchy a face. In his ground-breaking book, *The Power of Images in the Age of Augustus*, Paul Zanker sought to explain how the art of the Augustan age was implicated in the dissemination of a new and sophisticated ideology, centred on the person of the emperor (Zanker 1988). Zanker describes the evolving imagery of Augustus's regime during his unusually long reign, from the civil war period to the consolidation of his power and attempt to ensure dynastic succession before his death in 14 CE. At the heart of Augustan ideological imagery is a concern with legitimisation. The 19-year-old Octavian, who was an unexpected entrant into the civil war after the assassination of his uncle Julius Caesar in 44 BCE, was consistently associated with his ancestors (who included the goddess Venus) and with the mythical origins of Rome. He linked himself to the more respectable of the Graeco-Roman Olympian gods, particularly the sun-god Apollo and moon-goddess Diana. His reign was presented as ushering in a new *saeculum* formally declared in 17 BCE, a divinely sanctioned golden age associated with renewal, peace and abundance. In due course Augustus's nominated successors, chosen from his family or adoptive family, were presented as naturalised political heirs even though there was no such constitutional presumption – for example, their portraits are assimilated to Augustus's own, idealised image (on the range of imagery, besides Zanker, see generally Galinsky 1996).

The image of Augustus had a strong and enduring influence on the presentation of later rulers, not only during the dynasty founded by Augustus himself, the Julio-Claudians (14–68 CE), but throughout the imperial period. Indeed the title 'Augustus' and even his family name 'Caesar' came to be near synonyms meaning 'emperor'. Similarly, much of the repertoire of artistic imagery that emerged during his reign continued to be used in later imperial portraiture and public monuments.

Augustan ideological imagery was not usually actively disseminated by the imperial court, and in fact most imperial political art was commissioned in the form of honorific monuments, by patrons and artists who were attuned to what was desirable or expected. No doubt they took their cues from the emperor and his circle, however. At any rate, the Augustan artistic 'language' was remarkably successful, even if it is difficult to gauge its impact on its varied audiences. The keynote of this imagery was the manipulation of Greek styles and iconographical motifs which had originated in earlier centuries. The sort of stylistic pluralism that we now encounter in early imperial art recalls that of the 'Altar of Domitius Ahenobarbus', but it is arguably pursued in a more systematic and meaningful way (Zanker 1988: 239–63; Hölscher 2004). Writers of this period exhibit a self-conscious sophistication about the traditions of Greek literary and rhetorical style, in some cases expressing a strong preference for 'classical' styles that characterised the fifth and fourth centuries BCE. It is possible that a similar awareness of the positive and negative associations of particular artistic styles was also in patrons' minds and famous works of art from the classical Greek past were even cited explicitly as analogues for rhetorical style (Zanker 1988: esp. 245–50; Hölscher 2004: esp. 97). Thus, for example, the late first-century BCE Greek writer Dionysios of Halikarnassos opines 'δοκεῖ δή μοι μὴ ἀπὸ σκοποῦ τις ἂν εἰκάσαι τὴν μὲν Ἰσοκράτους ῥητορικὴν τῇ Πολυκλείτου τε καὶ Φειδίου τέχνῃ κατὰ τὸ σεμνὸν καὶ μεγαλότεχνον καὶ ἀξιωματικόν' ('it seems to me that it would not be inaccurate if one were to liken the rhetoric of Isokrates to the art of Polykleitos and Pheidias with respect to sanctity, grandeur, and dignity' (*On the Attic Orators*, *Isocrates*, 3), and a century or so later Quintilian associates Polykleitos's statue the *Doryphoros* ('spear-bearer') with the virtues of 'seriousness' and 'sanctity' (*Institutio Oratoria*, 5.12.21). It may also be the case that artists and their customers more or less instinctively knew what styles of art would carry the right connotations in particular circumstances (Hölscher 2004: 98–9).

The positive ethical associations of classical Greek styles can be detected in overtly political Augustan art, the most famous example of which is the Prima Porta statue of Augustus (Figure 8.3) (Zanker 1988:

Figure 8.3 The marble statue of Augustus from Prima Porta, *c.* early first century CE. Rome, Musei Vaticani. Open source. Available at https://arachne.dainst.org/entity/6480692.

98–100, 185–92; Galinsky 1996: 24–8, 155–64). The portrait statue shows the emperor in the traditional classical contrapposto pose, with weight on his right leg. His head turns to his right and he raises his right arm in what is probably a gesture of authority or address. He would have held a spear or similarly shaped object in the left hand. Over a tunic Augustus wears a cuirass with figural relief on the front and a cloak is wrapped around his middle. This is an elaborate version of the armour which Roman army

Figure 8.4 Portrait typology for the emperor Augustus. (a) Marble portrait of the emperor Augustus, from Roman theatre of Mérida, Spain, first century CE. Mérida, Museo Nacional de Arte Romano. © Peter Stewart, by permission of museum. (b) Marble portrait of Augustus from Kastro Tigani, Samos, Greece, first century CE. © DAI Athens/ Werner Technau, D-DAI-ATH-Samos 910.

officers wore. It had been used before for statues and would later become one of the stock body-types for statues of imperial men. In other ways the statue is innovative. It portrays the emperor as more than an ordinary man: his feet are bare and the structural support at his right leg takes the form of a cupid riding on a dolphin (strictly speaking Cupid, the child of Venus, was a distant relative of Augustus, if his claim to divine ancestry was to be believed!). Moreover, it has often been observed that beneath its armour the emperor's athletic body closely resembles Roman copies of Polykleitan statues, specifically copies traditionally identified with the *Doryphoros* (Pollini 1995, with detailed discussion of the implications). This is probably not to be viewed as an overt allusion to that specific work, but a harnessing of the ethical resonances of sculpture of that period which Quintilian evokes.

Similarly the head of the Prima Porta statue portrays Augustus with idealised youthful features and restrained, comma-shaped locks of hair. With its individualism played down in favour of emotionally restrained, generic good looks, the portrait recalls the ideal faces of the fifth century BCE. Faces of precisely this design are in fact the most frequently attested among sculptural portraits of Augustus (Figure 8.4). (The type is today

Figure 8.5 Breastplate, detail from the marble statue of Augustus from Prima Porta, *c.* early first century CE. Rome, Musei Vaticani. © Forschungsarchiv für Antike Plastik, Cologne/H. Kähler, https://arachne.dainst.org/entity/6480637.

named after this particular statue: the 'Prima Porta Type'). In this way the classical Greek tradition offered a venerable model for the portraiture of a ruler who had come to power when he was still extremely – perhaps shockingly – young (Zanker 1988: 98–100; Boschung 1993 on the portrait typology).

The relief breastplate of the statue conveys messages about Augustan success which are bolder, even if the specifics are vague and much debated (Figure 8.5) (Zanker 1988: 189–92; see Squire 2013 for a recent critical overview). In the centre of the scene is an image of Roman domination: a man in what is usually taken to be Parthian dress hands a Roman legionary standard over to a figure in a Roman officer's clothing and flanked by a hound. This is taken to be a reference to Augustus's diplomatic victory of 20/19 BCE, when Rome's age-old enemy the Parthians surrendered the standards which they had captured in battles over the previous 33 years (against this: Simpson 2005). The gods of heaven and earth frame the ceremony with a cosmic setting and offer their divine approval: above is probably Caelus, the god of heaven, with the canopy of the sky held above his head. The sun-god Sol gallops onto the scene from the left in his chariot, while a torch-holding Luna, the moon, rides on the back of Aurora (dawn) to the right. At the bottom it is probably Tellus, the Earth, who reclines with a cornucopia. On the emperor's hips are, respectively, the figures of his patron deities Apollo (on a griffin) and Diana (on a stag). And above them on each side are captive barbarian prisoners, interpreted either as general representatives or specific personifications of the peoples subdued by Augustus's armies. To an extent the Prima Porta statue's cuirass takes on a life of its own, almost independent from the rest of the subtly meaningful portrait, but complementing its moral associations. It sets out across Augustus's chest a symbolic tableau offering a vision of imperial dominion built on military success and the unambiguous sanction of heaven. These were themes that would dominate imperial imagery for centuries to come.

We do not know anything for sure about the origins of this statue. Very unusually it was found on property of the imperial family, at the villa of Augustus's wife, Livia, at Prima Porta, near Rome. Most scholars believe that it is a copy of a statue designed for more public display. Certainly, most imperial statues are honorific, though the imagery of the cuirass could communicate with the emperor's own circle as much as a wider audience.

Rarely do we find evidence of Augustus's own intentions, but these are explicitly described in his *Res Gestae*, an account of 'things accomplished', which survives from inscribed versions in the eastern provinces. The *Res Gestae* enumerates Augustus's building activities in Rome, among which was an act of personal self-promotion justified by the republican tradition of aristocrats piously constructing and restoring temples (*Res Gestae Divi Augusti*, 19–21). The Forum of Augustus, an adjunct to the old forum in the centre of Rome, was a porticoed complex centred on the temple of

Mars Ultor (Mars the Avenger), which Augustus had first vowed to build during the civil war. As he boasts, the temple and forum were built on land that he personally acquired ('in privato solo': *Res Gestae Divi Augusti*, 21), so this personal act undoubtedly reflects his ideas about his regime and the empire. The statues on the inside and outside of the temple (now lost) seem once again to associate the Olympian gods with Augustus's rule and family. Statues in the porticoes offered a sanitised gallery of Roman history going back to the founding heroes Romulus and Aeneas and culminating, it seems, in an image of Augustus riding a four-horse chariot in the centre of the Forum. The architectural decoration drew on classical Greek precedents and included, for instance, caryatids copied from the fifth-century BCE Temple of Erechtheus on the Athenian acropolis (for full discussions see: Zanker 1968; 1988: 194–215; Spannagel 1999; Geiger 2008).

It is interesting to note that elements from the Forum of Augustus were widely copied elsewhere. There is some evidence, particularly in Spain, for the imitation of a few of the statues and architectural sculptures in provincial colonies (Roman veteran settlements with a privileged status) (De la Barrera and Trillmich 1996). The statue of Aeneas escaping with his family from the mythical sack of Troy was even more widely imitated and becomes a funerary emblem, apparently carrying associations of virtue and piety in the adornment of monuments in the European provinces (Noelke 1976; Zanker 1988: 209–210; Spannagel 1999). In this way, as Zanker argues, imperial political imagery was internalised in the lives of the imperial population (Zanker 1988: 210; cf. 265–95). As ideological art it may have been all the more effective for its ability to migrate from the political sphere. In general, however, the art of empire does not so directly reflect the art and ideology of the ruling power. The provinces offer a more complicated and diffuse picture. With that in mind let us turn to the art of the provinces.

An imperial art

In the first and second centuries CE, when Rome was permanently under the authority of a ruler, the empire became a vast territory. By 120 CE its provinces embraced the lands of around 40 modern nation states. Roman art – the repertoire of monumental types, styles and iconography which, as we have seen, the Romans had inherited and adapted from the Greek world – was disseminated to almost every part of this empire. The word 'disseminated' is perhaps misleading. Certainly Italy and the Roman state had some role in this process of cultural diffusion. Sometimes Roman art was patronised by the legionary soldiers, or by colonists (military veterans), or other people coming to the provinces from Italy, whose world-view might be regarded as more particularly Romano-centric – aligned with that of the ruling elite. But in general provincial art was the product of the mainly indigenous provincial populations themselves. There was no centralised dissemination of imagery.[2] Roman provincial art therefore represents the adoption of Roman visual and material culture by the diverse peoples who had come under Roman rule.

It should be stressed that the annexed provinces included those of Greece and the Greek-speaking, eastern parts of the Mediterranean, from which, as we have seen, many aspects of Roman art had originated in the first place. In those lands Greek artistic traditions continued, but were sometimes reinvented and reorientated according to the new tastes and requirements of imperial society. For instance, Italian tastes in luxurious villa-decoration, which included assemblages of mythological imagery and marble 'ideal sculpture' with divine and mythological subjects, were 're-exported' back into Greece. One lavish example is the villa of Herodes Atticus at Loukou in the Peloponnese (Spyropoulos 2001), which represents an 'international style' of Hellenised luxury living. Is this a Greek villa, or a Roman villa, Roman culture in Greece or Hellenism of the Roman Empire? By the second century CE, in the selectively homogenised culture of the empire, such ethnic labels have largely ceased to be meaningful when applied to art. In fact the aristocratic owner of this villa, Herodes Atticus (*c.*101–177 CE), was himself a very 'international' figure: an Athenian who was also a Roman senator and consul, and lived for long periods both in both Greece and Rome.

At first sight, the imperial art that resulted from this process of Roman cultural expansion is remarkably consistent. It is true that it attests to a surprisingly thorough and persistent spread of Roman artistic culture across the empire. Perhaps we see this most clearly in honorific portraits set up for the emperor and his family. Statues and busts survive in significant numbers, but many more once existed and there were also honorific paintings virtually all of which are lost. While it is tempting to see imperial portraits across the empire as a form of propaganda, it is essential to remember that (with the exception of coin-portraits) the images of the emperor and his family were not centrally produced nor mandated, but commissioned spontaneously by provincial communities wishing to express their loyalty and devotion (Stewart 2006). Yet there does seem to have been a strong desire by provincial commissioners of images to get these portraits 'right', even though very few had ever seen the emperor in real life. They did this by quite consistently reproducing

Figure 8.6 Floor mosaic with image of cupid riding dolphin, from palatial villa at Fishbourne, England, *c.* late first century CE. © Matt Buck, CC BY-SA 2.0, by kind permission of the Sussex Archaeological Society.

portrait-types – established portrait designs – which were presumably officially approved at the imperial court (see e.g. Pfanner 1989; Smith 1996; Stewart 2008: 80–9). Even the details of individual locks of hair in these portrait-types could be carefully replicated, so that we can find the same type reproduced at opposite ends of the empire (Figure 8.4).

Many other Roman monumental types and art forms, both public and private, were adopted throughout the empire. Floor mosaics have already been mentioned as a good example of wide distribution of what had become a characteristic Roman form of decoration. The examples illustrated in Figures 8.6 and 8.7, picturing a cupid riding on a dolphin, also show how widely established Graeco-Roman iconography travelled within and across media. The same can be said of certain types of funerary monument, despite the enormous local and regional variety that also existed. The *stela* or gravestone, for example, is one of the most ubiquitous funerary forms. It had origins in the Hellenistic period and earlier but was adopted in Italy and many provinces of the empire, often adorned with a commemorative relief. One of the most widely favoured and enduring sculptural themes was the so-called funerary banquet (sometimes called by the German term *Totenmahl*). Typically the funerary banquet represents the deceased drinking or dining, and

Figure 8.7 Floor mosaic with image of cupid riding dolphin, from the House of Amphitrite at the site of Bulla Regia, Tunisia, second century CE. © bumihills/Shutterstock.com.

accompanied by one or more slaves and family members. This idealising, aspirational imagery originated in the eastern Mediterranean and Near East, but by the second century it was being used across the empire, from the eastern Mediterranean to northern Britain (Fabricius 1999; Stewart 2009). The details and execution vary, as does the usage by different local communities in the provinces (Stewart 2009), but the iconography is representative of the common visual 'language' that could be offered by traditional Graeco-Roman imagery in an empire divided by actual languages (Latin in the west, Greek in the east and numerous regional languages). The above examples, with their wide range of dates between the first and fourth centuries CE, also show how enduring the classical iconographical repertoire could be during the Roman imperial period.

Wall painting is another example of a kind of artistic homogeneity across the Roman Empire. Fresco painting – mural painting on carefully prepared wet plaster, which was often characteristic of stone-built, rectangular Roman buildings – represents both the technical and iconographical spread of Roman art on a large scale. Though less conspicuous it is perhaps the underlying plaster technique that speaks most clearly of the dissemination of Roman art,[3] but amidst the diversity of imagery it is also possible to find widely dispersed preferences for very similar decorative forms.

Examples such as these, selective as they are, might seem to point to a more or less universal Romanisation of artistic production in the provinces annexed by Rome, and that perception is partly true, especially if we restrict ourselves to looking for similarities in particular artistic media rather than considering material culture as a whole. But the concept of 'Romanisation' has been much criticised in the last 25 years for a number of reasons, especially by British and North American archaeologists, to the extent that it has almost wholly been removed from the archaeological vocabulary (see e.g. David J. Mattingly 2010: esp. 38–41, and Chapter 11 this volume). The word implies a very clear sense of what 'Roman' and 'Roman culture' mean, whereas in fact these are slippery and complex labels, as we have already seen. It also implies a Rome-centred view of empire, even perhaps a centralised interest in the Romanisation of the empire's peripheries in antiquity, which is hard to support with evidence. This is a one-sided view of cultural change. Another problem with the idea of Romanisation is that the pursuit of it in the art of the provinces, or other aspects of their material culture, can mean ignoring or marginalising the 'non-Roman' aspects of the Roman provinces. Classical archaeologists are trained to order, identify and date objects by means of typologies and analogies, and so perhaps tend to privilege sameness and consistency over variety, difference and discrepancy. And since we are *classical* archaeologists, it is the classical-*looking* evidence that we tend to pursue most actively, feeding a form of confirmation bias.

There are, of course, examples of Roman provincial art that conspicuously defy any impression of homogeneity in imperial art. For example, the art of Roman Egypt sometimes combines classical and Egyptian visual traditions in a striking juxtaposition of the naturalistic and abstract. The mummy portraits which were used by some members of the Graeco-Roman community in Roman Egypt contributed an often highly realistic painted portrait of the deceased, of the kind familiar in other parts of the Roman world, to traditional Egyptian embalming techniques (even sometimes to conventional mummy-casing with its Egyptian-style representations of gods of the afterlife). Here two artistic 'technologies' from different cultures complement each other in the effort to ensure life after death (Walker and Brierbrier 2000; Riggs 2005).

This is, however, an exceptional case. Usually the diversity of Roman provincial art is more subtle and less easy to categorise as cultural 'hybridity'. The province of Britain (Britannia) participated in the empire-wide artistic culture, and we find examples there of all the art forms and monumental types already mentioned above. Romano-British sculpture seems to be a particularly good example of 'Romanisation' because relatively little sculpture in stone or bronze existed in Britain before the Roman conquest in 43 CE. When we look at the pattern of distribution of imperial sculptures, however, we see that there is a bias towards particular parts of the provincial population. Sculpture occurred particularly in the larger towns and at military sites, including the two second-century defensive walls to the north of the province: Hadrian's Wall and the Antonine Wall. In other words, the use of Roman types of sculpture in Britain was largely an urban and military phenomenon, not so much that of the general, indigenous population (Stewart 2010). We could create different maps for other artistic media and other regions which would show similar variability in other ways. This is a complex human geography of acculturation belied by the totalising words like 'diffusion' or 'dissemination'.

Yet even where we do find provincial sculptures serving the same functions as in the Mediterranean area, the *form* of these works is often very different. In Britain and in all the other fringe provinces of the Roman Empire, there is a preponderance of sculptures that appear relatively simple or even crude in their technique and execution in comparison with the metropolitan sculptures of the urban Mediterranean. These local sculptures, carved mostly in local stones, by craftsmen whose skills were circumscribed by their training or expectations, exemplify a form of 'provincialism' (Stewart 2010). By this often derogatory word 'provincialism' I do not imply that the provincial sculptures were ineffective or unsuccessful works of art. They are not 'bad' works in that sense. But because of their makers' ability, cultural assumptions, or level of specialist know-how, they only selectively adhere to the stylistic and technical protocols of the Graeco-Roman sculptural tradition. Sometimes, as in Roman Egypt, they positively adhere to quite different traditions.

It is frequently the iconography – the most obviously meaningful content of the imagery – which is most conventional. Gods like Mercury in Figure 8.8a can be recognised by an iconography that was universal in the Roman Empire (cf. Figure 8.8b). The young messenger-god's distinctive wand (*caduceus*) and winged hat, head or shoes would have been instantly recognisable to any viewer acculturated to the classical tradition. In the case of the little votive relief from Herefordshire – perhaps an amateur version of a votive object used universally in the empire – the deity even received a simplified dedicatory inscription in Latin: *DEO ME(rcurio)* ('to the god Mercury'). On one level it could hardly be more Roman. Yet in *form* and *execution* provincial sculptures like this one depart strikingly from traditional classical norms for the naturalistic depiction of gods in human shape.

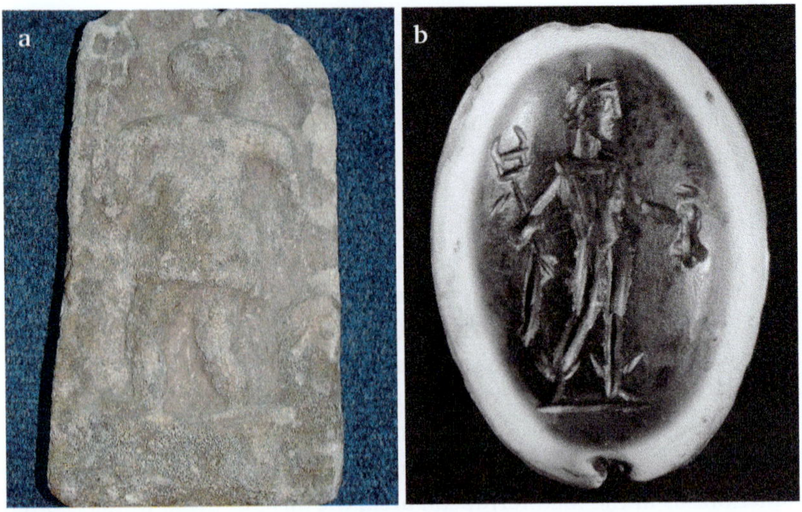

Figure 8.8 Mercury: an iconography standardised across the empire. (a) Votive relief sculpture for the god Mercury, from Staunton-on-Arrow, England, *c.* second to fourth century CE. Hereford Museum. Hartlebury, Worcester County Museum. Photo courtesy of the Museums. (b) Mercury on a Roman intaglio, first century CE. Banded agate. Malibu, J. Paul Getty Museum, inv. 81.AN.39.8. © J. Paul Getty Museum, Open Content Program.

A global art?

It would be tempting to see these examples of partial adherence to Roman artistic norms as evidence of the dissemination of Roman culture from the centre, becoming weaker and being transformed as it moves out towards the periphery. There is no doubt that examples of provincialism in art of the kind illustrated here are more common on the edges of the empire. But the picture is not so straightforward. 'Simplified' Roman art can be found anywhere in the empire, even in Italy, as a comparison with sculptures found in the Italian region of Campania shows (Figure 8.9). It would be misleading to call this water-basin decoration 'provincial' because it was made at the heart of the empire, not so very far from Rome; its simplicity reflects its humble function and the basic abilities of the carver who made it. Yet it does share some of the characteristics of Roman provincial sculpture. At the same time, very sophisticated, technically difficult works of art can be found in every region, even near the edges of the empire. So no simple model of centre and periphery or 'dissemination' of Roman culture is adequate to explain the dynamics of Roman imperial art.

Figure 8.9 Basalt fountain relief with depiction of a satyr. Pompeii, Via dell' Abbondanza (NW corner of Insula I 12), early first century CE. © Peter Stewart.

There would be some justification in invoking the modern concept of globalisation to help understand such complex patterns. 'Globalisation' has been very seriously discussed in recent years as a way of conceptualising the circulation of Greek and Roman culture in antiquity. The term is also subject to criticism, particularly because there is no clear agreement about what it means in the ancient context, and also because its associations are so obviously anachronistic (Hingley 2005; Gardner 2013: esp. 6–9; Versluys 2014; Pitts and Versluys 2015).

Nevertheless, the attraction of globalisation as a term is that it encourages us to conceptualise how cultures influence each other, how artistic traditions move around, are adopted and transformed, without resorting to simple cultural labels or imagining hierarchical, linear processes of cultural change. Globalisation does not offer a theoretical model for explaining Roman imperial art, but because of our own experience of globalism in the modern world, the concept can at least help us to imagine how certain kinds of imagery could *both* be associated with a specific cultural origin *and* at the same time circulate in more fluid and unpredictable ways around the empire without the people who used them necessarily thinking of them as 'Roman' in a very self-conscious way.

This is not the place to explore the problems and opportunities of the language of globalisation further (see further Versluys 2014), but they do raise a final question: to what extent should we see the art of an empire such as the Roman Empire as being commensurate with, or dependent on, the political limits of that empire? Despite the reservations stated above, there is no doubt that the Roman Empire does exhibit a high degree of artistic cohesion in particular respects. It is not inevitable – or even very obviously explicable – that the material culture of an empire should be characterised by such conformity. It is not the case, for example, with the contemporary Kushan Empire in Central Asia and northern Indian, which encompassed a number of connected but formally very different artistic traditions, notably those of Gandhara and Mathura.[4] It is most particularly not the case with the art of Rome's eastern neighbour, the Parthian Empire.

In fact, looking at the very eastern edge of the Roman Empire, exemplified here by the frontier town of Dura-Europos, helps us to ask whether Roman art and the Roman Empire were coterminous. Dura-Europos began its life as a Greek settlement within the Hellenistic Seleukid Kingdom. Between the first century BCE and second century CE it was mostly under Parthian control. Finally between 165 CE and its destruction in 257 CE it was a Roman garrison town (see generally Rostovtzeff 1938; Perkins 1973; Brody and Hoffman 2011).

Dura is famous for the remarkable preservation of its extraordinary vivid wall paintings, which were used to decorate religious buildings belonging to very different cultic communities. These paintings are rich in paradoxes for the modern viewer approaching them with cultural designations in mind. For example, in Dura's Roman synagogue a third-century (244/5 CE) narrative scene from the Jewish Bible shows the High Priest Aaron's tabernacle for the Ark of the Covenant in the Sinai wilderness (*Exodus* 40) (Kraeling 1956: esp. 125–31, pl. 60) (Figure 8.10). Here the temporary cult structure of the scriptural account has been visualised as a classical stone temple, with Corinthian columns and figures of Victory as acroteria. However, what would otherwise be quite a conventional

Figure 8.10 Scene of Aaron and the tabernacle. Wall painting from the Synagogue in Dura Europos, 244/5 CE. National Museum of Damascus. (Gouache reproduction by Herbert J. Gute, 1933–5, after Kraeling 1956, pl. 60.) Photo: https://upload.wikimedia.org/wikipedia/commons/5/51/Herod%27s_Temple.jpg, by kind permission of Yale University Art Gallery.

Roman scene of sacrifice, albeit with distinctively Jewish ritual objects, is populated by figures in Parthian dress. The rather abstract rendering of the scene with its frontal figures on different scales also eschews naturalistic classical conventions. In contrast, a first-century painting from inside the Temple of the Palmyrene Gods shows a family with Greek names, wearing local, Syrian dress making offerings to the gods with the help of priests (Heyn 2011; Duchâteau 2013: 418–20; Baird 2018: 6, 26–7) (Figure 8.11). The illusionistic style of this large mural has some of its closest analogues in the contemporary wall paintings of Roman Pompeii, and perhaps these distant towns could be regarded as sharing an inheritance of Hellenistic Greek art. Thus both classical and Parthian imagery are present in these two paintings from before and during the period of Roman rule. Would these paintings exist in the form they take without having been made under Roman or Parthian rule? How meaningful is it, really, to call them either 'Roman' or 'Parthian'? Is this the right question to ask about them? And if it is the wrong question for Dura-Europos, is it also the wrong question for Roman imperial art produced elsewhere?

Figure 8.11 Scene of offerings by Conon and his family. Wall painting from the Temple of the Palmyrene Gods, second half of first century CE. Damascus, National Museum. © Pierre Leriche.

With that in mind, let us finish with an extreme limit-case for testing how far the name of 'Roman art' might be detached from an association with the political entity of the Roman Empire. As has been much discussed since the nineteenth century, the Buddhist architectural sculpture of Gandhara in the Kushan Empire (roughly in the area of northern Pakistan) displays close associations with the Graeco-Roman artistic tradition, to the extent that some scholars in the past conceived of it as 'the Roman provincial art of Gandhara' (in the words of Lippe 1960: 179) despite the thousands of kilometres that separated these two empires (see also e.g. Wheeler 1949; Soper 1955; Stewart 2020).[5] It goes without saying that this claim is deeply flawed (at best it is as misleading as calling the art of the Roman provinces 'Greek' because of their Hellenic antecedents). But this provoking suggestion does perhaps open our minds to the idea of a globally circulating repertoire of Roman styles and imagery, which cannot be simply confined by calling it Roman imperial art. Empire was the vehicle for this art tradition, not simply its container.

Notes

1 On the victor's appropriation of a 'conquered' culture, with global historical parallels, see Veyne (1979).

2 This is notwithstanding the famous and contentious comment by Tacitus that his father-in-law Agricola, when governor of Britain between 77 and 85 CE, actively urged the local aristocracy to 'Romanise' by 'encouraging them privately and assisting them with public funds to construct temples, fora, and houses' (Tacitus, *Agricola* 21). Compare also Arrian's wholly exceptional request (as governor in Cappadocia) for the emperor Hadrian to send out a good-quality statue of himself to replace an inferior local one at Trapezus (Arrian, *Periplus Maris Euxini, 1-2*).

3 I owe the observation to the late Sharon Cather.

4 There is a notable lack of academic discussions of the art of the Kushan Empire as such, the exception being Rosenfield (1967). Gandhara and Mathura have nearly always been regarded as discrete regional artistic 'schools', albeit with global connections. Note also Schlumberger (1960a; 1960b) arguing for the transcendent connections between these and other Indo-European traditions.

5 For more on Gandharan art and its cross-cultural affinities, see e.g. Nehru (1989); Luczanits (2008).

References

Baird, Jennifer A. 2018. *Dura-Europos*. London: Bloomsbury.

Beard, Mary and John Henderson. 2001. *Classical Art: From Greece to Rome*. Oxford: Oxford University Press.

Bieber, Margarete and Gerhard Rodenwaldt. 1911. 'Die Mosaiken des Dioskurides von Samos', *Jahrbuch des Deutschen Archäologischen Instituts* 26: 1–22.

Boschung, Dietrich. 1993. *Die Bildnisse des Augustus*. Berlin: Mann.

Brendel, Otto. 1979. *Prolegomena to the Study of Roman Art*. New Haven, CT and London: Yale University Press. (Mainly reprint of article in *Memoirs of the American Academy in Rome* 21 (1953): 7–73.)

Brody, Lisa and Gail Hoffman (eds). 2011. *Dura Europos: Crossroads of antiquity*. Boston, MA: McMullen Museum of Art.

Calabi Limentani, Ida. 1958. *Studi sulla società romana: il lavoro artistico*. Milan and Varese: Istituto Editoriale Cisalpino.

De la Barrera, José Luis and Walter Trillmich. 1996. 'Eine Wiederhollung der Aeneas-Gruppe vom Forum Augustum samt ihrer Inschrift in Mérida (Spanien)', *Mitteilungen des Deutschen Archäologischen Instituts, Römische Abteilung* 103: 119–38.

Duchâteau, Marie-Emmanuelle. 2013. *Les divinités d'Europos-Doura: personnalité et identité (~301 av. N.È.–256 de N.È.)*. Paris: Geuthner.

Dunbabin, Katherine. 1999. *Mosaics of the Greek and Roman World*. Cambridge: Cambridge University Press.

Fabricius, Johanna. 1999. *Die hellenistischen Totenmahlreliefs: Grabrepräsentation und Wertvorstellungen in ostgriechischen Städten*. Munich: Pfeil.

Galinsky, Karl. 1996. *Augustan Culture: An interpretative introduction*. Princeton, NJ: Princeton University Press.

Gardner, Andrew. 2013. 'Thinking about Roman imperialism: postcolonialism, globalisation and beyond', *Britannia* 44: 1–25.

Geiger, Joseph. 2008. *The First Hall of Fame: A study of the statues in the Forum Augustum*. Leiden: Brill.

Gruen, Erich. 1992. *Culture and National Identity in Republican Rome*. Ithaca, NY: Cornell University Press.

Harris, William V. 2015. 'Prolegomena to a study of the economics of Roman art', *American Journal of Archaeology* 119: 395–417.

Hellenkemper Salies, Gisela, with Hans-Hoyer von Prittwitz und Gaffron and Gerhard Bauchhenß (eds). 1994. *Das Wrack: Der antike Schiffsfund von Mahdia*, 2 vols. Cologne: Rheinland-Verlag.

Heyn, Maura. 2011. 'The Terentius Frieze in context'. In *Dura Europos: Crossroads of antiquity*, edited by Lisa Brody and Hoffman, Gail, 221–33. Boston, MA: McMullen Museum of Art.

Hingley, Richard. 2005. *Globalizing Roman Culture: Unity, diversity and empire*. London and New York: Routledge.

Holliday, Peter. 2002. *The Origins of Roman Historical Commemoration in the Visual Arts*. Cambridge: Cambridge University Press.

Hölscher, Tonio. 2004. *The Language of Images in Roman Art*. Cambridge: Cambridge University Press. (Translated from German original, *Römische Bildsprache als semantisches System*. Heidelberg: Carl Winter Universitätsverlag, 1987.)

Kleiner, Diana. 1992. *Roman Sculpture*. New Haven, CT and London: Yale University Press.

Kraeling, Carl H. 1956. *The Excavations at Dura-Europos. Final Report 8.1: The synagogue*. New Haven, CT: Yale University Press.

Lippe, Aschwin. 1960. 'The sculpture of greater India', *The Metropolitan Museum of Art Bulletin* (February): 177–92.

Luczanits, Christian. 2008. *Gandhara: The Buddhist heritage of Pakistan. Legends, monasteries, and paradise*. Bonn: Kunst- und Ausstellungshalle der Bundesrepublik Deutschland.

Marvin, Miranda. 1993. 'Copying in Roman sculpture: the replica series', In *Roman Art in Context: An anthology*, edited by Eve D'Ambra, 161–88. Englewood Cliffs, NJ: Prentice-Hall.

Maschek, Dominik. 2018. 'Not *census* but *deductio*: reconsidering the "*Ara* of Domitius Ahenobarbus"', *Journal of Roman Studies* 108: 27–52.

Mattingly, David J. 2010. *Imperialism, Power and Identity: Experiencing the Roman Empire*. Princeton, NJ: Princeton University Press.

Nehru, Lolita. 1989. *Origins of the Gandhāran Style: A study of contributory influences*. Delhi: Oxford University Press.

Noelke, Peter. 1976. 'Aeneasdarstellungen in der römischen Plastik der Rheinzone', *Germania* 54: 409–39.

Perkins, Ann. 1973. *The Art of Dura-Europos*. Oxford: Clarendon Press.

Pfanner, Michael. 1989. 'Über das Herstellen von Porträts: ein Beitrag zu Rationalisierungsmassnahmen un Produktionsmechanismen von Massenware im späten Hellenismus und in der römischen Kaiserzeit', *Jahrbuch des Deutschen Archäologischen Instituts* 104: 157–257.

Pitts, Martin and Miguel J. Versluys (eds). 2015. *Globalisation and the Roman World: World history, connectivity and material culture*. Cambridge: Cambridge University Press.

Pollini, John. 1995. 'The Augustus from Prima Porta and the transformation of the Polykleitan heroic ideal: the rhetoric of art'. In *Polykleitos, the Doryphoros, and Tradition*, edited by Warren Moon, 262–82. Madison, WI: University of Wisconsin Press.

Pollitt, Jerome. 1978. 'The impact of Greek art on Rome', *Transactions of the American Philological Association* 108: 155–74.

Riggs, Christina. 2005. *The Beautiful Burial in Roman Egypt: Art, identity, and funerary religion*. Oxford: Oxford University Press.

Rosenfield, John. 1967. *The Dynastic Arts of the Kushans*. Berkeley, CA: University of California Press.

Rostovtzeff, Michael I. 1938. *Dura-Europos and Its Art*. Oxford: Clarendon Press.

Rutledge, Stephen. 2012. *Ancient Rome as a Museum: Power, identity, and the culture of collecting*. Oxford: Oxford University Press.

Schlumberger, Daniel. 1960a. 'Descendants non-méditerranéens de l'art grec' (part 1), *Syria* 37(1–2): 131–66.

Schlumberger, Daniel. 1960b. 'Descendants non-méditerranéens de l'art grec' (part 2), *Syria* 37(3–4): 253–319.

Simpson, Christopher. 2005. 'Where is the Parthian? The Prima Porta statue of Augustus revisited', *Latomus* 64: 82–90.

Smith, Roland R.R. 1981. 'Greeks, foreigners, and Roman republican portraits', *Journal of Roman Studies* 71: 24–38.

Smith, Roland R.R. 1996. 'Typology and diversity in the portraits of Augustus', *Journal of Roman Archaeology* 9: 30–47.

Soper, Alexander. 1955. 'The Roman style in Gandhāra', *American Journal of Archaeology* 55: 301–19.

Spannagel, Martin. 1999. *Exemplaria Principis: Untersuchungen zu Entstehung und Ausstattung des Augustusforums*. Heidelberg: Archäologie und Geschichte.

Spyropoulos, Georgios. 2001. *Drei Meisterwerke der griechischen Plastik aus der Villa des Herodes Atticus zu Eva/Loukou*. Frankfurt: Lang.

Squire, Michael. 2013. 'Embodied ambiguities on the Prima Porta Augustus', *Art History* 36: 242–79.

Stewart, Peter. 2003. *Statues in Roman Society: Representation and response*. Oxford: Oxford University Press.

Stewart, Peter. 2006. 'The image of the Roman emperor'. In *Presence: The inherence of the prototype within images and other objects*, edited by R. Maniura and R. Shepherd, 243–58. Aldershot: Ashgate.

Stewart, Peter. 2008. *The Social History of Roman Art*. Cambridge: Cambridge University Press.

Stewart, Peter. 2009. '*Totenmahl* reliefs in the northern provinces: a case-study in imperial sculpture', *Journal of Roman Archaeology* 22: 253–74.

Stewart, Peter. 2010. 'Geographies of provincialism in Roman sculpture', *Research Institutes in the History of Art Journal* (2010), https://doi.org/10.11588/riha.2010.0.68533.

Stewart, Peter. 2020. 'Roman sarcophagi and Gandhāran sculpture'. In *The Global Connections of Gandhāran Art*, edited by W. Rienjang and P. Stewart, 50–85. Oxford: Archaeopress.

Strong, Donald. 1989. *Roman Art* (2nd edition). London: Penguin.

Tanner, Jeremy. 2000. 'Portraits, power, and patronage in the late Roman republic', *Journal of Roman Studies* 90: 18–50.

Tanner, Jeremy. 2006. *The Invention of Art History in Ancient Greece: Religion, society, and artistic rationalisation*. Cambridge: Cambridge University Press.

Versluys, Miguel J. 2014. 'Romanisation 2.0 and its alternatives', *Archaeological Dialogues* 21: 1–64, incorporating responses by R. Hingley, T. Hodos, T. Stek, P. van Dommelen and G. Woolf.

Veyne, Paul. 1979. 'The Hellenization of Rome and the question of acculturations', *Diogenes* 27: 1–27.

Walker, Susan and Maurice Brierbrier. 2000. *Ancient Faces: Mummy portraits from Roman Egypt*. London: British Museum Press.

Wallace-Hadrill, Andrew. 2008. *Rome's Cultural Revolution*. Cambridge: Cambridge University Press.

Wheeler, Mortimer. 1949. 'Romano-Buddhist art: an old problem restated', *Antiquity* 23: 4–19.

Zanker, Paul. 1968. *Forum Augustum: das Bildprogramm*. Tübingen: Wasmuth.

Zanker, Paul. 1988. *The Power of Images in the Age of Augustus*. Ann Arbor, MI: University of Michigan Press. (First published as *Augustus und die Macht der Bilder*. Munich: Beck, 1987.)

Zanker, Paul. 2010. *Roman Art*. Los Angeles, CA: J. Paul Getty Museum. (Originally published as *Arte romana*. Rome and Bari: Laterza, 2008.)

9 Materialising imperial ideology and religion in the Roman world

Ton Derks

> For this ... cult to be effective, it needed to be supported by a minimal form of materiality ... (Schnapp 1993: 53; author's translation)

Introduction: towards a material-oriented history of Roman religion

In the Roman empire, politics and religion were closely intertwined. Both in Rome and in the conquered territories of Italy and the provinces, the collective group of citizens making up the city-state was protected by a set of patron gods which are hence called state gods or 'civic' gods. The cults of these gods were run by officially appointed priests and the expenses for these public cults were borne by the treasury of Rome or, in the case of cults in the communities of Italy and the provinces, by that of the respective municipal town. In Rome, the senate decided which gods were to receive a state cult; in the municipal communities of the empire (the *civitates* in the west and the *poleis* in the east), the decision which cults were civic or public was the responsibility of the local magistrates (Crawford 1996: no. 25, *Lex coloniae Genetivae*, Ch. 64; González and Crawford 1986: *Lex Irnitana*, ch. 77). This political or social dimension of Roman religion, in which the religious practice of the individual is determined by membership of a community or group rather than by personal conviction, was first described thoroughly by German historian Georg Wissowa (Wissowa 1912). Despite recent pleas to bring the individual rather than the community into the centre of attention (Rüpke

2015; Albrecht et al. 2018), in my view the institutional framework of interpretation remains vital for understanding the standard collective practices that set the norm for individual religious behaviour and still has great explanatory power for most of our evidence (cf., for instance, Van Andringa 2009; for a reply to critics of the polis model, Scheid 2016).

Aside from casual references to the domestic shrines of Pompeii or to votive statues, altar reliefs and coins (e.g. Wissowa 1912: 7–8), the material objects of religion play no part in Wissowa's handbook. Another striking feature is that Wissowa left religion in the Roman provinces virtually undiscussed. Central is the Roman state religion as documented in sacred laws, religious calendars, or in the acts of a public priesthood such as the Arval Brethren. Following Rome's military expansion in Italy and beyond, the religion of Rome itself changed. Given the scarce availability of sources for the conquered territories, Wissowa's focus remained on Rome itself and on distinguishing 'foreign', especially Etruscan and Greek, influences on traditional Roman religion (cf. Wissowa 1912: 14–16). A final characteristic is the teleological nature of Wissowa's historical narrative, which describes the development of Roman religion in terms of a decline of the pagan cults of the Roman state that gradually lost their attraction and made way for the personal salvation religions of the so-called 'oriental' cults and, finally, Christianity (Rives 2010).

This lack of interest in the material dimension of religion, and in the religions of the conquered territories of the expanding empire, in Wissowa's work replicated in that of many later authors (e.g. Latte 1960), was surely not determined by an absence of archaeological research on religious sites: the dominant Western colonialist concept of religion, in which belief and the religious experience of the individual are paramount, played at least an equally important role (Orsi 2011). It made archaeologists thoroughly sceptical of being able to penetrate into the religious world of past societies. A classic example is Christopher Hawkes' 'ladder of inferences', which arranged various domains of past societies according to their accessibility to the archaeologist: that he placed religion on the top rung of the ladder, and considered it hardly accessible even to a text-aided archaeologist, must be explained by the implicit focus on beliefs of the individual rather than the – repeated – ritual practices of a social group (Hawkes 1954).

The last decades have seen a gradual but important change, first with the development of cognitive archaeology, which comprised the first systematic archaeological approach to the study of religion (Renfrew 1994), then with a material turn in anthropology, in which the focus shifted away from belief systems to the 'materiality of ritual and religion' (Insoll 2011), that is, to 'the very concrete ways through which humans fabricate ... a sense of the presence of something beyond' (Meyer 2014: 22), and finally with the inclusion of bioarchaeological studies (e.g. Schwartz 2017). Subjects of research from this material-oriented perspective range from the ways in which sacred space was ordered and the gods were made present and visible through cult images and temples, to the selection of sacrificial animals, the slaughtering procedures of victims, the offering of man-made objects deemed appropriate as gifts to the gods, and curse tablets and the role of magic (cf. contributions in Raja and Rüpke 2015). This material approach will be the one adopted here, but rather in addition to, than as a replacement of, the historical and institutional framework of interpretation developed by Wissowa. As my examples will make clear, visibility, locality and temporality are the most important structuring principles linked up with materiality.

The remainder of this chapter consists of two parts. In the first part, we will investigate what role material forms of religion played in the legitimisation and acceptance of the new political order introduced with the reign of Augustus. While the literature on the ruler cult in the Roman empire is vast (e.g. Fishwick 1987–2005), the religious and material foundation of it has received limited attention. We will investigate in what way monuments like the Pantheon and Ara Pacis in Rome not only reflected the new order of the Principate, but also were instrumental in creating, communicating and maintaining the sacrosanct power and prominence of the first emperor and the imperial family.

The second part of the chapter discusses the question of how Roman rule affected the religions of subject territories at different levels of organisation. We will look at the introduction of the imperial cult in the capitals of the provinces as well as in individual cities of the empire, then consider the composition and re-ordering of the pantheon venerated by civic communities, and finally review changes at grassroot level through the lens of the important rituals of coming of age of boys in a provincial town.

Religion and the legitimisation of imperial power at Rome

After Rome had been a Republic for almost five centuries, a new form of government was introduced in 27 BCE known as the Principate, a designation which refers to the position of the new sovereign as *princeps inter pares*. While the Princeps took over the leadership of the state, he was supposed to seek cooperation with his peers in the senate. With the vicissitudes of the civil war still fresh in mind, the Roman state and in particular the Roman senate took a risk with this political experiment. The first emperor Augustus sought to legitimise the new form of government by presenting it as a restoration of the Republic, as a continuation of the existing order. He secured the pre-eminent position of himself and his family by claiming divine descent and by anchoring his dominant position in a cosmological order. Let us look at two prominent buildings from the time of Augustus designed with the explicit goal of providing the new political order of the nascent Principate with a firm religious foundation through monumental material forms and ritual: the Pantheon and the Altar of Augustan Peace.

The Pantheon is without doubt the best-preserved and most widely known ancient monument in Rome. Consisting of a drum covered by a dome, the height of which exactly matches the rotunda's diameter, the building forms an architectural masterpiece unrivalled in the ancient world (De Fine Licht 1968; Marder and Wilson Jones 2015; Thomas 2017). Construction of the building as we know it was started by the emperor Trajan and completed by Hadrian (Hetland 2015), but the origin of the monument reaches back to the early Augustan period. The first building on the site was constructed at the initiative of Augustus' son-in-law M. Agrippa and was dedicated in 25 BCE (Dio 53.27.2-4; *CIL* VI.896 = 31196; Boatwright 2013). Excavations in the entrance hall (1892–3) and along the façade (1996–7) have provided solid evidence that the outline of Agrippa's building anticipated the shape, size and orientation of its successor (La Rocca 2015; for the original inscription mentioning Agrippa's name, cf. Suet., *Aug*. 97.1). On the elevation of the Augustan Pantheon, little can be said beyond Pliny's observation that it had bronze columns in the shape of Caryatides as well as bronze capitals (*HN* 36.38; 34.13); we are not even sure whether or not the circular space was covered (La Rocca 2015: 64ff.; Waddell 2015: 135). Given the purpose of this chapter, our focus here is on the design and furnishing of the building and the question how these worked to materially anchor the newly established Principate and the position of its first incumbent in a cosmological order.

An essential source is the description of the building in Cassius Dio's Roman History, written *c*.200 CE:

> Meanwhile Agrippa beautified the city at his own expense. … At that time he completed the Pantheon as it is called. It is known by this name, perhaps because it received images (*eikones*) of many

> gods among the statues (*agalmata*), that of Mars and that of Venus; but, I believe, because, being like a *tholos*, it resembles the heavens. Agrippa, for his part, wished to place Augustus there too and to bestow on him the honour of having the structure named after him; but when the emperor would not accept either honour, he installed there statues (*andriantes*) of the former Caesar and in the pronaos of Augustus and himself. (Dio 53.27.2–3; translation Cary (Loeb), emended)

Dio's account of Agrippa's monument is tersely written, and it is hard to separate historical facts from speculation or personal observation of the monument as it existed in his own time, but three things stand out.

First, there is a tension between the original plan for the design of the temple and the eventual execution. Following a Hellenistic model (see below), Agrippa's plan was to put up statues of Julius Caesar, Augustus and himself amid the statues of the gods in the Pantheon's interior. Given its importance, Augustus must have been informed of the plan at an early stage and have given his consent. His wish to alter the design thus most likely was inspired by changed circumstances. One factor may have been the inauguration of the temple of Divus Julius in the Forum Romanum. In 42 BCE, Julius Caesar had been granted the privilege of being the first mortal in Roman history ever to be officially divinised and received among the gods (Koortbojian 2013: 21). The temple, which had been voted for in 40 BCE (Dio 47.18.2–4), was inaugurated only in 29 BCE (Dio 51.22), a few years before the completion of the Pantheon. The new experience with the cult statue of the first Divus may have changed the acceptability of honorific statues of living mortals among the gods. However this may have been, Augustus ordered the statues of himself and his son-in-law to be installed in the Pantheon's porch, probably in the niches on either side of the entrance to the *cella*, assuming that the porch of Agrippa's building featured similar niches to those of the present building (Gros 1976: 146). Such a liminal position on the threshold between the profane world of his subjects outside the temple and the sacred world of the gods in the *cella*, corresponded with his status as a living ruler and fitted with his image as protagonist of old republican values. With distinctive honours being paid to a living emperor and his deified dead predecessor, the model for the imperial cult was set, being followed, for example by Augustus' successor Tiberius (Suet., *Tib.* 26).

Second, Agrippa had conceptualised the building as a *Pantheum*. The use of this Greek loan word in contemporary Latin sources[1] implies a conceptual transfer from the Hellenistic east where the concept was

Figure 9.1 Augustus. Silver denarius, 12 BCE. AVGVSTVS - Head of Augustus, bare, right/L LENTVLVS FLAMEN MARTIALIS, triumvir monetalis: Augustus, laureate and togate, right, resting on shield inscribed *C(lupeum) V(irtutis)*, 'Shield of Virtue', placing a star on divinized Julius Caesar, in 'hip mantle', left, holding spear and Victoriola on globe. *RIC* I² 415. Courtesy of the American Numismatic Society (1944.100.38345).

used for the association of a divinised king with 'all the gods'(Thomas 2004; id. 2017: 180–8; La Rocca 2015: 71–5). However, notwithstanding the literal meaning of the term by which the temple was designated, the circle of gods that accompanied the deified Caesar was not unlimited, but probably consisted of the Twelve Gods of Mount Olympus (Thomas 2017: 186). These gods were also identified with planets and signs of the zodiac. Their images, which perhaps filled the exedrae along the wall of the rotunda, may be recognised in the anonymous *eikones* mentioned by Dio. While Dio's comment that the Pantheon derived its name from its resemblance to the vault of heavens (Dio 53.27.2) was probably sparked off by the hemispherical interior and the gilded bronze stars which supposedly decorated the dome's coffers of the building in his own time (La Rocca 2015: 67–71, esp. 69; Thomas 2017: 184–5 with fig. 32), the interpretation may have been further inspired by the circle of statues of these celestial gods.

Third, Roman temples were normally devoted to one or more explicitly named deities who were considered the titular gods of the sanctuary. Consequently, scholars have distrusted the idea that the term 'Pantheon' was the building's original name. Nevertheless, in Dio's account two of the many images present in the building, those of Mars and Venus, are singled out as cult images (*agalmata*).[2] This fact together with the

Figure 9.2 'Algiers relief', marble, Museum of Antiquities, Algiers, representing Venus, Cupid, Mars Ultor, resting on shield decorated with wreath of oak leaves, and Julius Caesar in hip mantle, stretched right arm (proffering statuette of Victoria?); hole above the forehead with traces of metal fitting for star, now lost. Photo: R. Laev (https://arachne.dainst.org/entity/3618118). © German Archaeological Institute, Rome.

well-known claims by the Julian House to trace their descent from Mars and Venus (Zanker 1988: 167ff., esp. 192–215), suggests that, despite the name by which the temple was known, Mars and Venus were the titular gods of the Pantheon. It is these two gods who must have had a place in, or just in front of, the principal exedra opposite the entrance to the building.

An unsolved problem concerns the status of Caesar's statue. When his temple on the Forum Romanum was eventually dedicated in 29 BCE, it certainly had a proper cult statue which represented Caesar as a god. The status change probably was first and foremost made visible by a star that Augustus had 'added as an adornment to the head of the statue of Caesar' (Plin., *HN* 2.94; Suet., *Div.Jul.* 88; Ramsey and Licht 1997: 159), a reference to the appearance of the Julian Star (*sidus Iulium*), which, according to Augustus' memoirs, the people of Rome believed to signal Caesar's apotheosis. The conventionalised form was reached only after experimentation as becomes clear from two coin series issued *c.*36 BCE, which depict the as yet unbuilt temple of Divus Julius with the cult statue in two variants, one togate and one in hip mantle (*RRC* 540; Koortbojian 2013: 9, 41–9, 136). The ultimately canonised form shows the Divus Julius in hip mantle while proffering on the palm of his right hand a small statuette of Victory (Figure 9.1). If Caesar had thus been conceptualised as a god before, it seems unlikely that, despite the conclusions that have been drawn from Dio's words, the statue in the Pantheon would not portray him like that (Koortbojian 2013: 234–5; differently, Fishwick 1992: 331–2). If we accept the conclusions of recent research that the statuary group of the Pantheon is replicated, amongst others, in the so-called 'Algiers relief' (Figure 9.2), the star which is thought to have been attached to the metal fitting still present in the hole of Caesar's forehead is clear proof that the statue in the Pantheon indeed represented him as a god (Pollini 2012: 133ff., with fig. III.13b; Koortbojian 2013: 45–9, 134–7; Thomas 2017: 153ff.).

Drawing all the evidence together we can conclude that, by reallocating the statues of Augustus and Agrippa to the porch, close to but at a respectful distance from the gods, and by juxtaposing the statue of the divinised Caesar with the cult statues of his ancestral gods, the Pantheon came to work as a dynastic temple which presented the existing political order as god-given and natural, one which therefore would be hard to challenge.

The position of the first Emperor and his family was also anchored by linking them to the religious architecture of altars and the commemorative practices associated with them. The most important example is the Altar of Augustan Peace, the Ara Pacis Augustae (Figure 9.3).[3] The Senate voted for its construction after Augustus' victorious return to Rome from the western provinces, on 4 July 13 BCE. After Augustus had refused to accept an earlier proposal to erect the altar in the Senate itself (Dio 54.25.3), it was eventually built in the northern part of the Campus Martius, on the Via Flaminia less than one mile north of the pomerium, the sacred boundary between the competence areas of magistrates with supreme military and supreme civil power respectively (Dio 53.17.4, 51.19.6; Wissowa 1912: 146; Torelli 1982: 29–30, 32–3). The site of the altar was thus located on the last stretch of the returning army's march into the city from the north, just before it reached the Field of Mars where it would be dissolved. The monument was inaugurated on 30 January 9 BCE.

The altar had the typical U-shaped plan, was set on a high square podium and crowned by a rectangular table designed to receive big blood sacrifices. The altar's sacred area was delimited by a screen wall

Figure 9.3 Ara Pacis Augustae, cut away drawing. Western front side with steps leading to the entrance to the U-shaped inner altar and north side with processional frieze. After Giuseppe Moretti, *The Ara Pacis* (Rome, 1967), p. 17.

with two entrances with doorways on the short sides. Both the altar itself and the precinct wall were richly decorated with fine marble reliefs – sacrificial scenes on the table of the inner altar (Koeppel 1987: 137–41, 144–5, figs. 27–31, 34–5; Rossini 2012: 28–9), imitations of a wooden fence with suspended festoons and bucrania on the precinct's interior wall, and a festive procession, scenes of Rome's mythological past and representations of the personified goddesses Roma and Tellus Italiae, on its exterior. While the artistic and historical significance of these reliefs have evoked much scholarship (Koeppel 1987; 1988 with the older literature; Rossini 2012), my focus here will be on the ritual observances and commemorative practices associated with the monument and the potential these had to positively affect the Roman people's perception of the emperor and his family and enhance the acceptance of their special position.

The procession depicted on the long walls of the precinct moves on both sides in the same direction towards the entrance to the sacrificial altar on the monument's short west side. While there is consensus that the scenes on both walls reflect the same procession as seen from opposite sides of the route, the question as to what occasion it relates to remains controversial. Many have assumed that the procession was linked to a

Figure 9.4 Ara Pacis Augustae, 9 BCE. Processional frieze, North wall, right side. Taking part in the procession is a *camillus*, bearing an incense box and wine jug. *Victimarii* and sacrificial animals are absent. Photo: B. Malter (https://arachne.dainst.org/entity/74140). © German Archaeological Institute, Rome.

sacrifice associated with either the *constitutio*, the senatorial decree to build the monument, voted for on 4 July 13 BCE, or to the *dedicatio*, the monument's actual inauguration, on 30 January 9 BCE. Others argued that the reliefs depicted the inauguration of the as yet unbuilt plot on which the altar had to be erected.

Fundamental objections can be raised against each of these interpretations individually (Billows 1993),[4] but a problem faced by all three is that the sacrifice in which the procession supposedly culminated

Figure 9.5 Ara Pacis Augustae, 9 BCE. Processional frieze, North wall, left side. By the wreathed heads and the sprigs of laurel borne by some of the figures the procession may be identified as a *supplicatio* to the gods, in this case held for the victorious return of the emperor Augustus. Photo: N. Hannestad (https://arachne.dainst.org/entity/6121104). © German Archaeological Institute, Rome.

is not depicted or alluded to at all: victims, cult personnel that would help with performing the sacrifice, sacrificial implements – none of these standard features of Roman sacrificial scenes is present. Instead, we see *camilli*, young serving boys, carrying incense boxes, a jug and a libation bowl (Figure 9.4, right), paraphernalia needed for the offering of incense and wine. Although it is true that great sacrifices are normally preceded by such smaller offerings during the so-called *praefatio* (Scott Ryberg 1955: e.g. figs 17, 38, 86; Scheid 1990: 326–39), it is inconceivable that the inauguration would not have been accompanied by a blood sacrifice. Crucial clues for an escape from this aporia are the sprigs of laurel that many participants, their heads wreathed, hold in their hands (Figure 9.5), an unequivocal indication that what is depicted here is a so-called *supplicatio*, a public thanksgiving ordered by the consuls or the Senate (Liv. 40.37.3; Wissowa 1912: 423–6; Billows 1993: 88–9). During such a ceremony all members of society were supposed to perform an offering of incense and wine; the temples of the gods which were thought to have been instrumental in achieving the goals that were the object of the *supplicatio* were opened for the occasion, with the incense and wine necessary for the offering being provided by the state (Liv. 10.23.1; *CIL* XII.4333; Wissowa 1912: 423ff.).

The processional friezes on the long walls commemorate in an idealised fashion the *supplicatio* held to express the widely shared feelings of joy for the victorious return of the emperor. The celebration must have been decided soon after the emperor's arrival, perhaps by the same *senatus-consultum* with which the altar was voted for. In conformity with the republican values he wished to promote, Augustus figures here as *primus inter pares* amid magistrates and their lictors, priests and ordinary senators. What is extraordinary, however, is the appearance of the emperor's family led by his wife Livia (on the south wall) and his daughter Iulia (on the north wall) (Figure 9.4). Two aspects are noteworthy: first, this is the first appearance of the imperial family (*domus augusta*) on a public monument and, second, its appearance is directly associated with the military success of the emperor leaving the implicit message that the future well-being and prosperity of the state are also dependent on the emperor's wife and children.

Monuments by nature intend to keep the memory of particular events alive long after they took place. Some monuments, however, are more effective in achieving this goal than others. Augustus' choice to opt for an altar as the focus for commemorative practices celebrating his military achievements was prompted by a deliberate communicative strategy. Generations of Roman generals had used the pomp of a triumph for self-representation and self-aggrandisement (Versnel 1970; Brilliant 1999; Östenberg 2009). After the battle of Actium, however, Octavian-Augustus had refused to accept any further triumphs. He wanted to present himself as different from the late republican generals, that is, as modest and pious, as a responsible magistrate who thought more of the interest of his country than of personal gain. By its religious nature and modest size, the altar as a monument served this purpose very well. Furthermore, rather than triumphal arches, which after their inauguration could easily lapse into 'dead' monuments, the altar remained a living thing: the senatorial decree by which the construction of the Ara Pacis was voted for included the order that an annual sacrifice (*anniversarium sacrificium*) be performed by the magistrates, priests and Vestal Virgins (*RG* 12). And, finally, in the absence of a cult statue of a deity which could be seen as the sacrifice's prime recipient, that same sacrifice, though officially made for

Figure 9.6 Divus Augustus. Bronze as, Rome mint, struck under Tiberius, 22–30 CE. DIVVS AVGVSTVS PATER, radiate head, left/The Ara Providentiae: ornate altar enclosure with double panelled door, PROVIDENT in exergue, S C across field (*RIC* I^2 81). Courtesy of the American Numismatic Society (1937.158.458).

Pax Augusta, became indirectly associated with the figure of the Princeps. While Augustus and his successors had to be considerate of the Senate for whom worship of the living emperor was unacceptable, cults to the emperor's divine power or will, that is, to his Genius or his Numen, or to imperial virtues were permitted (Torelli 1982: 63ff.).[5] The absence of a cult image or a directly related temple which housed the god for whom the sacrifice was intended created a deliberate ambiguity, suggesting that the tribute paid by the sacrifice was intended as much for Augustus as for the personified Pax Augusta, the Peace brought about by Augustus (Elsner 1991).

One final point that deserves mentioning here is the choice of the anniversary days. The decree to vote for the altar had to be taken while the memories of Augustus' glorious return to the capital were still fresh, but the inauguration day could be manipulated and so it was: by choosing the birthday of the empress Livia (30 January), the wife of the emperor was linked up with the successes of her husband. That this was a deliberate policy is not only to be derived from the inclusion of the imperial family in the processional frieze, but also from Ovid's verses which exhort the priests to pledge their vows at the ceremony in January not just for the emperor, but for the entire imperial house to persist in peace (Ovid, *Fasti* 1.709–10, 719–22, esp. 721–2).

Altars such as the Ara Pacis Augustae, devoted not to the emperor himself, but to an abstract imperial virtue or divine quality associated

Figure 9.7 Nero. Bronze as, Lugdunum (Lyon) mint, struck 62-68 CE. IMP NERO CAESAR AVG PONTIF MAX TRIB POT PP, bare head left, globe at point of bust/The Ara Pacis: ornamented altar enclosure with double door; ARA PACIS in exergue (*RIC* I^2 527). Courtesy of the American Numismatic Society (1953.171.1292).

with him (e.g. Pax, Providentia, Pietas), gave a crucial material basis to the religious sanctioning of the monarchy. The religious legitimisation was of particular importance for the first emperors, as is clear from the example of the Ara Providentiae (Figure 9.6), which was inaugurated on the day (26 June) that Augustus had adopted Tiberius (Scheid 1998: 28ff., no. 12c, lines 52–7); the altar commemorated Augustus' foresight (*providentia*) throughout his reign in promoting a number of consecutive successors by adoption, when one after the other candidate prematurely died (Fishwick 2010). Once the Principate had been firmly established, the Julian dynasty well enshrined, and the sacrifices and festivals related to the first emperor and his family routinised, these altars lost their specific association with Augustus and acquired generic significance: this explains why after Claudius no new altars were built: later successors, such as the emperor Nero, who released a coin series with the Ara Pacis on the reverse, simply put themselves in the Augustan tradition by using the existing monuments (Figure 9.7).

Provincial centres of imperial cult

The most significant impact of the Roman conquest on the religions of Rome's subject communities was the introduction of the imperial cult (Price 1984; Fishwick 1987-2005). The Augustan period saw the creation of centres for emperor worship in the capitals of all provinces of the empire. The initiative for these cults came from the provincial communities themselves (Coşkun 2014: 59-61; Eck 2015), though all proposals needed imperial approval. The example was set by the provinces of Asia and Bithynia. In 29 BCE, just after he had gained absolute power as sole ruler of the empire, Octavian-Augustus gave Roman residents of these provinces permission to build sanctuaries for Rome and his deified father Divus Julius in the towns of Ephesus and Nicomedia respectively, and at the same time allowed the indigenous population to initiate cults for Rome and himself in Pergamum and Nicomedia. These first grants of permission sparked a competition in demonstrations of loyalty to the new ruler between provincial communities (Tac., *Ann.* 4.37-38; Coşkun 2014, 59). Augustus refused any ruler cult for his person in Rome and accepted one in the provinces only under the condition that he be worshipped in partnership with the goddess Rome.[6] Judging by the titles of priesthoods connected with these cults, the imperial instructions were followed.[7] The rights and duties of the provincial priests were centrally regulated as is suggested by the so-called *Lex de flamonio provinciae Narbonensis*, in origin an imperial edict or senatorial decree from Rome (*CIL* XII.6038; Fishwick 1987, vol. 1.2: 240–3; 2002, vol. 3.2: 3–15). In line with these instructions, the ingredients for the imperial cult were everywhere pretty much the same: festive days with sacrifices, supplications, and games in honour of Rome and Augustus, making the ruler and his (nearly) godly power present and visible to his subjects. Yet, as the archaeology of the diverse examples from Lugdunum-Lyon in the West and Ancyra-Ankara in the East demonstrates, in their material forms no two cult centres were the same.

The focal point of the imperial cult of the Three Gallic provinces in Lyon in France was an altar dedicated, according to our sources, to Rome and Augustus (Fishwick 1987, vol. 1.1: 97–137; 2004, vol. 3.3: 105–27; *CAG* 69/2, 278–80, 288–98, 405–6). It was inaugurated by Drusus, Augustus' stepson and legate in Gaul, on 1 August 12 BCE, the anniversary of Octavian's triumph at Actium and of the self-chosen death of Antony. Although the cult thus started during Augustus' reign, sacrifices made here were probably not directed at the living emperor, but at his Genius (Scheid 2010; 2021). The precise site of the altar has not been ascertained, but it is supposed to have been on the slope of the steep hill overlooking the confluence of the Saone and Rhone rivers (Desbat 2016). Landscape and architecture were most effectively put to use here for the monument to send a message of power. Our best evidence for the physical appearance of the altar is the obverse of several series of bronze coins

Figure 9.8 Augustus. Bronze sestertius, Lugdunum (Lyon) mint, struck 10–14 CE. CAESAR AVGVSTVS DIVI F PATER PATRIAE, laureate head right/The Altar of the Three Gauls: front side, decorated with the *corona civica* between laurels, flanked by laurel crowns with hanging fillets; to left and right, Victories on columns, facing one another, ROM ET AVG in exergue (*RIC* I^2 231a). Courtesy of the American Numismatic Society (1944.100.39130).

issued by the imperial mint at Lyon in the period from Augustus down to Nero (Fishwick 1986: 91; 1987: 104 with plates 1, 11–17) (Figure 9.8). Depicted is the front side of the altar itself decorated with the typical symbols of Augustan peace: the oak swag (*corona civica*), which was granted Augustus 'for the saving of the citizens', in the centre, flanked by laurel trees and, on the extreme ends, laurel crowns with hanging fillets (for these symbols, cf. *RG* 34.2; *RIC* 277–9; Zanker 1988: 89–98). According to Strabo (4.3.2), the altar bore an inscription mentioning the names of the 60 tribes participating in the cult. Two high columns crowned by winged victories flank the altar. The coin images are lent some support by archaeological finds of a gilded bronze laurel wreath and columns of Egyptian granite used as spolia nearby (Fishwick 1987, vol. 1.1: pl. 2 and 5). Marble panels with carvings of suspended festoons found on the site remind us of the interior of the screen wall of the Ara Pacis (Fishwick 1987, vol. 1.1: pl. 6b and 7). This visual symbolism and the scenery created by its landscape and architectural setting broadcast the message that the Augustan peace which the Princeps gained by his victory at Actium had now been brought to the provinces of Gaul!

At Ancyra, the provincial capital of Galatia, modern Turkey, the central element of the sanctuary was not an altar, but a large (c.54 × 36 m) Greek temple (Figure 9.9) (Krencker and Schede 1936; Pinna

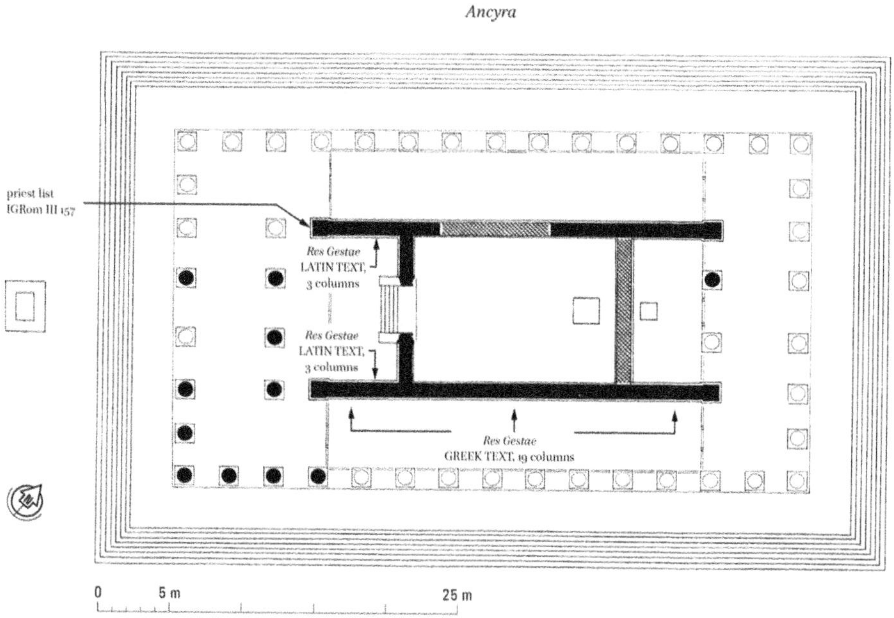

Figure 9.9 Simplified plan of the temple of Augustus and Roma at the provincial cult centre of Galatia at Ankara with indication of the places of the Greek and Latin inscribed texts of Augustus' *Res Gestae* and the list of priests. Black: original parts in situ; hatched: original foundations; white: reconstruction. Drawing: © Vrije Universiteit Amsterdam, Bert Brouwenstijn.

Caboni 2018). Its construction is firmly dated in the Augustan period (Weigand 1937; Fittschen 1985: 314–5; Pinna Caboni 2018: 170ff). Following the list of annual priests inscribed on the left anta of the pronaos, the cult started in 5 BCE when the first priest held office, but construction of the temple can only have begun after the fourth priest had donated the building plot as one of the benefactions of his priesthood in 2 BCE. The temple was inaugurated by the 19th priest in 14 CE, the year Augustus died and was deified (Coşkun 2014). Following examples in Rome the temple walls were decorated with gold paint proclaiming the golden age of the Augustan reign (Coşkun 2014: 36; Zink and Piening 2009). Augustus' rule was further glorified by the carving of copies of the 'Deeds of the Deified Augustus' in both Latin and Greek into the walls of the pronaos and the cella respectively (cf. Figure 9.9). Several layers of rectangular blocks with their distinct margins had to be smoothed in order to create a proper writing surface demonstrating that the inscriptions were a later addition to the original design, probably added shortly after the inauguration. An intriguing question is how Roma and Augustus were materially made present in the temple. The title of the priesthood as recorded in the heading of the list of priests mentions the cult partners, compared to normal practice, in reverse order: 'Of the Galatians, men who have been priest for the god Augustus and the goddess Rome'. Since the heading and the following 18 names of priests were added only secondarily, most probably after the recording of priests had come to an end in 18 CE (Coşkun 2014: 50), it remains uncertain whether the emperor was treated as a god and given precedence over his cult partner directly from the start of the cult, i.e. during his lifetime, or only after his death and subsequent deification. Unfortunately, nothing remains of the two cult statues themselves nor of the bases that supported them. We can thus only speculate about their relative sizes and places. If the two cult statues were of unequal size, the larger one must have stood in the cella and most probably embodied the Deified Augustus, whereas a smaller one of the goddess Rome had its place in the rear part of the temple, the opisthodomos. Anyway, for visitors who entered the pronaos a deliberate association was created between the text of Augustus' Deeds and his cult statue in the interior of the temple. While the imperial cult centres at Lugdunum and Ancyra served the same purposes as centres of worship and loyalty to the emperor, their material forms are very different: an altar versus a temple, and visual imagery versus text on gold painted walls as the main forms of communication. These differences may be partly understood by different experiences with ruler cults in the eastern and western half of the empire (Roels 2018).

Imperial cult organised by cities in the empire

Apart from the imperial cult at the provincial level, emperor worship was also organised at the level of individual city-states. In Asia Minor, for instance, a priesthood for Rome and Augustus or for Augustus alone is documented for some 34 different cities (Price 1984: 58). In the Three Gauls, nearly half of all cities have produced attestations for a priesthood attached to a civic cult of Roma and Augustus (Derks 2020: fig. 1). If we consider that such distributions reflect the state of preservation rather than actual historic occurrences, it seems likely that public cults of emperor worship existed in all civic communities across the empire. Since these forms of emperor worship were basically local initiatives which were exempt from imperial permission, they often took on slightly different forms. Temples linked with the imperial cult are normally located in the forum, the central public square of the town (Hänlein-Schäfer 1985: 23ff., esp. 26). Among the best-preserved examples is the temple in the forum of Colonia Iulia Pola, modern Pula, Croatia, with a dedication on the entablature 'to Rome and Augustus Caesar, son of the Deified, father of the fatherland' (*CIL* V.18), dating the building to between 2 BCE and 14 CE. The mentioning of the title 'father of the fatherland' may be taken as an indication that the formal addressee of the cult was the Genius Augusti. From the temple in the forum of Colonia Augusta Raurica, modern Augst, Switzerland, only the foundations remain, but the sculptured decoration of the altar in front of the temple with oak swag and eagle point to the imperial cult, most probably in the form of a civic cult for Roma and Augustus (Bossert-Radtke 1992: 37–50, pl. 14–8; Hufschmid 2009: 185–91);[8] the altar is stylistically dated to around the mid-first century CE.

With the progressive development of the Principate, the imperial cult began to include other members of the *domus augusta*. The process can be closely followed in the emergence and gradual change of dynastic statuary groups which, following the first monumental representation of the imperial family in the frieze of the Ara Pacis Augustae in Rome, began to appear in fora and temples of the imperial cult in Italy and the provinces (Boschung 2002; Cesarano 2015). As early as 1 BCE, the Koinon of the Galatians at Ancyra, for instance, received statues (andriantes) of the emperor Augustus and his wife Iulia Augusta (Livia) (Krencker and Schede 1936: 53; Coşkun 2014: 51–53), whereas in the early Tiberian period the more than life-sized enthroned statues of Roma and Augustus of the temple in the forum of Leptis Magna were accompanied by four pairs of statues: Tiberius and his mother Livia, as well as the designated successors to the throne, Germanicus and Drusus the Younger, and their respective wives and mothers (Hänlein-Schäfer 1985: 226–30; Boschung 2002: 8–24). Such cycles of statues which heightened the public awareness of the imperial family beyond the emperor paved the way for the expansion of the cult of Roma and Augustus into one for the *domus divina*. An early illustration of this is the temple of Rome and Augustus in the forum of Vienne in France. As can be seen from the expansion of the original building inscription over the temple's architrave (*CIL* XII.1845 = *ILN* 5.1, no. 34; Derks 2020: fig. 2), after the death and deification of Augustus' wife Livia, the original cult for Rome and Augustus was expanded to include the deified empress. The rededication of the temple implies that in the cella, beside the cult statue of Augustus, a statue of the Diva Augusta was erected (Cesarano 2015:

186). The example shows how the vicissitudes of the imperial family in Rome found a material resonance in the changing interior designs of forum temples across the empire.

Just as the imperial cult organized by the provincial assemblies, the cults dedicated to emperor worship in the cities in Italy and the provinces were a completely new phenomenon. The religious landscape of the conquered territories was, however, no tabula rasa. From a post-colonial perspective, recent research focuses on the religious encounter between coloniser and colonised, the fertile breeding ground where new hybrid forms of culture are constantly being created (Webster 1995; 2001; 2003; Glinister 2006: 23ff; van Dommelen 2006). As far as the civic cults are concerned, the creative process is visible in the selective adoption of cults from the Roman pantheon which, with the pre-existing cults, were fused into a new pantheon. This fusion often implied a change of status, identity and hierarchy of the pre-existing cults. The process started as early as the earliest expansion of Rome over its neighbours. To what extent the civic pantheons of the conquered communities were homogenised can be judged from a comparison between extant monumental stone calendars from Italian cities, mostly dating from the late republican and early imperial period. While these calendars retain many imperial festive days common to all of them, after several centuries of Roman dominion, each of these communities still recorded festivals which were tied to gods specific to them alone. The Fasti Praenestini (Degrassi 1963: no. 17; Bertinetti 2013), for instance, note on 9–10 April a two-day festival for Fortuna Primigenia, the city's patron goddess, who had an impressive terraced sanctuary on the hill above the town from where she literally kept a watch over her community (Miano 2018: 17ff.); according to the calendar, the magistrates (*duoviri*), on behalf of the civic community, sacrificed a calf to her.

In the provinces, pre-existing local cults which were to become civic cults were often first transformed and assimilated to Roman cults (Derks 1998: 73ff.; 2020; Van Andringa 2002: 131–58). The process of assimilation implied the translation of indigenous representations of the past into Roman terms. Local sets of myths were interwoven with Roman ones. For example, when an expat community of Remi, a tribe from Northern Gaul, settled on the Rhine and put up a monument for their patron deity, they assimilated him to Roman Mars. In the inscription, the god is presented as Mars Camulus, the second name probably being his old indigenous name now serving as a kind of epithet to Mars (Figure 9.10). How the articulation was made is often unknown, but in the case of the Remi one could think of a hypothetical mythical ancestor Remus

Figure 9.10 Dedication to Mars Camulus, the patron deity of the *civitas* of the Remi, by citizens of the community settled on the Rhine. The laurel trees on the side panels and the wreath of oak leaves (*corona civica*) with the centred abbreviation *o(b) c(ives) s(ervatos)* ('for the saving of the citizens') on the rear side refer to the imperial ideology from the age of Augustus. © Butzon & Bercker GmbH, Kevelaer.

who was identified with Romulus' brother (Derks 1998: 107–10). The decoration of the monument for Mars Camulus, with a laurel tree on both sides and a laurel wreath as well as the expression *o(b) c(ives) s(ervatos)* ('for the saving of the citizens') at the back, is a quote from the Augustan visual imagery we have seen before at the altar of Lyon and a sign of the profound conceptual changes of the original indigenous god. The example is typical for the patron deities of the civic communities.

* * *

Since the Roman conquest changed the very idea of community, it was unavoidable that the rites of passage, through which members of the community were 'fabricated', changed as well. I focus here on the coming-of-age rituals for boys. Thanks to historical information, we have a fairly good idea of the course of action of the Roman ritual, as it was performed by imperial princes and the sons of the Roman elite (Dolansky 2008). In the morning, the boy offered the *bulla*, the amulet holder which had served to protect him from his earliest childhood, to the household gods. In addition, he changed clothes, taking off the children's *toga praetexta* and donning the manly toga of the adult Roman male. In the afternoon, the boy went

Figure 9.11 Inscribed base of a stone statuette put up by a father reading 'To Mars Iovantucarus for the well-being of Mercurialis, his son. Secundius Secundinus. He paid his vow willingly and deservedly' (inv. no. ST_9724). Votive from the sanctuary of Iovantucarus at Trier. © GDKE/Rheinisches Landesmuseum Trier, Th. Zühmer.

to the Forum of Augustus, where he first appeared in public in his new attire to perform his first sacrifice as a full member of Roman society. The setting was pregnant with symbolism (Zanker 1988: 192ff). In the semi-circular exedrae, statues of the mythical ancestors of Rome were exhibited, whereas the porticoes on both long sides of the square were full of statues for illustrious men from Rome's glorious past (Geiger 2008). These were the examples for the new adult worthy to imitate. Sometimes, he himself, his parents or his friends decided to erect, in commemoration of the rite, a lasting monument, often a statue representing the boy in his new status as an adult *togatus* (Derks 2006: table 4; to be supplemented with *CIL* X.688 (Sorrento) and a new inscription from Pompeii, on which, see Osanna, *JRA* 32, 2018).

There is some historical evidence that the Roman rite was adopted by the provincial nobility for the ritual transformation of their sons (*P.Mich*.VII, 433; Plin., *Ep*. 10.116; Plut., *Sertorius* 14; Tac., *Agr*. 21), but we should be cautious to extrapolate from this to such a rite for all young males in the empire. If we bear in mind that only families with Roman citizenship could perform the rite of the *toga virilis* – as wearing the toga was a prerogative of Roman citizens – non-citizens and perhaps in general families of middle or lower classes should have performed a different rite. What alternative can we think of?

Some 1300 km north of Rome, in the sanctuary of the patron deity of the Treveri, (Lenus) Mars Iovantucarus, located just outside the Roman

Figure 9.12 Anepigraphical stone statuette (inv.no. ST-9732 = ST-9759b). Votive from the sanctuary of Iovantucarus at Trier. © GDKE/Rheinisches Landesmuseum Trier, Th. Zühmer.

town of Trier, Germany, archaeologists made a chance discovery of a cache of eight inscribed statuette bases as well as a set of statuettes of boys without inscription (Binsfeld et al. 1988: nos. 183–7, 434, 485A, 503). This series of votives has often been interpreted as thanksgivings for healing by a distinctively 'Celtic' deity, but, as I have argued elsewhere (Derks 2006), a different reading may be more plausible. One of the inscribed bases still shows the bare feet of a child, the image of which has become lost (Figure 9.11). Originally, it must have looked quite similar to the better-preserved statuettes without inscriptions (Figure 9.12). This suggests that the two types of monuments, inscribed and uninscribed, are in a sense complementary. The statuettes may be interpreted as genre representations of playing children used as emblems for a happy childhood, the prototypes of which are to be found in Classical and Hellenistic Greece. If we compare the texts of the inscriptions, a number of recurring patterns may be

Figure 9.13 Terracotta statuettes (inv.no. 1899.1004; 1899.1364; 1899.1365). Votives from the sanctuary of Iovantucarus at Trier. © GDKE/Rheinisches Landesmuseum Trier, Th. Zühmer.

observed. All inscriptions mention a vow as the context of the dedication. All monuments are dedicated to (Mars) Iovantucarus, who is the local patron god in his capacity as 'caretaker of the youth'. With one possible exception for which this information is not explicitly given, all monuments were set up by parents or by a father. As far as the reason for the dedication is given, this is always 'for' (*pro*) or 'for the well-being of' (*pro salute*) the child. With one exception, all statuettes were set up for sons.

The monuments were set up by parents to thank the god for having protected their children during their childhood period. Simple terracotta statuettes representing the same type of a half-naked boy holding a bird or other toy may have functioned as cheap alternatives to the stone ones (Figure 9.13). The repeated erection or deposition of such stone and terracotta statuettes may be related to a coming-of-age ritual. In absence of any historical information we are unable to reconstruct the precise course of action, but from its material manifestation we can conclude that it had nothing in common with the donning of the *toga virilis*. Given the absence of any martial symbolism, it must also have been very different from the old warrior initiation rites which we may assume for the preceding Late Pre-Roman Iron Age (Derks 1998: 45ff., esp. 54). Whereas the small upper stratum of urban elites adopted the example of the Roman nobility and tried to emulate them, other segments of the urban community – and, for that matter, most of the rural population – created new ritual forms and material symbols to express their children's transition to the age group of adults.

Conclusion

This chapter has focused on the question how material forms of temples, altars and statues helped the first emperor legitimise the new order of his reign in Rome, Italy and the provinces. It also investigated the effects of conquest on the religions of subject peoples. The reign of Augustus was clearly a time of change and experimentation; the most effective material forms of expression needed time to crystallise, as is illustrated, for instance, by the development of an image of the divinised Caesar, the reallocation of the human statues of Augustus and Agrippa from the Pantheon's interior to its porch, and the creation of altars for personified abstractions associated with the emperor, inaugurated on days with a marked relevance for the imperial house. The building of the Ara Pacis as a commemorative monument for Augustus' military successes in the western provinces in 9 BCE proved to be a very effective means to provide the new political order with a religious foundation: it consecrated Augustus' military achievements to the gods and through the annual sacrifice kept on recalling the cause for the monument's erection long afterwards. By having the inauguration coincide with the birthday of Augustus' wife Livia, and by including the imperial family in the frieze commemorating the supplications of thanks for Augustus' return, the foundation was laid for the concept of the *domus augusta*, the dynastic 'imperial house', which included, apart from the emperor, the intended successors to the throne and their mothers and wives. In a similar vein, the deification of Livia, the wife of the first emperor, was a first step towards the development of a *domus divina*, a 'divine house' of deified emperors and empresses. While the cycles of dynastic statuary groups erected in the fora and entrance halls of temples across the empire embodied the *domus augusta*, the *domus divina* was materialised by the erection of proper cult statues in temple interiors.

Regarding the effects of conquest on the religion of the conquered peoples, it has been argued that the pantheons of the civic communities were drastically changed. New cults selected from the state cults of Rome were added, and the gods of the pre-existing cults changed status, identity and hierarchical position. An example of the deep transformation of the pre-existing cults is the monument set up by *cives Remi* to the patron god of their community. This monument is decorated with symbols of the imperial ideology which were now associated with this originally indigenous Gallic god. As for coming-of-age rituals of boys, we established that whereas the ritual forms adopted by the provincial nobility were similar to the ones used by the Roman elite documented in the written sources, the ordinary people of the medium and lower classes, many of whom had no Roman citizenship and thus no access to the described elite forms, invented new rituals with new material forms, borrowed from classical visual language, to mark their transition to a new age group.

Acknowledgements

I would like to thank the editors for inviting me as a contributor to the original conference and this volume. I am grateful to Andrew Lawrence (Bern) and Nico Roymans (Amsterdam) for comments on a draft of this chapter.

Notes

1 Coarelli (1983: 42, 45), Fishwick (1992: 334–5) and Koortbojian (2013: 135) suppose that the building was originally called *Pantheum Augustum*, which was subsequently shortened to *Pantheum*. The earliest mention of the *Pantheum* is in the Acta of the Fratres Arvales for the year 59 CE (Scheid 1998: no. 27, lines 49–50). The ancient sources are collected by De Fine Licht (1968: 180–4); *LTUR* IV (1999: 54 (Ziolkowski)).

2 For the distinction between cult statues and other statues of gods, see Price (1984: 176–9); Fishwick (1992); Cesarano (2015: 187). The arguments put forward by Thomas (2017: 151–3) to play down the distinctions are unconvincing.

3 Others are, for instance, the Ara Fortunae Reducis, the Ara Gentis Iuliae, the Ara Providentiae and the Ara Claudiae; on the renewed popularity of the altar as the architectural form for new foundations of sanctuaries in the Augustan period (Wissowa 1912: 470). The literature on the Ara Pacis is abundant; cf. Koeppel (1987) (with the older literature); Rossini (2012). Ancient sources on the Ara Pacis: *RGDA* 12; Dio 54.23.3–4; Degrassi (1963) *Inscriptiones Italiae* XIII.2, no. 8 (Fasti Caeretani), no. 17 (Fasti Praenestini), no. 22 (Fasti Verulani), no. 25 (Fasti Amiterni), no. 26 (Fasti Antiates), no. 44 (Feriale Cumanum).

4 An argument against an association with the *dedicatio* not mentioned by Billows is that at the moment of the monument's inauguration in 9 BCE, Agrippa had been dead for three years. For the improbability of a sacrifice accompanying the *constitutio*, see Wissowa (1904) and Torelli (1982: 30).

5 For the development of the material forms of the cult of the Genius Augusti and that of the closely related Lares Augusti in the early decades of the Principate, see Rosso (2021).

6 Wissowa (1912: 80–81, 341–2); Fishwick (1987, vol. 1.1: 126–30). Ancient sources: Dio, 51.20.6–8; 56.25.6; Suet., *Aug*. 52. Tac., *Ann*. 4.37–8. In Rome, altars like the Ara Pacis Augustae carefully avoided to directly address the living emperor as the recipient of cult.

7 The priests were generally named *flamines Romae et Augusti*, merely indicating that they were attached to Rome and Augustus without specifying the exact modality of their cults. As the priestly title remained unchanged after the death and deification of Augustus and even

after other deified emperors had been included in the cult, the title itself cannot be taken as evidence for worship of the person of the living emperor (Scheid 2019: 192). See also the argument on the inscription of Pula, above p. 249.

8 It should be remembered that the first founder of the town was the senator L. Munatius Plancus (*CIL* X.6078), who in the memorable senatorial meeting of 16 January 27 BCE took the initiative to grant Octavian the title Augustus and have his house decorated with the *corona civica* and two laurel trees (Vell.Pat. 2.91.1; Gros 1976: 36). A civic cult for Rome and Augustus therefore seems more plausible than a cult for Jupiter.

Abbreviations

CAG: *Carte Archéologique de la Gaule*. Paris: Académie des Inscriptions et Belles-Lettres and Fondation Maison des Sciences de l'Homme, 1988–.

CIL: *Corpus Inscriptionum Latinarum*. Berlin: Berlin-Brandenburg Academy of Sciences and Humanities, 1863–.

LTUR: *Lexicon Topographicum Urbis Romae*, vols I–VI. Roma: Edizioni Quasar, 1993–2000.

References

Albrecht, Janico et al. 2018. 'Religion in the making: the lived ancient religion approach', *Religion* 48: 568–93.

Bertinetti, Marina. 2013. 'Fasti Praenestini'. In *Palazzo Massimo alle Terme: le collezioni*, edited by Carlo Gasparri and Rita Paris, 90–2. Milano: Electa.

Billows, Richard. 1993. 'The religious procession of the Ara Pacis Augustae: Augustus' supplication in 13 B.C', *Journal of Roman Archaeology* 6: 80–92.

Binsfeld, Wolfgang, Karin Goethert-Polaschek and Lothar Schwinden. 1988. *Katalog der römischen Steindenkmäler des Rheinischen Landesmuseums Trier. 1: Götter und Weihedenkmäler*. Trierer Grabungen und Forschungen XII(1) = CSIR Deutschland IV(3). Mainz am Rhein: Philipp von Zabern.

Boatwright, Mary. 2013. 'Hadrian and the Agrippa inscription of the Pantheon'. In *Hadrian: Art, politics and economy*, edited by Thorsten Opper, 19–30. British Museum Research Publication 175. London: British Museum.

Boschung, Dietrich. 2002. *Gens Augusta: Untersuchungen zu Aufstellung, Wirkung und Bedeutung der Statuengruppen des julisch-claudischen Kaiserhauses*. Monumenta artis romanae 32. Mainz am Rhein: Philipp von Zabern.

Bossert-Radtke, Claudia. 1992. *Die figürlichen Rundskulpturen und Reliefs aus Augst und Kaiseraugst*. Forschungen in Augst 16 = CSIR Schweiz III. Augst: Römermuseum.

Brilliant, Richard. 1999. '"Let the trumpets roar!" The Roman triumph', *Studies in the History of Art* 56: 220–9.

Cesarano, Mario. 2015. *In honorem domus divinae: Introduzione allo studio dei cicli statuari giulio-claudii a Roma e in Occidente*. Roma: Quasar.

Coarelli, Filippo. 1983. 'Il Pantheon, l'apoteosi di Augusto e l'apoteosi di Romolo'. In *Città e architettura nella Roma imperiale, Atti del seminario del 27 Ottobre 1981 nel 25° anniversario dell'Accademia di Danimarca*, edited by Kjeld de Fine Licht, 41–6. Analecta Romana Instituti Danici, Suppl. 10. Roma: Accademia di Danimarca.

Coşkun, Altay. 2014. 'Neue Forschungen zum Kaiserkult in Galatien. Edition der Priester-Inschriften des Ankyraner Sebasteions (Dittenberger II 1903/70, 533 = Bosch 51) und Revision der frühen Provinzialgeschichte'. In *Der Beitrag Kleinasiens zur Kultur- und Geistesgeschichte der griechisch-römischen Antike, Akten des Internationalen Kolloquiums, Wien, 3.-5. November 2010*, edited by Joseph Fischer, 35-73. Vienna: Österreichische Akademie der Wissenschaften.

Crawford, Michael. 1996. *Roman Statutes*. Bulletin of the Institute of Classical Studies Supplementary Series 64. London: Institute of Classical Studies.

De Fine Licht, Kjeld. 1968. *The Rotunda in Rome: A study of Hadrian's Pantheon*. Copenhagen: Nordlundes Bogtrykkeri.

Degrassi, Atilio, 1963. *Inscriptiones Italiae vol. XIII, Fasti et elogia, fasciculus II. Fasti anni Numani et Iuliani*. Roma: Libreria dello Stato.

Derks, Ton. 1998. *Gods, Temples and Ritual Practices: The transformation of religious ideas and values in Roman Gaul*. Amsterdam Archaeological Studies 2. Amsterdam: Amsterdam University Press.

Derks, Ton. 2006. 'Le grand sanctuaire de Lenus Mars à Trèves et ses dédicaces privées: une réinterprétation'. In *Sanctuaires, pratiques cultuelles et territoires civiques dans l'Occident romain*, edited by Monique Dondin-Payre and Marie-Thérèse Raepsaet-Charlier, 239–70. Bruxelles: Timperman.

Derks, Ton. 2020. 'The impact of the empire on cult places and ritual practices in Roman Gaul and Germany'. In *Pervading Empire: Relationality and diversity in the Roman provinces*, edited by Vladimir Mihajlovic and Marko Jankovic, 281–98. Potsdamer Altertumswissenschaftliche Beiträge 73. Stuttgart: Franz Steiner.

Desbat, Armand. 2016. 'Le sanctuaire des Trois Gaules et la question du forum provincial', *Revue Archéologique de l'Est* 65: 303–23.

Dolansky, Fanny. 2008. '*Togam virilem sumere*: coming of age in the Roman world'. In *Roman Dress and the Fabrics of Roman Culture*, edited by Jonathan Edmondson and Alison Keith, 47–70. Phoenix Supplementary Volume 46. Toronto: University of Toronto Press.

Eck, Werner. 2015. 'Römische Amtsträger und die Entwicklung des Herrscherkultes in den Provinzen des Imperium Romanum in der frühen Kaiserzeit'. In *L'Augusteum di Narona*, edited by Giuseppe Zecchini, 145–58. Roma: L'Erma di Bretschneider.

Elsner, John. 1991. 'Cult and sculpture: sacrifice in the Ara Pacis Augustae', *Journal of Roman Studies* 81: 50–61

Fishwick, Duncan, 1986. 'L'autel des Trois Gaules: le témoignage des monnaies', *Bulletin de la Société Nationale des Antiquaires de France*, 1986: 90–111.

Fishwick, Duncan. 1987–2005. *The Imperial Cult in the Latin West: Studies in the ruler cult of the western provinces of the Roman Empire*. Leiden: Brill,

Fishwick, Duncan. 1992. 'The statue of Julius Caesar in the Pantheon', *Latomus* 51: 329–36.

Fishwick, Duncan. 2010. 'Agrippa and the Ara Providentiae', *Zeitschrift für Papyrologie und Epigraphik* 174: 251–58.

Fittschen, Klaus. 1985. 'Zur Datierung des Augustus-Roma-Tempels in Ankara', *Archäologischer Anzeiger* 1985: 309–15.

Geiger, Joseph. 2008. *The First Hall of Fame: A study of the statues in the Forum Augustum*. Mnemosyne Supplements 295. Leiden: Brill.

Glinister, Fay. 2006. 'Reconsidering "religious Romanization"'. In *Religion in Republican Italy*, edited by Celia Schultz and Paul Harvey Jr., 10–33. Yale Classical studies 33. Cambridge: Cambridge University Press.

González, Julián and Michael Crawford. 1986. 'The Lex Irnitana: a new copy of the Flavian municipal law', *Journal of Roman Studies* 76: 147–243.

Gros, Pierre. 1976. *Aurea templa: Recherches sur l'architecture religieuse de Rome à l'époque d'Auguste*. BEFAR 231. Rome: École Française de Rome.

Hänlein-Schäfer, Heidi. 1985. *Veneratio Augusti: Eine Studie zu den Tempeln des ersten römischen Kaisers*. Archaeologica 39. Roma: G. Bretschneider.

Hawkes, Christopher. 1954. 'Archeological theory and method: some suggestions from the Old World', *American Anthropologist* 56: 55–168.

Hetland, Lise. 2015. 'New perspectives on the dating of the Pantheon'. In *The Pantheon: From antiquity to the present*, edited by Tod Marder and Mark Wilson Jones, 79–98. New York: Cambridge University Press.

Hufschmid, Thomas. 2009. *Amphitheatrum in provincia et Italia: Architektur und Nutzung römischer Amphitheater von Augusta Raurica bis Puteoli*. Forschungen in Augst 43. Augst: Römermuseum.

Insoll, Timothy (ed.). 2011. *The Oxford Handbook of the Archaeology of Ritual and Religion*. Oxford: Oxford University Press.

Koeppel, Gerhard. 1987. 'Die historischen Reliefs der römischen Kaiserzeit V. Ara Pacis Augustae, Teil 1', *Bonner Jahrbücher* 187: 101–57.

Koeppel, Gerhard. 1988. 'Die historischen Reliefs der römischen Kaiserzeit V. Ara Pacis Augustae, Teil 2', *Bonner Jahrbücher* 188: 97–106.

Koortbojian, Michael. 2013. *The Divinization of Caesar and Augustus: Precedents, consequences, implications*. Cambridge: Cambridge University Press.

Krencker, Daniel and Martin Schede. 1936. *Der Tempel in Ankara*. Berlin: Archäologisches Institut des Deutschen Reiches.

La Rocca, Eugenio. 2015. 'Agrippa's Pantheon and its origin'. In *The Pantheon: From antiquity to the present*, edited by Tod Marder and Mark Wilson Jones, 49–78. New York: Cambridge University Press.

Latte, Kurt. 1960. *Römische Religionsgeschichte*. Handbuch der Altertumswissenschaft 5(4). München: Beck.

Marder, Tod and Mark Wilson Jones (eds). 2015. *The Pantheon: From antiquity to the present*. New York: Cambridge University Press.

Meyer, Birgit. 2014. 'An author meets her critics: around Birgit Meyer's "Mediation and the genesis of presence: toward a material approach to religion"', *Religion and Society: Advances in Research* 5: 205–54.

Miano, Daniele. 2018. *Fortuna: Deity and concept in archaic and republican Italy*. Oxford: Oxford University Press.

Moretti, Giuseppe. 1967. *Ara Pacis Augustae* (3rd edition). Translation by Veronica Priestley. Roma: Istituto Poligrafico dello Stato – Libreria dello Stato.

Östenberg, Ida. 2009. *Staging the World: Spoils, captives, and representations in the Roman triumphal procession*. Oxford and New York: Oxford University Press.

Orsi, Robert. 2011. 'Belief', *Material Religion* 7: 10–16.

Pinna Caboni, Beatrice. 2018. 'Considerazioni sull'architettura del tempio di Roma e Augusto'. In *Progetto ANCYRA. Il tempio di Augusto e Roma ad Ankara*, edited by Paula Botteri, 127– 333. Trieste: Edizioni Università di Trieste.

Pollini, John. 2012. *From Republic to Empire: Rhetoric, religion, and power in the visual culture of ancient Rome*. Norman, OK: University of Oklahoma Press.

Price, Simon. 1984. *Rituals and Power: The Roman imperial cult in Asia Minor*. Cambridge: Cambridge University Press.

Raja, Rubina and Jörg Rüpke (eds). 2015. *A Companion to the Archaeology of Religion in the Ancient World*. Hoboken, NJ: Wiley Blackwell.

Ramsey, John and Lewis Licht. 1997. *The Comet of 44 BC and Caesar's Funeral Games*. American Classical Studies 39. Atlanta GA: Scholars Press.

Renfrew, Colin. 1994. 'The archaeology of religion'. In *The Ancient Mind: Elements of cognitive archaeology*, edited by Colin Renfrew and Ezra Zubrow, 47–54. Cambridge: Cambridge University Press.

Rives, James. 2010. 'Graeco-Roman religion in the Roman Empire: old assumptions and new approaches', *Currents in Biblical Research* 8: 240–99.

Roels, Evelien. 2018. 'The Queen of Inscriptions Contextualized: The Presence of Civic Inscriptions in the pronaos of Ancient Temples in Hellenistic and Roman Asia Minor (Fourth Century BCE–Second Century CE)'. In *Sacred Thresholds. The door to the Sanctuary in Late Antiquity*, edited by Emilie van Opstall, 221–253. Religions in the Graeco-Roman World 185. Leiden: Brill.

Rossini, Orietta. 2012. *Ara Pacis, Guide* (3rd expanded edition). Milan: Electa.

Rosso, Emmanuelle. 2021. 'Représenter le *Genius Augusti* sous les Julio-Claudiens'. In *L'empereur romain, un mortel parmi les dieux*, edited by Manuella Lambert, 84–91. Nîmes: Musée de la Romanité.

Rüpke, Jörg. 2015. 'Individual choices and individuality in the archaeology of ancient religion'. In *A Companion to the Archaeology of Religion in the Ancient World*, edited by Rubina Raja and Jörg Rüpke, 437–50. Hoboken, NJ: Wiley Blackwell.

Scheid, John. 1990. *Romulus et ses frères: Le collège des frères Arvales, modèle du culte public dans la Rome des Empéreurs*. BEFAR 275. Rome: École Française de Rome.

Scheid, John. 1998. *Commentarii fratrum arvalium qui supersunt: Les copies épigraphiques des protocoles annuels de la confrérie arvale (21 ap. J.C.–304 ap. J.C.)*. Recherches archéologiques à La Magliana; Roma antica 4. Rome: École Française de Rome.

Scheid, John. 2010. 'Epigraphie et rituel: de quelques formulations ambiguës relatives au culte impérial', *Cahiers Gustave Glotz* 21, 285–91.

Scheid, John. 2016. *The Gods, the State and the Individual: Reflections on civic religion in Rome*. Translated and with a foreword by Clifford Ando. Philadelphia, PA: University of Pennsylvania Press.

Scheid, John. 2021. 'Les célébrations et les rites effectués en l'honneur de *Genius* de l'empereur régnant et des *Divi*'. In *L'empereur romain, un mortel parmi les dieux*, edited by Manuella Lambert, 84–91. Nîmes: Musée de la Romanité.

Schnapp, Alain. 1993. *La conquête du passé. Aux origines de l'archéologie*. Paris: Carré.
Schwartz, Glenn. 2017. 'The archaeological study of sacrifice', *Annual Review of Anthropology* 46: 223–40.
Scott Ryberg, Inez. 1955. *Rites of the State Religion in Roman Art*. Memoirs of the American Academy in Rome 22. Rome: American Academy in Rome.
Thomas, Edmund. 2004. 'From the pantheon of the gods to the Pantheon of Rome'. In *Pantheons: Transformations of a monumental idea*, edited by Richard Wrigley and Matthew Craske, 11–34. Aldershot: Ashgate.
Thomas, Edmund. 2017. 'The cult statues of the Pantheon', *Journal of Roman Studies* 107: 146–212.
Torelli, Mario. 1982. *Typology and Structure of Roman Historical Reliefs*. Ann Arbor, MI: University of Michigan Press.
Van Andringa, William. 2002. *La religion en Gaule romaine: Piété et politique (Ier-IIIe siècle apr. J.-C.)*. Paris: Errance.
Van Andringa, William. 2009. *Quotidien des dieux et des hommes: La vie religieuse dans les cités du Vésuve à l'époque romaine*. BEFAR 337. Rome: École Française de Rome.
van Dommelen, Peter. 2006. 'Colonial matters: material culture and postcolonial theory in colonial situations'. In *Handbook of Material Culture*, edited by Christopher Tilley, Webb Keane, Susanne Küchler, Michael Rowlands and Patricia Spyer, 104–25. London: Sage.
Versnel, Hendrik. 1970. *Triumphus: An inquiry into the origin, development, and meaning of the Roman triumph*. Leiden: Brill.
Waddell, Gene. 2015. 'Sources and parallels for the design and construction of the pantheon'. In *The Pantheon: From antiquity to the present*, edited by Tod Marder and Mark Wilson Jones, 132–59. Cambridge: Cambridge University Press.
Webster, Jane. 1995. '*Interpretatio*: Roman word power and the Celtic gods', *Britannia* 26: 153–61.
Webster, Jane. 2001. 'Creolizing the Roman provinces', *American Journal of Archaeology* 105: 209–25.
Webster, Jane. 2003. 'Art as resistance and negotiation'. In *Roman Imperialism and Provincial Art*, edited by Sarah Scott and Jane Webster, 24–51. Cambridge: Cambridge University Press.
Wissowa, Georg. 1904 'Constitutio area', *Hermes* 39: 156–60.
Wissowa, Georg. 1912 (1902). *Religion und Kultus der Römer* (2nd edition). Handbuch der klassischen Altertumswissenschaft 5(4). München: Beck.
Zanker, Paul. 1988. *The Power of Images in the Age of Augustus*. Translated by Alan Shapiro. Ann Arbor, MI: University of Michigan Press.

10
Empires and their boundaries: the archaeology of Roman frontiers

Andrew Gardner

Introduction: framing the Roman frontiers

As with so many aspects of Roman imperial culture, the frontiers of the empire have cast a long shadow in later times. Whether in the sense of the idea of a boundary between 'civilisation' and 'barbarism', or in relation to the physical remains of Roman military occupation and garrisoning of border regions, concepts of the frontiers have been influential on scholarly and popular perceptions of the Roman Empire as a whole. The importance of frontier regions in the definition and transformation of Roman culture is indeed profound, and will be the major theme of this chapter, even if some of the stereotypes about the nature of Rome's imperial boundaries within both academic and wider discourse are open to question. Indeed, the significance of the Roman frontiers lies not in stout defences or resistance to outside influence, but precisely the opposite. The flow of interaction along and across the frontiers, facilitated very much by the military (even as it undoubtedly served in a protective role at times), was crucial to the political and cultural transformation of the empire from the Principate (first to early third centuries CE) to the Dominate (late third to fifth centuries), and beyond into the early Middle Ages. Misunderstanding of the character of Roman frontiers has come about largely because their study has been closely entwined with the politics of more recent empires since the beginnings of Roman military archaeology in the eighteenth century, but also partly because Roman literary writers themselves had a skewed understanding of their role – when they wrote about them at all. In both cases, the predominant colonial ideology of boundaries beyond which lay feared, but also coveted, lands and peoples is foremost. The archaeology of the borderlands tells another story.

Roman concepts of the frontiers developed over time and are less well understood than attitudes to the boundaries of cities, to which they bear some relation. This is not surprising when we consider the limited experience many Roman writers had of the frontier provinces, even if military campaigns were a major theme in their narratives. Indeed, the very idea of limits to Roman power was not always acknowledged before the Principate; in the Republic, when the majority of what became the Roman Empire was actually conquered (or otherwise came under Roman control), there was no *limes*. The more relevant limitation was the extent of a regional governor's power – their *provincia* – which was also not clearly defined and was articulated more in terms of authority over peoples than sections of land (Roman cartography similarly dealt in peoples, places and routeways rather than anything like an abstract Cartesian landscape) (Lintott 1981; Whittaker 1994: 10–38; Elton 1996: 1–28; Edwell 2012). Interestingly, this stands in some contrast to the considerable ritual significance accorded to lines around civic communities (Esmonde Cleary 2005; Pinder 2011). Just as the early Principate saw the organisation of governors and provinces start to become more formalised and territorialised, so too did the frontiers start to acquire a more specific terminology – the *limes/limites* – but initially this referred primarily to military roads built in such areas. Only from the later first century CE does the meaning of 'boundary' start to accrue to this word, and with specific reference to land borders – riverine or maritime boundaries are *ripae* – but not to any defences that might be found upon them. In the period of the Dominate, from the late third century, the term *limes* appears much more frequently and forms part of the military/administrative terminology of frontier regions, but still does not relate to defensive architecture, even though by now this was quite prevalent (Isaac 1988). In a way this exemplifies the remoteness of the writers of Roman literature from the frontiers, but the fact that their use of language does change over time is also revealing of some of the cultural processes that occurred in these regions. The rest of this chapter will demonstrate how the much more extensive archaeological record of those processes can help us to understand them.

Studying the frontiers: a history of research

It is probably no accident that the origins of the modern sub-discipline of Roman *limes* studies coincided with the emergence of the nation-states of central and western Europe in the eighteenth and nineteenth centuries. I refer here not simply to the broad correlation of archaeology with modernity, but more specifically to a developing interest in the defended borders of a 'civilised' empire at the time when various European nations were seeking to define their own boundaries while simultaneously engaging in imperial projects (cf. Hingley 2000; Díaz-Andreu 2007). These points relate particularly to Germany and the United Kingdom, but can be extended to France, Italy, Austria, Hungary and some Balkan nations too. The Roman frontier installations in northern England, and along the Rhine and Danube, sometimes corresponded quite directly with disputed modern boundaries, such as between England and Scotland or Germany and France, and some of the first surveys of some of these sites were undertaken by military personnel involved in those disputes. In North Africa and the Middle East, similar activity occurred, though here in a colonial context with European domination of these regions being legitimised by the Roman remains (Mattingly 1996; Díaz-Andreu 2007: 99–118). Across the former Roman Empire, the mix might be different, but the same ingredients were involved – a cocktail of nationalism, imperialism, militarism and chauvinism, seeking certainties based on the admired Roman past for an uncertain present. As toxic as this ideological mixture sounds, there was important work conducted in this period. General Sir William Roy, for example, working in the Hadrian's Wall region in the late eighteenth century, conducted detailed topographical studies of numerous fort sites (Bidwell 1997: 11–27; James 2002: 7–12; Hingley 2008: 139–48) (Figure 10.1). Of course, in such border areas, cartography and engineering were very much connected to the military, and the overlap between modern military personnel and archaeology on the Roman frontiers continued into the twentieth century, up to and including the Second World War. By this time, while there had been much methodological development, study of the Roman military and its frontier bases had begun to be quite detached from the archaeology of Roman cities and farms, particularly as this was practised in the Mediterranean, but even in frontier provinces like Britain, too. The '*limes* school', as it came to be defined, was typically very much interested in the fortified aspects of frontiers and the structure of the military formations deployed there; it was not concerned with the political, social or economic aspects of these regions or their relationships to the empire as a whole (James 2001, 2002; Collins 2012: 1–5). As such it was influenced by a very particular modern attitude to military experience – the perspective of the officer class – and the nature of national boundaries (even though scholars in the school retained strong international links). This would only begin to change in the 1970s.

Archaeology in the United Kingdom, and in North America, went through many changes in the 1960s and 1970s. The New Archaeology prioritised a generalising, comparative approach to create a more scientific and anthropologically relevant subject. Perhaps inevitably, this sort of perspective had less impact initially in historical, particularistic sub-disciplines like Roman archaeology, and doubly so outside of the Anglosphere in continental European classical scholarship (Dyson 1993a; Andrén 1998: 20–5; Trigger 2006: 500–2). By the 1980s, however, aspects of this school of thought were beginning to appear in studies of the Roman economy, for example (also under the influence of similar changes in history), and indeed in a few works on the frontiers. Although Roman frontier research had long employed implicit comparisons between ancient and modern, studies such as that of Brad Bartel (1980) represented an explicit attempt to derive models of frontier dynamics from cross-cultural studies. In a similar spirit, Stephen Dyson invoked the theory of America's frontier culture put forward by Frederick Jackson Turner in the nineteenth century, to define Rome as a 'frontier society' (Dyson 1985, 1988, 1993b). This revolutionary period in archaeology was not just theoretical, but methodological and empirical, in the sense that it made the most of – and helped further expand – a much larger database than had supported traditional interpretations (cf. Trigger 2006: 5–26). This enabled much more detailed study of frontier societies far from the reach of ancient writers, with new approaches to economy and trade building on much improved information about supply and consumption – including finds beyond the frontier in Germany, Scandinavia and elsewhere – which in turn inspired the use of world-systems theory to link these contexts (e.g. Cunliffe 1988). Increased understanding of cross-frontier communication (e.g. Hedeager 1987; cf. Wells 1980; Barrett et al. 1989) also helped to encourage the development of theories about the political transformation of societies in frontier regions of the empire, again within a comparative anthropological context (e.g. Mattingly 1992). Many of these themes remain crucial in contemporary frontier research, but they have been further complemented by some different developments in the 1990s.

Although a more critical and analytical approach to the nature and function of Roman frontiers had thus emerged by this point, the most prominent group of people usually associated with the frontiers – the

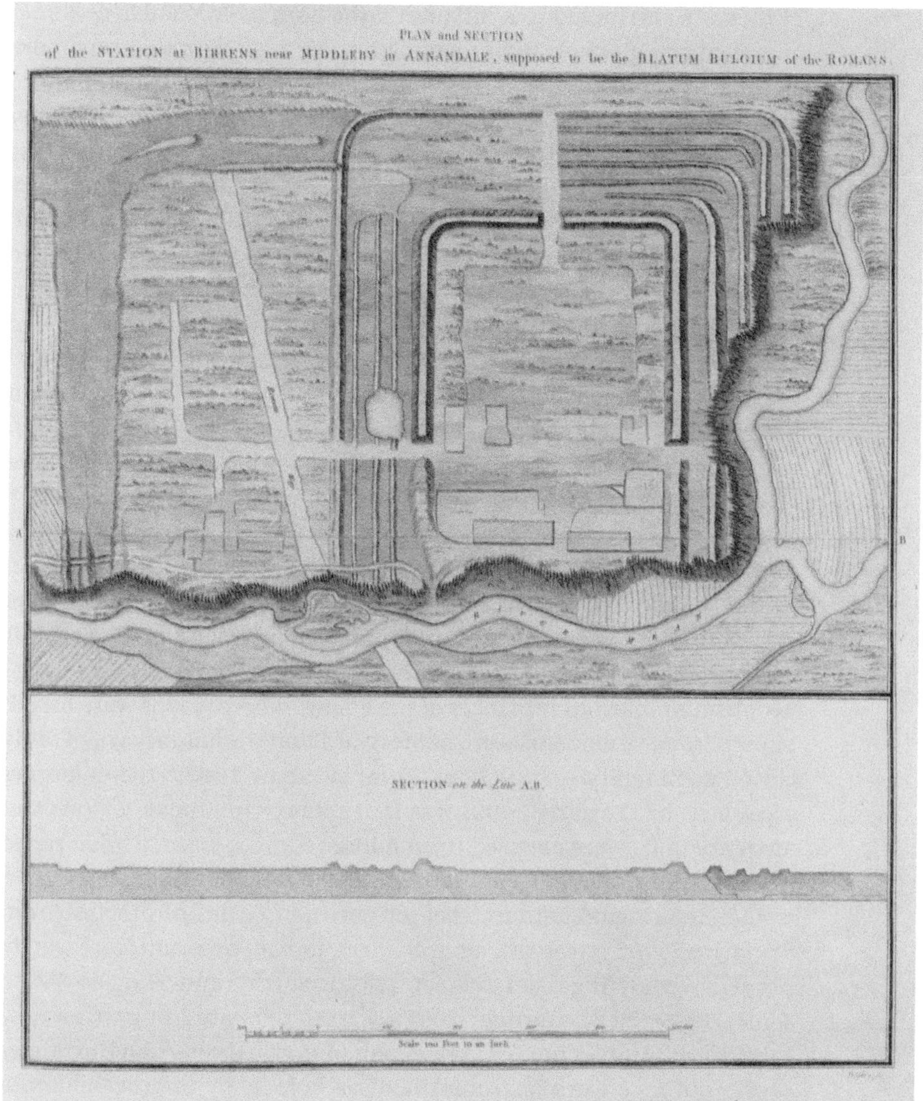

Figure 10.1 Survey of the fort at Birrens, just north of Hadrian's Wall, by William Roy, 1793. Reproduced with the permission of the National Library of Scotland.

Roman military – did not really figure in this wave of anthropological studies. Military archaeology remained firmly bound by traditional perspectives focused on a top-down, structural approach to the institutions of Roman armies and to the archaeology of military sites.

This can be attributed to a mixture of the aforementioned aversion to new theory in Roman studies generally combined with the even more closed community of the *limes* scholars and their continued preference for the authority of military experience over other sources of inspiration (Scott 1993; James 2002). These factors would keep military specialists somewhat apart even from other Roman archaeologists – particularly those in Britain, usually working closely with prehistorians – well into the 1990s, with significant consequences for the study of Roman Britain in particular, as we will see below. In this decade, however, and with the passing of the last members of a generation who had experienced national military service, things did begin to change, and a number of studies of Roman military archaeology – from what might be called a sociological perspective – began to appear (James 2001). Like other branches of Roman archaeology in this period, these were often influenced by aspects of post-processual archaeology, which emerged as a more humanistic and particularistic response to the New Archaeology, largely among prehistorians, and in the UK especially, in the early 1980s. A major theme in these new approaches to the Roman military was the construction of military identity, and how open this was to influence not just from the Roman imperial elite, but from local people in the various provinces of the empire where troops were based. Though some arguments were put forward that the military was a fairly closed community (e.g. Pollard 1996; cf. Shaw 1983), the emerging consensus by the early 2000s was that soldiers in Roman legions and auxiliary units were exposed to, and indeed encouraged, a wide range of interactions. While the military was the pre-eminent state institution in the empire, and held to a shared series of norms of practice from Britain to Egypt, it was also quite changeable over time and increasingly prone to centrifugal tendencies (Goldsworthy and Haynes 1999; James 1999, 2014; Gardner 2007a). Although based in part on new theoretical interest in identity and community, these changing views of the military were also informed, as before, by improvements in archaeological method (detailed finds recording in buildings, for example, supplementing the traditional interest in structural plans), and by interrogation of some of the documentary evidence that Roman military bureaucracy had created (e.g. Birley 2002; cf. Isaac 1993; Alston 1995). Investigation into the everyday lives of soldiers, and those they lived with, continues, but the question of how this relates to the broader themes of frontier dynamics leads us to consider the overall current situation, and where it might be going next.

Future frontiers: new theories and new discoveries

As research on the Roman military has gradually been brought up to date in relation to archaeology more generally, and comparably to other trends in Roman archaeology, some persistent fault-lines have nonetheless become obvious. The segregation of military archaeology from other aspects of Roman studies has continued even as the approaches used by scholars, whether studying forts, towns or farms, have come to be held more in common. Partly this situation is the legacy of the preceding decades already described, but it also owes something to the fact that the major trends in 'civilian' Roman archaeology of the last few years, especially but by no means only in Romano-British studies, have had little to say about the role of the frontiers. Post-colonial approaches to the resistance to and/or influence on Roman culture from conquered peoples, and 'globalisation' approaches to the increased connectivity and interaction between local and 'global' culture in the empire, have both been important trends in the last couple of decades (e.g. Webster and Cooper 1996; Hingley 2005; Pitts and Versluys 2015; cf. Gardner 2013; Versluys 2014). They have rightly worked towards 'decentring' the empire from a traditional perspective that simply reproduced that of the Mediterranean Roman elite. They have largely ignored the role of the military and the frontiers, however, even as they have grappled with the very nature of Roman imperialism. This is understandable in the sense that seeking the perspective of the less powerful in the empire meant initially moving away from the institutions of imperial power, which had also been dominant in traditional historical accounts. However, in trying to understand the process of Roman imperialism such a schism is highly problematic and a reconciliation between these different domains is long overdue. Indeed, just as in the social sciences at large, globalisation theory has had to acknowledge that we live increasingly in, not a 'borderless' world, but one which is 're-bordering' (Bude and Dürrschmidt 2010), so such approaches in Roman studies need to encompass how the frontiers of the empire defined it (cf. Breeze 2018; Fernández-Götz et al. 2020). This 'definition' operates on many levels, as I will explain in the rest of this chapter, and fortunately there are a number of theoretical and methodological tools to help us analyse this process.

As with previous steps forward in Roman archaeology, new approaches are being forged from the interaction of new data, new theories and new questions which are framed by contemporary social and political concerns. In terms of new data, there have been recent

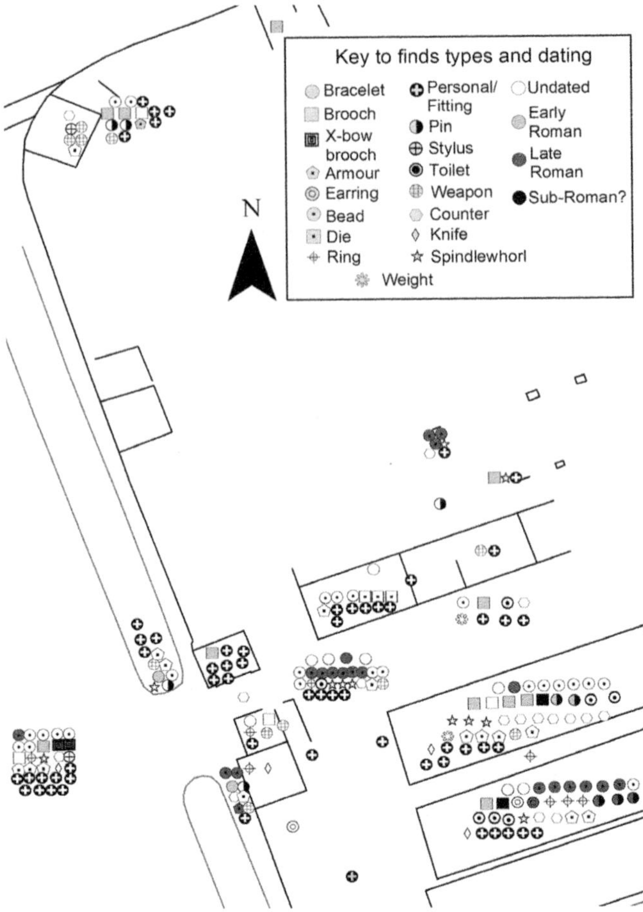

Figure 10.2 Artefact distribution analysis at Birdoswald fort, with small finds plotted in their area of deposition, showing changing patterns in the use of space. © Andrew Gardner, based on data in Wilmott 1997.

improvements at a number of different scales. At the level of individual people, developments in skeletal analysis are important, particularly the application of new methods in bone chemistry which use isotopic signatures to infer information about where a person grew up. This has begun to be invaluable in tracking migration around the Roman world, which is certainly a topic relevant to the military, and to cross-frontier interaction (e.g. Eckardt 2010; Cahill Wilson et al. 2014). At the site level, as already mentioned, excavations in the last couple of decades have been much better than those of previous generations at carefully recording finds and stratigraphy within forts and their associated villages (*vici*). This allows much more effective reconstruction of everyday life in these communities, and how it changed over time (Figure 10.2; e.g. Gardner 2007b; Birley 2013). A further development at this scale has been the much-increased use of geophysical survey to chart the extent of many of the unexcavated portions of military settlements (e.g. Hopewell 2005). Furthermore, thanks in part to the wave of developer-funded excavations in the UK in particular, recent years have seen large areas of the more general settlement map that had hitherto been quite blank begin to be filled in. Where these occur in borderland regions, such as on the Northumberland coastal plain to the north of Hadrian's Wall (Hodgson et al. 2012), they are particularly significant, but the wider new synthesis of rural settlement archaeology (Smith et al. 2016) is important for understanding the nature of a province like Britain as a frontier zone in a more encompassing sense. The application of ever-more sophisticated techniques is enabling of, and developing in response to, some of the new questions and ideas alluded to already.

These questions prioritise issues like identity and the experience of different groups within the empire of political and cultural change, themes which are themselves timely in the twenty-first century. Of particular relevance to the frontiers, however, is an interdisciplinary field of scholarship which has yet to make much of an impact in Roman archaeology, but will surely contribute much to the future theoretical agenda (cf. Boozer 2013; Gardner 2017a; Hingley 2018). 'Border Studies' has some pedigree in geography, anthropology and political science but has flourished recently across these and a range of other disciplines as opposition to globalisation has emerged since the beginning of the present century (Kolossov 2005; Newman 2006; Parker et al. 2009). This has been a period of quite intense 're-bordering' in some regions of the world, including south-eastern Europe and the southern United States, where new physical barriers have been erected or are planned. In many other regions, the 'control' of nation-states over their borders and their citizenry has been asserted in different ways, from the EU Referendum in the UK to the electoral success of nationalist parties in several countries (cf. Gardner 2017b; Niklasson and Hølleland 2018). While to many people these seem to be troubling developments, understanding them is certainly necessary, as they perhaps indicate that there is a persistent tension in human societies between fluidity and boundedness. This is what many scholars working on borders and frontiers are seeking to analyse. While, like any broad interdisciplinary field, difficult to summarise, Border Studies has been much concerned with the productive role of boundaries in affecting social formations, and indeed individuals. Rather than treating them as marginal, accidental phenomena, which simply delineate the interesting substance of culture, or of psychology, we are encouraged to see boundaries and liminality as profoundly shaping that substance. The role of borderlands is thus placed at centre-stage in our analysis of a society, and social boundaries become essential to understanding the constitution of the individual (Kearney 1991; Mignolo and Tlostanova 2006; Parker 2006; Rumford 2006; Mezzadra and Neilson 2013). More specific theoretical tools have also been developed, and we will explore some of these concepts in the following discussion of the nature and role of Roman frontiers.

Case studies: the frontiers of Roman Britain

Development of the British frontiers

A new wave of comparative frontier studies informed by aspects of these approaches is already emerging in archaeology. Among the broader, anthropological volumes (e.g. Mullin 2011; Feuer 2016; Beule 2017), the Introduction to *Untaming the Frontier* summarises cogently three of the processes we might look at in different contexts: 'the emergence of the frontier in relation to a "center" or "core area" ...; the mutually structuring interactions between frontier and core area ...; the development of social exchange, merger, or conflict between previously separate populations brought together on the frontier' (Rodseth and Parker 2005: 4). Traditional approaches to the Roman frontier have focused mainly on the third point, and then primarily on conflict; the new evidence we have, along with the sympathetic inter-disciplinary developments in Border Studies, allow us to say much more about all of the other processes which this quotation encapsulates. In what follows I will focus on Roman Britain as a case study of a frontier region which itself encompassed three different frontier zones, while also making reference to the adjoining frontier in Gaul and to the wider context of changing imperial cultures (Figure 10.3). This focus is necessary not only because the frontiers of the Roman Empire are so extensive, but also because they are very diverse, and Britain is convenient in exemplifying some of this variation in its different frontiers. Moreover, Britain has been studied in more detail than most other parts of the empire, and in a relatively consistent fashion, whereas several of the other major frontier regions are divided between different modern states with different traditions of archaeological research. For all the

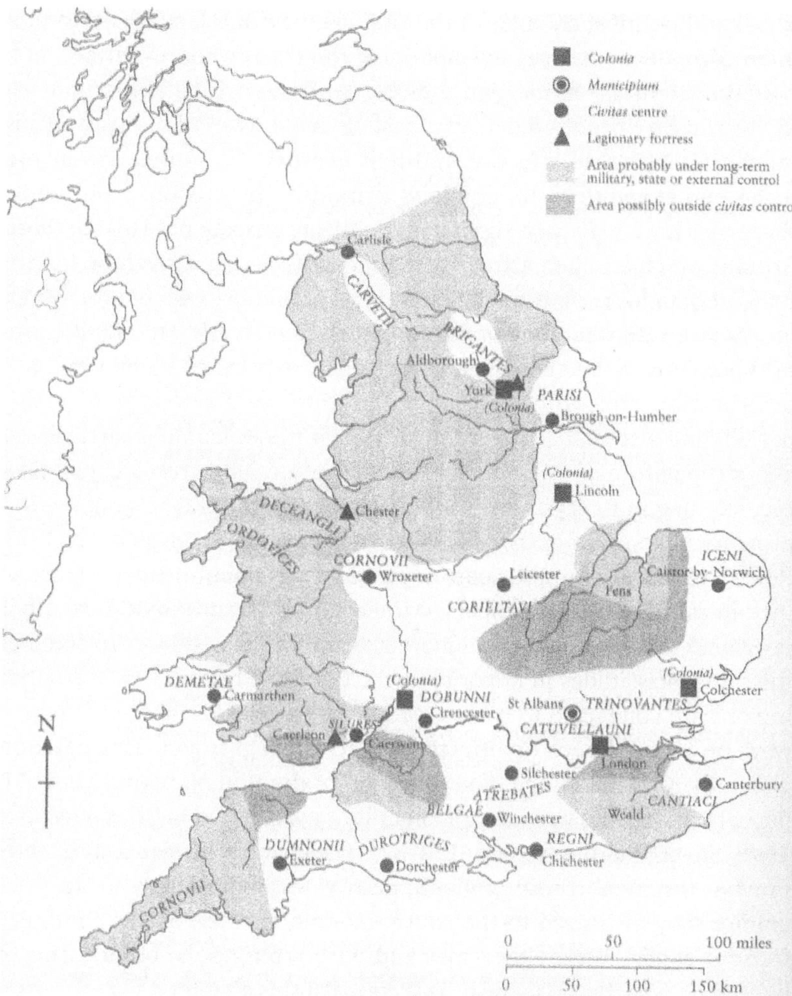

Figure 10.3 General map of Roman Britain. After Mattingly (2006: 262); © David J. Mattingly.

parochialism of Romano-British archaeology, therefore (Fulford 2007; cf. Versluys 2014), it does constitute a useful arena in which to explore imperial frontier processes.

Britain is a somewhat unusual part of the empire, however, and part of the reason for this is how it fits into the chronology of Roman imperialism. As already noted in the Introduction to this chapter, Rome had an empire before it had an emperor. Indeed, the crisis of the late Republic from which Augustus emerged as the first emperor, and the social and political changes of the first century BCE leading up to that point, are all themselves exemplary of the transformative effect on a society of military expansion into new territories. Britain is unusual in that it was conquered in the Principate, under Claudius and his immediate successors in the mid-first century CE. Julius Caesar did make two expeditions to mainland Britain in the 50s BCE, and while these may have had quite significant political consequences for southern Britain, which are increasingly being recognised (e.g. Creighton 2000), the Claudian invasion brought a new level of military occupation, which was to last until sometime in the early fifth century CE. The significance of this relatively late conquest is that many aspects of Roman military organisation and provincial administration were developing in this period, and also that some of the ideas that the Roman elite articulated about the nature of their empire, and its cultural significance, had only recently begun to crystallise (Woolf 1995; Dench 2005). Compared to provinces like some of those in North Africa or in Spain that had been Roman territories for 200 years or more by this point, the experience of Britain can therefore be expected to be somewhat different. Like other provinces, however, once conquered, *Britannia* was subject to some of the same vicissitudes in imperial interest and the histories of its frontier regions are connected to others, particularly those on the Rhine, where wars often had knock-on effects on the British garrison. This garrison generally remained large, and for much of the Roman period about 10 per cent of the whole of the Roman military was based in Britain (Millett 1990: 56–60; Mattingly 2006: 128–32). These troops lived predominantly in what is now northern England, and Wales; increasingly in the later empire they also lived in the south. Examining each of these military frontier zones, at varying scales and with reference to other forms of boundary, will comprise the next sections of this chapter.

Even though the conquest of Britain came late in the process of Roman expansion, and shortly after the practice of the construction of long-term military bases in frontier areas became more typical, the British frontiers took some time to take their most recognisable form. Indeed, that form was always changing, once we begin to look at it closely. The invasion force in 43 CE was large for a Roman army – four legions totalling 20,000 soldiers and a similar number of auxiliaries, in smaller units – and it soon spread out across southern Britain. Early forts and fortresses were generally short-lived (e.g. Alchester; Sauer et al. 2000), with some becoming towns in due course. The campaigns in the upland regions of Wales and the north were more protracted than the conquest of the lowlands; the latter took a handful of years (notwithstanding the Boudican revolt of 60/61 CE), while the former took several decades, concluding only in the 70s for Wales and the 80s for the north, although the whole of the mainland was never fully occupied (James 2011). Throughout this period, Wales was an active conflict zone, with garrisons and roads gradually being established in several areas while others remained resistant. Various of the roads built across England may have been provisional frontiers, such as the Fosse Way and the Stanegate (Hodgson 2000; Burnham and Davies 2010: 37–48), but in the 120s, the emperor Hadrian took the drastic step of initiating construction of a wall, running just north of the Stanegate, right across the width of Britain between Newcastle and Carlisle. One might think this was to be a permanent frontier, but just 20 years later Antoninus Pius launched a campaign into what is now Scotland which led to a new, replacement wall being constructed between Edinburgh and Glasgow. This only lasted for a decade or so, however, before Hadrian's Wall was reoccupied and its forts became the permanent garrison line, supported by numerous forts to the south, and a few to the north (Hodgson 2017: 70–100). Later expeditions did head north, such as that under the emperor Septimius Severus in 208–10, but Hadrian's Wall was not abandoned again for some 250 years. In the meantime, the garrison of Wales had been reduced as the north became the major conflict zone in the early second century, and this too then remained fairly static until the fourth century, when it would be complemented with coastal forts like those which had begun to be built in the third century around the south-eastern coast of England. The latter, though accumulating somewhat gradually, seem ultimately to have been designated as the 'Saxon Shore' frontier command. This too lasted until the end of Roman administration of Britain early in the fifth century (Pearson 2002). The military archaeology of Britain therefore relates to multiple frontiers – provisional and permanent, land and maritime, and external and internal (with some of the Saxon Shore forts facing similar Channel-defence forts in northern Gaul). What was happening in each of these zones, and how the military institutions related to other aspects of the province, can now be considered in a little more detail.

Wales and the Irish Sea zone

To begin in the west, with the region that experienced the longest period as a frontier zone, Wales is actually a dual frontier even in just the military sense. On the one hand it faces outwards, toward Ireland and further unconquered (but not unknown) peoples; on the other hand it faces inwards, as a region which was never left unsupervised by the colonial authority, and which was therefore divided from lands to the east (Figure

10.4). Two legionary fortresses, at Caerleon in the south and Chester in the north, were initially located in the 70s CE to support the fairly extensive network of roads and auxiliary forts across Wales. Once this had dwindled half a century later to a handful of forts, these fortresses remained occupied as the front-line of an internal boundary between the largely military-administered Welsh highlands and the civilian *civitates* (administrative regions) of lowland Britain – much like York in the north. The Welsh landscape became somewhat internally fractured as well, between communities in and around forts that were nominally closely linked to the Roman state, and pastoral and agricultural communities whose engagement with the changes to material culture in Britain in this period was patchy until the third and fourth centuries (White 2007: 123–47). Yet there was interaction between these communities, through supply and recruitment as well as the organisation of taxation and other state demands, such that boundaries were crossed as well as made. This is evident at the military sites themselves, where sites like Caernarfon and Caerleon are the locations of much less distinctive practices in the fourth century than in the second (Gardner 2007a: 217–53; cf. Haynes 2013). This is not just a product of the social processes taking place within the Welsh frontier zone, but also the connections stretching beyond it – to the wider province and the Roman state, also changing over time, and crucially across the Irish Sea to the people of Ireland. While long-neglected, there is increasing awareness of the evidence for contacts between Ireland and other regions – Gaul, Scotland and Roman Britain, with Wales being the most immediate link to the latter (Cahill Wilson 2014). This evidence, including numerous finds of metalwork and other objects, some in significant contexts like burials and ritual sites, supports an interpretation along the lines of some of the anthropological theory mentioned earlier, that Irish societies changed in response to the nearby presence of the Roman Empire. This seems to have fed a cycle of more and more contact, via raiding and/or migration, that explains the new Roman forts in Wales (e.g. at Cardiff) from the late third century, and also the inscribed stones bearing Irish script ('ogham', itself inspired by Latin), in the fifth century (Newman 1998; Edwards 2001; Rance 2001; cf. Ferguson and Whitehead 2000; Gardner 2022). The inherent dynamism of the frontier zone and its complex interactions between different groups of people can be expected to produce just this mixture of boundary-making, driven by conflict, and boundary-crossing, driven by co-operation; the two processes frequently go hand-in-hand (Donnan and Wilson 1999; Barth 2000). This then influenced the 'other side' of the frontier zone, enhancing the differences between Wales and England (cf.

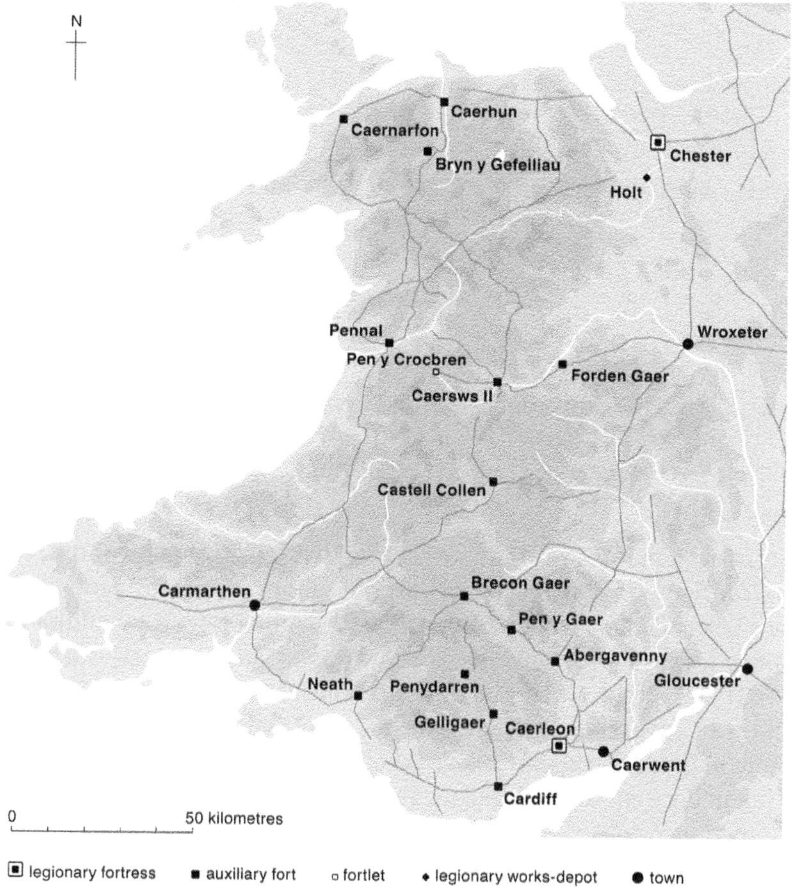

Figure 10.4 Location map of main forts in Wales, mid-second century CE. Drawn by Christina Unwin, after Burnham and Davies (2010: 53); © Christina Unwin.

White 2007: 195–207). Whether this degree of fluidity can also be found in a frontier based not on a sea channel but on a land wall is an interesting question, to which we can turn by looking at northern England.

The northern frontier zone

The Hadrian's Wall frontier is one of the best-known, in both popular and academic contexts, in the empire (Figure 10.5). Yet important aspects of the linear barrier itself, and of the communities living on and around it, are still unclear, or have only recently been elucidated. This might seem

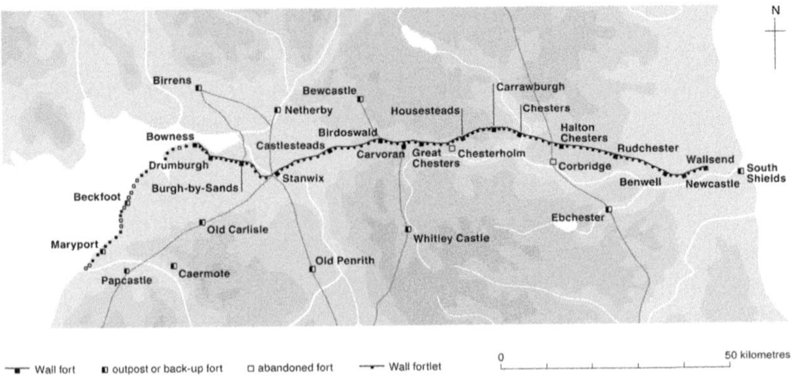

Figure 10.5 Location map of Hadrian's Wall and environs. Drawn by Christina Unwin, after Jones and Mattingly (1990: 114); © Christina Unwin.

surprising, but it is worth remembering that the attribution of the Wall to Hadrian was only settled just over a century ago, many generations of earlier scholars having been confused by the presence of additional linear features (especially the so-called *vallum*, an earthwork behind the Wall) and rather unclear references in ancient sources, itself revealing of the relative ignorance of Roman and early Medieval writers about the frontier defences (Breeze 2014). What is well understood now is that the Wall underwent several changes even during its construction, including to its dimensions, and the replacement of turf sections to the west in stone. Most significant of these changes, though, was the movement of forts up to the Wall itself, the initial plan seemingly being to keep the pre-existing garrisons on the Stanegate road, just to the south. Along with the milecastles and turrets – fortlets at regular intervals all along the Wall – the curtain of the Wall was thus heavily garrisoned when completed. In front of it lay a ditch, and there is increasing evidence from excavation for spiked defences on the strip of ground between ditch and Wall (Hodgson 2017: 161–4). Behind it lay a military road, and the *vallum*, comprising a ditch and two banks. Overall, the completed system appears to be the definitive protective frontier of the Roman period, more elaborate than any of the other linear land frontiers elsewhere in the empire. However, the positioning of the forts on the Wall was itself probably in part designed to facilitate easier deployment to its north side. Furthermore, each milecastle had a gate through the Wall, and others were provided at key routeways. Meanwhile, the *vallum* was not maintained throughout the life of the Wall, being breached at the time of the Antonine advance, then reinstated, but then allowed to lapse again in the third century (Hodgson 2017: 173–5). Together with the forts which lay both to the north and the south of the Wall on major roads, all of these factors help us place the Wall in context as but one element of a frontier zone.

Debate about the precise balance of exclusion and accommodation that the Wall allowed continues (Bidwell 2008; Symonds 2013, 2021; Breeze 2014: 109–34; Hodgson 2017: 157–75), and probably both were important at different times and in different circumstances along the length of the frontier. Other forms of evidence similarly suggest a complementarity between processes of division and of connection. Rural settlement archaeology, as already mentioned, has come a long way in recent years in the regions surrounding Hadrian's Wall, and this shows some notable differences in the landscapes to north and south of the fortification. A cleared zone of about 10 miles seems to have been created north of the Wall, with pre-existing settlements here being abandoned as the frontier line was built. Beyond this, the settlement pattern of what is now Scotland is complex, but while evidence for Roman contact with these areas certainly exists, it is mainly in the form of metalwork and coins. This material seems to have been monopolised by an elite in society which increasingly concentrated political power, and perhaps – as in Ireland – controlled more centralised groupings. In Scotland, the Picts would emerge as the named group that subsumed others in the later Roman period (Hunter 2007a). Meanwhile, to the south, although many rural settlements looked fairly similar to those in the north, others were developing into villa-style farms such as those popular in the south of *Britannia* with the civic elite class; examples in the Tees valley, about 30 miles south of the Wall, have recently been discovered (e.g. Ingleby Barwick; Willis and Carne 2013). However, for all these indications of a meaningful political and, perhaps, cultural frontier, there are at least two strands of evidence which highlight a more unifying aspect of the borderlands. One of these is the existence of a range of types of metalwork which reflect indigenous traditions but which span the frontier region and, indeed, well beyond to the south, while also being quite common finds in forts. These tend to be items of personal adornment, such as brooches, suggesting that – as indeed in some of their more martial equipment – Roman soldiers adopted many local fashions wherever they were stationed (and as, over time, they were recruited more locally too) (Hunter 2007b, 2008; Collins 2010; James 2014; cf. Leahy 2007; Coulston 2010). The spread of such items among other members of the provincial and 'free' populations suggests some degree of shared identity, perhaps contrasting with other influences from the wider empire, with which soldiers were also in contact. The second category of evidence, which perhaps explains how this commonality emerged, comes from forts themselves, where finds and architectural changes attest to local interactions. The *vici* epitomise this, but later – when these were largely abandoned in the later third century (Hodgson 2017: 150–3) – finds attesting to market and communal feasting activity can be found within the forts, at the same time that many structures were being modified in their functions. These suggest that the military was a broad-based and permeable community (Gardner 2007a; Collins 2012; Petts 2013; cf. Hodgson and Bidwell 2004). The military, much like the Wall itself, was a liminal entity that both divided and united society in a province like *Britannia* and – because it was a key element of the Roman state – this had repercussions all the way to Rome.

The 'Saxon Shore' and internal frontiers

An inkling of how these frontier phenomena affected the whole of the Roman Empire can be gleaned from one of the events associated with the third case-study region, the so-called 'Saxon Shore' (Figure 10.6). This is a maritime frontier somewhat like the Irish Sea, except that the immediately facing coast of northern Gaul was also a part of the empire, and the 'external' face of the frontier was probably, in conjunction with forts on the Gallic coast, directed to the east and to regions beyond the Rhine frontier. However, for a period in the late third century, when several of the Shore forts were built, it may be that these fortifications were used against the empire itself, as in this period Britain was home to one of the break-away states which were a feature of this period of Roman history. The so-called 'British empire' ruled by Carausius and Allectus followed on from the Gallic empire of the 260s and 270s, which was contemporary with the briefly independent Palmyrene kingdom in the east (Casey 1994; Smith 2013). What these entities had in common is instructive; in none of them was Roman culture or the concept of Roman power rejected; they were all situations where local leaders sought to assume a portion of Roman imperial power over a smaller area that might be self-sufficient in military (and other) means. As such, they symbolise the way in which frontier regions were – precisely because of the combination of factors operating around the frontier – coming to be more coherent, and beginning to influence the 'centre' in a more profound way. All were reintegrated into the empire by the reign of Diocletian (284-305 CE), although through the fourth century and into the fifth similar sorts of processes were to play out on numerous occasions. In this period,

Figure 10.6 Coastal bases of the later Roman period in Britain. Drawn by Christina Unwin, after Pearson (2002: 56); © Christina Unwin.

the 'Saxon Shore' resumed its purpose of defence against coastal raiding, and its archaeology bears some comparison with the Welsh frontier, with the interesting difference that the string of a dozen forts along the coast were very much part of the 'civilian' province. Many of these forts, and their counterparts across the English Channel, like Oudenburg in Belgium (Vanhoutte 2015), were characterised by a later Roman style of defensive architecture, distinct from the forts of the Wall and indeed the earliest Shore forts like Reculver, in Kent. Whereas the second-century forts were built more as protected encampments intended to be used offensively, later third and fourth century forts had a more defensive aspect, with projecting towers and higher walls (Pearson 2002: 67–77). Their plans also seem to have been more flexible – or simply built in more ephemeral materials – than those of the older forts, as barracks have rarely been clearly identified in any of the excavated Shore forts. There is artefactual and burial evidence for quite mixed communities, in terms of gender and age, which is also true on the Wall, and has often been interpreted as relating to reduced unit sizes in the fourth century – but families residing in forts may well not only be a late Roman phenomenon (Cunliffe 1975; Vanhoutte 2015; cf. Driel-Murray 1995; Allison 2013; Hodgson 2017: 119–20). The key point is that the idea of the fort as a focus for interaction, rather than a bastion of isolation, is reinforced by evidence from both sides of the Channel.

The emergence of a militarised internal frontier along the Channel coasts in the later third and fourth centuries fits into a broader pattern of changes to provincial society in Britain, and parts of Gaul, in this period. While we need to be cautious about the narratives of 'decline and fall' popularised by some late Roman – and many more modern – writers, the imperial state was certainly under some strain in this era. Whether this was due to 'barbarian' threats, or the internal tensions generated by increasing economic and political power at the fringes, eclipsing that of the centre, is an interesting question, and in either case the frontiers are key to the narrative (cf. Miller 1996; James 2014). In Britain, as across the empire, what had initially been one province had been sub-divided, first into two and then into four, superficially as part of efforts to dilute local gubernatorial power by emperors who were anxious about usurpers. This seems also, however, part of a trend to attempt to scrutinise local elites, who administered the *civitates*, more closely. This may explain two important archaeological trends of the fourth century, where towns seem to be increasingly devoid of civic spending by elites, which had hitherto equipped them with public buildings – many now falling out of use – while some of the villas in the south of England become spectacular in scale (Mattingly 2006: 325–50; Gerrard 2013: 118–55). Across the landscape, then, internal boundaries, both physical and social, were being reconfigured in this period – between new provincial jurisdictions, between fortified towns and the villas and villages of the countryside, and between social classes. The external frontiers, notionally protecting this landscape against external threats, now equally frequently furnished troops for usurpers in the vein of Carausius (e.g. Magnentius in the 350s, Magnus Maximus in the 380s), directed at more firmly wresting imperial power from the emperor in Rome (or one of the other imperial capitals of the period) (Gerrard 2013: 15–72). The presence of imperial frontiers in Britain thus, over time, led to economic and cultural changes that were a direct contributor to the political fragmentation of the western empire, but also of Britain itself, laying the foundations of diverse local states that would emerge as British and Saxon kingdoms, once that empire had withdrawn.

Conclusion: borderland processes and Rome

The frontier archaeology of Roman Britain thus exemplifies the central role that the peripheries of the empire played in its transformation over time. As already noted, Britain is in some respects unusual – in its geographical situation, its military presence and indeed in the history of research within it – but as a case study in frontier formation, development and process, it is fairly typical. Across the empire, the configuration of frontier installations was varied, but in every region military communities interacted with local people, both friendly and hostile, and mediated change to both those localities and the wider culture of the Roman state (cf. Alston 1995; Esmonde Cleary 2013; Smith 2013). Beyond the empire, too, whether in Germany, Mesopotamia or the Sudan, the frontier impinged upon, but also enabled, political changes such as those we have noted in Ireland and Scotland. The influence of Roman material culture, whether understood as such or not, and the simple presence of the empire, interacted with indigenous agencies to shape the emergence of a number of cultural formations from Persia to Scandinavia (see e.g. papers in González Sánchez and Guglielmi 2013; Wells 1999). And within the empire, the borderlands also exerted their influence. In the later Roman Empire, although power still derived from some of the traditional symbols of Roman culture in its narrow sense, new forms of 'being Roman' came from the periphery. Some of these developments were resisted in the centre, as is evident for example in late Roman laws banning 'barbarian' fashions (in reality now military fashions) in Rome (Gardner 2007a: 234–6; James 2014). Others were embraced, eventually at least, particularly the new religions redolent with the exoticism of the eastern fringes of empire – the Egyptian Isis, the Persian Mithras and ultimately Christianity (Bispham 2008: 225–33). At the broadest scale, then, a history of the Roman Empire can be written from its frontiers.

At the smaller scales, however, challenges and problems remain. The evidence drawn upon in this chapter to characterise the different frontiers within Roman Britain highlights inconsistencies and tensions, and some gaps too. Somewhat contradictory lines of evidence, for example about how defensive the Hadrian's Wall frontier was, might indicate that errors of interpretation require correction one way or another, or that new evidence needs to be discovered to help us decide one way or another. This may well be true, but it is equally likely that, when considering borderlands and frontier regions, we should *expect* contradiction. Frontiers are definitively liminal spaces inhabited by people who are sometimes one thing, and sometimes another; yet this makes them productive of the social formations which they ostensibly delimit (Nail 2016: 1–21). Militarised frontiers are often erected to prevent interaction – of which conflict is one form – yet interaction often erodes them to the point of collapse (Donnan and Wilson 1999: 87–150). We do, however, need to undertake further, detailed research to understand more precisely how social practices changed over time in the vicinity of forts and other installations, and to learn more about the mobility of the military within Britain, and therefore its engagement with other groups across the province, in contexts from recruitment, to supply, to exploitation (cf. Given 2004). The consciousness of the frontier of ordinary Romano-Britons in the centre of what is now England is also something we know little about. Beyond the frontier, there is also much research still to be done to continue the pioneering studies of recent years into changing material culture and settlement archaeology (e.g. Hunter 2007a; Cahill Wilson 2014). As well as enhancing our understanding of the influence of Rome beyond the *limes*, this is essential for shifting our viewpoint on how Rome itself changed over time. Traditionally, study of the frontiers has been dominated by a narrow archaeology of the military which has become alienated from the archaeology of the empire as a whole. Hopefully the directions of research pointed to in this chapter show that we are beginning to turn that perspective around and see how, looking from the frontier regions inward, it is the periphery which should be central to future accounts of Roman imperialism.

Acknowledgements

Many thanks to Jeremy Tanner and Rui Pang for taking care of by far the lion's share of organisation for the conference at which this chapter was presented, and to Jeremy for comments on this chapter. My thinking about frontiers has been influenced by many friends and colleagues, including Richard Hingley, Kerstin Hofmann, Fraser Hunter, Bill Sillar and Jake Weekes. Part of the research for this chapter was completed during a fellowship at the Römisch-Germanische Kommission in Frankfurt in January 2018, and I would like to thank all of the colleagues there for their welcome and discussion.

References

Allison, Penelope M. 2013. *People and Spaces in Roman Military Bases*. Cambridge: Cambridge University Press.

Alston, Richard. 1995. *Soldier and Society in Roman Egypt: A social history*. London: Routledge.

Andrén, Anders. 1998. *Between Artifacts and Texts: Historical archaeology in global perspective*. Trans. A. Crozier. New York: Plenum Press.

Barrett, John C., Andrew P. Fitzpatrick and Lesley Macinnes (eds). 1989. *Barbarians and Romans in North-West Europe*. BAR International Series 471. Oxford: British Archaeological Reports.

Bartel, Brad. 1980. 'Colonialism and cultural responses: problems related to Roman provincial analysis', *World Archaeology* 12(1): 11–26.

Barth, Fredrik. 2000. 'Boundaries and connections'. In *Signifying Identities: Anthropological perspectives on boundaries and contested values*, edited by Anthony P. Cohen, 17–36. London: Routledge.

Beule, Christine D. (ed.). 2017. *Frontiers of Colonialism*. Gainesville: University Press of Florida.

Bidwell, Paul. 1997. *Roman Forts in Britain*. London: Batsford/English Heritage.

Bidwell, Paul. 2008. 'Did Hadrian's Wall have a wall-walk?' In *Understanding Hadrian's Wall*, edited by Paul Bidwell, 129–43. Kendal: The Arbeia Society.

Birley, Anthony. 2002. *Garrison Life at Vindolanda: A band of brothers*. Stroud: Tempus.

Birley, Andrew. 2013. 'The fort wall: a great divide?' In *Breaking Down Boundaries: Hadrian's Wall in the 21st century*, edited by Rob Collins and Matthew Symonds, 85–104. JRA Supplementary Series, 93. Portsmouth, RI: Journal of Roman Archaeology.

Bispham, Edward. 2008. 'Religions'. In *Roman Europe*, edited by Edward Bispham, 203–33. Oxford: Oxford University Press.

Boozer, Anna L. 2013. 'Frontiers and borderlands in imperial perspectives: exploring Rome's Egyptian frontier', *American Journal of Archaeology* 117(2): 275–92.

Breeze, David J. 2014. *Hadrian's Wall: A history of archaeological thought*. Kendal: Cumberland and Westmorland Antiquarian and Archaeological Society.

Breeze, David J. 2018. 'The value of studying Roman frontiers', *Theoretical Roman Archaeology Journal* 1(1), 1–17, https://doi.org/10.16995/traj.212.

Bude, Heinz and Jörg Dürrschmidt. 2010. 'What's wrong with globalization? Contra "flow speak" – towards an existential turn in the theory of globalization', *European Journal of Social Theory* 13: 481–500.

Burnham, Barry C. and Jeffrey L. Davies. 2010. *Roman Frontiers in Wales and the Marches*. Aberystwyth: Royal Commission on the Ancient and Historic Monuments of Wales.

Cahill Wilson, Jacqueline. 2014. 'Romans and Roman material in Ireland: a wider social perspective'. In *Late Iron Age and 'Roman' Ireland*, edited by Jacqueline Cahill Wilson, Ger Dowling, Michael Ann Bevivino and Philippa Barry, 11–58. Dublin: Wordwell/The Discovery Programme.

Cahill Wilson, Jacqueline, Christopher Standish and Elizabeth O'Brien. 2014. 'Investigating mobility and migration in the later Irish Iron Age'. In *Late Iron Age and 'Roman' Ireland*, edited by Jacqueline Cahill Wilson, Ger Dowling, Michael Ann Bevivino and Philippa Barry, 127–49. Dublin: Wordwell/The Discovery Programme.

Casey, Patrick John. 1994. *Carausius and Allectus: The British usurpers*. London: Batsford.

Collins, Rob. 2010. 'Brooch use in the 4th to 5th century frontier'. In *Finds from the Frontier: Material culture in the 4th–5th centuries*, edited by Rob Collins and Lindsay Allason-Jones, 64–77. Research Report 162. York: Council for British Archaeology.

Collins, Rob. 2012. *Hadrian's Wall and the End of Empire: The Roman frontier in the 4th and 5th centuries*. London: Routledge.

Coulston, John C.N. 2010. 'Military equipment of the "long" 4th century on Hadrian's Wall'. In *Finds from the Frontier: Material culture in the 4th–5th centuries*, edited by Rob Collins and Lindsay Allason-Jones, 50–63. Research Report 162. York: Council for British Archaeology.

Creighton, John. 2000. *Coins and Power in Late Iron Age Britain*. Cambridge: Cambridge University Press.

Cunliffe, Barry. 1975. *Excavations at Portchester Castle, I: Roman*. London: Society of Antiquaries.

Cunliffe, Barry. 1988. *Greeks, Romans and Barbarians: Spheres of interaction*. London: Guild Publishing.

Dench, Emma. 2005. *Romulus' Asylum: Roman identities from the age of Alexander to the age of Hadrian*. Oxford: Oxford University Press.

Díaz-Andreu, Margarita. 2007. *A World History of Nineteenth Century Archaeology: Nationalism, colonialism, and the past*. Oxford: Oxford University Press.

Donnan, Hastings and Thomas M. Wilson. 1999. *Borders: Frontiers of identity, nation and state*. Oxford: Berg.

Driel-Murray, Carol van. 1995. 'Gender in question'. In *Theoretical Roman Archaeology: Second conference proceedings*, edited by Peter Rush, 3–21. Aldershot: Avebury.

Dyson, Stephen L. 1985. *The Creation of the Roman Frontier*. Princeton, NJ: Princeton University Press.

Dyson, Stephen L. 1988. 'Frederick Jackson Turner and the Roman frontier in Italy', *Revue des Archéologues et Historiens d'Art de Louvain* 21: 7–17.

Dyson, Stephen L. 1993a. 'From new to New Age archaeology: archaeological theory and classical archaeology – a 1990s perspective', *American Journal of Archaeology* 97(2): 195–206.

Dyson, Stephen L. 1993b. 'The Roman frontier in comparative perspective: the view from North America'. In *Frontières d'Empire: Nature et signification des frontières romains*, edited by Patrice Brun, Sander van der Leeuw and Charles R. Whittaker, 149–57. Nemours: APRAIF/CNRS.

Eckardt, Hella (ed.). 2010. *Roman Diasporas: Archaeological approaches to mobility and diversity in the Roman Empire*. JRA Supplementary Series 78. Portsmouth, RI: Journal of Roman Archaeology.

Edwards, Nancy. 2001. 'Early-medieval inscribed stones and stone sculpture in Wales: context and function', *Medieval Archaeology* 45: 15–39.

Edwell, Peter M. 2012. 'Definitions of Roman imperialism'. In *A Companion to Roman Imperialism*, edited by Dexter Hoyos. Leiden: Brill. https://doi.org/10.1163/9789004236462_004.

Elton, Hugh. 1996. *Frontiers of the Roman Empire*. London: Batsford.

Esmonde Cleary, Simon. 2005. 'Beating the bounds: ritual and the articulation of urban space in Roman Britain'. In *Roman Working Lives and Urban Living*, edited by Ardle Mac Mahon and Jennifer Price, 1–17. Oxford: Oxbow Books.

Esmonde Cleary, Simon. 2013. *The Roman West AD 200–500: An archaeological study*. Cambridge: Cambridge University Press.

Ferguson, R. Brian. and Neil L. Whitehead. 2000. 'The violent edge of empire'. In *War in the Tribal Zone: Expanding states and indigenous warfare* (2nd edition), edited by R. Brian Ferguson and Neil L. Whitehead, 1–30. Santa Fe, NM: School of American Research Press/Oxford: James Currey.

Fernández-Götz, Manuel, Dominik Maschek, and Nico Roymans. 2020. 'The dark side of the empire: Roman expansionism between object agency and predatory regime', *Antiquity* 94(378): 1630–9.

Feuer, Bryan. 2016. *Boundaries, Borders and Frontiers in Archaeology*. Jefferson, NC: McFarland.

Fulford, Michael. 2007. 'An insular obsession', *Britannia* 38: 367–9.

Gardner, Andrew. 2007a. *An Archaeology of Identity: Soldiers and society in late Roman Britain*. Walnut Creek, CA: Left Coast Press.

Gardner, Andrew. 2007b. 'Artefacts, contexts and the archaeology of social practices'. In *Promoting Roman Finds: Context and theory*, edited by Richard Hingley and Steven Willis, 128–39. Oxford: Oxbow Books.

Gardner, Andrew. 2013. 'Thinking about Roman imperialism: postcolonialism, globalisation and beyond?' *Britannia* 44: 1–25.

Gardner, Andrew. 2017a. 'Roman Britain from the outside: comparing Western and Northern frontier cultures'. In *'Romans' and 'Barbarians' Beyond the Frontiers: Archaeology, ideology and identities in the north*, edited by Sergio González Sánchez and Alexandra Guglielmi, 34–47. Oxford: Oxbow Books.

Gardner, Andrew. 2017b. 'Brexit, boundaries, and imperial identities – a comparative view', *Journal of Social Archaeology* 17(1): 3–26.

Gardner, Andrew. 2022. 'Practicing the borders: structure and creativity on the Roman frontiers'. In *Sozialität – Materialität – Praxis/Sociality – Materiality – Practice*, edited by Tobias Kienlin and Richard Bußmann, 321–34. Köln: Kölner Beiträge zu Archäologie und Kulturwissenschaften.

Gerrard, James. 2013. *The Ruin of Roman Britain: An archaeological perspective*. Cambridge: Cambridge University Press.

Given, Michael. 2004. *The Archaeology of the Colonized*. London: Routledge.

Goldsworthy, Adrian and Ian Haynes (eds). 1999. *The Roman Army as a Community*. JRA Supplementary Series 34. Portsmouth, RI: Journal of Roman Archaeology.

González Sánchez, Sergio and Alexandra Guglielmi (eds). 2013. *'Romans' and 'Barbarians' Beyond the Frontiers: Archaeology, ideology and identities in the north*. Oxford: Oxbow Books.
Haynes, Ian 2013. *Blood of the Provinces: The Roman auxilia and the making of provincial society from Augustus to the Severans*. Oxford: Oxford University Press.
Hedeager, Lotte. 1987. 'Empire, frontier and the barbarian hinterland: Rome and Northern Europe from AD 1–400'. In *Center and Periphery in the Ancient World*, edited by Michael Rowlands, Mogens T. Larsen and Kristian Kristiansen, 125–40. Cambridge: Cambridge University Press.
Hingley, Richard. 2000. *Roman Officers and English Gentlemen: The imperial origins of Roman archaeology*. London: Routledge.
Hingley, Richard. 2005. *Globalizing Roman Culture: Unity, diversity and empire*. London: Routledge.
Hingley, Richard. 2008. *The Recovery of Roman Britain 1586–1906: A colony so fertile*. Oxford: Oxford University Press.
Hingley, Richard. 2018. 'Frontiers and mobilities: the frontiers of the Roman Empire and Europe', *European Journal of Archaeology* 21(1): 78–95.
Hodgson, Nick. 2000. 'The Stanegate: a frontier rehabilitated', *Britannia* 31: 11–22.
Hodgson, Nick. 2017. *Hadrian's Wall: Archaeology and history at the limit of Rome's empire*. Marlborough: Robert Hale.
Hodgson, Nick and Paul T. Bidwell. 2004. 'Auxiliary barracks in new light: recent discoveries on Hadrian's Wall', *Britannia* 35: 121–58.
Hodgson, Nick, Jonathan McKelvey and Warren Muncaster. 2012. *The Iron Age on the Northumberland Coastal Plain: Excavations in advance of development 2002–2010*. Newcastle upon Tyne: TWM Archaeology/The Arbeia Society.
Hopewell, David. 2005. 'Roman fort environs in North-West Wales', *Britannia* 36: 225–69.
Hunter, Fraser. 2007a. *Beyond the Edge of the Empire: Caledonians, Picts and Romans*. Rosemarkie: Groam House Museum.
Hunter, Fraser. 2007b. 'Artefacts, regions and identities in the Northern British Iron Age'. In *The Later Iron Age in Britain and Beyond*, edited by Colin Haselgrove and Tom Moore, 286–96. Oxford: Oxbow Books.
Hunter, Fraser. 2008. 'Celtic art in Roman Britain'. In *Rethinking Celtic Art*, edited by Duncan Garrow, Chris Gosden and J.D. Hill, 129–45. Oxford: Oxbow Books.
Isaac, Benjamin. 1988. 'The meaning of the terms *limes* and *limitanei*', *Journal of Roman Studies* 78: 125–47.
Isaac, Benjamin. 1993. *The Limits of Empire: The Roman army in the east*. Oxford: Clarendon Press.
James, Simon. 1999. 'The community of the soldiers: a major identity and centre of power in the Roman Empire'. In *TRAC 98: Proceedings of the Eighth Annual Theoretical Roman Archaeology Conference, Leicester 1998*, edited by Patricia Baker, Colin Forcey, Sophia Jundi and Robert Witcher, 14–25. Oxford: Oxbow Books.
James, Simon. 2001. 'Soldiers and civilians: identity and interaction in Roman Britain'. In *Britons and Romans: Advancing an Archaeological Agenda*, edited by Simon James and Martin Millett, 77–89. Research Report 125. York: CBA.
James, Simon. 2002. 'Writing the legions: the development and future of Roman military studies in Britain', *The Archaeological Journal* 159: 1–58.
James, Simon. 2011. '"*Perdomita Britannia*...": Roman and indigenous strategies and their outcomes in Britain from Caesar to Domitian and beyond'. In *Fines Imperii – Imperium Sine Fine?* Römische Okkupations- und Grenzpolitik im frühen Principat, edited by Günther Moosbauer and Rainer Wiegels, 87–105. Rahden: Verlag Marie Leidorf GmbH.
James, Simon. 2014. 'The "Roman-ness" of the soldiers: barbarized periphery or imperial core?' In *Roman in the Provinces: Art on the periphery of empire*, edited by Lisa R. Brody and Gail L. Hoffman, 91–107. Chesnut Hill, PA: McMullen Museum of Art.
Jones, Barri and David J. Mattingly. 1990. *An Atlas of Roman Britain*. Oxford: Blackwell.
Kearney, Michael. 1991. 'Borders and boundaries of state and self at the end of empire', *Journal of Historical Sociology* 4(1): 52–74.
Kolossov, Vladimir. 2005. 'Border studies: changing perspectives and theoretical approaches', *Geopolitics* 10(4): 606–32.
Leahy, Kevin. 2007. 'Soldiers and settlers in Britain, fourth to fifth century – revisited'. In Collectaea Antiqua*: Essays in memory of Sonia Chadwick Hawkes*, edited by Martin Henig and Tyler J. Smith, 133–43. B.A.R. International Series 1673. Oxford: Archaeopress.
Lintott, Andrew. 1981. 'What was the "Imperium Romanum"?', *Greece and Rome* 28(1): 53–67.

Mattingly, David J. 1992. 'War and peace in Roman North Africa: observations and models of state-tribe interaction'. In *War in the Tribal Zone: Expanding states and indigenous warfare*, edited by R. Brian Ferguson and Neil L. Whitehead, 31–60. Santa Fe, NM: School of American Research Press.

Mattingly, David J. 1996. 'From one colonialism to another: imperialism and the Maghreb'. In *Roman Imperialism: Post-colonial perspectives*, edited by Jane Webster and Nick Cooper, 49–69. Leicester: University of Leicester School of Archaeological Studies.

Mattingly, David J. 2006. *An Imperial Possession: Britain in the Roman Empire, 54BC–AD409*. London: Penguin.

Mezzadra, Sandro and Brett Neilson. 2013. *Border as Method, or, the Multiplication of Labor*. Durham, NC: Duke University Press.

Mignolo, Walter D. and Madina V. Tlostanova. 2006. 'Theorizing from the borders: shifting to geo- and body-politics of knowledge', *European Journal of Social Theory* 9(2): 205–21.

Miller, David H. 1996. 'Frontier societies and the transition between late antiquity and the early Middle Ages'. In *Shifting Frontiers in Late Antiquity*, edited by Ralph W. Mathisen and Hagith S. Sivan, 158–71. Aldershot: Variorum.

Millett, Martin. 1990. *The Romanization of Britain*. Cambridge: Cambridge University Press.

Mullin, David (ed.). 2011. *Places in Between: The archaeology of social, cultural and geographical borders and borderlands*. Oxford: Oxbow Books.

Nail, Thomas. 2016. *Theory of the Border*. Oxford: Oxford University Press.

Newman, Conor. 1998. 'Reflections on the making of a 'royal site' in early Ireland', *World Archaeology* 30(1): 127–41.

Newman, David. 2006. 'Borders and bordering: towards an interdisciplinary dialogue', *European Journal of Social Theory* 9(2): 171–86.

Niklasson, Elisabeth and Herdis Hølleland. 2018. 'The Scandinavian far-right and the new politicisation of heritage', *Journal of Social Archaeology* 18(2): 121–48.

Parker, Bradley J. 2006. 'Toward an understanding of borderland processes', *American Antiquity* 71(1): 77–100.

Parker, Noel, Nick Vaughan-Williams, et al. 2009. 'Lines in the sand? Towards an agenda for critical border studies', *Geopolitics* 14: 582–7.

Pearson, Andrew. 2002. *The Roman Shore Forts: Coastal defences of southern Britain*. Stroud: Tempus.

Petts, David. 2013. 'Military and civilian: reconfiguring the end of Roman Britain in the north', *European Journal of Archaeology* 16(2): 314–35.

Pinder, Isobel. 2011. 'Constructing and deconstructing Roman city walls: the role of urban enceintes as physical and symbolic borders'. In *Places in Between: The archaeology of social, cultural and geographical borders and borderlands*, edited by David Mullin, 67–79. Oxford: Oxbow Books.

Pitts, Martin and Miguel John Versluys (eds). 2015. *Globalisation and the Roman World: World history, connectivity and material culture*. Cambridge: Cambridge University Press.

Pollard, Nigel. 1996. 'The Roman army as a "total institution" in the Near East? A case study from Dura Europos'. In *The Roman Army in the East*, edited by David Braund and D.L. Kennedy, 211–27. JRA Supplementary Series 18. Portsmouth: Journal of Roman Archaeology.

Rance, Philip. 2001. 'Attacotti, Déisi and Magnus Maximus: the case for Irish federates in late Roman Britain', *Britannia* 32: 243–70.

Rodseth, Lars and Bradley J. Parker. 2005. 'Introduction: theoretical considerations in the study of frontiers'. In *Untaming the Frontier in Anthropology, Archaeology, and History*, edited by Bradley J. Parker and Lars Rodseth, 3–21. Tucson, AZ: University of Arizona Press.

Rumford, Chris. 2006. 'Introduction: theorizing borders', *European Journal of Social Theory* 9(2): 155–69.

Sauer, Eberhard W., Nicholas J. Cooper, Geoffrey B. Dannell, Brenda Dickinson, Patrick Erwin, Annie Grant, Martin Henig, Alison W. McDonald and Mark Robinson. 2000. 'Alchester, a Claudian "vexillation fortress" near the western boundary of the Catuvellauni: new light on the Roman invasion of Britain', *Archaeological Journal* 157(1): 1–78.

Scott, Eleanor. 1993. 'Writing the Roman Empire'. In *Theoretical Roman Archaeology: First conference proceedings*, edited by Eleanor Scott, 5–22. Aldershot: Avebury.

Shaw, Brent D. 1983. 'Soldiers and society: the army in Numidia', *Opus* 2: 133–57.

Smith, Andrew M. 2013. *Roman Palmyra: Identity, community and state formation*. Oxford: Oxford University Press.

Smith, Alex T., Martyn Allen, Tom Brindle and Michael Fulford. 2016. *New Visions of the Countryside of Roman Britain, Vol. 1: The rural settlement of Roman Britain*. London: Society for the Promotion of Roman Studies.

Symonds, Matthew. 2013. 'Gateways or garrisons? Designing, building and manning the milecastles'. In *Breaking Down Boundaries: Hadrian's Wall in the 21st century*, edited by Rob Collins and Matthew Symonds, 53–70. JRA Supplementary Series 93. Portsmouth, RI: Journal of Roman Archaeology.

Symonds, Matthew. 2021. *Hadrian's Wall: Creating division*. London: Bloomsbury.

Trigger, Bruce G. 2006. *A History of Archaeological Thought* (2nd edition). Cambridge: Cambridge University Press.

Vanhoutte, Sofie. 2015. 'The late Roman coastal fort of Oudenburg (Belgium): spatial and functional transformations within the fort wall'. In *Roman Military Architecture on the Frontiers*, edited by Rob Collins, Matthew Symonds and Meike Weber, 62–75. Oxford: Oxbow Books.

Versluys, Miguel John. 2014. 'Understanding objects in motion: an archaeological dialogue on Romanization' (with comments and reply), *Archaeological Dialogues* 21(1): 1–64.

Webster, Jane and Nick Cooper (eds). 1996. *Roman Imperialism: Post-colonial perspectives*. Leicester: University of Leicester School of Archaeological Studies.

Wells, Peter S. 1980. 'Contact and change: an example on the fringes of the classical world', *World Archaeology* 12(1): 1–10.

Wells, Peter S. 1999. *The Barbarians Speak: How the conquered peoples shaped Roman Europe*. Princeton, NJ: Princeton University Press.

White, Roger. 2007. Britannia Prima*: Britain's Last Roman Province*. Stroud: Tempus.

Whittaker, Charles R. 1994. *Frontiers of the Roman Empire: A social and economic study*. Baltimore, OH: Johns Hopkins University Press.

Willis, Steven and Peter Carne (eds). 2013. *A Roman Villa at the Edge of Empire: Excavations at Ingleby Barwick, Stockton-on-Tees, 2003–4*. Research Report 170. York: CBA.

Wilmott, Tony. 1997. *Birdoswald: excavations of a Roman fort on Hadrian's Wall and its successor settlements: 1987-92*. London: English Heritage.

Woolf, Greg. 1995. 'The formation of Roman provincial cultures'. In *Integration in the Early Roman West: The role of culture and ideology*, edited by Jeannot Metzler, Martin Millett, Nico Roymans and Jan Slofstra, 9–18. Luxembourg: Musée National d'Histoire et d'Art.

11

Imperial power and its limits: social and cultural integration and resistance in the Roman Empire

David J. Mattingly

Introduction: material culture perspectives on the limits of empire

One of the problems with delineating the cultural limits of empire is that modern scholarship is still entangled in a colonialist discourse about empire that imposes many assumptions on the evidence before we start (Mattingly 2011: 3–40; cf. Webster and Cooper 1996; Goff 2003; Terrenato 2008: 234–40; Vasunia 2013). A mundane but striking example concerns the similarities between ancient and modern attitudes to colonised territories, illustrated by the personification of conquered territory as a naked and defenceless woman, as in many examples of Roman provinces or Spanish images of the discovery of America (Mattingly 2011: 100). Such attitudes emphasise unilateral aspects of imperial power and cultural change in a colonial setting, while stressing the primitiveness and malleability of provincial societies.

Traditional approaches in Roman archaeology have reinforced inherent biases and underlying assumptions about the cultural impact of Roman civilisation (see Liberati and Bourbon 2001 for a typical example). The emphasis of study has tended to be on elite sites and public monuments, the efficiency and order of the army and its role in protecting provincials, the high culture of empire (architecture, statuary, sculpture, mosaics, wall paintings, silver plate, jewellery, the epigraphic footprint of empire and so on). All these aspects combine to give a sense of uniformity and a common cultural agenda in the Roman Empire and 'a false cultural intimacy' between ancient and modern empires (Mol 2023) – generally articulated by the concept of Romanisation, which since the early twentieth century has been the guiding paradigm (see Haverfield 1912 for the classic early articulation).

> What, then, was the general civilisation of the western Empire, the conditions of which were so similar in all its districts? The general answer is easily given. The whole area in varying degrees became Romanised. In speech, literature, in fashions, in art and architecture – in short in the whole fabric of life – it adopted Roman ways. Put that broadly, the statement is almost too familiar to convey any definite impression. (Haverfield and MacDonald 1924: 173)

The answer to the question of the cultural impact and reach of the Roman Empire is perhaps less easy to give today. Nonetheless, there is no doubt that there was a considerable degree of cultural and structural similarity to be found across the empire, as the other contributions in this volume demonstrate. The large-scale production of highly standardised manufactured goods (Van Oyen, Chapter 7), but also coinage (Howgego, Chapter 3), was complemented by long-distance trade networks (Wilson, Chapter 4). Road networks (Laurence, Chapter 1) also enhanced connectivity and commonality, as did the shared structures of the Roman army and frontiers (Gardner, Chapter 10), the deployment of Latin as the key language of governance (Pearce, Chapter 2) and the near ubiquity of urban based systems of provincial government (Revell, Chapter 5). Yet scratch beneath the surface and much local variability is immediately apparent – perhaps most evident in matters like religion (Derks, Chapter 9) and artistic output in the provinces (Stewart, Chapter 8). As a result of recent work, the presentation of the Roman world is becoming a good deal more complex and diverse. This chapter presents a personal perspective on cultural identity and cultural limits in empires, though I have tried to reflect wider debates in the bibliography referenced.

However, the stereotypical views of Romans in popular books, TV programmes and museum displays still draw predominantly on the older tradition of the Roman Empire as a culturally homogenous world, with simplified models of typical Roman lives – though in fact these generally relate to selected and limited subgroups: a cosmopolitan elite, the army and some niche elements like gladiators (again for a typical example, selected at random, see Farmer 1993). What the remaining 90 per cent of society were up to in terms of cultural behaviours is rarely explored in any detail.

The defining characteristics of the Roman Empire cannot be understood in isolation, but rather they need to be reviewed within comparative frameworks of study (Alcock et al. 2001; Parsons 2010; Shaw 2022; see Burbank and Cooper 2010: 23–59 for an explicit comparison). Moreover, post-colonial scholarship of the last decades has transformed our understanding of how empires worked, how they were perceived and resisted by subject populations (Ashcroft et al. 1995; 1998; Schwarz and Ray 2000). Archaeological studies of colonialism and the impacts of colonisation have broadened the scope of research (van Dommelen 1998; Lyons and Papadopoulos 2002; Given 2004; Gosden 2004; Hurst and Owen 2005; Stein 2005; Hodos 2006; Dietler 2010). Empires represent a key development in the structural embedding (and scale) of inequality in societies (Flannery and Marcus 2012; Altaweel and Squitieri 2018), and this gives significance to our efforts to understand their operation in both political and cultural terms. A key argument of my chapter is that, in empires like Rome, there was a link and a parallelism between the operation of power and the drivers of cultural change (in this respect I diverge from Terrenato 2008, who sees cultural change in the Roman Empire as predominantly antedating or happening independently of annexation). Just as imperial power operated under certain constraints, so, I suggest, cultural 'soft power' also ran up against limits. Cultural exchange was in any event neither unidirectional nor an easily controllable process.

Studies of imperial systems often recognise three significant drivers – the actions emanating from the metropolitan core of the empire, peripheral effects relating to the reactions of provincials/neighbours and systemic effects of empire (Mattingly 2011: 15–16). The systemic effects can often be linked to the actions (sometimes transgressive) of imperial agents at the fringes of empires with long and slow communication lines. The plans and desires of the imperial power are often thrown off course by what happens at the edge of empire – unwanted wars with neighbouring peoples, revolts and coups (see Doyle 1986 on imperial drivers in general and for a variety of interpretations of Rome's motivation, Badian 1968; Harris 1978; 1984; Rich 1995).

In a similar way, I want to suggest that cultural drivers at play included metropolitan, provincial and systemic elements (Table 11.1). The imperial court and ruling elite will tend to present a cultural

Imperialism model/key locale	*Behaviours*	*Cultural driver*	*Behaviours*
Metrocentric/ metropolitan core	Imperial actions	Metropolitan fashions	Diffusion of Roman elements
Pericentric/ peripheral or frontier zones	Provincial reactions	Provincial/ regional traditions	Assimilation and spread of regional culture
Systemic/dispersed	Transgressive effects	Globalisation	Systemic effects of cultural change in a globalised world

Table 11.1 Comparison of different drivers and locales of imperialism and cultural impacts in the Roman Empire.

benchmark that is carried into provincial territories by the agents of the state and will be emulated by local elite groups seeking position within the empire's power structures. However, regional cultural traditions will also be influential and in some cases may be fostered as a form of cultural resistance to imperial power or an assertion of regional identity. We should think neither in terms of a uniformly positive response to imperial power nor of enduring resistance. Integration and resistance are points on a broad spectrum of possible responses and we need to recognise the inherent probability of multiple and diverse local strategies encompassing resistance, accommodation, adaptation, flight and so on (Stark and Chance 2012). While we might expect regional traditions to remain quite localised with empires, there are also systemic effects that can facilitate their spread and adoption more widely. Globalisation is the obvious term to capture this (for studies of globalisation and the Roman world, see *inter alia*, Hingley 2005; Hitchner 2008; Pitts and Versluys 2015; Hodos 2016). However, another element of large spatial changes in culture concerns the patterns of enhanced migration (voluntary or forced) that were often a feature of empires.

In Table 11.2, I present the three elements of the power dynamic – intentional acts of the imperial state, the consequential acts and responses of the provincial community, and the systemic effects that often complicate the business of empire (see further Mattingly 2014: 25–8). This illustrates how the ideal operation of power can easily be thrown off track. In the same way, I argue that the scale and diversity of the empire complicated the cultural impact of empire. It is debatable that there was ever a coherent cultural mission of the Roman Empire.

Intentional acts (Imperial structure)	*Systemic effects (unforeseen consequences)*	*Consequential acts (native agency)*
Acts of conquest	Power imbalances, collateral damage, transgressive behaviours	Resistance (armed and cultural) & flight, surrender & compliance
Garrison deployments	Brutality, transgressive behaviours	Resistance & compliance, redefining of identities, behaviour modifications
Census taking	Resentment at intrusion, corruption	Resistance (economic)
Tax settlements	Corruption/extortion	Tax payment/avoidance
Legal frameworks	Legal abuses	Reinforced social hierarchy
Urban promotions and monumentality	Bribery, fiscal over-commitments of towns,	Elite competition for imperial favour
Land confiscation, survey & re-assignment	High potential of corruption & arbitrary actions, leading to protracted legal argument	Emergence of greater regional and community differences
Creation of imperial estates & exploitation of natural resources	Conflicts of interest between locals and officials/chief tenants	Loss of valuable resources to community
Language of government	Exclusive & socially excluding nature	Linguistic and educational choices to access power
Enslavement	Human trafficking & exploitation	Increase in slave ownership
Military recruitment	Loss of men to community	Recruits absorbed into military community
Operation of imperial economy	Unequal economic opportunities	Investment in province from outside & inside

Table 11.2 The potential for systemic effects arising from intentional acts of imperial power and/or consequential responses in a provincial setting.

Nonetheless, the governance of far-flung territories had a significant cultural dimension, and the army garrisons and other imperial agents (including local elites delivering elements of local government) are often disproportionately represented in the archaeological evidence from the provinces. This is the part of the spectrum that has been most explored through the concept of Romanisation. Since Martin Millett's famous redefinition of Romanisation in the 1990s, the focus has shifted to some

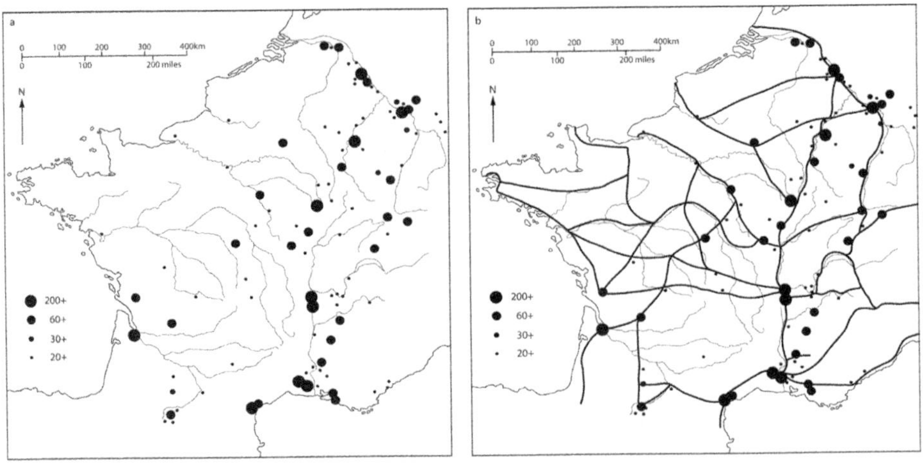

Figure 11.1 Latin inscriptions and their distribution in Roman Gaul: (a) clusters of 20 or more Latin inscriptions from Gaul; (b) the same distribution superimposed on the main road network. Maps by Mike Hawkes from author's roughs, developed after two separate maps in Woolf (1998). © David J. Mattingly.

extent to the agency implicit in 'native'/local reaction to Rome (Millett 1990; Woolf 1998; Wells 1999; van Dommelen and Terrenato 2007). What is less examined is the relationship between that local agency and the systemic effects due to empire, globalisation and migration.

Cultural choices in imperial situations can thus be seen to be constrained by the same sort of factors as imperial power – articulated here as the interplay between imperial and local perceptions of cultural behaviour and systemic effects of the interaction between the two. The unsurprising result of this is that cultural heterogeneity is likely to far outweigh homogeneity in imperial situations – though this runs counter to the key assumptions of models like Romanisation.

My final introductory point is to stress that observed *cultural behaviours* need to be calibrated by the evidence of *imperial infrastructures*. Figure 11.1a shows the distribution of clusters of 20 or more Latin inscriptions in Gaul. The distribution seems to reflect a general engagement with and take-up of the language and its associated epigraphic practices (Woolf 1998: 82–91). Figure 11.1b (produced by combining separate maps from Woolf 1998: 87 and 89) reveals an underlying structure focused on the major harbours and the communication lines (roads and rivers), especially those connecting the Mediterranean and the Roman frontier installations along the river Rhine in Germany. This combined map highlights large areas of Gaul with far lower engagement with 'becoming Roman', raising questions about how far the distribution of inscriptions relates to acculturation in general and how far to the location within Gaul of groups of privileged actors.

Integration and resistance: Romanisation and its alternatives

Culture change (or the lack of it) in the Roman Empire has often been presented as a binary opposition between integration and resistance. Such dichotomies serve to support a colonialist narrative of Roman progress and 'native' backwardness (Mattingly 1997: 7–20). Quality judgements, in part born out of a connoisseurship tradition of art historical study, have tended to emphasise the more cosmopolitan and aesthetically celebrated productions over provincial art – though the latter have perhaps more to tell us about the cultural impact of Rome in the provinces (Scott and Webster 2003; Stewart, Chapter 8 this volume).

Like many Roman archaeologists who completed their PhDs before the 1990s, I initially accepted the appropriateness of the Romanisation concept without question (see Jones and Mattingly 1990: 151–8). However, from the early 1990s onwards in common with others in the UK I became interested in post-colonial theory and this opened my eyes to the problems of Romanisation as a guiding paradigm. In my more recent work I have actively rejected the continued use of the Romanisation concept (Mattingly 2004; 2006: 14–16; 2011: 38–41, 203–7; 2023).

Before moving on to new approaches to investigating material culture, I need to briefly outline some of the perceived defects of Romanisation. It has been defined and redefined multiple times as a concept in attempts to make it still function as a valid shorthand term – however, a paradigm that has different meanings to different people is no longer a workable paradigm. Romanisation is also an unhelpful term in that it implies cultural change was unilateral and unilinear. The term encourages a top-down way of looking at the world, placing its prime emphasis on elite sites, Roman state monuments and elite culture. This in turn leads us to focus on the degree of sameness across provinces, rather than the degree of difference/divergence between areas. There was, of course, a fair degree of commonality, but more than a century of Romanisation studies have explored that terrain in some detail, whereas divergent patterns and behaviours have tended to be neglected. 'Romanisation' is also used to describe both a process and the end result of cultural change, which creates a dangerous circularity of argument, wherein a dubious concept is its own proof. Finally, and in some respects most critically, Romanisation has to be recognised as part of a modern colonial discourse on the nature of empire, as I think the following quote illustrates:

> The instrument of civilisation used by Rome in achieving such results was the town and the many-sided attainments of amenity and social grace which successful civic organisation involves. No false modesty or feeling for others inhibited the Roman belief in their own hybrid civilisation ... The normal method for introducing the instrument in Celtic lands ... was through aristocratic families. These were encouraged to adopt Roman ways and to give their sons a Roman education, absorbing these things as the inward stamp of a new civilisation whose outward habits and equipment possessed the magnetism of novelty and the prestige of success. Once this movement got underway, the rest would follow. (Richmond 1955: 66–7)

Essentially similar attitudes towards and justifications of imperialism underpinned nineteenth- and early twentieth-century colonialism (Mattingly 2011: 43–72 for an overview of North Africa). When Haverfield (1912: 9–10) stated that the Romans 'wrought for the betterment of mankind' it was without irony, though in a post-colonial age it seems to very much echo the paternalistic idea of the 'white man's burden' in the colonies (Hingley 2021). The Roman Empire is often portrayed by 'imperial enthusiasts ... as the model for future empires' (Parsons 2010: 5), though it proved a troubling archetype for modern colonial regimes to compare themselves with: 'No modern Imperialist nation has, however, shown powers of assimilation at all comparable to those displayed by the Romans' (Baring 1910: 77, with following examples 77–114). While Baring's explanation focused on modern issues of race, nationalism, religion and so on that have hindered the cultural project of colonisers, it is also apparent that he, and others, have tended to overestimate considerably the assimilative and integrationist successes of the Roman Empire.

The critique of Romanisation has become well established in UK scholarship and this body of work increasingly argues for the abandonment of the term (see *inter alia*, Webster 2001; James 2001a; Keay and Terrenato 2001; Mattingly 2002; Gardner 2013; 2016; 2021). Jean-Miguel Versluys' (2014) attempt to reboot it as 'Romanisation 2.0' is a rare recent counter-argument, but one that ducks the key objections outlined here (see now also the volume of papers edited by Belvedere and Bergemann 2021). My position is that we need to stop using the term – which directs our thinking in unhelpfully unilateral and unilinear paths and also because it was invented as part of a modern colonial-era discourse. We also need to look across a wider range of society than Romanisation has traditionally focused on and more actively explore the evidence for cultural diversity to set alongside what we have long established as homogenous elements of Roman culture.

Different identities

My favoured alternative to Romanisation is to use well-established frameworks of post-colonial and identity theory to look afresh at the cultural changes of the Roman Empire (Said 1978; 1992; Sen 2006). While we need to recognise the potential difficulties implicit in the varied ways of defining social/group identity (Brubaker and Cooper 2000), identity has been a key concept in archaeological research. There has been considerable interest in the potential of investigating identity representation through archaeological evidence in general (Shennan 1994; Meskell 2001; Gardner 2002; Díaz-Andreu et al. 2005; Insoll 2007a; 2007b; Hales and Hodos 2010) and in Roman archaeology in particular (Berry and Laurence 1998; Huskinson 2000; Gardner 2004; Pitts 2007; Revell 2009; 2016). In a number of publications, I have articulated my own approach to this as 'discrepant identity'– perhaps also to be understood as plural or different identities – though I prefer the edginess of the term 'discrepant' (for the evolution of the idea, see especially Mattingly 1997; 2004; 2006; 2011; 2014; 2023). Identities can perhaps be thought of as flexible, like the choice of clothing (Rothe 2009) or strategies of bilingualism (Adams 2003). By changing costume or language, people can signal a switch in their identity display. Code-switching has been recognised as an important aspect of plural identity presentation (Mullen 2013) and the idea is also being applied to artefacts and other aspects of identity construction (Revell 2013; 2016; Winther-Jacobsen 2013).

A starting point for thinking about the complexities of multiple identities is to reflect on how higher-order group identities might have been shaped in the Roman Empire (Mattingly 2014). A series of higher-order identity markers can be suggested that may have operated individually or in combinations to define identity groups: ethnicity, pre-existing states and kingdoms, Roman citizenship, language and/or bilingualism (Latin, Greek, many others), association with particular cities, *civitates*, *nationes*, provinces, religion/religious preferences, communities (real and imagined), gender and age groups. The crucial point is that for most people in antiquity there was no one identity affiliation that outweighed all others, something that makes the Roman Empire very different from the modern world, which is much more prone to nationalistic or overarching religious affiliations. The interplay between local and global influences is particularly pertinent in the case of imperial and colonial societies (Hodos 2010; Mattingly 2010).

Ethnicity was probably far less developed than in later eras (Emberling 1997; Hall 1997; Jones 1997; Brubaker 2004; Isaac 2004; Roymans 2004; Derks and Roymans 2009) and was in many cases externally observed and applied – thus groups like the Phoenicians, Celts, Germans and Britons were primarily constructs of the Romans (see *inter alia*, James 1999a; Quinn 2018). The differences between emic and etic ascriptions of identity in our literary source material are frequently not recognised in scholarly discussions (Hall 1997). Regional populations were more likely to self-identify in relation to smaller scale pre-existing states and peoples at the level of the city or the 'tribe', though these units might share a language and aspects of material culture in common with other groups. In many parts of the Mediterranean the prevalence of city-states informed later cultural preferences for stressing the city of birth (Hall 2002). Local loyalties and affiliations continued long into the Roman Empire, especially in the eastern provinces, with its ancient urban cultures and distinctive traditions (Millar 1998; Ball 2000; Versluys 2008; Hoffman 2011). The evolution of 'Greek' identity under Roman rule is a particular focus of discussion (Woolf 1994; Wallace-Hadrill 2008; Whitmarsh 2010). Overall, the Roman Empire has yielded little evidence of an enthusiasm for expressing identity in terms of provincial units – *Britannia*, *Africa* and so on (Modéran 2011). Religion always had the potential to create a sense of groupness, but in reality this was more relevant to the monotheistic communities of Jews, Christians and later Moslems than the accommodating accretions of paganism (Rives 2007). Roman citizenship was an important discriminator of status that cut across geographical, language, ethnic, social and cultural groupings (Dench 2005). Because of the massive expansion of the empire and its citizenship by the first century CE, it is debateable to what extent Roman citizens really constituted an identity group as such, as opposed to a diverse set of people with specific legal rights and privileges – they were more akin to a group of Platinum credit card holders than a community.

The Roman army is the best example from the ancient world of an 'imagined community' (Anderson 1991; cf. James 1999b; Gardner, Chapter 10 this volume) – though widely scattered through the provinces and composed of a polyglot and culturally diverse manpower, the garrisons exhibited a distinctive set of behaviours and cultural preferences that were designed to set them apart from ordinary people (Goldsworthy and Haynes 1999). Some groups of civilians who were closely associated with the army became culturally enmeshed in the military community (especially those living adjacent in garrison settlements), but the wider rural community exhibit less signs of engagement (James 2001b). In the army and beyond, linguistic and literate skills served to set some people apart from others in society – creating cultural groupings that were highly dependent on the imperial power networks. Apart from soldiers, minority groups of enslaved people proved adept at constructing identity in the narrow spaces allowed them, sometimes taken to further extremes in their self-reinvention as freedmen and freedwomen (Webster 2005; Joshel 2010; Redfern, Chapter 6 this volume). Gender and age are important division lines in many societies, though often less overtly deployed in projecting a sense of higher-order identity (Harlow and Laurence 2002; Herring and Lomas 2009; Carroll 2013a).

How can we best operationalise the investigation of identity in imperial societies? One approach is to explore evidence for different identity groups in provinces under Roman rule. This involves us in recognising differing levels of social conformity in Roman society and in delineating some broad communities (military/imperial servants and officials, urban communities and rural populations are obvious starting categories). The investigation needs to take account of both inter- and intra-communal differences (for an insightful case study of cultural diversity at Dura-Europos, see Hoffman 2011). For example, some towns and townspeople behaved in distinctive ways that differentiated them from the wider urban community. In this way, for the British (Mattingly 2006) and African provinces (Mattingly 2011: 236–45; 2023), I have sought to detect gross differences between these groups in terms of material culture and behaviour (clarifying identity markers of urban, rural and military communities). This has also highlighted internal variability in the use of material culture and dynamic change across time (with many actors evidently having a plurality of identities).

This has led me to consider two crucial aspects of identity. First, I draw attention to how the different ways of being 'Roman' reflected the place of an individual within the imperial power structures. The second important observation is that identity was often used in a relational

Identity marker	*Annobal Tapapius Rufus*
Status	Local aristocrat, non-citizen but aspirant
Wealth	High wealth (urban community)
Location	Lepcis Magna, free city
Employment	Local magistrate
Religion	Pagan (cosmopolitan range)
Origin	Libyphoenician
Links to imperial government	Ornamentor of town, early adopter
Whether living under civil/ military law	Civil law (but not yet a chartered town)
Languages and literacy	Latin/Neo-Punic/Libyan
Gender/age	Middle-aged male

Table 11.3 Identity matrix for Annobal Tapapius Rufus.

manner, to mark boundaries and differences between people, rather than similarity (Barth 1969). Romanisation theory has obscured this, but an important advantage of identity theory is the way it allows us to appreciate that differentiation and the creation of distance from other groups in society was often more important than emulation for some groups.

To explore these ideas further, I present the identity profiles we can develop for a series of individuals from different parts of the Roman Empire and different social groups. I have chosen to interrogate in each case an iconic 'Roman' object (statue, mausoleum, tombstone), together with associated epigraphy. The resulting identity matrices reveal considerable complexity behind the conventional categorisation as 'Roman'. My first example is a member of the urban community of Lepcis Magna in North Africa. Annobal Tapapius Rufus donated a theatre and a market built on Roman models to his home town under the emperor Augustus (see Mattingly 1995: 58, 161; Wilson 2012). At this point in time Lepcis was a free Libyphoenician city – a native *civitas* – though by the early second century CE it had been promoted twice to *municipium* and honorary *colonia*. From his inscriptions and his surviving statue we can reconstruct Annobal's identity matrix (Table 11.3).

He was evidently a very wealthy man and very invested in the Roman project – though a non-Roman citizen, he had Latinised his Punic names, is depicted in a togate statue (Figure 11.2a) and recorded his beneficence in both Latin and Neo-Punic (*IRT* 319, 321–23). The religious preferences of the town at this date focused on the Phoenician tutelary gods, Melqart (Hercules) and Milkashdart (Liber Pater), but a huge temple of Rome and Augustus was soon to appear in the forum. Annobal is typical of a town

a) Annobal Tapapius Rufus

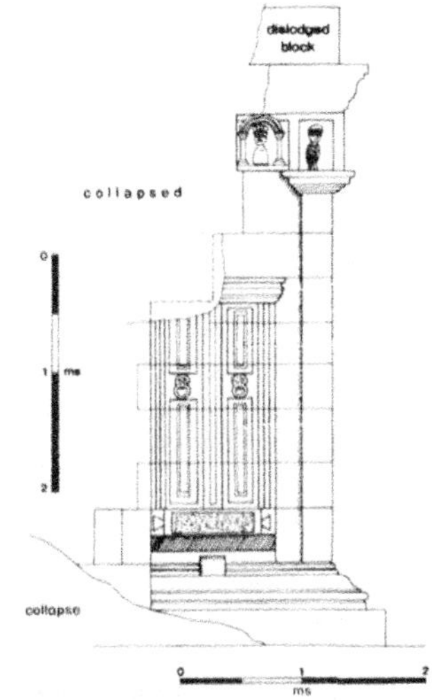

b) Tomb of Masaucan

c) Tombstone of Insus

d) Tombstone of Regina

Figure 11.2 Commemorative monuments from Roman North Africa and Britain: (a) statue of Annobal Tapapius Rufus, Lepcis Magna, Libya (David J. Mattingly); (b) mausoleum of Masaucan, Libyan pre-desert (from Barker et al. 1996); (c) tombstone of cavalryman Insus from Lancaster, UK (Simon James); (d) tombstone of freedwoman Regina, South Shields, UK (David J. Mattingly). © David J. Mattingly.

Identity marker	*Masaucan, son of Iyllul*
Status	Non-citizen
Wealth	High wealth (rural community)
Location	Large farm in Libyan pre-desert
Employment	Landowner/farmer
Religion	Pagan (ancestors, desert cults)
Origin	Libyan
Links to imperial government	Limited
Whether living under civil/ military law	Civil law?
Languages and literacy	Neo-Punic/Libyan/Latino-Punic funerary text
Gender/age	Middle-aged male

Table 11.4. Identity matrix for Masaucan, son of Iyllul.

of early adopters of Roman identity. The impetus of the Romano-mania appears to be local, but it was not all encompassing. Evidence of family funerary crypts for the Lepcitanian families show that they continued to inter the ashes of their dead in individual cinerary urns with the names written in Neo-Punic characters long after the official inscriptions in the town had switched to Latin only. Even when names on urns were written in Latin it was often the Punic cognomen of the individual that was given rather than the full *tria nomina* of the elite families who were full Roman citizens by the later decades of the first century CE. Some names indicate Libyan elements, reminding us that these families were trilingual in Latin, Punic and Libyan – no doubt with much socially contingent code switching (Mattingly 2014: 32–4).

My second example is from a rural settlement in the pre-desert zone south of Lepcis Magna. A man with a Libyan name was buried in an imposing mausoleum (Figure 11.2b) on a rural estate in the second century CE (Mattingly 1995: 164–5; Barker et al. 1996: 20–5). Again, we can reconstruct something of his identity profile (Table 11.4).

Masaucan was a non-citizen with a Libyan name and he recorded his patrilineal descent in a non-Roman way in the tomb inscription (*IRT* 906; Reynolds 1955: 141–2), which was cut in Latin letters, but utilising the Punic language. It is by no means certain that he spoke or understood Latin; in this region Punic and Libyan were the languages of rural society. There is little evidence of formal temples in the pre-desert region and there are indications that the tombs themselves were focal points in a local ancestor cult. Despite the classically inspired architecture of the tomb, there are remarkably few signs that Masaucan

Identity marker	*Insus, son of Vodullus*
Status	Cavalry trooper (in ala Aug)
Wealth	Good (among army ranks)
Location	Lancaster fort, Britain
Employment	Soldier (and head-hunter!)
Religion	Pagan
Origin	Treveran (from Gallia Belgica)
Links to imperial government	Military community
Whether living under civil/ military law	Military
Languages and literacy	Gallic, Latin, British?
Gender/age	Male/late 20s? (female heir)

Table 11.5 Identity matrix for Insus, son of Vodullus.

was actively engaged in a Roman 'project'. The funerary imagery stresses very distinctive local styles of dress and cultural preoccupations (Nikolaus 2017: 93, 237).

For my third example, I move to Britain, where the splendid tombstone (Figure 11.2c) of a Roman cavalryman was found at the fort of Lancaster (Tomlin and Hassall 2006: 468–71; Bull 2007; Shotter 2007; James 2011: 126 and pl. IV). Insus stands in here as a good example of a member of the military community (Table 11.5).

As an elite cavalry trooper, serving in an *ala*, Insus was among the higher-paid soldiers in the army – a fact perhaps reflected in the scale and detail of the tombstone. It portrays a classic stereotype of the Roman cavalryman riding down a defeated enemy – typically shown as a native 'barbarian'. The novel twist here is that not only has the defeated Briton lost his head, but Insus is actually riding off with it. Now, Insus was from Trier in north-eastern Gaul and, while the overall assemblage of tombstone, image and Latin inscription firmly articulate a military identity, there are some elements that remind us of a more complex identity lurking behind. The names of Insus and his father are Gallic; if the son of Insus also served he would have had Roman citizenship and perhaps been less recognisable to us as a Gaul. The inclusion of the unusual detail of Insus carrying off the severed head of the fallen foe does make me wonder if Insus had a specific reputation for this sort of decapitation/head-hunting practice or whether it was meant to reference ancient Celtic tradition (Shotter 2007: 26; Armit 2012). Evidently, the Treveri were notorious for their head-hunting proclivities in the time of Caesar (Cicero, *Letters to his Friends*, 7.13.2). Although his age is not explicitly mentioned on the

Identity marker	*Regina, freedwoman and wife of Barathes*
Status	Freedwoman
Wealth	Moderate wealth
Location	Northern frontier
Employment	Slave, then freedwoman/wife of merchant/ soldier
Religion	Pagan
Origin	Catuvellaunian (Briton)
Links to imperial government	Military community
Whether living under civil/ military law	Military law
Languages and literacy	British/Latin/Palmyrene
Gender/age	Female, 30

Table 11.6 Identity matrix for Regina, freedwoman and wife of Barathes.

tombstone, Insus was probably some way into his service term since he had a designated heir, Domitia – perhaps a common-law wife. This detail leads me on to my next example.

The tombstone of a woman called Regina (Figure 11.2d) is regularly held up as the archetype of a respectable Roman matron from Britain – a well-to-do woman enthroned in a niche, with her respectable style of dress, her wool basket, her jewel box (Liversidge 1973: 136, 152, 167; Allason-Jones 1989: 24–5). But Regina's story was altogether more complicated and messy (*RIB* 1065; Mattingly 2011: 217–18; Carroll 2013b). As Table 11.6 shows, she had started life as a freeborn member of the Catuvellaunian people, whose *civitas* centre was Verulamium (St Albans). At some point she became an enslaved person – perhaps sold into slavery from a poor family? She was evidently bought by a Syrian man Barathes, who may have been a merchant or a soldier. At any rate, his business was with the Roman army in northern Britain and he is attested on Regina's tombstone at South Shields and his own at Corbridge. He may well have from the outset exploited her sexually, as was not uncommon (Mattingly 2011: 114–18). In the course of time, Regina's relationship with Barathes was regularised by his freeing and marrying her. She died childless at 30 years of age and was commemorated as 'freedwoman and wife' by Barathes with a tombstone that bestowed a false gloss of respectability and normality on their relationship. An additional text in Palmyrene mentions only that she was his freedwoman. She is not a representative of the civil population of Britain at large, but rather someone whose life had become inextricably linked with the military community and the institution of slavery.

A reviewer of this chapter raised the question with me of how far the experience of being in the Roman Empire impacted on the identities presented above. In response, I want to emphasise the point that I think all of these different identities have to be understood as being shaped to some degree by the imperial/colonial context. The Roman world could widen horizons and dislocate people across its wide spaces, sometimes violently through forced migration. Moderating the globalising effects of empire (Hodos 2016), were the violent undertones of Roman imperialism and gross inequalities of its society (Fernández-Götz et al. 2020). For instance, empires enact epistemic damage on subjected peoples leading to cultural loss (Padilla Peralta 2020). Amartya Sen (2006: 31) has noted the difficulties of self-defining one's identity in the eyes of powerful others – as existed in an empire like Rome's. This has implications for the conceptualisation of local agency. I argue that the Roman Empire variously opened and narrowed the possible identities open to its servants and subject peoples, for some groups to an extent favouring certain cultural choices. In this sort of material world, the 'performance of identity' could over time come to be framed in relation to cosmopolitan material 'norms' (as also highlighted by Van Oyen, Chapter 7 this volume), though I emphasise that this was a far from inevitable or uniform result. I shall now turn to some further reflections on Roman materiality.

Identity and material culture

Identity clearly has a close relationship with material culture, but it is not a straightforward linear one. One of the problems with Romanisation theory is that it tends to see material adoptions in the provinces as a sign of cultural acceptance of broader beliefs and behaviours. As the examples just discussed have shown, both material culture choices and the associated behaviours could vary considerably across the Roman world. For example, styles of dress and display of elite women were regionally diverse, despite occasional echoes of metropolitan fashion in things like hairstyle (Rothe 2009). In this section, I shall look at a number of examples where we can identify broader social trends behind what at first sight seem to be simple material culture preferences. In recent years new approaches to the theorisation, analysis and interpretation of material culture have emerged, in what may be termed a 'materialist turn' in Roman archaeology (see *inter alia* Van Oyen and Pitts 2017; Pitts 2019; Mol 2023; Van Oyen, Chapter 7 this volume). In particular, New Materialist approaches have the potential to take us into less examined corners of Roman society, such as the lives of enslaved people and the poor and marginalised. As Mol (2023: 12) observes 'after such an interrogation we cannot unsee the darkness that speculatively resides in Roman material culture'.

Pottery is the most ubiquitous material cultural marker from the Roman provinces and the application of big data approaches to comparative study are starting to reveal interesting social patterning. A pioneering study of red slipped fineware (*terra sigillata*) from Britain by Willis (2011) has revealed differences in consumption preferences between urban, military and rural sites that seem to go beyond simple economic explanations (such as access to markets). Similarly, the work of Perring and Pitts on pottery (and other material assemblages) from a selection of sites in Essex dating to the mid to late first century CE has produced suggestive results. There are clear differences evident between the typical pottery assemblage of the military community, a British group associated with the *colonia* at Colchester and another at a small rural settlement (Perring and Pitts 2013). The differences relate not only to wealth or access to pottery, but to different approaches to storing, preparing and serving food and drink. The presence of some red slipped pottery at the British sites might in the past have been commented on as a sign of 'Romanisation', but the underlying patterns reflect strongly differentiated foodways and approaches to social display through acts of drinking and feasting.

My main examples in this section, however, relate to funerary practices. It is well known that the Roman world in the first century CE could broadly be divided into a western zone where cremation rites predominated and an eastern inhuming zone (Jones 1987; Morris 1992). This is a bit of a fudge, especially for Africa where there were both cremating (mainly coastal) and inhuming (mainly inland) traditions. Over time, there was a general shift towards inhumation in both the east and the west, predating the rise of Christianity, but undoubtedly accelerated by the eventual dominance of Christianity. One of the pitfalls of the broad trends in funerary practice is that we perhaps too readily adopt a mindset that Roman burial rites and behaviours, as well as funerary beliefs, became largely standardised – especially as represented by the practice of erecting tombstones to the departed (Carroll 2006). Thus from finds of tombstones in some parts of Britain that resemble those from other parts of the empire (see for

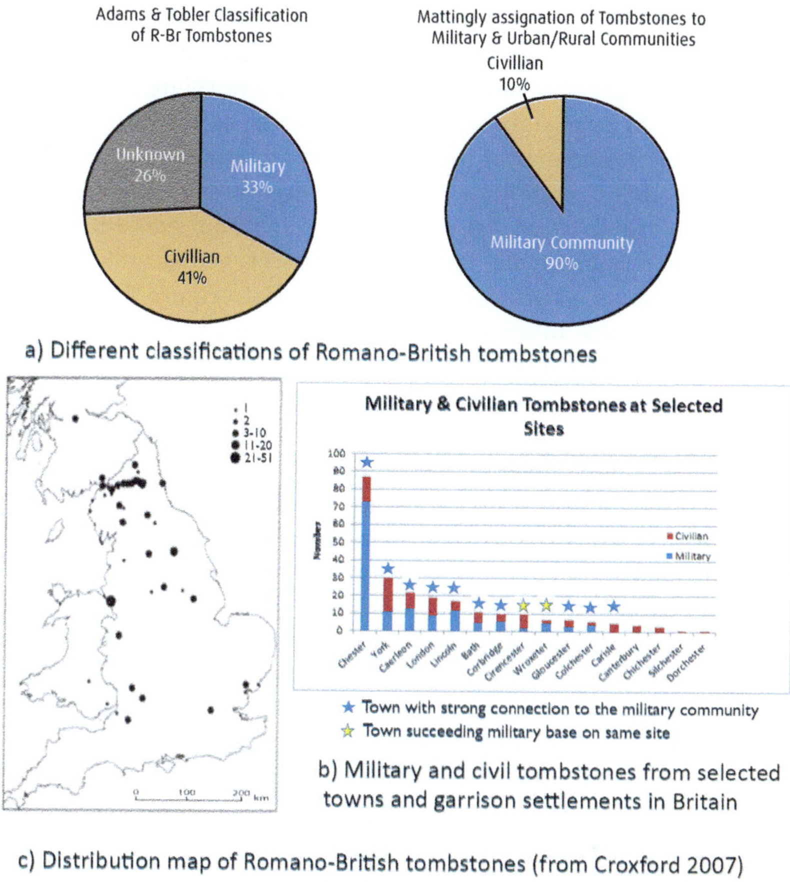

Figure 11.3 Classifications of Roman tombstones and their distribution in Roman towns and garrison settlements in Britain: (a) two different categorisations of Roman tombstones in Britain as pertaining to military or civilian communities, to left adapted from Adams and Tobler (2007) and to right my recategorisation based on site type; (b) analysis of military and civilian tombstones from selected garrison settlements and towns in Britain; (c) distribution map of Roman tombstones in Britain (from Croxford 2007). © David J. Mattingly.

example Figure 11.2c and d), it is often assumed that Britons adopted a normative approach to funerary commemoration and that the roads outside Roman towns in Britain were flanked by funerary monuments in an exactly similar way to say Italy – as illustrated in imaginative reconstruction drawings (Alcock 1996: 48–9).

In a study of *c.*140 Romano-British tombstones from the civil part of the province, Adams and Tobler (2007) classified the material between military, civilian and unknown others (Figure 11.3a, left pie chart). At first sight this certainly suggests a healthy uptake of funerary commemoration among the civilian population. The problem is that they defined as 'civilian' any woman and child, even though the majority of these tombstones came from sites with strong military associations – the legionary fortresses, veteran *coloniae* and so on. In my reclassification of this material (Figure 11.3a, right pie chart), I have taken the view that garrison settlements had a character that was quite distinct from civil urban centres and that funerary commemoration there essentially followed a military track. Accordingly I have reclassified tombstones of women and children from garrison settlements and those identified as wives and children of serving or ex-soldiers as pertaining to the military community. In this alternative reading of the data, there are remarkably few genuinely 'civilian' tombstones in Roman Britain.

The point is given further emphasis if one considers the distribution of all Roman tombstones found in Britain (following analysis by Croxford 2007), which is strongly biased towards military sites and garrison settlements in the north and west of the province, with a very thin distribution among the civil towns in the south-east (Figure 11.3c). Moreover, even in the cases where tombstones are attested in the civil towns, there is a significant percentage made up of military personnel or other agents of the imperial government (for a more detailed analysis, see Mattingly 2008). Of the remainder, quite a significant number of those commemorated on tombstones were identified as 'foreigners'. Urban tombstones come predominantly from the sites with the closest associations with the military community – the veteran *coloniae*, the provincial capitals, the major garrison settlements established by the legionary fortresses (Figure 11.3b). There are very few instances of native Britons, outside those associated with the military community, who were memorialised by a tombstone. The majority of the native *civitas* capitals have produced no tombstones, or at most only one or two exceptional finds. This is sometimes explained in terms of the availability of good stone, though the military community and foreigners at southern towns do seem to have been able to access suitable material. The more logical explanation of this pattern is that native British communities, both urban and rural, did not generally choose to adopt this supposedly normative Roman behaviour. Those groups in the province that were adopters – the army, imperial officials, foreigners – effectively used the erection of tombstones as a way of emphasising a crucial difference in identity display from the bulk of the population.

Vectors of change: direction, intensity, durability

There has never been dispute about the fact that Roman culture was transformed by her imperial encounters, most notably with the Greek world – perhaps best exemplified in Andrew Wallace-Hadrill's (2008) book *Rome's Cultural Revolution*. Such analyses have tended to privilege some cultural voices over others – intertwining Romanisation with Hellenisation – to the exclusion of proper consideration of more varied influences and material impacts. This is perhaps best witnessed in the religious sphere where Rome's pagan pantheon of the gods was vastly expanded and iconographically transformed between the late centuries BCE and the early centuries CE.

Yet, modern commentary on the cultural transformations remains somewhat blind to the directionality of change within the empire. To select just one recent example, from an essay accompanying an exhibition on *Roma Caput Mundi*, the paradigm of Romanisation remains to the fore:

> … since they were convinced that their culture was superior, they thought it natural that foreigners should make it their own. Individuals chose to become Romanised because they were attracted to Roman culture, because it raised their social status, because it allowed them access to local and public offices. (Giardina and Pesando 2012a: 33–34; note also the short essay on Romanisation in the same volume, Wallace-Hadrill 2012)

The implication is that it was the culture of the dominant power that was ultimately alluring and seductive for provincials, determining a circulation of Roman culture outwards from the metropolitan heart of empire.

What was really striking about the *Caput Mundi* exhibition and its catalogue, however, was the extent of the cultural flows in the reverse direction. The exhibition presented finds from Italy representing the integrationist success of the Roman Empire, with long sections on the impact of Eastern religions (Giardina and Pesando 2012b: 17–20, 49–64), foreigners in army and senate (39–42), Greeks and Greek culture (43–48), enslaved people (65–68). The migration (forced or voluntary)

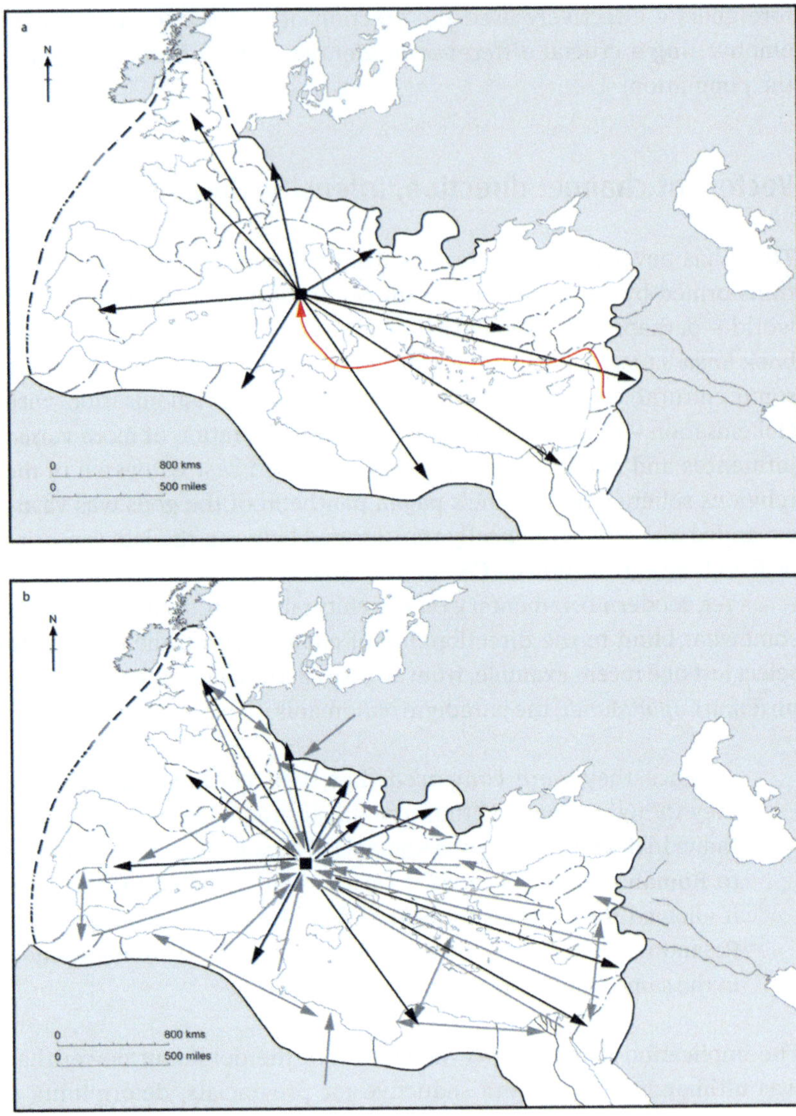

Figure 11.4 Contrasting models of cultural flow in the Roman Empire: (a) Rome-centred cultural dissemination model, with a recognised important reverse flow from the Greek world; (b) the 'cultural backwash' model, with cultural dissemination from the centre counterbalanced by multiple inward flows from provinces and additional inter-provincial flows providing further complexity. Maps by Mike Hawkes from author's roughs. © David J. Mattingly.

of people from all over the empire saw the import of many new cultural practices, languages and religions, and these are all too visible in the archaeological record, much as later imperial capitals, such as Paris and London, have been marked by the cultural specificities of former colonies.

In Figure 11.4a I characterise a traditional 'Romanisation' model of cultural flow from the centre, which also acknowledges a particular influence from the Greek East, following the argument of Wallace-Hadrill (2008). My alternative model, which I call 'cultural backwash', tries to communicate some of the cultural complexity of an empire and how this impacts on the promulgation of metropolitan cultural behaviours (Figure 11.4b). At the start of the chapter, I spoke of cultural behaviours being a complicated mixture of metropolitan fashions, provincial traditions and globalising trends. In this model, the unique position of the imperial capital (Rome, but later other centres too) is highlighted. While some cultural fashions emanated from here, the multiple inward transmissions of provincial traditions and innovations made Rome uniquely open to multiple influences and thus a node for transformation. The survival of the Roman Empire was to some extent contingent on its capacity to cope with cultural diversity and to assimilate change in the metropolitan culture at the empire's core. This is, I suggest, a paradox of empires in general.

Conclusion

In this chapter I advance a series of propositions for further reflection and discussion. First, I suggest that ancient empires were not able to enforce a cultural model on subject peoples (even if they had wanted to). A key concern of all empires is how to cope with the 'politics of difference' (Burbank and Cooper 2010: 11–13). As I have noted, Rome is often held up as an example of a homogenising empire, based on a distinctive culture that developed as Rome expanded (Burbank and Cooper 2010: 12). The high culture of the empire and its associated elite behaviours were undoubtedly alluring to some, but this was always in danger of dilution and transformation in the face of new cultural influences from elsewhere. The most striking example is perhaps the triumph of Christianity. Initially treated with suspicion and periodically persecuted for its evangelising brand of monotheism, from the fourth century CE Christianity came to be officially embraced and spread rapidly.

Second, and following from this, I argue that identities within empires were shaped by a range of cultural drivers – imperial examples, local traditions and choices and systemic effects of globalisation. I also suggest that these followed similar dynamics to the structures of power in empires.

Third, I have drawn attention to the inherent diversity of material culture in empires like Rome – and contrasted this with a superficial sense of sameness, which has been exaggerated by models like Romanisation.

The fourth aim of the chapter has been to show that the variance in identity markers and behaviours can be studied at different levels (regions, social groupings, chronological phases) and this can help us understand how individuals and groups sought to make sense of their place within the political and social structures of the empire. Another important conclusion is that cultural choices were made not solely to express similarity with others, but, rather, that the intention was often primarily to register difference and social distance from others in society.

Finally, I have argued that cultural flows between metropolitan centre and provinces, between province and province and between provinces and the metropolitan centre were very variable. There is a paradox that the greatest net cultural change in an imperial system was often located at its metropolitan centre due to the focusing there of the diverse cultural influences of *all* the provinces.

Abbreviations

IRT: Inscriptions of Roman Tripolitania (2021 online edition), https://irt2021.inslib.kcl.ac.uk/en/.

References

Adams, Geoffrey W. and Rebecca Tobler. 2007. *Romano-British Tombstones between the 1st and 3rd Centuries: Epigraphy, gender and familial relations*. British Archaeological Reports 437. Oxford: Archaeopress.

Adams, John N. 2003. *Bilingualism and the Latin Language*. Cambridge: Cambridge University Press.

Alcock, Joan P. 1996. *English Heritage Book of Life in Roman Britain*. London: English Heritage.

Alcock, Susan E., Terrence N. D'Altroy, Kathleen D. Morrison and Carla M. Sinopoli (eds). 2001. *Empires: Perspectives from archaeology and history*. Cambridge: Cambridge University Press.

Allason-Jones, Lindsay. 1989. *Women in Roman Britain*. London: British Museum Publications.

Altaweel, Mark and Andrea Squitieri. 2018. *Revolutionizing a World: From small states to universalism in the pre-Islamic Near East*. London: UCL Press.

Anderson, Benedict. 1991. *Imagined Communities: Reflections on the origins and spread of nationalism*. London and New York: Verso.

Armit, Ian. 2012. *Headhunting and the Body in Iron Age Europe*. Cambridge: Cambridge University Press.

Ashcroft, Bill, Gareth Griffiths and Helen Tiffin. 1995. *The Post-Colonial Studies Reader*. London: Routledge.

Ashcroft, Bill, Gareth Griffiths and Helen Tiffin 1998. *Key Concepts in Post-Colonial Studies*. London: Routledge.
Badian, Ernst. 1968. *Roman Imperialism in the Late Republic*. Oxford: Clarendon Press.
Ball, Warwick. 2000. *Rome in the East: The transformation of an empire*. London: Routledge.
Baring, Evelyn B. 1910. *Ancient and Modern Imperialism*. New York: Longmans, Green and Co.
Barker, Graeme W., David D. Gilbertson, Barri Jones and David J. Mattingly. 1996. *Farming the Desert: The UNESCO Libyan Valleys Archaeological Survey. Vol. 2, Gazetteer and pottery* (principal editor, D.J. Mattingly). Paris and London: UNESCO, Society for Libyan Studies.
Barth, Frederik (ed.). 1969. *Ethnic Groups and Boundaries: The social organisation of ethnic difference*. Boston, MA: Little Brown.
Belvedere, Oscar and Johannes Bergemann (eds). 2021. *Imperium Romanum: Romanization between colonization and globalization*. Palermo: Palermo University Press.
Berry, Joanne and Ray Laurence (eds). 1998. *Cultural Identity in the Roman Empire*. London: Routledge.
Brubaker, Rogers. 2004. *Ethnicity without Groups*. Cambridge: Cambridge University Press.
Brubaker, Rogers and Frederick Cooper. 2000. 'Beyond "identity"', *Theory and Society* 29: 1–47.
Bull, Stephen. 2007. *Triumphant Rider: The Lancaster Roman cavalry tombstone*. Lancaster: Lancashire Museums.
Burbank, Jane and Frederick Cooper. 2010. *Empires in World History: Power and the politics of difference*. Princeton, NJ: Princeton University Press.
Carroll, Maureen. 2006. *Spirits of the Dead: Roman funerary commemoration in Western Europe*. Oxford: Oxford University Press.
Carroll, Maureen. 2013a. 'Ethnicity and gender in Roman funerary commemoration: case studies from the empire's frontiers'. In Sarah Tarlow and Liv Nilsson Stutz (eds), *The Oxford Handbook of the Archaeology of Death and Burial*, 559–79. Oxford: Oxford University Press.
Carroll, Maureen. 2013b. 'The insignia of women: dress, gender and identity on the Roman funerary monument of Regina from Arbeia', *The Archaeological Journal* 169: 281–311
Croxford, Benjamin T. 2007. 'Sculpture from Roman Britain: aspects of origin, use, disuse and deposition'. Unpublished PhD thesis, Cambridge.
Dench, Emma. 2005. *Romulus' Asylum: Roman identities from the age of Alexander to the age of Hadrian*. Oxford: Oxford University Press.
Derks, Ton and Nico Roymans. 2009. *Ethnic Constructs in Antiquity: The role of power and tradition*. Amsterdam: Amsterdam University Press.
Díaz-Andreu, Margarita, Sam Lucy, Stasa Babić and David N. Edwards. 2005. *The Archaeology of Identity: Approaches to gender, age, status, ethnicity and religion*. London: Routledge.
Dietler, Michael. 2010. *Archaeologies of Colonialism: Consumption, entanglement, and violence in ancient Mediterranean France*. Berkeley, CA: University of California Press.
Doyle, Michael W. 1986. *Empires*. New York: Cornell University Press.
Emberling, Geoff. 1997. 'Ethnicity in complex societies: archaeological perspectives', *Journal of Archaeological Research* 5(4): 295–344.
Farmer, Alan. 1993. *Invaders and Settlers: Romans, Anglo-Saxons, Vikings*. Aylesbury: Ginn.
Fernández-Götz, Manuel, Dominic Maschek and Nico Roymans. 2020. 'The dark side of the Empire: Roman expansionism between object agency and predatory regime', *Antiquity* 94(378): 1630–39.
Flannery, Kent and Joyce Marcus. 2012. *The Creation of Inequality: How our prehistoric ancestors set the stage for monarchy, slavery and empire*. Cambridge, MA: Harvard University Press.
Gardner, Andrew. 2002. 'Social identity and the duality of structure in late Roman-period Britain', *Journal of Social Archaeology* 2(3): 323–51.
Gardner, Andrew (ed.). 2004. *Agency Uncovered: Archaeological perspectives on social agency, power, and being human*. London: UCL Press.
Gardner, Andrew. 2013. 'Thinking about Roman imperialism: postcolonialism, globalisation and beyond?', *Britannia* 44: 1–25.
Gardner, Andrew. 2016. 'Debating Roman imperialism: critique, construct, repeat?' In *TRAC 2015: Proceedings of the 25th Annual Theoretical Roman Archaeology Conference*, edited by Matthew Mandich, Thomas Derrick, Sergio González Sánchez, Giacommo Savani and Eleanora Zampieri, 1–14. Oxford: Oxbow.
Gardner, Andrew. 2021. 'Post-colonial Rome and beyond: religion, power and identity', *Revista de historiografía* 36: 309–20.

Giardina, Andrea and Fabrizio Pesando (ed.). 2012a. *Roma Caput Mundi: Una città tra dominio e integrazione*. Milan: Electa.

Giardina, Andrea and Fabrizio Pesando (eds). 2012b. *Roma Caput Mundi: La mostra*. Milan: Electa.

Given, Michael. 2004. *The Archaeology of the Colonized*. London: Routledge.

Goff, Barbara (ed.). 2003. *Classics and Colonialism*. London: Duckworth.

Goldsworthy, Adrian and Ian Haynes (eds). 1999. *The Roman Army as a Community*. JRA Supplementary Series 34. Portsmouth, RI: Journal of Roman Archaeology.

Gosden, Chris. 2004. *Archaeology and Colonialism: Cultural contact from 5000 BC to the present*. Cambridge: Cambridge University Press.

Hales, Shelley and Tamar Hodos (eds). 2010. *Material Culture and Social Identities in the Ancient World*. Cambridge, Cambridge University Press.

Hall, Jonathan. 1997. *Ethnic Identity in Greek Antiquity*. Cambridge: Cambridge University Press.

Hall, Jonathan. 2002. *Hellenicity: Between ethnicity and culture*. Chicago, IL: Chicago University Press.

Harris, William V. 1978. *War and Imperialism in Republican Rome 327–70 BC*. Oxford: Clarendon Press.

Harris, William V. (ed.). 1984. *The Imperialism of Mid-Republican Rome*. Papers and Monographs of the American Academy in Rome xxix. Rome: American Academy in Rome.

Harlow, Mary and Ray Laurence. 2002. *Growing Up and Growing Old in Ancient Rome: A life course* approach. London: Routledge.

Haverfield, Francis. 1912. *The Romanization of Roman Britain* (2nd edition). Oxford: Clarendon Press.

Haverfield, Francis and George MacDonald. 1924. *The Roman Occupation of Britain*. Oxford: Clarendon Press.

Herring, Edward and Kathryn Lomas. 2009. *Gender Identities in Italy in the First Millennium BC*. British Archaeological Reports S1983. Oxford: Archaeopress.

Hingley, Richard. 2005. *Globalising Roman Culture: Unity, diversity and empire*. London: Routledge.

Hingley, R. 2021. 'From colonial discourse to post-colonial theory: Roman archaeology and the province of Britannia'. In *Imperium Romanum: Romanization between colonization and globalization*, edited by Oscar Belvedere and Johannes Bergemann, 181–91. Palermo: Palermo University Press.

Hitchner, R. Bruce. 2008. 'Globalization avant la lettre: globalization and the history of the Roman empire', *New Global Studies* 2: 1–12.

Hodos, Tamar. 2006. *Local Responses to Colonization in the Iron Age Mediterranean*. London: Routledge.

Hodos, Tamar. 2010. 'Local and global perspectives in the study of social and cultural identities'. In *Material Culture and Social Identities in the Ancient World*, edited by Shelley Hales and Tamar Hodos, 3–31. Cambridge: Cambridge University Press.

Hodos, Tamar (ed). 2016. *The Routledge Handbook of Archaeology and Globalization*. London: Routledge.

Hoffman, Gail L. 2011. 'Theory and methodology: study of identities using archaeological evidence from Dura-Europos'. In *Dura Europos. Crossroads of Antiquity*, edited by Lisa R. Brody and Gail L. Hoffman, 45–69. Boston, MA: McMullen Museum of Art.

Hurst, Henry and Sara Owen (eds). 2005. *Ancient Colonizations: Analogy, similarity and difference*. London: Duckworth.

Huskinson, Janet. 2000. *Experiencing Empire: Culture, identity and power in the Roman Empire*. London: Routledge.

Insoll, Timothy (ed.). 2007a. *The Archaeology of Identities: A reader*. Abingdon: Routledge;

Insoll, Timothy. 2007b. 'Configuring identities in archaeology'. In *The Archaeology of Identities*, edited by Timothy Insoll, 1–18. Abingdon: Routledge;

Isaac, Benjamin. 2004. *The Origins of Racism in Classical Antiquity*. Princeton, NJ: Princeton University Press.

James, Simon. 1999a. *The Atlantic Celts: Ancient people or modern invention?* Madison, WI: University of Wisconsin Press.

James, Simon. 1999b. 'The community of the soldiers: a major identity and centre of power in the Roman empire'. In *TRAC 98: Proceedings of the Eighth Annual Theoretical Roman Archaeology Conference, Leicester, 1998*, edited by Patricia Baker, Colin Forcey, Sophia Jundi and Robert Witcher, 14–25. Oxford: Oxbow.

James, Simon. 2001a. 'Romanization and the peoples of Britain'. In *Italy and the West: Comparative issues in Romanization*, edited by Simon Keay and Nicolo Terrenato, 187–209. Oxford: Oxbow.
James, Simon. 2001b. 'Soldiers and civilians: identity and interaction in Roman Britain'. In *Britons and Romans: Advancing an archaeological agenda*, edited by Simon James and Martin Millett, 77–89. York: Council for British Archaeology.
James, Simon. 2011. *Rome and the Sword*. London and New York: Thames and Hudson.
Jones, Barri and David J. Mattingly. 1990. *An Atlas of Roman Britain*. Oxford: Blackwell.
Jones, Rick F.J. 1987. 'Burial customs of Rome and the provinces'. In *The Roman World*, vol 2, edited by John Wacher, 812–37. London: Routledge.
Jones, Sian. 1997. *The Archaeology of Ethnicity: Constructing identities in the past and present*. London: Routledge.
Joshel, Sandra R. 2010. *Slavery in the Roman World*. Cambridge: Cambridge University Press.
Keay, Simon J. and Nicola Terrenato (eds.). 2001. *Italy and the West: Comparative issues in Romanization*. Oxford: Oxbow.
Liberati, Anna Maria and Fabio Bourbon. 2001. *Rome: Splendours of an ancient civilisation*. London: Thames and Hudson.
Liversidge, Joan. 1973. *Britain in the Roman Empire*. Trowbridge: Redwood Press.
Lyons, Claire. L. and John K. Papadopoulos (eds.). 2002. *The Archaeology of Colonialism*. Los Angeles, CA: Getty Research Institute.
Mattingly, David J. 1995. *Tripolitania*. London: Batsford.
Mattingly, David J. (ed.). 1997, *Dialogues in Roman Imperialism: Power, discourse and discrepant experience in the Roman Empire*. JRA Supplementary Series 23. Portsmouth, RI: Journal of Roman Archaeology.
Mattingly, David J. 2002. 'Vulgar and weak "Romanization", or time for a paradigm shift?' *Journal of Roman Archaeology* 15: 536–40.
Mattingly, David J. 2004. 'Being Roman: expressing identity in a provincial setting', *Journal of Roman Archaeology* 17: 5–25.
Mattingly, David J. 2006. *An Imperial Possession: Britain in the Roman Empire*. London: Penguin.
Mattingly, David J. 2008. 'Urbanism, epigraphy and identity in the towns of Britain under Roman rule'. In *A Roman Miscellany: Essays in honour of Anthony R. Birley on his seventieth birthday*, edited by Hans Michael Schellenberg, Vera-Elisabeth Hirschmann and Andreas Krieckhaus, 53–71. Gdansk: Akanthina 3, Department of Archaeology Gdansk University.
Mattingly, David J. 2010. 'Cultural cross-overs: global and local identities in the Classical world'. In *Material Culture and Social Identity in the Roman World*, edited by Shelley Hales and Tamar Hodos, 283–95. Cambridge: Cambridge University Press.
Mattingly, David J. 2011. *Imperialism, Power and Identity: Experiencing the Roman Empire*. Princeton, NJ: Princeton University Press.
Mattingly, David J. 2014. 'Identities in the Roman world: discrepancy, heterogeneity, hybridity and plurality'. In Lisa R. Brody and Gail L. Hoffmann (eds.), *Roman in the Provinces. Art on the Periphery of Empire*, 32–61. Boston: McMullen Museum of Art.
Mattingly, David J. 2023. *Between Sahara and Sea: Africa in the Roman Empire*. Ann Arbor, MI: Michigan University Press.
Meskell, Lynn. 2001. 'Archaeologies of identity'. In *Archaeological Theory Today*, edited by Ian Hodder, 187–213. Cambridge: Polity Press.
Millar, Fergus. 1998. *The Roman Near East 31 BC–AD 337*. Cambridge, MA: Harvard University Press.
Millett, Martin. 1990. *The Romanization of Britain: An essay in archaeological interpretation*. Cambridge: Cambridge University Press.
Modéran, Yves. 2011. 'La province, troisième patrie'. In *Provinces et identités provinciales dans l'Afrique romaine*, edited by Claude Briand-Ponsart and Yves Modéran, 9–40. Caen: Centre de recherches archéologiques et historiques anciennes et médiévales.
Mol, Eva. 2023. 'New materialism and posthumanism in Roman archaeology: when objects speak for others', *Cambridge Archaeological Journal*, 1–15, https://doi.org/10.1017/S0959774323000124.
Morris, Ian. 1992. *Death Ritual and Social Structure in Classical Antiquity*. Cambridge: Cambridge University Press.
Mullen, Alex. 2013. 'The bilingualism of material culture? Thoughts from a linguistic perspective', *HEROM. Journal of Hellenistic and Roman Material Culture* 2: 21–43.

Nikolaus, Julia. 2017. 'Roman funerary reliefs and North African Identity: a contextual investigation of Tripolitanian mausolea and their iconography'. Unpublished PhD thesis, University of Leicester.

Padilla Peralta, Dan-el. 2020. 'Epistemicide: the Roman case', *Classica* 33(2): 151–86.

Parsons, Timothy H. 2010. *The Rule of Empires: Those who built them, those who endured them and why they always fall*. Oxford: Oxford University Press.

Perring, Dominic and Martin Pitts. 2013. *Alien Cities: Consumption and the origins of urbanism in Roman Britain*. Monograph 7. Portslade: SpoilHeap.

Pitts, Martin. 2007. 'The emperor's new clothes? The utility of identity in Roman archaeology', *American Journal of Archaeology* 111(4): 693–713

Pitts, Martin. 2019. *The Roman Object Revolution: Objectscapes and intra-cultural connectivity in Northwest Europe*. Amsterdam: Amsterdam University Press.

Pitts, Martin, and Miguel-John Versluys (eds). 2015. *Globalisation and the Roman World: Perspectives and opportunities*. Cambridge: Cambridge University Press.

Quinn, Josephine. 2018. *In Search of the Phoenicians*. Princeton, NJ: Princeton University Press.

Revell, Louise. 2009. *Roman Imperialism and Local Identities*. Cambridge: Cambridge University Press.

Revell, Louise. 2013. 'Code-switching and identity in the western provinces', *HEROM. Journal of Hellenistic and Roman Material Culture* 2: 123–41.

Revell, Louise. 2016. *Ways of Being Roman: Discourses of identity in the Roman west*. Oxford: Oxbow Books.

Reynolds, Joyce. 1955. 'Inscriptions of Roman Tripolitania (IRT): a supplement', *Papers of the British School at Rome* 23: 124–27.

Rich, John. 1995. 'Fear, greed and glory: the causes of Roman war-making in the middle Republic'. In John Rich and Graham Shipley (eds.), *War and Society in the Roman World*, 38–68. London: Routledge.

Richmond, Ian. 1955. *Roman Britain*. Harmondsworth: Penguin.

Rives, James B. 2007. *Religion in the Roman Empire*. Oxford: Blackwell.

Rothe, Ursula. 2009. *Dress and Cultural Identity in the Rhine-Moselle Region of the Roman Empire*. British Archaeological Reports S2038. Oxford: Archeopress.

Roymans, Nico. 2004. *Ethnic Identity and Imperial Power: The Batavians in the early Roman Empire*. Amsterdam: Amsterdam University Press.

Said, Edward W. 1978. *Orientalism*. Harmondsworth: Penguin.

Said, Edward W. 1992. *Culture and Imperialism*. London: Vintage.

Schwarz, Henry and Sangeete Ray (ed.). 2000. *A Companion to Postcolonial Studies*. Oxford: Blackwell.

Scott, Sarah and Jane Webster (eds). 2003. *Roman Imperialism and Provincial Art*. Cambridge: Cambridge University Press.

Sen, Amartya. 2006. *Identity and Violence: The illusion of destiny*. New York: Norton.

Shaw, Brent D. 2022. 'Global empires and the Roman imperium', *American Journal of Philology* 143(3)(571): 505–34.

Shennan, Stephen (ed.). 1994. *Archaeological Approaches to Cultural Identity*. London: Routledge.

Shotter, David. 2007. 'A Roman cavalry tombstone from Lancaster', *Contrebis* 31: 23–8.

Stark, Barbara L. and John K. Chance. 2012. 'The strategies of provincials in empires'. In *The Comparative Archaeology of Complex Societies*, edited by Michael E. Smith, 192–237. Cambridge: Cambridge University Press.

Stein, Gil J. (ed.). 2005. *The Archaeology of Colonial Encounters: Comparative perspectives*. Santa Fe, NM: School of American Research Press.

Terrenato, Nicola. 2008. 'The cultural implications of Roman conquest'. In *Roman Europe*, edited by Edward Bishpam, 234–64. Oxford: Oxford University Press.

Tomlin, Roger and Mark Hassall. 2006. 'Roman Britain in 2005: inscriptions', *Britannia* 37: 467–88.

van Dommelen, Peter. 1998. *On Colonial Grounds: A comparative study of colonialism and rural settlement in 1st millennium BC west central Sardinia*. Leiden: University of Leiden.

van Dommelen, Peter and Nicola Terrenato (eds). 2007. *Articulating Local Cultures: Power and identity under the expanding Roman republic*. JRA Supplementary Series 63. Portsmouth, RI: Journal of Roman Archaeology.

Van Oyen, Astrid and Martin Pitts (eds). 2017. *Materialising Roman Histories*. Oxford: Oxbow Books.

Vasunia, Phiroze. 2013. *The Classics and Colonial India*. Oxford: Oxford University Press.

Versluys, Miguel-John. 2008. 'Exploring identities in the Phoenician, Hellenistic and Roman east', *Bibliotheca Orientalis* 65(3–4): 341–56.

Versluys, Miguel-John. 2014. 'Understanding objects in motion: an archaeological dialogue on Romanization'. *Archaeological Dialogues* 21(1): 1–64 (includes responses by Hingley, Hodos, Stek, van Dommelen, Woolf).

Wallace-Hadrill, Andrew. 2008. *Rome's Cultural Revolution*. Cambridge: Cambridge University Press.

Wallace-Hadrill, Andrew. 2012. 'Romanizzazione'. In *Roma Caput Mundi: Una città tra dominio e integrazione*, edited by Andrea Giardina and Fabrizio Pesando, 111–16. Milan: Electa.

Webster, Jane. 2001. 'Creolising the Roman provinces', *American Journal of Archaeology* 105(2): 209–25.

Webster, Jane. 2005. 'Archaeologies of slavery and servitude: bringing 'New World' perspectives to Roman Britain', *Journal of Roman Archaeology* 18: 161–79.

Webster, Jane and Nicholas Cooper (eds). 1996. *Roman Imperialism: Post-colonial perspectives*. Leicester: School of Archaeological Studies.

Wells, Peter. 1999. *The Barbarians Speak*. Princeton, NJ: Princeton University Press.

Whitmarsh, Timothy (ed). 2010. *Local Knowledge and Microidentities in the Imperial Greek World*. Cambridge: Cambridge University Press.

Willis, Steven. 2011. 'Samian ware and society in Roman Britain and beyond', *Britannia* 42: 167–242.

Wilson, Andrew I. 2012. 'Neo-Punic and Latin inscriptions in Roman Tripolitania: function and display'. In *Multilingualism in the Graeco-Roman Worlds*, edited by Alex Mullen and Patrick James, 265–316. Cambridge: Cambridge University Press.

Winther-Jacobsen, Kristina. 2013. 'Artefact variability, assemblage differentiation and identity negotiation: debating code switching in material culture: introduction', *HEROM. Journal of Hellenistic and Roman Material Culture* 2: 11–20.

Woolf, Greg. 1994. 'Becoming Roman, staying Greek: culture, identity and the civilizing process in the Roman East', *Proceedings of the Cambridge Philological Society* 40: 116–43.

Woolf, Greg. 1998. *Becoming Roman: The origins of provincial civilization in Gaul*. Cambridge: Cambridge University Press.

Index

References to images are in *italics*.

Printed and bound by CPI Group (UK) Ltd, Croydon, CR0 4YY
19/05/2025
01876495-0001